D1017089

WEBSTER'S 21ST CENTURY WORLD ATLAS

The Editors of AND Cartographic

BARNES
&NOBLE
BOOKS
NEW YORK

Contents

Produced by AND Cartographic Publishers Ltd
Alberto House, Hogwood Lane
Finchampstead, Berks, RG40 4RF
United Kingdom

1999 Barnes & Noble Books

ISBN 0-7607-1658-7 casebound
ISBN 0-7607-1659-5 paperback

Originated by AND Cartographic Publishers Ltd.

Printed and bound in China

99 00 01 02 MC 9 8 7 6 5 4 3 2 1
99 00 01 02 MP 9 8 7 6 5 4 3 2 1

4   Key map and legend

6   World flags and statistics

30   World: Political

32   North America: Political

34   Canada

36   United States

38   United States: Northwest

40   United States: Northeast

42   United States: Southeast

44   United States: Southwest

46   Central America
and the Caribbean

48   South America: Political

50   South America: North

52   South America: South

54   Europe: Political

56   Scandinavia

58   Central Europe

60 Germany

62 Benelux

64 British Isles

66 France

68 Spain and Portugal

70 The Alpine States

72 Italy

74 The Balkans

76 Greece and Western Turkey

78 European Russia

80 Asia: Political

82 Asia: Northwest

84 Asia: Northeast

86 Asia: East

88 Japan and Korea

90 Asia: Southeast

92 Malaysia and Indonesia

94 Asia: South

96 The Middle East

98 Turkey

100 Israel and the Gulf States

102 Africa: Political

104 Africa: Northeast

106 Africa: Northwest

108 Africa: West

110 Africa: Central

112 Africa: Southern

114 Oceania: Political

116 Australia

118 New Zealand

120 Polar Regions

121 Glossary

122 Index

Legend and key map

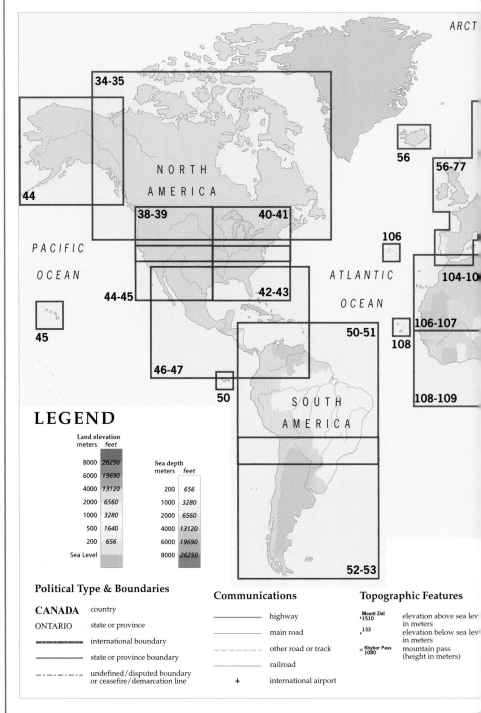

ARCT

34-35

NORTH
AMERICA

56

56-77

44

38-39

40-41

PACIFIC

106

OCEAN

104-10

ATLANTIC

44-45

42-43

OCEAN

45

50-51

106-107

108

46-47

50

SOUTH

108-109

AMERICA

LEGEND

Land elevation
meters / feet

8000	26250
6000	19690
4000	13120
2000	6560
1000	3280
500	1640
200	656
Sea Level	

Sea depth
meters / feet

200	656
1000	3280
2000	6560
4000	13120
6000	19690
8000	26250

52-53

Political Type & Boundaries

CANADA   country

ONTARIO   state or province

———————— international boundary

———————— state or province boundary

– – – – – – – undefined/disputed boundary
or ceasefire/demarcation line

Communications

———————— highway

———————— main road

– – – – – – – other road or track

················ railroad

✈   international airport

Topographic Features

▲ Mount Ziel
1510   elevation above sea lev
in meters

▾ 133   elevation below sea lev
in meters

× Khyber Pass
1080   mountain pass
(height in meters)

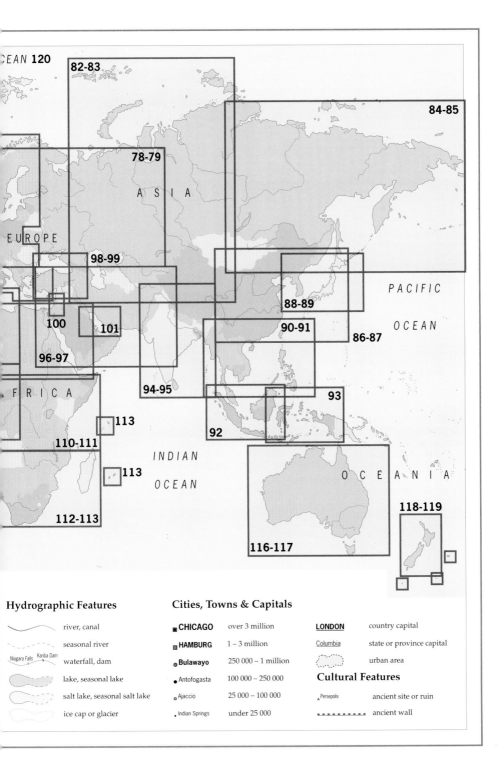

CEAN **120**
82-83
84-85
78-79
A S I A
98-99
E U R O P E
100
101
88-89
PACIFIC
96-97
90-91
OCEAN
86-87
F R I C A
94-95
93
113
92
110-111
INDIAN
113
OCEAN
O C E A N I A
112-113
118-119
116-117

Hydrographic Features

	river, canal
	seasonal river
Niagara Falls Kariba Dam	waterfall, dam
	lake, seasonal lake
	salt lake, seasonal salt lake
	ice cap or glacier

Cities, Towns & Capitals

■ **CHICAGO**	over 3 million
▣ **HAMBURG**	1 – 3 million
◉ **Bulawayo**	250 000 – 1 million
● Antofogasta	100 000 – 250 000
◦ Ajaccio	25 000 – 100 000
· Indian Springs	under 25 000

LONDON	country capital
Columbia	state or province capital
⬚	urban area

Cultural Features

| ▴ Persepolis | ancient site or ruin |
| ┉┉┉┉ | ancient wall |

5

World Flags and Statistics

National populations: United Nations, Population Division, Dept. of Economic & Social Affairs, 1998

NORTH AND CENTRAL AMERICA

Antigua and Barbuda

Area: 171 sq. mi.
Population: 67,000
Capital: St John's (*pop:* 22,342)
Religions: Protestant,
Roman Catholic
Languages: English, Creole
Political system: Constitutional monarchy
Economy: Tourism, fishing
GNP per capita: US$7,380
Currency: East Caribbean dollar

Canada

Area: 3,849,674 sq. mi.
Population: 30,563,000
Capital: Ottawa
(*pop:* 1,010,288)
Religions: Roman Catholic, Protestant
Languages: English, French
Political system: Constitutional monarchy
Economy: Light industries
GNP per capita: US$19,290
Currency: Canadian dollar

Bahamas, The

Area: 5,358 sq. mi.
Population: 296,000
Capital: Nassau
(*pop:* 172,196)
Religions: Protestant, Roman Catholic
Languages: English, Creole
Political system: Constitutional monarchy
Economy: Tourism, banking
GNP per capita: US$11,940
Currency: Bahamian dollar

Costa Rica

Area: 19,730 sq. mi.
Population: 3,841,000
Capital: San José
(*pop:* 1,186,417)
Religion: Roman Catholic
Languages: Spanish, English, Creole
Political system: Republic
Economy: Agriculture, coffee
GNP per capita: US$2,640
Currency: Costa Rican colón

Barbados

Area: 166 sq. mi.
Population: 268,000
Capital: Bridgetown
(*pop:* 108,000)
Religions: Protestant, Roman Catholic
Languages: English, Creole
Political system: Constitutional monarchy
Economy: Sugar, tourism
GNP per capita: US$6,560
Currency: Barbados dollar

Cuba

Area: 42,804 sq. mi.
Population: 11,116,000
Capital: Havana
(*pop:* 2,175,888)
Religion: Roman Catholic
Languages: Spanish, English
Political System: Republic
Economy: Sugar
GNP per capita: US$1,250
Currency: Cuban peso

Belize

Area: 8,763 sq. mi.
Population: 230,000
Capital: Belmopan
(*pop:* 44,087)
Religion: Christian
Languages: English, Spanish, Creole
Political system: Constitutional monarchy
Economy: Agriculture, tourism
GNP per capita: US$2,740
Currency: Belize dollar

Dominica

Area: 290 sq. mi.
Population: 71,000
Capital: Roseau
(*pop:* 16,243)
Religions: Roman Catholic, Protestant
Languages: English, Creole
Political system: Republic
Economy: Bananas, tourism
GNP per capita: US$3,120
Currency: East Caribbean dollar

Dominican Republic

Area: 18,816 sq. mi.
Population: 8,232,000
Capital: Santo Domingo
(*pop:* 2,134,779)
Religions: Roman Catholic, Protestant
Main language: Spanish
Political system: Republic
Economy: Mining, sugar
GNP per capita: US$1,670
Currency: Dominican Republic peso

Haiti

Area: 10,714 sq. mi.
Population: 7,952,000
Capital: Port-au-Prince
(*pop:* 690,168)
Religions: Roman Catholic, Protestant
Languages: Creole, French
Political system: Republic
Economy: Dependent on foreign aid
GNP per capita: US$330
Currency: Gourde

El Salvador

Area: 8,124 sq. mi.
Population: 6,032,000
Capital: San Salvador
(*pop:* 422,570)
Religions: Roman Catholic, Protestant
Main language: Spanish
Political system: Republic
Economy: Coffee, foreign aid
GNP per capita: US$1,810
Currency: El Salvador colón

Honduras

Area: 43,277 sq. mi.
Population: 6,147,000
Capital: Tegucigalpa
(*pop:* 670,000)
Religions: Roman Catholic, others
Languages: Spanish, English
Political system: Republic
Economy: Bananas, coffee
GNP per capita: US$700
Currency: Lempira

Grenada

Area: 133 sq. mi.
Population: 93,000
Capital: St George's
(*pop:* 4,788)
Religions: Roman Catholic, Protestant
Languages: English, Creole
Political system: Constitutional monarchy
Economy: Spices, cocoa
GNP per capita: US$3,000
Currency: East Caribbean dollar

Jamaica

Area: 4,243 sq. mi.
Population: 2,538,000
Capital: Kingston
(*pop:* 103,962)
Religions: Christian, others
Languages: English, Creole
Political system: Constitutional monarchy
Economy: Bauxite, tourism
GNP per capita: US$1,560
Currency: Jamaican dollar

Guatemala

Area: 42,042 sq. mi.
Population: 10,801,000
Capital: Guatemala City
(*pop:* 1,675,589)
Religion: Christian
Languages: Spanish, Indian languages
Political system: Republic
Economy: Agriculture, sugar
GNP per capita: US$1,500
Currency: Quetzal

Mexico

Area: 756,066 sq. mi.
Population: 95,831,000
Capital: Mexico City
(*pop:* 15,047,685)
Religions: Roman Catholic, Protestant
Languages: Spanish, Indian languages
Political system: Republic
Economy: Oil, cash crops
GNP per capita: US$3,680
Currency: Peso

Nicaragua

Area: 50,193 sq. mi.
Population: 4,807,000
Capital: Managua (*pop:* 608,020)
Religions: Roman Catholic, others
Languages: Spanish, English
Political system: Republic
Economy: coffee, sugar
GNP per capita: US$410
Currency: Córdoba

Panama

Area: 29,157 sq. mi.
Population: 2,767,000
Capital: Panama City
(*pop:* 445,902)
Religions: Roman Catholic, others
Languages: Spanish, Creole
Political system: Republic
Economy: Banking, insurance
GNP per capita: US$3,080
Currency: Balboa

St Kitts-Nevis

Area: 101 sq. mi.
Population: 39,000
Capital: Basseterre (*pop:* 14,161)
Religion: Protestant
Languages: English, Creole
Political system: Constitutional monarchy
Economy: Sugar, tourism
GNP per capita: US$6,160
Currency: East Caribbean dollar

St Lucia

Area: 240 sq. mi.
Population: 150,000
Capital: Castries
(*pop:* 56,000)
Religions: Roman Catholic, others
Languages: English, Creole
Political system: Constitutional monarchy
Economy: Agriculture
GNP per capita: US$3,620
Currency: East Caribbean dollar

St Vincent and the Grenadines

Area: 150 sq. mi.
Population: 112,000
Capital: Kingstown (*pop:* 33,694)
Religions: Protestant,
Roman Catholic
Languages: English, Creole
Political system: Constitutional monarchy
Economy: Agriculture
GNP per capita: US$2,500
Currency: East Caribbean dollar

Trinidad and Tobago

Area: 1,981 sq. mi.
Population: 1,283,000
Capital: Port of Spain
(*pop:* 50,878)
Religions: Christian, Hindu, Muslim
Main language: English
Political system: Republic
Economy: Oil, gas
GNP per capita: US$4,230
Currency: Trinidad and Tobago dollar

United States

Area: 3,615,276 sq. mi.
Population: 274,028,000
Capital: Washington DC
(*pop:* 7,051,495)
Religions: Protestant, Roman Catholic, Jewish
Languages: English, Spanish
Political system: Republic
Economy: Manufacturing, agriculture
GNP per capita: US$28,740
Currency: US dollar

SOUTH AMERICA

Argentina

Area: 1,073,518 sq. mi.
Population: 36,123,000
Capital: Buenos Aires
(*pop:* 10,686,163)
Religions: Roman Catholic, Jewish, others
Languages: Spanish, English
Political system: Republic
Economy: Beef, wheat
GNP per capita: US$8,570
Currency: Peso

Bolivia

Area: 424,165 sq. mi.
Population: 7,957,000
Capital: Sucre (*pop:* 144,994)
Religions: Roman Catholic, others
Languages: Spanish, Quechua, Aymará
Political system: Republic
Economy: Mining, oil
GNP per capita: US$950
Currency: Boliviano

Ecuador

Area: 109,484 sq. mi.
Population: 12,175,000
Capital: Quito
(*pop:* 1,387,887)
Religions: Roman Catholic, others
Languages: Spanish, Quechua
Political system: Republic
Economy: Bananas, oil
GNP per capita: US$1,590
Currency: Sucre

Brazil

Area: 3,300,171 sq. mi.
Population: 165,851,000
Capital: Brasilia (*pop:* 1,601,094)
Religion: Christian
Main language: Portuguese
Political system: Republic
Economy: Mining industry
GNP per capita: US$4,720
Currency: Real

Guyana

Area: 83,000 sq. mi.
Population: 850,000
Capital: Georgetown
(*pop:* 250,000)
Religions: Christian, Hindu, Muslim
Languages: English, Creole
Political system: Republic
Economy: Bauxite, gold
GNP per capita: US$800
Currency: Guyana dollar

Chile

Area: 292,135 sq. mi.
Population: 14,824,000
Capital: Santiago
(*pop:* 5,257,937)
Religions: Roman Catholic, Protestant
Languages: Spanish, Indian languages
Political system: Republic
Economy: Copper, wine
GNP per capita: US$5,020
Currency: Chilean peso

Paraguay

Area: 157,048 sq. mi.
Population: 5,222,000
Capital: Asuncion
(*pop:* 718,690)
Religions: Roman Catholic, other
Languages: Spanish, Guaraní
Political system: Republic
Economy: Agriculture, electricity
GNP per capita: US$2,010
Currency: Guaraní

Colombia

Area: 439,737 sq. mi.
Population: 40,803,000
Capital: Bogotá (*pop:* 8,000,000)
Religions: Roman Catholic, others
Languages: Spanish, Indian languages
Political system: Republic
Economy: Coffee, coal
GNP per capita: US$2,280
Currency: Colombian peso

Peru

Area: 496,225 sq. mi.
Population: 24,797,000
Capital: Lima (*pop:* 6,483,901)
Religions: Roman Catholic, others
Languages: Spanish, Quechua, Aymará
Political system: Republic
Economy: Minerals, fishing
GNP per capita: US$2,460
Currency: New Sol

Surinam

Area: 63,037 sq. mi.
Population: 414,000
Capital: Paramaribo
(*pop:* 200,970)
Religions: Christian, Hindu, Muslim
Languages: Dutch, Sranang Tongo, Hindi
Political system: Republic
Economy: Aluminium, bauxite
GNP per capita: US$1,240
Currency: Surinam guilder

Andorra

Area: 175 sq. mi.
Population: 72,000
Capital: Andorra la Vella
(*pop:* 16,151)
Religions: Roman Catholic, others
Languages: Catalan, French, Spanish
Political system: Constitutional principality
Economy: Tourism, banking, commerce
GNP per capita: US$14,000
Currency: French franc, Spanish peseta

Uruguay

Area: 68,500 sq. mi.
Population: 3,289,000
Capital: Montevideo
(*pop:* 1,383,660)
Religions: Roman Catholic, Protestant, Jewish
Main language: Spanish
Political system: Republic
Economy: Agriculture, livestock
GNP per capita: US$6,020
Currency: New Uruguayan peso

Austria

Area: 32,378 sq. mi.
Population: 8,140,000
Capital: Vienna (*pop:* 1,806,737)
Religions: Roman Catholic,
Protestant
Main language: German
Political system: Republic
Economy: Manufacturing industry
GNP per capita: US$27,980
Currency: Schilling

Venezuela

Area: 352,145 sq. mi.
Population: 23,242,000
Capital: Caracas (*pop:* 2,784,042)
Religions: Roman Catholic,
Protestant
Languages: Spanish, Indian languages
Political system: Republic
Economy: Oil, coal, bauxite
GNP per capita: US$3,450
Currency: Bolívar

Belarus

Area: 80,155 sq. mi.
Population: 10,315,000
Capital: Minsk
(*pop:* 1,687,400)
Religions: Russian Orthodox, Roman Catholic
Languages: Belarusian, Russian
Political system: Republic
Economy: Food processing
GNP per capita: US$2,150
Currency: Rouble

EUROPE

Albania

Area: 11,099 sq. mi.
Population: 3,119,000
Capital: Tirana (*pop:* 244,153)
Religions: Muslim, Greek Orthodox
Languages: Albanian, Greek
Political system: Republic
Economy: Oil, gas
GNP per capita: US$750
Currency: Lek

Belgium

Area: 11,783 sq. mi.
Population: 10,141,000
Capital: Brussels (*pop:* 960,324)
Religions: Roman Catholic, others
Languages: Flemish, French
Political system: Constitutional monarchy
Economy: Steel, glassware
GNP per capita: US$26,490
Currency: Belgian franc

Bosnia-Herzegovina

Area: 19,741 sq. mi.
Population: 3,675,000
Capital: Sarajevo
(*pop:* 415,631)
Religion: Muslim
Languages: Serbo-Croat, Croato-Serb
Political system: Republic
Economy: Manufacturing industry
GNP per capita: US$2,600
Currency: Convertible marka

Bulgaria

Area: 42,823 sq. mi.
Population: 8,336,000
Capital: Sofia (*pop:* 1,188,563)
Religions: Christian, Muslim, Jewish
Languages: Bulgarian, Turkish
Political system: Republic
Economy: Agriculture, wine
GNP per capita: US$1,140
Currency: Lev

Croatia

Area: 34,022 sq. mi.
Population: 4,481,000
Capital: Zagreb
(*pop:* 867,717)
Religions: Roman Catholic, Protestant
Languages: Croato-Serb, Serbo-Croat
Political system: Republic
Economy: Manufacturing
GNP per capita: US$4,610
Currency: Kuna

Czech Republic

Area: 30,450 sq. mi.
Population: 10,282,000
Capital: Prague (*pop:* 1,216,568)
Religions: Roman Catholic,
Protestant
Languages: Czech, Slovak
Political system: Republic
Economy: Heavy industry
GNP per capita: US$5,200
Currency: Koruna

Denmark

Area: 16,639 sq. mi.
Population: 5,270,000
Capital: Copenhagen
(*pop:* 1,353,333)
Religions: Evangelical, Lutheran, others
Main language: Danish
Political system: Constitutional monarchy
Economy: Industry, agriculture
GNP per capita: US$32,500
Currency: Kroner

Estonia

Area: 17,413 sq. mi.
Population: 1,429,000
Capital: Tallinn (*pop:* 447,672)
Religions: Evangelical, Lutheran
Languages: Estonian, Russian
Political system: Republic
Economy: Machinery, shipping
GNP per capita: US$3,330
Currency: Kroon

Finland

Area: 130,559 sq. mi.
Population: 5,154,000
Capital: Helsinki
(*pop:* 1,016,291)
Religions: Evangelical, Lutheran, Greek Orthodox
Languages: Finnish, Swedish
Political system: Republic
Economy: Engineering
GNP per capita: US$24,080
Currency: Markka

France

Area: 212,935 sq. mi.
Population: 58,683,000
Capital: Paris (*pop:* 9,319,367)
Religions: Roman Catholic,
Protestant
Main language: French
Political system: Republic
Economy: Steel, chemicals
GNP per capita: US$26,050
Currency: Franc

Germany

Area: 137,735 sq. mi.
Population: 82,133,000
Capital: Berlin *(pop:* 3,472,009)
Religions: Protestant,
Roman Catholic
Main language: German
Political system: Republic
Economy: Cars, engineering
GNP per capita: US$28,260
Currency: Deutsche mark

Ireland, Republic of

Area: 27,137 sq. mi.
Population: 3,681,000
Capital: Dublin
(pop: 952,700)
Religions: Roman Catholic, Protestant
Languages: English, Irish
Political system: Republic
Economy: Agriculture
GNP per capita: US$18,280
Currency: Punt

Greece

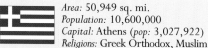

Area: 50,949 sq. mi.
Population: 10,600,000
Capital: Athens (pop: 3,027,922)
Religions: Greek Orthodox, Muslim
Main language: Greek
Political system: Republic
Economy: Tourism, shipping
GNP per capita: US$12,010
Currency: Drachma

Italy

Area: 116,320 sq. mi.
Population: 57,369,000
Capital: Rome (pop: 2,693,383)
Religions: Roman Catholic, other
Main language: Italian
Political system: Republic
Economy: Industry design, textiles
GNP per capita: US$20,120
Currency: Lira

Hungary

Area: 35,920 sq. mi.
Population: 10,116,000
Capital: Budapest
(pop: 2,002,121)
Religions: Roman Catholic, Protestant
Languages: Magyar, German
Political system: Republic
Economy: Industry, agriculture
GNP per capita: US$4,430
Currency: Forint

Latvia

Area: 24,942 sq. mi.
Population: 2,424,000
Capital: Riga (pop: 847,976)
Religions: Evangelical,
Lutheran, others
Languages: Latvian, Russian
Political system: Republic
Economy: Transport, defence equipment
GNP per capita: US$2,430
Currency: Lats

Iceland

Area: 39,769 sq. mi.
Population: 276,000
Capital: Reykjavik (pop: 153,210)
Religions: Evangelical, Lutheran, others
Languages: Icelandic, Danish
Political system: Republic
Economy: Fishing
GNP per capita: US$27,580
Currency: Icelandic króna

Liechtenstein

Area: 62 sq. mi.
Population: 32,000
Capital: Vaduz (pop: 5,072)
Religions: Roman Catholic,
Protestant
Main language: German
Political system: Constitutional monarchy
Economy: Banking, dental products
GNP per capita: US$33,500
Currency: Swiss franc

Lithuania

Area: 25,174 sq. mi.
Population: 3,694,000
Capital: Vilnius
(*pop:* 581,500)
Religions: Roman Catholic, others
Languages: Lithuanian, Russian
Political system: Republic
Economy: Textiles, engineering
GNP per capita: US$2,230
Currency: Litas

Moldova

Area: 13,012 sq. mi.
Population: 4,378,000
Capital: Chisinau
(*pop:* 667,100)
Religions: Romanian Orthodox, Jewish
Languages: Moldovan, Russian
Political system: Republic
Economy: Wine, tobacco, cotton
GNP per capita: US$540
Currency: Leu

Luxembourg

Area: 998 sq. mi.
Population: 422,000
Capital: Luxembourg
(*pop:* 76,446)
Religions: Roman Catholic, others
Languages: Letzebuergesch, French, German
Political system: Constitutional monarchy
Economy: Steel-making
GNP per capita: US$45,440
Currency: Luxembourg franc

Monaco

Area: 0.4 sq. mi.
Population: 33,000
Capital: Monaco (*pop:* 27,063)
Religions: Roman Catholic, others
Languages: French, Italian
Political system: Constitutional monarchy
Economy: Tourism, gambling
GNP per capita: US$16,000
Currency: French franc

Macedonia

Area: 9,928 sq. mi.
Population: 1,999,000
Capital: Skopje
(*pop:* 448,229)
Religions: Christian, Muslim
Languages: Macedonian, Serbo-Croat
Political system: Republic
Economy: Reliant on foreign aid
GNP per capita: US$1,090
Currency: Dinar

Netherlands

Area: 15,770 sq. mi.
Population: 15,678,000
Capital: Amsterdam
(*pop:* 1,100,764)
Religions: Roman Catholic, Protestant, others
Main language: Dutch
Political system: Constitutional monarchy
Economy: Machinery, chemicals
GNP per capita: US$25,820
Currency: Guilder

Malta

Area: 122 sq. mi.
Population: 384,000
Capital: Valletta (*pop:* 9,144)
Religions: Roman Catholic, Anglican
Languages: Maltesse, English
Political system: Republic
Economy: Tourism
GNP per capita: US$11,000
Currency: Maltese lira

Norway

Area: 125,050 sq. mi.
Population: 4,419,000
Capital: Oslo (*pop:* 758,949)
Religions: Evangelical, Lutheran, others
Main language: Norwegian
Political system: Constitutional monarchy
Economy: Oil, gas
GNP per capita: US$36,090
Currency: Krone

Poland

Area: 124,808 sq. mi.
Population: 38,718,000
Capital: Warsaw (*pop:* 1,643,203)
Religions: Roman Catholic, others
Main language: Polish
Political system: Republic
Economy: Heavy industry
GNP per capita: US$3,590
Currency: Zloty

San Marino

Area: 24 sq. mi.
Population: 26,000
Capital: San Marino (*pop:* 4,251)
Religions: Roman Catholic, Protestant
Main language: Italian
Political system: Republic
Economy: Tourism, light industry
GNP per capita: US$20,000
Currency: Italian lira

Portugal

Area: 35,514 sq. mi.
Population: 9,869,000
Capital: Lisbon (*pop:* 2,561,225)
Religions: Roman Catholic,
Protestant
Main language: Portuguese
Political system: Republic
Economy: Agriculture, wine
GNP per capita: US$10,450
Currency: Escudo

Slovakia

Area: 18,924 sq. mi.
Population: 5,377,000
Capital: Bratislava (*pop:* 451,272)
Religions: Roman Catholic, Protestant
Languages: Slovak, Hungarian, Czech
Political system: Republic
Economy: Heavy industry
GNP per capita: US$3,700
Currency: Koruna

Romania

Area: 92,043 sq. mi.
Population: 22,474,000
Capital: Bucharest
(*pop:* 2,060,551)
Religions: Romanian Orthodox, Roman Catholic
Main language: Romanian
Political system: Republic
Economy: Heavy industry
GNP per capita: US$1,420
Currency: Leu

Slovenia

Area: 7,821 sq. mi.
Population: 1,993,000
Capital: Ljubljana
(*pop:* 330,000)
Religions: Roman Catholic, Muslim
Languages: Slovene, Hungarian, Italian
Political system: Republic
Economy: Manufacturing, tourism
GNP per capita: US$9,680
Currency: Tolar

Russia

Area: 6,592,850 sq. mi.
Population: 147,434,000
Capital: Moscow
(*pop:* 8,663,142)
Religions: Russian Orthodox, Jewish, Muslim
Main language: Russian
Political system: Republic
Economy: Oil, gas
GNP per capita: US$2,740
Currency: Rouble

Spain

Area: 195,365 sq. mi.
Population: 39,628,000
Capital: Madrid (*pop:* 3,084,673)
Religions: Roman Catholic, others
Languages: Spanish, Basque
Political system: Constitutional monarchy
Economy: Agriculture, industry
GNP per capita: US$14,510
Currency: Peseta

Sweden

Area: 173,732 sq. mi.
Population: 8,875,000
Capital: Stockholm
(*pop:* 1,532,803)
Religions: Evangelical, Lutheran, Roman Catholic
Main language: Swedish
Political system: Constitutional monarchy
Economy: Car industry, electronics
GNP per capita: US$26,220
Currency: Swedish krona

Switzerland

Area: 15,940 sq. mi.
Population: 7,299,000
Capital: Bern (*pop:* 321,932)
Religions: Roman Catholic, Protestant
Languages: German, French, Italian
Political system: Republic
Economy: Banking, tourism
GNP per capita: US$44,430
Currency: Swiss franc

Ukraine

Area: 233,090 sq. mi.
Population: 50,861,000
Capital: Kiev (*pop:* 2,646,100)
Religions: Ukrainian Orthodox, others
Languages: Ukrainian, Russian
Political system: Republic
Economy: Heavy industry
GNP per capita: US$1,040
Currency: Hryvna

United Kingdom

Area: 94,248 sq. mi.
Population: 58,649,000
Capital: London
(*pop:* 6,962,319)
Religions: Protestant, Roman Catholic, others
Main language: English
Political system: Constitutional monarchy
Economy: Financial services, defence
GNP per capita: US$20,710
Currency: Pound

Vatican City

Area: 0.2 sq. mi.
Population: 1,000
Capital: Vatican City (*pop:* 480)
Religion: Roman Catholic
Main language: Italian
Political system: Absolute rule
Economy: Investment
GNP per capita: not available
Currency: Italian lira

Yugoslavia

Area: 39,449 sq. mi.
Population: 10,635,000
Capital: Belgrade
(*pop:* 1,136,786)
Religions: Orthodox Catholic, Muslim
Languages: Serbo-Croat, Albanian, Hungarian
Political system: Republic
Economy: Largely barter
GNP per capita: US$1,400
Currency: New dinar

AFRICA

Algeria

Area: 919,595 sq. mi.
Population: 30,081,000
Capital: Algiers (*pop:* 3,250,000)
Religions: Muslim, Christian
Languages: Arabic, Berber, French
Political system: Republic
Economy: Oil, gas
GNP per capita: US$1,490
Currency: Algerian dinar

Angola

Area: 481,354 sq. mi.
Population: 12,092,000
Capital: Luanda (*pop:* 475,328)
Religions: Roman Catholic, Protestant
Main language: Portuguese
Political system: Republic
Economy: Oil, diamonds
GNP per capita: US$340
Currency: Readjusted kwanza

Benin

Area: 43,484 sq. mi.
Population: 5,781,000
Capital: Porto Novo
(*pop:* 179,138)
Religions: Traditional beliefs, Muslim
Languages: French, Fon, Bariba, Yoruba
Political system: Republic
Economy: Subsistence farming
GNP per capita: US$380
Currency: Franc CFA

Cameroon

Area: 183,569 sq. mi.
Population: 14,305,000
Capital: Yaoundé (*pop:* 653,670)
Religions: Traditional beliefs,
Christian
Languages: French, English
Political system: Republic
Economy: Oil, timber, cocoa
GNP per capita: US$650
Currency: Franc CFA

Botswana

Area: 224,607 sq. mi.
Population: 1,570,000
Capital: Gaborone (*pop:* 133,468)
Religions: Traditional beliefs, Anglican
Languages: Setswana, English
Political system: Republic
Economy: Diamonds, copper
GNP per capita: US$3,260
Currency: Pula

Cape Verde

Area: 1,557 sq. mi.
Population: 408,000
Capital: Praia (*pop:* 80,000)
Religions: Roman Catholic,
Protestant
Languages: Portuguese, Creole
Political system: Republic
Economy: Subsistence farming
GNP per capita: US$1,090
Currency: Escudo

Burkina

Area: 105,792 sq. mi.
Population: 11,305,000
Capital: Ouagadougou
(*pop:* 634,479)
Religions: Traditional beliefs, Muslim
Languages: French, Mossi, Fulani, Tuareg
Political system: Republic
Economy: Agriculture
GNP per capita: US$240
Currency: Franc CFA

Central African Republic

Area: 240,535 sq. mi.
Population: 3,485,000
Capital: Bangui (*pop:* 473,817)
Religions: Christian, traditional
beliefs
Languages: French, Sango
Political system: Republic
Economy: Subsistence farming, gold
GNP per capita: US$320
Currency: Franc CFA

Burundi

Area: 10,747 sq. mi.
Population: 6,457,000
Capital: Bujumbura
(*pop:* 235,440)
Religions: Roman Catholic, traditional beliefs
Languages: Kirundi, French, Kiswahili
Political system: Republic
Economy: Agriculture
GNP per capita: US$180
Currency: Burundi franc

Chad

Area: 495,755 sq. mi.
Population: 7,270,000
Capital: Ndjamena
(*pop:* 179,000)
Religions: Muslim, Christian
Languages: French, Arabic, Sara
Political system: Republic
Economy: Subsistence farming
GNP per capita: US$240
Currency: Franc CFA

Comoros

Area: 863 sq. mi.
Population: 658,000
Capital: Moroni (*pop:* 17,267)
Religions: Muslim, Roman Catholic
Languages: French, Arabic, Comoran
Political system: Republic
Economy: Subsistence farming
GNP per capita: US$400
Currency: Comorian franc

Egypt

Area: 386,662 sq. mi.
Population: 65,978,000
Capital: Cairo (*pop:* 13,000,000)
Religions: Muslim, others
Main language: Arabic
Political system: Republic
Economy: Oil, gas
GNP per capita: US$1,180
Currency: Egyptian pound

Congo

Area: 132,047 sq. mi.
Population: 2,785,000
Capital: Brazzaville
(*pop:* 596,200)
Religions: Roman Catholic, traditional beliefs
Languages: French, Lingala, Kikongo
Political system: Republic
Economy: Oil, sugar, coffee
GNP per capita: US$660
Currency: Franc CFA

Equatorial Guinea

Area: 10,831 sq. mi.
Population: 431,000
Capital: Malabo (*pop:* 30,418)
Religions: Roman Catholic, others
Languages: French, Spanish
Political system: Republic
Economy: Timber, cocoa, oil
GNP per capita: US$1,050
Currency: Franc CFA

Congo, Democratic Republic of

Area: 905,355 sq. mi.
Population: 49,139,000
Capital: Kinshasa
(*pop:* 2,664,309)
Religions: Christian, traditional beliefs
Languages: Swahili, Lingala, French
Political system: Republic
Economy: Minerals
GNP per capita: US$110
Currency: Congolese franc

Eritrea

Area: 45,406 sq. mi.
Population: 3,577,000
Capital: Asmara
(*pop:* 358,100)
Religions: Coptic Christian, Muslim, others
Languages: English, Arabic
Political system: Republic
Economy: Subsistence farming, gold
GNP per capita: US$210
Currency: Nakfa

Djibouti

Area: 8,958 sq. mi.
Population: 623,000
Capital: Djibouti
(*pop:* 340,700)
Religions: Christian, others
Languages: Arabic, French, Somali
Political system: Republic
Economy: Sea trade
GNP per capita: US$1,000
Currency: Djibouti franc

Ethiopia

Area: 426,373 sq. mi.
Population: 59,649,000
Capital: Addis Ababa
(*pop:* 2,316,400)
Religions: Muslim, Christian
Languages: Amharic, English, Arabic
Political system: Republic
Economy: Subsistence farming
GNP per capita: US$110
Currency: Ethiopian birr

Gabon

Area: 103,347 sq. mi.
Population: 1,167,000
Capital: Libreville *(pop:* 251,000)
Religions: Roman Catholic, Protestant
Languages: French, Fang, Eshira
Political system: Republic
Economy: Oil, timber, cocoa
GNP per capita: US$4,230
Currency: Franc CFA

Gambia, The

Area: 4,361 sq. mi.
Population: 1,229,000
Capital: Banjul *(pop:* 109,986)
Religions: Muslim, Christian
Languages: English, Mandinka, Fula, Wollof
Political system: Republic
Economy: Agriculture, fishing
GNP per capita: US$350
Currency: Dalasi

Ghana

Area: 92,098 sq. mi.
Population: 19,162,000
Capital: Accra *(pop:* 738,498)
Religions: Traditional beliefs, Muslim
Languages: English, Twi, Fanti
Political system: Republic
Economy: Cocoa, timber, gold
GNP per capita: US$370
Currency: Cedi

Guinea

Area: 94,926 sq. mi.
Population: 7,337,000
Capital: Conakry *(pop:* 763,000)
Religions: Muslim, Christian
Languages: French, Susu, Malinké
Political system: Republic
Economy: Cash crops
GNP per capita: US$570
Currency: Guinea franc

Guinea-Bissau

Area: 13,948 sq. mi.
Population: 1,161,000
Capital: Bissau *(pop:* 109,214)
Religions: Traditional beliefs,
Muslim
Languages: Portuguese, Creole
Political system: Republic
Economy: Subsistence farming
GNP per capita: US$240
Currency: Franc CFA

Ivory Coast

Area: 124,504 sq. mi.
Population: 14,292,000
Capital: Yamoussoukro
(pop: 126,191)
Religions: Traditional beliefs, Muslim
Main language: French
Political system: Republic
Economy: Cash crops, timber
GNP per capita: US$690
Currency: Franc CFA

Kenya

Area: 224,081 sq. mi.
Population: 29,008,000
Capital: Nairobi *(pop:* 1,400,000)
Religions: Roman Catholic,
Protestant
Languages: Swahili, English
Political system: Republic
Economy: Tourism, tea
GNP per capita: US$330
Currency: Kenya shilling

Lesotho

Area: 11,720 sq. mi.
Population: 2,062,000
Capital: Maseru *(pop:* 288,951)
Religions: Roman Catholic,
Protestant
Languages: Sesotho, English
Political system: Constitutional monarchy
Economy: Subsistence farming
GNP per capita: US$670
Currency: Loti

Liberia

Area: 43,000 sq. mi.
Population: 2,666,000
Capital: Monrovia
(*pop:* 421,053)
Religions: Traditional beliefs, Muslim
Languages: English, many ethnic languages
Political system: Republic
Economy: Unstable
GNP per capita: US$850
Currency: Liberian dollar

Mali

Area: 478,841 sq. mi.
Population: 10,694,000
Capital: Bamako (*pop:* 658,275)
Religions: Muslim, traditional beliefs
Languages: French, Bambara, Fulani
Political system: Republic
Economy: Farming, herding, fishing
GNP per capita: US$260
Currency: Franc CFA

Libya

Area: 679,362 sq. mi.
Population: 5,339,000
Capital: Tripoli
(*pop:* 1,000,000)
Religions: Muslim, others
Languages: Arabic, Tuareg
Political system: Republic
Economy: Oil
GNP per capita: US$7,000
Currency: Libyan dinar

Mauritania

Area: 395,956 sq. mi.
Population: 2,529,000
Capital: Nouakchott
(*pop:* 850,000)
Religion: Muslim
Languages: Arabic, French, Pulaar
Political system: Republic
Economy: Agriculture, mining
GNP per capita: US$450
Currency: Ouguiya

Madagascar

Area: 226,658 sq. mi.
Population: 15,057,000
Capital: Antananarivo
(*pop:* 377,600)
Religions: Traditional beliefs, Christian
Languages: Malagasy, French
Political system: Republic
Economy: Coffee, vanilla
GNP per capita: US$250
Currency: Franc malgache

Mauritius

Area: 788 sq. mi.
Population: 1,141,000
Capital: Port Louis
(*pop:* 144,776)
Religions: Hindu, Roman Catholic, Muslim
Languages: Creole, English, French, Hindi
Political system: Republic
Economy: Sugar, tourism
GNP per capita: US$3,800
Currency: Mauritius rupee

Malawi

Area: 45,747 sq. mi.
Population: 10,346,000
Capital: Lilongwe (*pop:* 233,973)
Religions: Protestant, traditional
beliefs
Languages: Chichewa, English
Political system: Republic
Economy: Tobacco, tea
GNP per capita: US$220
Currency: Kwacha

Morocco

Area: 172,414 sq. mi.
Population: 27,377,000
Capital: Rabat (*pop:* 1,220,000)
Religion: Muslim
Languages: Arabic, Berber, French, Spanish
Political system: Constitutional monarchy
Economy: Phosphates, tourism
GNP per capita: US$1,250
Currency: Dirham

Mozambique

Area: 309,496 sq. mi.
Population: 18,880,000
Capital: Maputo (*pop:* 882,601)
Religions: Traditional beliefs, Christian
Main language: Portuguese
Political system: Republic
Economy: Foreign aid
GNP per capita: US$90
Currency: Metical

Rwanda

Area: 10,169 sq. mi.
Population: 6,604,000
Capital: Kigali (*pop:* 156,000)
Religions: Roman Catholic,
traditional beliefs
Languages: Kinyarwanda, French, English
Political system: Republic
Economy: Coffee, oil, gas
GNP per capita: US$210
Currency: Rwanda franc

Namibia

Area: 318,261 sq. mi.
Population: 1,660,000
Capital: Windhoek (*pop:* 147,056)
Religions: Christian, others
Languages: English, Afrikaans, German
Political system: Republic
Economy: Uranium, diamonds
GNP per capita: US$2,220
Currency: Namibian dollar

São Tomé and Príncipe

Area: 372 sq. mi.
Population: 141,000
Capital: São Tomé
(*pop:* 43,420)
Religions: Roman Catholic, others
Languages: Portuguese, Creole
Political system: Republic
Economy: Cocoa, coffee, palm oil
GNP per capita: US$270
Currency: Dobra

Niger

Area: 489,191 sq. mi.
Population: 10,078,000
Capital: Niamey (*pop:* 392,169)
Religions: Muslim, traditional beliefs
Languages: French, Hausa, Djerma, Fulani
Political system: Republic
Economy: Uranium
GNP per capita: US$200
Currency: Franc CFA

Senegal

Area: 75,955 sq. mi.
Population: 9,003,000
Capital: Dakar (*pop:* 1,641,358)
Religions: Muslim, traditional beliefs
Languages: French, Wolof, Fulani, Serer
Political system: Republic
Economy: Farming, mining
GNP per capita: US$550
Currency: Franc CFA

Nigeria

Area: 356,669 sq. mi.
Population: 106,409,000
Capital: Abuja (*pop:* 378,671)
Religions: Muslim, Christian
Languages: English, Hausa, Yoruba, Ibo
Political system: Republic
Economy: Oil
GNP per capita: US$260
Currency: Naira

Seychelles

Area: 176 sq. mi.
Population: 76,000
Capital: Victoria
(*pop:* 24,324)
Religions: Roman Catholic, others
Languages: French, English, Creole
Political system: Republic
Economy: Tourism
GNP per capita: US$6,880
Currency: Rupee

Sierra Leone

Area: 27,699 sq. mi.
Population: 4,568,000
Capital: Freetown (*pop:* 469,776)
Religions: Traditional beliefs, Muslim
Languages: English, French, Krio
Political system: Republic
Economy: Subsistence farming
GNP per capita: US$200
Currency: Leone

Swaziland

Area: 6,704 sq. mi.
Population: 952,000
Capital: Mbabane (*pop:* 38,290)
Religions: Protestant, others
Languages: Siswati, English
Political system: Absolute monarchy
Economy: Cash crops, asbestos
GNP per capita: US$1,440
Currency: Lilangeni

Somalia

Area: 246,201 sq. mi.
Population: 9,237,000
Capital: Mogadishu (*pop:* 1,000,000)
Religions: Sunni Muslim, others
Languages: Somali, Arabic, English
Political system: Republic
Economy: Foreign aid
GNP per capita: US$500
Currency: Somali shilling

Tanzania

Area: 341,217 sq. mi.
Population: 32,102,000
Capital: Dodoma (*pop:* 88,474)
Religions: Traditional beliefs, Muslim
Languages: Swahili, English
Political system: Republic
Economy: Agriculture, cash crops
GNP per capita: US$210
Currency: Shilling

South Africa

Area: 471,445 sq. mi.
Population: 39,357,000
Capital: Pretoria (*pop:* 525,583)
Religions: Protestant, Roman Catholic, others
Languages: English, Afrikaans, Zulu, Xhosa
Political system: Republic
Economy: Manufacturing, agriculture
GNP per capita: US$3,400
Currency: Rand

Togo

Area: 21,925 sq. mi.
Population: 4,397,000
Capital: Lomé (*pop:* 366,476)
Religions: Traditional beliefs, Christian
Languages: French, Ewe
Political system: Republic
Economy: Agriculture, coffee
GNP per capita: US$330
Currency: Franc CFA

Sudan

Area: 967,500 sq. mi.
Population: 28,292,000
Capital: Khartoum (*pop:* 924,505)
Religions: Muslim, traditional beliefs
Languages: Arabic, English
Political system: Republic
Economy: Cash crops
GNP per capita: US$280
Currency: Sudanese dinar

Tunisia

Area: 63,170 sq. mi.
Population: 9,335,000
Capital: Tunis (*pop:* 1,394,749)
Religions: Muslim, Christian
Languages: Arabic, French, English
Political system: Republic
Economy: Oil, gas
GNP per capita: US$2,090
Currency: Tunisian dinar

Uganda

Area: 93,065 sq. mi.
Population: 20,554,000
Capital: Kampala (*pop:* 750,000)
Religions: Roman Catholic,
Protestant, others
Languages: English, Swahili
Political system: Republic
Economy: Coffee, mining
GNP per capita: US$330
Currency: Uganda shilling

Zambia

Area: 290,587 sq. mi.
Population: 8,781,000
Capital: Lusaka (*pop:* 982,362)
Religions: Christian,
traditional beliefs
Languages: English, Nyanja, Tonga, Beruba
Political system: Republic
Economy: Subsistence farming
GNP per capita: US$380
Currency: Kwacha

Zimbabwe

Area: 150,872 sq. mi.
Population: 11,377,000
Capital: Harare
(*pop:* 1,189,103)
Religions: Christian, traditional beliefs
Languages: English, Shona, Ndebele
Political system: Republic
Economy: Self-sufficient
GNP per capita: US$750
Currency: Zimbabwe dollar

ASIA

Afghanistan

Area: 251,773 sq. mi.
Population: 21,354,000
Capital: Kabul
(*pop:* 1,424,400)
Religions: Sumi, Muslim
Languages: Dari, Pushtu
Political system: Republic
Economy: Agriculture
GNP per capita: US$300
Currency: Afghani

Armenia

Area: 11,506 sq. mi.
Population: 3,536,000
Capital: Yerevan
(*pop:* 1,254,000)
Religions: Armenian Apostolic, others
Languages: Armenian, Russian
Political system: Republic
Economy: Mining, agriculture
GNP per capita: US$530
Currency: Dram

Azerbaijan

Area: 33,436 sq. mi.
Population: 7,669,000
Capital: Baku
(*pop:* 1,149,000)
Religions: Muslim, Armenian Apostolic
Languages: Azerbaijani, Russian
Political system: Republic
Economy: Oil, gas
GNP per capita: US$510
Currency: Manat

Bahrain

Area: 268 sq. mi.
Population: 595,000
Capital: Manama
(*pop:* 140,401)
Religions: Shi'a Muslim, Christian
Languages: Arabic, English
Political system: Constitutional monarchy
Economy: Oil, gas
GNP per capita: US$7,840
Currency: Bahraini dinar

Bangladesh

Area: 55,598 sq. mi.
Population: 124,774,000
Capital: Dhaka (*pop:* 3,397,187)
Religions: Muslim, Hindu
Languages: Bengali, English
Political system: Republic
Economy: Foreign aid, jute
GNP per capita: US$270
Currency: Taka

Bhutan

Area: 18,147 sq. mi.
Population: 2,004,000
Capital: Thimphu (*pop:* 15,000)
Religions: Buddhist, Hindu
Languages: Dzongkha, English
Political system: Absolute monarchy
Economy: Subsistence farming
GNP per capita: US$400
Currency: Ngultrum

Brunei

Area: 2,226 sq. mi.
Population: 315,000
Capital: Bandar Seri Begawan
(*pop:* 49,902)
Religions: Muslim, Buddhist, Christian
Languages: Malay, English
Political system: Absolute monarchy
Economy: Oil, gas
GNP per capita: US$14,500
Currency: Brunei dollar

Cambodia

Area: 69,898 sq. mi.
Population: 10,716,000
Capital: Phnom Penh (*pop:* 832,000)
Religions: Buddhist, Muslim
Languages: Khmer, Chinese, Vietnamese
Political system: Constitutional monarchy
Economy: Rubber, timber
GNP per capita: US$300
Currency: Riel

China

Area: 3,705,408 sq. mi.
Population: 1,240,658,000
Capital: Beijing (*pop:* 7,362,426)
Religions: Confucian, Buddhist
Languages: Mandarin Chinese, Cantonese
Political system: Republic
Economy: Agriculture, industry
GNP per capita: US$860
Currency: Yuan

Cyprus

Area: 3,572 sq. mi.
Population: 771,000
Capital: Nicosia (*pop:* 188,800)
Religions: Greek Orthodox, Muslim
Languages: Greek, Turkish
Political system: Republic
Economy: Tourism, shipping
GNP per capita: US$11,500
Currency: Cyprus pound

Georgia

Area: 26,911 sq. mi.
Population: 5,059,000
Capital: Tbilisi (*pop:* 1,268,000)
Religion: Georgian Orthodox
Languages: Georgian, Russian, Armenian
Political system: Republic
Economy: Food processing
GNP per capita: US$840
Currency: Lari

India

Area: 1,269,346 sq. mi.
Population: 982,223,000
Capital: New Delhi
(*pop:* 301,297)
Religions: Hindu, Muslim, Christian
Languages: Hindi, English, others
Political system: Republic
Economy: High-tech industry, clothing
GNP per capita: US$390
Currency: Indian rupee

Indonesia

Area: 735,358 sq. mi.
Population: 206,338,000
Capital: Jakarta (*pop:* 9,160,500)
Religions: Muslim, Christian, others
Languages: Bahasa Indonesian, Dutch, English
Political system: Republic
Economy: Timber, minerals
GNP per capita: US$1,110
Currency: Rupiah

Iran

Area: 630,577 sq. mi.
Population: 65,758,000
Capital: Tehran
(*pop:* 6,750,043)
Religion: Shi'a Muslim
Languages: Persian, Turkish, Kurdish, Arabic
Political system: Republic
Economy: Oil
GNP per capita: US$1,780
Currency: Rial

Iraq

Area: 169,235 sq. mi.
Population: 21,800,000
Capital: Baghdad
(*pop:* 3,841,268)
Religion: Shi'a Muslim
Languages: Arabic, Kurdish, Turkic, Aramaic
Political system: Republic
Economy: Oil, collapsed due to UN sanctions
GNP per capita: US$1,800
Currency: Dinar

Israel

Area: 8,130 sq. mi.
Population: 7,020,000
Capital: Jerusalem (*pop:* 662,700)
Religions: Jewish, Muslim
Languages: Hebrew, Arabic
Political system: Republic
Economy: Industry, agriculture
GNP per capita: US$15,900
Currency: Shekel

Japan

Area: 145,870 sq. mi.
Population: 126,281,000
Capital: Tokyo (*pop:* 11,927,457)
Religions: Shinto, Buddhism
Main language: Japanese
Political system: Constitutional monarchy
Economy: Electronics
GNP per capita: US$37,850
Currency: Yen

Jordan

Area: 37,738 sq. mi.
Population: 6,304,000
Capital: Amman
(*pop:* 1,270,000)
Religions: Muslim, Christian
Languages: Arabic, English, French
Political system: Constitutional monarchy
Economy: Phosphates, chemicals
GNP per capita: US$1,570
Currency: Jordanian dinar

Kazakhstan

Area: 1,049,156 sq. mi.
Population: 16,319,000
Capital: Astana
(*pop:* 292,000)
Religions: Muslim, Russian Orthodox
Languages: Kazakh, Russian
Political system: Republic
Economy: Gas, oil, coal, uranium
GNP per capita: US$1,340
Currency: Tenge

Kuwait

Area: 6,880 sq. mi.
Population: 1,811,000
Capital: Kuwait
(*pop:* 400,000)
Religions: Muslim, Christian
Languages: Arabic, English
Political system: Constitutional monarchy
Economy: Oil, gas
GNP per capita: US$17,390
Currency: Kuwaiti dinar

Kyrgyzstan

Area: 76,641 sq. mi.
Population: 4,643,000
Capital: Bishkek (*pop:* 627,800)
Religions: Muslim, Russian
Orthodox
Languages: Kirghiz, Russian
Political system: Republic
Economy: Collective farming, coal
GNP per capita: US$440
Currency: Som

Laos

Area: 91,429 sq. mi.
Population: 5,163,000
Capital: Vientiane (*pop:* 120,000)
Religions: Buddhist, Christian
Languages: Lao, French
Political system: Republic
Economy: Timber, mining
GNP per capita: US$400
Currency: Kip

Lebanon

Area: 4,015 sq. mi.
Population: 3,191,000
Capital: Beirut (*pop:* 1,500,000)
Religions: Muslim, Christian
Languages: Arabic, French, English
Political system: Republic
Economy: Banking, services
GNP per capita: US$3,350
Currency: Lebanese pound

Malaysia

Area: 127,320 sq. mi.
Population: 21,410,000
Capital: Kuala Lumpur
(*pop:* 1,145,075)
Religions: Muslim, Buddhist
Languages: Malay, English, Chinese, Tamil
Political system: Constitutional monarchy
Economy: Electronics, cars
GNP per capita: US$4,680
Currency: Malaysian dollar

Maldives

Area: 115 sq. mi.
Population: 271,000
Capital: Male (*pop:* 62,973)
Religion: Sunni Muslim
Main language: Maldivian
Political system: Republic
Economy: Tourism, fishing
GNP per capita: US$1,150
Currency: Rufiyaa

Mongolia

Area: 604,829 sq. mi.
Population: 2,579,000
Capital: Ulan Bator
(*pop:* 515,100)
Religions: Buddhist, Muslim
Languages: Mongolian, Kazakh
Political system: Republic
Economy: Agriculture, oil, coal
GNP per capita: US$390
Currency: Tugrik

Myanmar (Burma)

Area: 261,228 sq. mi.
Population: 44,497,000
Capital: Rangoon
(*pop:* 2,513,023)
Religions: Buddhist, Muslim
Languages: Burmese, English, Shan, Karen
Political system: Republic
Economy: Teak, rice
GNP per capita: US$1,000
Currency: Kyat

Nepal

Area: 56,827 sq. mi.
Population: 22,847,000
Capital: Kathmandu (*pop:* 419,073)
Religions: Hindu, Buddhist
Main language: Nepali
Political system: Constitutional monarchy
Economy: Agriculture
GNP per capita: US$210
Currency: Nepalese rupee

North Korea

Area: 46,540 sq. mi.
Population: 23,348,000
Capital: Pyongyang
(*pop:* 2,000,000)
Religions: Traditional beliefs, Buddhist
Main language: Korean
Political system: Republic, one-party state
Economy: Manufacturing, agriculture
GNP per capita: US$1,000
Currency: Won

Oman

Area: 82,030 sq. mi.
Population: 2,382,000
Capital: Muscat
(*pop:* 400,000)
Religions: Ibadi Muslim, Hindu
Languages: Arabic, Qarra, Mahra
Political system: Absolute monarchy
Economy: Oil, gas
GNP per capita: US$4,820
Currency: Rial

Pakistan

Area: 307,374 sq. mi.
Population: 148,166,000
Capital: Islamabad (*pop:* 350,000)
Religions: Sunni Muslim, Hindu
Languages: Punjabi, Urdu, Sindi, Pushto
Political system: Republic
Economy: Cotton, rice, oil
GNP per capita: US$490
Currency: Pakistan rupee

Philippines

Area: 115,831 sq. mi.
Population: 72,944,000
Capital: Manila
(*pop:* 8,594,150)
Religions: Roman Catholic, Protestant
Languages: Filipino, English
Political system: Republic
Economy: Agriculture
GNP per capita: US$1,220
Currency: Philippine peso

Qatar

Area: 4,247 sq. mi.
Population: 579,000
Capital: Doha (*pop:* 217,294)
Religions: Sunni Muslim, Hindu
Languages: Arabic, English
Political system: Absolute monarchy
Economy: Oil, gas
GNP per capita: US$11,600
Currency: Qatar riyal

Saudi Arabia

Area: 830,000 sq. mi.
Population: 20,181,000
Capital: Riyadh (*pop:* 1,800,000)
Religions: Sunni Muslim
Languages: Arabic, English
Political system: Absolute monarchy
Economy: Oil, gas
GNP per capita: US$7,040
Currency: Saudi riyal

Singapore

Area: 239 sq. mi.
Population: 3,476,000
Capital: Singapore
Religions: Buddhist, Christian,
Muslim
Languages: Malay, Mandarin, Tamil, English
Political system: Republic
Economy: Finance, banking
GNP per capita: US$32,940
Currency: Singapore dollar

South Korea

Area: 38,330 sq. mi.
Population: 46,109,000
Capital: Seoul (*pop:* 10,776,201)
Religions: Mahayana Buddhist,
Protestant
Main language: Korean
Political system: Republic
Economy: Ship-building, cars
GNP per capita: US$10,550
Currency: Won

Sri Lanka

Area: 25,332 sq. mi.
Population: 18,455,000
Capital: Colombo
(*pop:* 615,000)
Religions: Buddhist, Hindu, Christian
Languages: Sinhala, Tamil, English
Political system: Republic
Economy: Tea, tourism
GNP per capita: US$800
Currency: Sri Lankan rupee

Syria

Area: 71,498 sq. mi.
Population: 15,333,000
Capital: Damascus
(*pop:* 1,549,000)
Religions: Sunni Muslim, Christian
Languages: Arabic, Kurdish, Turkish
Political system: Republic
Economy: Oil
GNP per capita: US$1,150
Currency: Syrian pound

Taiwan

Area: 13,800 sq. mi.
Population: 21,700,000
Capital: Taipei (*pop:* 2,607,010)
Religions: Buddhist, Confucian, Taoist
Languages: Mandarin Chinese, Taiwanese
Political system: Republic
Economy: Manufacturing, electronics
GNP per capita: US$12,000
Currency: New Taiwan dollar

Tajikistan

Area: 55,251 sq. mi.
Population: 6,015,000
Capital: Dushanbe
(*pop:* 602,000)
Religion: Sunni Muslim
Languages: Tajik, Uzbek, Russian
Political system: Republic
Economy: Carpet-making
GNP per capita: US$330
Currency: Tajik rouble

Thailand

Area: 198,115 sq. mi.
Population: 60,300,000
Capital: Bangkok
(*pop:* 5,876,000)
Religions: Buddhist, Muslim
Languages: Thai, Chinese, Khmer, Malay
Political system: Constitutional monarchy
Economy: Manufacturing, rice, rubber
GNP per capita: US$2,800
Currency: Baht

Turkey

Area: 299,158 sq. mi.
Population: 64,479,000
Capital: Ankara (*pop:* 3,103,000)
Religion: Muslim
Main language: Turkish
Political system: Republic
Economy: Textiles, manufacturing
GNP per capita: US$3,130
Currency: Turkish lira

Turkmenistan

Area: 188,456 sq. mi.
Population: 4,309,000
Capital: Ashkhabad
(*pop:* 407,000)
Religion: Muslim
Languages: Turkmenian, Russian, Uzbek
Political system: Republic
Economy: Cotton, gas
GNP per capita: US$630
Currency: Manat

United Arab Emirates

Area: 32,278 sq. mi.
Population: 2,353,000
Capital: Abu Dhabi
(*pop:* 450,000)
Religion: Sunni Muslim
Languages: Arabic, English
Political system: Federation of absolute monarchies
Economy: Oil, gas
GNP per capita: US$17,400
Currency: Dirham

Uzbekistan

Area: 172,742 sq. mi.
Population: 23,574,000
Capital: Tashkent
(*pop:* 2,094,000)
Religions: Muslim
Languages: Uzbek, Russian
Political system: Republic
Economy: Agriculture, oil, gas
GNP per capita: US$1,010
Currency: Sum

Vietnam

Area: 128,066 sq. mi.
Population: 77,562,000
Capital: Hanoi (*pop:* 3,056,146)
Religions: Buddhist, Roman Catholic
Languages: Vietnamese, French, English
Political system: Republic
Economy: Steel, gas, oil
GNP per capita: US$320
Currency: Đông

Yemen

Area: 203,850 sq. mi.
Population: 16,887,000
Capital: San'a (*pop:* 926,595)
Religion: Sunni Muslim
Main language: Arabic
Political system: Republic
Economy: Oil, gas
GNP per capita: US$270
Currency: Riyal

AUSTRALIA AND OCEANIA

Australia

Area: 2,988,902 sq. mi.
Population: 18,520,000
Capital: Canberra
(*pop:* 307,100)
Religions: Protestant, Roman Catholic
Main Language: English
Political system: Constitutional monarchy
Economy: Mining, agriculture
GNP per capita: US$20,540
Currency: Australian dollar

Fiji

Area: 7,056 sq. mi.
Population: 796,000
Capital: Suva (*pop:* 141,273)
Religions: Christian, Hindu,
Muslim
Languages: Fijian, Hindi
Political system: Republic
Economy: Sugar, gold, timber
GNP per capita: US$2,470
Currency: Fiji dollar

Kiribati

Area: 280 sq. mi.
Population: 81,000
Capital: Bairiki (*pop:* 17,921)
Religions: Roman Catholic,
Protestant
Languages: I-Kiribati, English
Political system: Republic
Economy: Coconuts, copra
GNP per capita: US$910
Currency: Australian dollar

Marshall Islands

Area: 70 sq. mi.
Population: 60,000
Capital: Dalap-Uliga-Darrit
(*pop:* 20,000)
Religions: Protestant, Roman Catholic
Languages: Marshallese, English
Political system: Republic
Economy: Copra, tuna-fishing
GNP per capita: US$1,770
Currency: US dollar

Micronesia, Federated States of

Area: 271 sq. mi.
Population: 114,000
Capital: Palikir
Religions: Roman Catholic,
Protestant
Languages: English, Yapese, Ulithian, Woleaian
Political system: Republic
Economy: Fishing, US aid
GNP per capita: US$1,980
Currency: US dollar

Nauru

Area: 8 sq. mi.
Population: 11,000
Capital: Yaren
Religions: Christian, others
Languages: Nauruan, English
Political system: Republic
Economy: Phosphate
GNP per capita: US$10,000
Currency: Australian dollar

New Zealand

Area: 104,454 sq. mi.
Population: 3,796,000
Capital: Wellington
(*pop:* 326,900)
Religions: Protestant, Roman Catholic
Languages: English, Maori
Political system: Constitutional monarchy
Economy: Agriculture, wool
GNP per capita: US$16,480
Currency: New Zealand dollar

Solomon Islands

Area: 11,157 sq. mi.
Population: 417,000
Capital: Honiara
(*pop:* 40,000)
Religions: Christian, others
Main language: English
Political system: Constitutional monarchy
Economy: Palm oil, copra, cocoa
GNP per capita: US$900
Currency: Solomon Islands dollar

Palau

Area: 177 sq. mi.
Population: 19,000
Capital: Koror (*pop:* 10,493)
Religions: Christian,
traditional beliefs
Languages: Palauan, English
Political system: Republic
Economy: Coconuts, US aid
GNP per capita: US$2,260
Currency: US dollar

Tonga

Area: 288 sq. mi.
Population: 98,000
Capital: Nuku'alofa
(*pop:* 29,018)
Religions: Protestant, Roman Catholic
Languages: Tongan, English
Political system: Constitutional monarchy
Economy: Cash crops
GNP per capita: US$1,830
Currency: Pa'anga

Papua New Guinea

Area: 178,704 sq. mi.
Population: 4,600,000
Capital: Port Moresby
(*pop:* 173,500)
Religions: Christian, others
Languages: English, Pidgin English
Political system: Constitutional monarchy
Economy: Gold, copper, oil
GNP per capita: US$940
Currency: Kina

Tuvalu

Area: 10 sq. mi.
Population: 11,000
Capital: Fongafale
(*pop:* 2,856)
Religions: Protestant, others
Languages: Tuvaluan, English
Political system: Constitutional monarchy
Economy: Fishing, foreign aid
GNP per capita: US$600
Currency: Australian dollar

Samoa

Area: 1,093 sq. mi.
Population: 174,000
Capital: Apia (*pop:* 36,000)
Religions: Protestant,
Roman Catholic
Languages: Samoan, English
Political system: Constitutional monarchy
Economy: Agriculture, banking
GNP per capita: US$1,150
Currency: Tala

Vanuatu

Area: 4,706 sq. mi.
Population: 182,000
Capital: Port-Vila (*pop:* 26,100)
Religions: Protestant, Roman Catholic
Languages: Bislama, English, French
Political system: Republic
Economy: Copra, cocoa
GNP per capita: US$1,310
Currency: Vatu

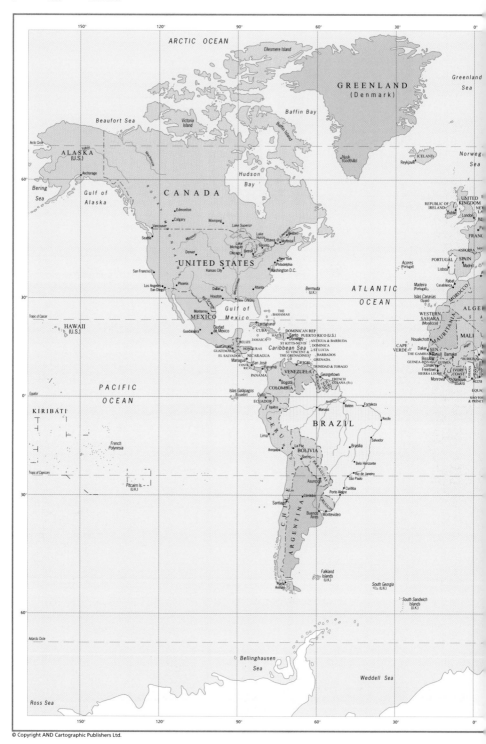

Equatorial Scale 1 : 154 000 000

0   1000   2000   3000   4000 km

0   1000   2000 miles

ARCTIC OCEAN

Ellesmere Island

GREENLAND
(Denmark)

Greenland
Sea

Baffin Bay

Beaufort Sea

Victoria
Island

Baffin Island

Arctic Circle

ALASKA
(U.S.)

Nuuk
(Godthåb)

ICELAND

Norweg
Sea

ReykJavik

Anchorage

Bering
Sea

Gulf of
Alaska

Hudson
Bay

CANADA

UNITED
KINGDOM

REPUBLIC OF
IRELAND

Dublin

London

NE

Edmonton

Calgary

Winnipeg

Lake Superior

Vancouver

Lake
Huron

Quebec

FRANC

Seattle

Lake
Michigan

Ottawa

Toronto

Montreal

ANDORRA

Denver

Chicago

Detroit

PORTUGAL

SPAIN

San Francisco

UNITED STATES

Kansas City

New York

Philadelphia

Açores
(Portugal)

Lisbon

Madrid

Washington D.C.

Los Angeles
San Diego

Phoenix

Dallas

Atlanta

Bermuda
(U.K.)

ATLANTIC

Madeira
(Portugal)

Casablanca

Rabat

MOROCCO

Houston

New Orleans

OCEAN

Islas Canarias
(Spain)

Tropic of Cancer

HAWAII
(U.S.)

MEXICO

Gulf of
Mexico

THE
BAHAMAS

WESTERN
SAHARA
(Morocco)

ALGE

Monterrey

La Habana

CUBA

Nouakchott

MALI

Guadalajara

Ciudad
de Mexico

DOMINICAN REP.
Santo
Domingo

PUERTO RICO (U.S.)

CAPE
VERDE

Dakar

SEN.

MAURITANIA

BELIZE

HAITI

ANTIGUA & BARBUDA

Banjul

Bamako

ST KITTS-NEVIS

DOMINICA

THE GAMBIA

GUATEMALA

JAMAICA

GUINEA-BISSAU

GUINEA

BURKINA

HONDURAS

Caribbean Sea

ST LUCIA

Bissau

Conakry

IVORY

EL SALVADOR

NICARAGUA

ST VINCENT &
THE GRENADINES

BARBADOS

Freetown

Yamoussoukro

COAST

Accra

San José

GRENADA

SIERRA LEONE

Monrovia

Managua

COSTA
RICA

TRINIDAD & TOBAGO

LIBERIA

PANAMA

Panama

Caracas

Georgetown

VENEZUELA

FRENCH
GUIANA (Fr.)

EQUA

SÃO TO
& PRINCI

PACIFIC

Islas Galápagos
(Ecuador)

Bogotá

COLOMBIA

KIRIBATI

OCEAN

Equator

ECUADOR

Quito

Iquitos

Manaus

Belém

Fortaleza

Amazon

Recife

French
Polynesia

Lima

PERU

BRAZIL

La Paz

BOLIVIA

Brasília

Salvador

Arequipa

Sucre

Belo Horizonte

Tropic of Capricorn

Pitcairn Is.
(U.K.)

PARAGUAY

Rio de Janeiro

Asunción

São Paulo

Curitiba

Córdoba

URUGUAY

Porto Alegre

Santiago

CHILE

Buenos
Aires

Montevideo

ARGENTINA

Falkland
Islands
(U.K.)

Punta
Arenas

South Georgia
(U.K.)

South Sandwich
Islands
(U.K.)

Antarctic Circle

Bellinghausen
Sea

Weddell Sea

Ross Sea

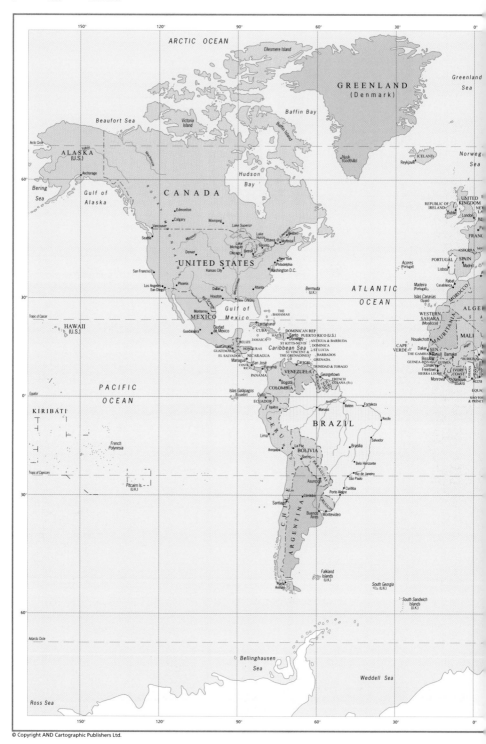

© Copyright AND Cartographic Publishers Ltd.

30

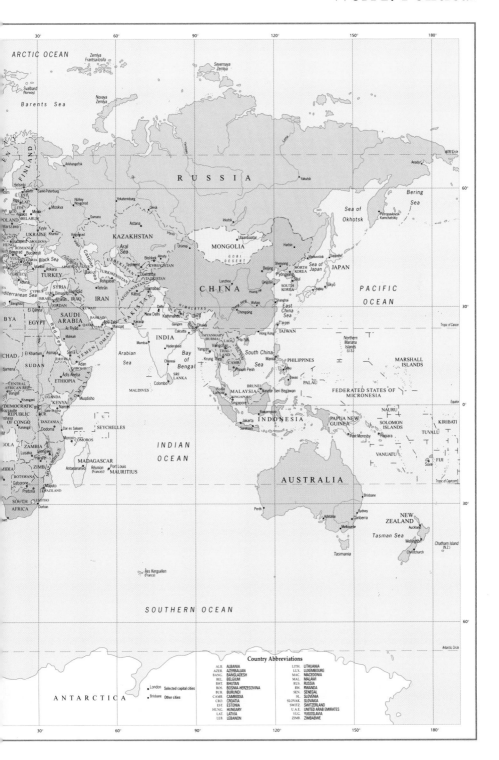

Scale 1 : 47 600 000

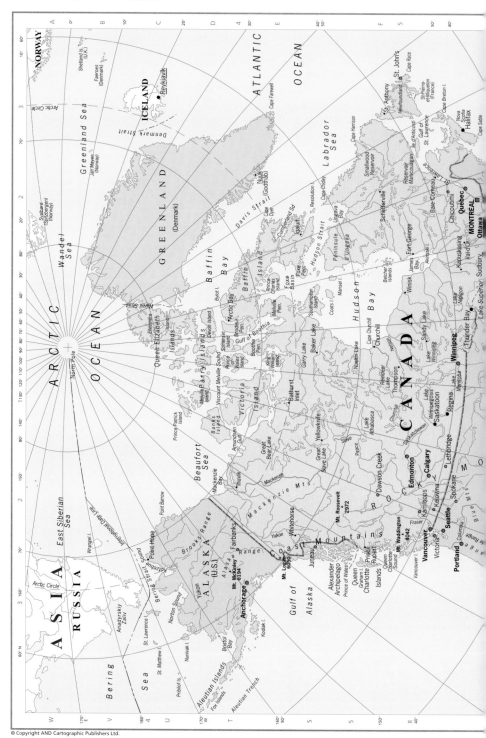

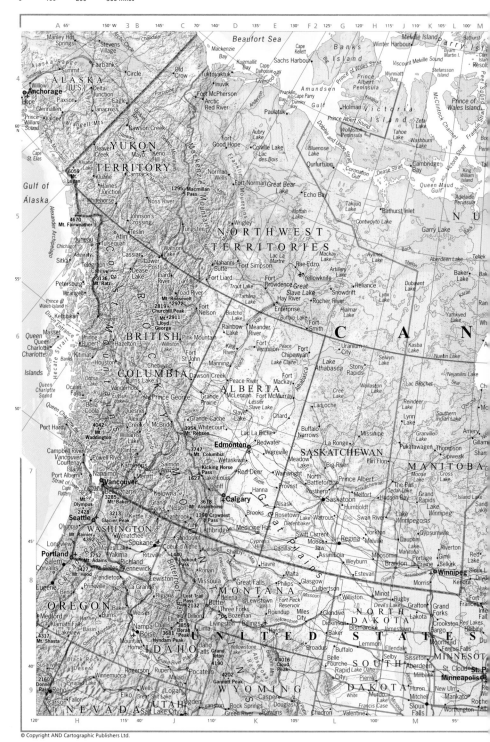

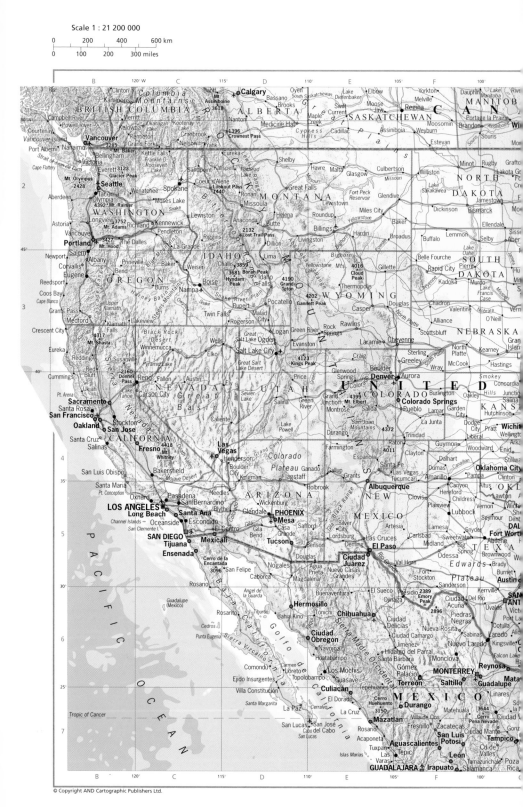

© Copyright AND Cartographic Publishers Ltd.

Scale 1 : 21 200 000

| 0 | 200 | 400 | 600 km |
| 0 | 100 | 200 | 300 miles |

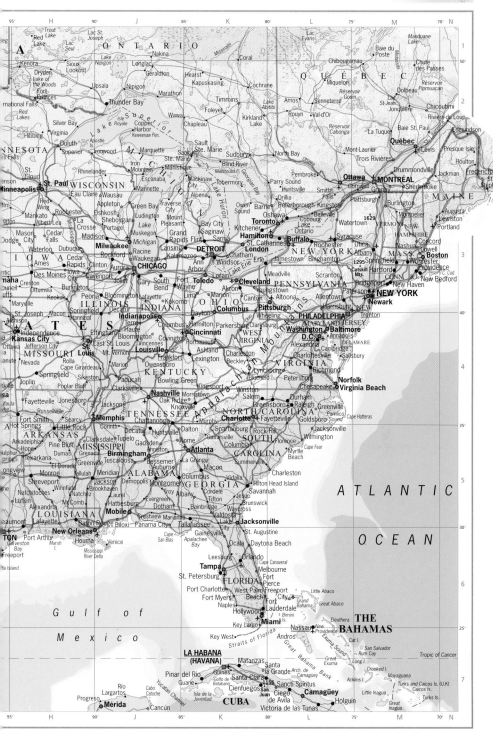

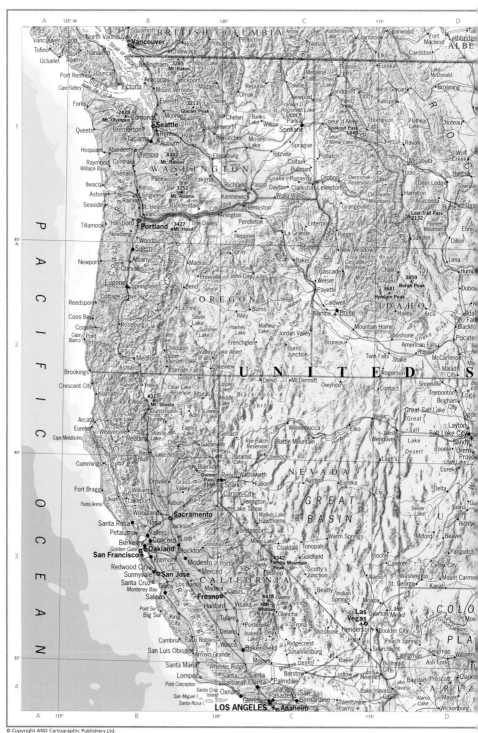

Scale 1 : 9 900 000

0   100   200   300 km

0   50   100   150 miles

© Copyright AND Cartographic Publishers Ltd.

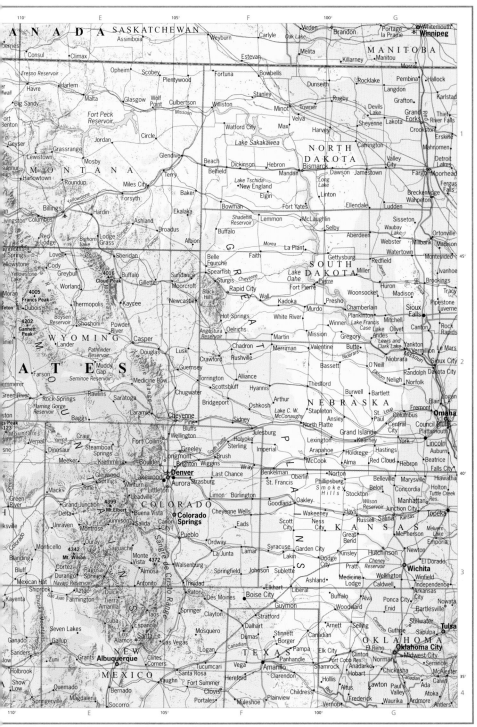

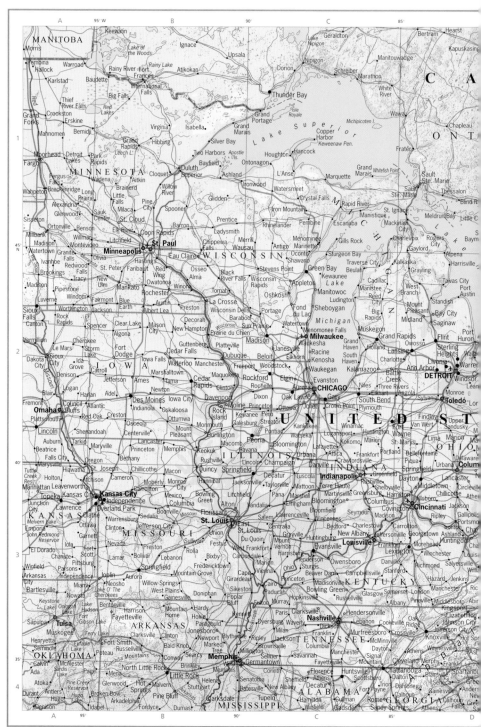

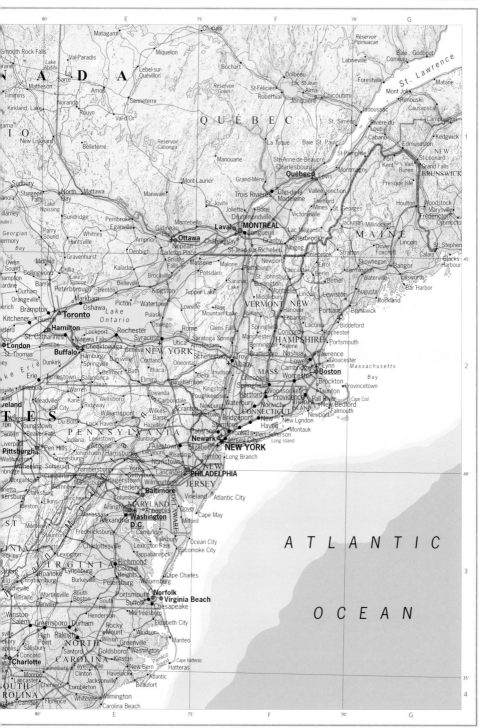

Scale 1 : 9 900 000

| 0 | 100 | 200 | 300 km |

| 0 | 50 | 100 | 150 miles |

© Copyright AND Cartographic Publishers Ltd.

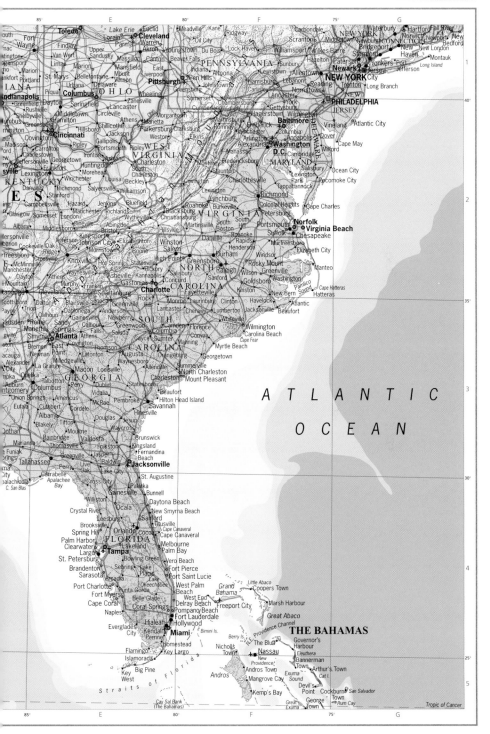

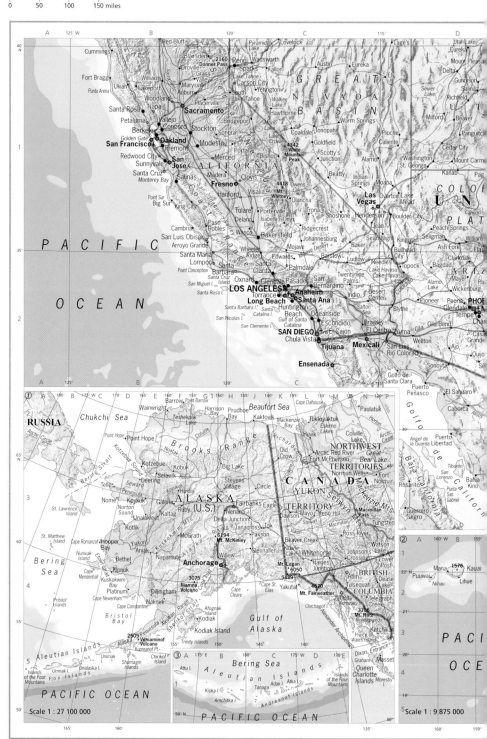

Scale 1 : 9 900 000

| 0 | 100 | 200 | 300 km |
| 0 | 50 | 100 | 150 miles |

A 125° W   **B** 120°   **C** 115°   **D**

40°
N

Red Bluff · Pyramid · Lovelock · Cage's · Utah Lake
Cummings · Blairsden · Lake · Eureka
Oroville · 2160 · Reno · Wadsworth · Mount Pleas.
Fort Bragg · Donner Pass · Sparks · Fallon · Austin · Eureka · Delta
Grass · Lake Tahoe · Yerington · Carson City · G R E A T · Ely · Gunnison · Salina
Punta Arena · Williams · Valley · South · Walker · N E V A D A · Sever · Richfield
Santa Rosa · Marysville · Lake Tahoe · Lake · B A S I N · Warm Springs · Milford · Beaver
Napa · Placerville · Mono · Hawthorne · Bridgeport · Lake · Coaldale · Tonopah · Pioche · Panguitch
Petaluma · Vallejo · Stockton · Sonora · Crowl? · Goldfield · Caliente · Cedar City
Berkeley · Concord · 4342 · White · Goldfield · Alamo · Mount Carm.
Golden Gate · Oakland · Fremont · Modesto · Mountain · Scotty's · Washington · St. George · Kanab
San Francisco · Merced · Peak · Junction · Alamo · COLO.
Redwood City · Sunnyvale · San · C A L I F O R N I A · Beatty · Indian · U N
Santa Cruz · Jose · Madera · Clovis · Springs · Moapa · P L A T
Monterey Bay · Salinas · Fresno · 4418 · Owens · Las · Overton Lake · Peach Springs
Point Sur · Hanford · Visalia · Mt. · Olancha · Vegas · Lake · Seligman · William
Big Sur · King City · Whitney · Ironn? · Shoshone · Henderson · Mead · Ash Fork · Clarkdale
Tulare · Porterville · Isabella · Onyx · Boulder City · Bullhead · Topock · A R I Z.
Cambria · Paso · Deland · Lake · Johannesburg · Searchlight · City · Kingman · Bagdad · Pa
Robles · Wasco · Ridgecrest · Baker · Lake Havasu · Mayer · Wickenburg
San Luis Obispo · Wheeler · Mojave · Desert · Ludlow · Lake Havasu · City · Pioneer · Peena · PHOE.
Arroyo Grande · Ridge · Edwards · Barstow · Desert · Alamo · Glendale · EN.
Santa Maria · Santa · Santa · Palmdale · Twentynine · Center · Lake · Blythe · Tempe
Lompoc · Barbara · Clarita · San · Palms · Indio · Gila Bend · Chan.
Point Conception · Santa Cruz I. · Oxnard · Glendale · Pasadena · Bernardino · Salton · Casa
San Miguel I. · Island · LOS ANGELES · Anaheim · Sea · Brawley · Grande
Santa Rosa I. · Torrance · Santa Ana · El Centro · Yuma · Gila · Quijo
Long Beach · Huntington · Oceanside · Wellton · Ajo.
Santa Barbara I. · Beach · Escondido · El Centro · San Luis · Sonoyta
San Nicolas I. · Gulf of Santa · SAN DIEGO · El Cajon · Rio Colorado
San Clemente I. · Catalina · Chula Vista · Mexicali · Golfo de
Tijuana · Santa Clara · El Saharo
Ensenada · Puerto · Caborca
Peñasco

P A C I F I C

O C E A N

© Copyright AND Cartographic Publishers Ltd.

44

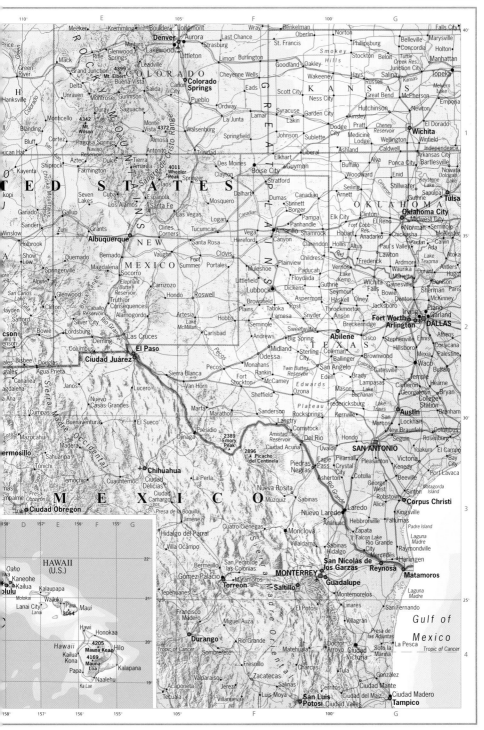

Scale 1 : 22 100 000

| 0 | 200 | 400 | 600 km |
| 0 | 100 | 200 | 300 miles |

A   115° W   B   110°   C   105°   D   100°   E   95°   F   90°

Santa
Maria Bakersfield Las
1 Oxford Mojave Desert Vegas Henderson *Colorado*
35° N CALIFORNIA Boulder Grand *P l a t e a u*
Long Kingman Flagstaff
Beach LOS ANGELES San Bernardino Needles A R I Z O N A
Santa Ana Glendale Blythe Wickenburg
2 Oceanside San PHOENIX Mesa
Clemente I. SAN DIEGO Tucson Safford
Tijuana Mexicali Green Benson
Ensenada Cerro de la Valley Douglas
Encantada Nogales Agua Prieta
3096 San Felipe Magdalena

COLORADO
Durango La Junta Lamar Dodge Newton St. Louis
4372 Trinidad Garden City Wichita Ottawa Jefferson Rolla
Farmington Raton City Liberal Pratt Wellington Chanute Nevada City
Española Santa Fe Clayton Dalhart Woodward Enid Arkansas Bartlesville Joplin Polar Bluff
Albuquerque Las Vegas Guymon Canadian City Broken Arrow
N E W Tucumcari Amarillo Dumas Clinton TULSA Oklahoma City ARKANSAS
Belen Hereford Pampa Childress Fort Little Rock Memphis
M E X I C O Clovis Atus O K L A H O M A Smith
Silver City Artesia Lubbock Wichita Falls Ardmore Durant Sherman El Dorado
Lordsburg Las Cruces Lamesa Seymour Texarkana Greenville
Ciudad El Paso Carlsbad Snyder Sweetwater FORT DALLAS Shreveport Jackson
Juárez Val Horn Midland Abilene Big Brownwood WORTH Longview MISSISSIPPI
Odessa Corsicana Tyler Monroe Natchitoches Brookhaven
Alpine Fort T E X A S Temple Waco AUSTIN Lufkin Alexandria Natchez Hattiesburg
Sanderson Stockton Edwards Kerrville Huntsville LOUISIANA Baton Rouge
Presidio Plateau Del Rio HOUSTON Beaumont North Iberia NEW
Emory Peak Ciudad Uvalde SAN ANTONIO Galveston Houma Orleans
2389 Acuña Victoria Bay Freeport Marsh Venice
2896 Nueva Rosita Cotulla Port Lavaca Island
Sabinas Alice Beeville Matagorda Island
Nuevo Laredo Laredo Corpus Christi
Monclova Kingsville Padre Island

Guadalupe
(Mexico)
Rosario
3 Cedros Bahía
Punta Eugenia Kino Tónichi
Tiburón

Angel de
la Guarda
Isla Nuevo Casas Grandes
Chihuahua
Hermosillo Buenaventura
Caborca El Sueco
Ciudad Ciudad Camargo
Obregón Villa
Navojoa Ahumada
Huatabampo Jiménez
Hidalgo del Parral
Los Mochis

GULF OF
MEXICO

La Paz Santa
Margarita
Tropic of Cancer
4 San José del Cabo El Dorado
San Lucas Cabo La Cruz
San Lucas 3150 Durango
Cerro
Huehuento
Mazatlán

Villa
Constitución
Guasave
Culiacán
Guamúchil Tepehuanes
Gómez
Palacio
Torreón Saltillo
MONTERREY Guadalupe Reynosa
Linares Harlingen
Brownsville
Matamoros

Islas Revillagigedo
(Mexico)
I. San
Benedicto
I. Socorro
I. San
5 I. Clarión Bahía de Banderas
Cabo Corrientes
GUADALAJARA
Nevado
de Colima
4339
Punta San Telmo
Bahía de
Petacalco
Lázaro Cárdenas

Rosario
Acaponeta
Tepic
Zacatecas
Fresnillo Matehuala
Río Grande
Ciudad
Victoria
3644 Soto la Marina
Cerro Laguna
Peña Nevada Madre
Villa Ciudad Mante
de Cos Ciudad Madero
M E X I C O Gonzales Tampico
Aguascalientes San Luis Cd. de Valles
León Potosí
Irapuato Salamanca Poza Tuxpan
Celaya Rica
Morelia Querétaro Pachuca Papantla
CIUDAD Jalapa
DE MÉXICO PUEBLA Enriquez
Cuernavaca Popocatépetl Córdoba Veracruz
Uruapan 5452 Coatzacoalcos
Chilpancingo Minatitlán
Acapulco Oaxaca Istmo
3395 de
Zempoaltépetl Tehuantepec
Juchitán

Cabo Rojo
Río Larga
Progreso
Mérida Valladolid
Campeche Yucatán
Ciudad
del Carmen Escárcega
Chetumal
Frontera
Villahermosa
Belmopan
Tuxtla Melchor
Gutiérrez de Mencos BELIZE
Cintalapa San Cristóbal Puerto
Tonalá de las Casas Barrios
Bahía de Golfo de Cobán
Campeche Tehuantepec Volcán 4220
Tajumulco San
Tapachula Pedro
Quezaltenango H O N D U R A S
Sierra Madre del Sur Puerto GUATEMALA Santa
Ángel Nueva San Salvador Ana
GUATEMALA San Salvador San Miguel
EL SALVADOR Golfo de
Fonseca

Bahía de
Campeche

Clipperton I.
(France)

P A C I F I C   O C E A N

Equator

B   110°   C   105°   D   100°   E   95°   F   90°

Scale 1 : 38 400 000

0   500   1000   1500 km
0   250   500   750 miles

© Copyright AND Cartographic Publishers Ltd.

48

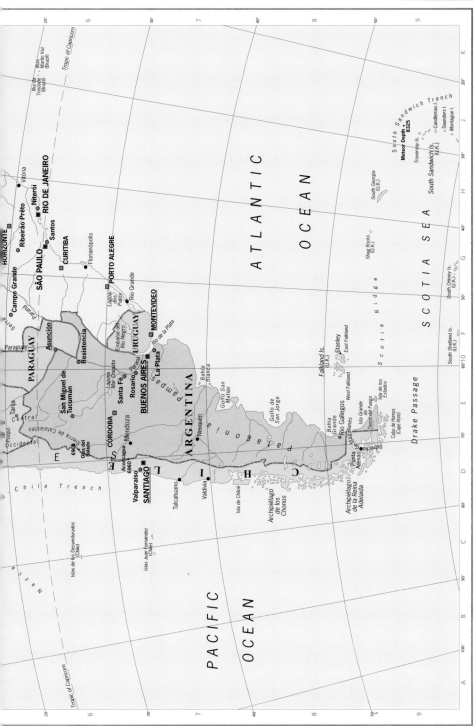

South America: North

ATLANTIC OCEAN

Countries & regions

ANA
SURINAM
FRENCH GUIANA
AMAPÁ
PARÁ
MARANHÃO
CEARÁ
PIAUÍ
RIO GRANDE DO NORTE
PARAÍBA
PERNAMBUCO
ALAGOAS
SERGIPE
BAHIA
TOCANTINS
MATO GROSSO
GOIÁS
DISTRITO FEDERAL
MINAS GERAIS
ESPÍRITO SANTO
MATO GROSSO DO SUL
SÃO PAULO
RIO DE JANEIRO
BRAZIL (...AZIL)
Planalto Central
Mato Grosso

Cities & towns

Georgetown
New Amsterdam
Corriverton
Nieuw Nickerie
Apoera
Albina
Nieuw Amsterdam
Iracoubo
St. Laurent
Kourou
Paramaribo
Brokopondo
W. J. van Blommestein-meer
Embalse
Toekomstig
Juliana Top 1230
Cayenne
Camopi
Oiapoque
Calcoene
Amapá
Cabo Norte
Porto Grande
Pôrto Santana
Macapá
Chaves
Ilha de Marajó
Baía de Marajó
Salinópolis
Ilha Grande de Gurupá
BELÉM
Vigia
Bragança
Para
Castanhal
Camiranga
Mazagão
Afuá
Breves
Portel
Cametá
Acará
Badajós
Baião
São Luís
Ilha de São Luís
Rosário
Pindaré Mirim
Itapecuru Mirim
Luziândia
Camocim
Sobral
Itapipoca
Caucaia
FORTALEZA
Bacabal
Pedreiras
Codó
Pirapiri
Campo Maior
Canindé
Aracati
Areia Branca
Macau
Cabo de São Roque
Obidos
Monte Alegre
Prainha
Almeirim
Santarém
Altamira
Faro
Parintins
Itacoatiara
Itaituba
Marabá
Caxias
Timon
Teresina
Mossoró
RIO GRANDE DO NORTE
Natal
Imperatriz
Barra do Corda
Amarante
Taua
Iguatu
Ourinhos Novos
Araras
São Félix
Grajaú
Pastos Bons
Floriano
Picos
Juàzeiro do Norte
Crato
Sousa
Guarabira
João Pessoa
Campina Grande
Pôrto Franco
Uruçuí
Oeiras
Ouricuri
Caruaru
RECIFE
Jaboatão
Olinda
Conceição do Araguaia
Santa Maria das Barreiras
Carolina
Balsas
Canto do Buriti
São Raimundo Nonato
Petrolina
Juàzeiro
Garanhuns
Palmares
Maceió
Pedro Afonso
Alto Parnaíba
Gilbués
Barragem de Sobradinho
Paulo Afonso
Macaúba
Palmas
Pôrto Nacional
Barra
Xique Xique
Senhor do Bonfim
Jacobina
Tucano
Serrinha
Aracaju
Dianópolis
Peixe
Paraná
Barreiras
Ibotirama
Irecê
Mundo Novo
Esplanada
Estância
Porangatu
Bom Jesus da Lapa
Itaberaba
SALVADOR
Baía de Todos os Santos
Niquelândia
Posse
Uruaçu
Ceres
Formosa
Manga
Guanambi
Brumado
Ibiá
Vitória da Conquista
Itabuna
Ilhéus
Ubaitaba
Gandu
Santo Antônio de Jesus
Jequié
Camaçari
Alagoinhas
Goiás
BRASÍLIA
Anápolis
Cristalina
Januária
Monte Azul
Janaúba
Pedra Azul
Itapebi
Belmonte
Pôrto Seguro
Goiânia
Pires do Rio
Ipameri
Paracatu
Montes Claros
Bocaiuva
Salinas
Prado
Caravelas
Jataí
Itumbiara
Rio Verde
Araguari
Minas Novas
Diamantina
Itambacuri
Nanuque
Uberlândia
Ituiutaba
Patos de Minas
Curvelo
Pico do Itambé 2033
Teófilo Otoni
Governador Valadares
ESPÍRITO SANTO
Araxá
Sete Lagoas
Itabira
Ipatinga
Linhares
Uberaba
Pará de Minas
Campo Grande
Ribas do Rio Pardo
Paranaíba
Fernandópolis
Barretos
Divinópolis
BELO HORIZONTE
Manhuaçu
Cariacica
Vitória
Cachoeiro de Itapemirim
Campos
Andradina
Rio Preto
França
Passos
Formiga
Lavras
Ubá
Muriaé
Dourados
Presidente Prudente
Marília
Araçatuba
Lins
Bauru
SÃO PAULO
Assis
Piracicaba
Limeira
Ribeirão Prêto
São Carlos
Três Corações
Juiz de Fora
Volta Redonda
Agu1has Negras
Nova Iguaçu
RIO DE JANEIRO
Niterói
Pico da Bandeira 2890
Pedro Juan Caballero
Ponta Porã
Paranaval

Physical features

Serra Acari
Serra Tumucumaque
Serra dos Carajás
Serra Formosa
Serra do Cachimbo
Serra do Roncador
Serra dos Dois Irmãos
Chapada Diamantina
Planalto do Mato Grosso
Pantanal
Mouths of the Amazon
Baía de Marajó
Amazonas (Amazon)
Tocantins
Xingu
Araguaia
Tapajós
São Francisco
Equator
I. Fernando de Noronha
Atol das Rocas
1850
2033
2890
2792

BADOS
getown
1230

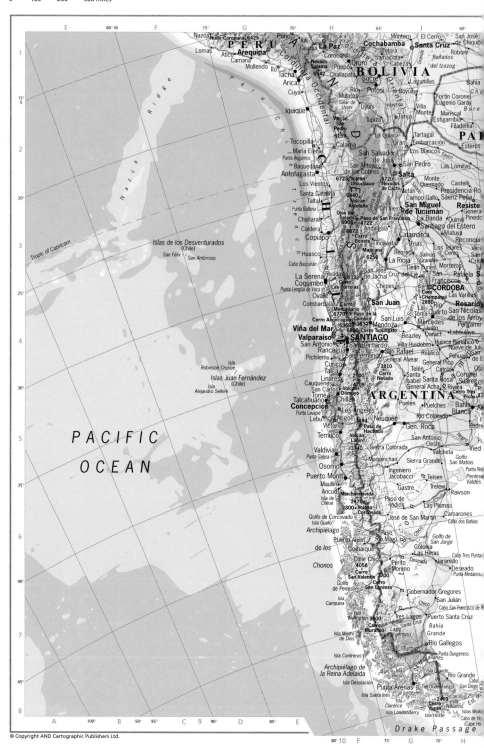

© Copyright AND Cartographic Publishers Ltd.

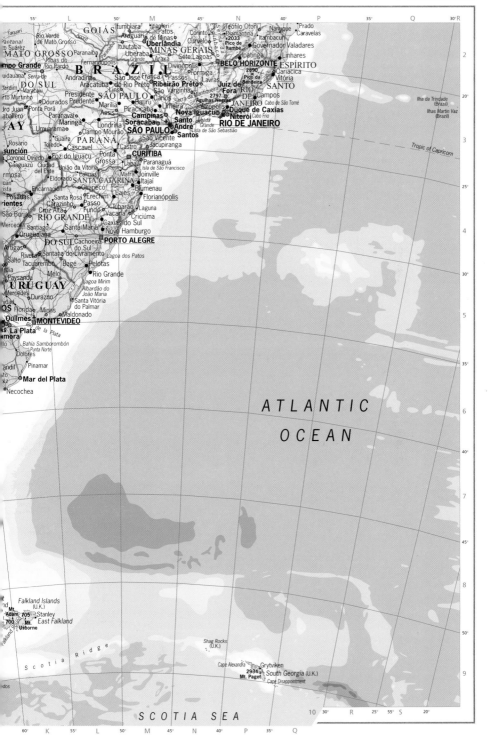

ATLANTIC

OCEAN

SCOTIA SEA

Major places shown on the map:

GOIÁS · Taquari · Rio Verde de Mato Grosso · MATO GROSSO · Pantanal · to Suárez · uidauana · Jardim · DO SUL · Maracaju · Iro Juan · Dourados · Prudente · Ponta Porã · aballero · Paranavaí · AY · Umuarama · Campo Mourão · Rosario · Guaíra · Toledo · unción · Coronel Oviedo · Cascavel · Foz do Iguaçu · Caaguazú · Ciudad del Este · rmosa · Eldorado · uan · Palmas · ista · Encarnación · Posadas · Santa Rosa · rientes · Carazinho · São Borja · Cruz Alta · Mercedes · Santiago · Uruguaiana · Santa Maria · Artigas · Rivera · DO SUL · Salto · Tacuarembó · Bagé · Pelotas · dia · Paysandú · Melo · Rio Grande · URUGUAY · Mercedes · Durazno · idad · Florida · Minas · Maldonado · OS · Quilmes · MONTEVIDEO · s La Plata · amora · Dolores · andil · Pinamar · to · ez · Mar del Plata · Necochea

Ibiá · Araxá · Uberlândia · MINAS GERAIS · Uberaba · Divinópolis · Francia · BELO HORIZONTE · BRAZIL · Andradina · São José do Rio Preto · Passos · Lavras · Araçatuba · Lins · São Varginha · Juiz de Fora · SÃO PAULO · Bauru · Carlos · Limeira · Marília · Piracicaba · RIO DE JANEIRO · Assis · Campinas · Santo · Londrina · Soracaba · André · PARANÁ · SÃO PAULO · Santos · São Vicente · Jacupiranga · Castro · CURITIBA · Ponta Grossa · Lapa · Paranaguá · União da Vitória · Mafra · Joinville · SANTA CATARINA · Chapecó · Itajaí · Erechim · Blumenau · Passo · Lajes · FLorianópolis · Fundo · Tubarão · Laguna · Vacaria · Criciúma · RIO GRANDE · Caxias do Sul · Santa Maria · Novo Hamburgo · DO SUL · Cachoeira do Sul · PORTO ALEGRE · Santana do Livramento · Lagoa dos Patos · Lagoa Mirim · Albardão do João Maria · Santa Vitória do Palmar

Teófilo Otoni · Diamantina · Itambacuri · Governador Valadares · Pico da Bandeira · ESPÍRITO · Vitória · SANTO · Campos · RIO · JANEIRO · Nova Iguaçu · Duque de Caxias · Niterói · RIO DE JANEIRO · Prado · Caravelas · Ilha da Trindade (Brazil) · Ilhas Martin Vaz (Brazil)

Tropic of Capricorn

Falkland Islands (U.K.) · Mt. Adam 705 · Stanley · East Falkland · Mt. Usborne · 700

Scotia Ridge · Shag Rocks (U.K.) · Cape Alexandra · Grytviken · 2934 · South Georgia (U.K.) · Mt. Paget · Cape Disappointment

Scale 1 : 27 700 000

| 0 | 250 | 500 | 750 | 1000 km |

| 0 | 100 | 200 | 300 | 400 | 500 miles |

60° N A 1 30° W B 20° C 70° 10' D 0° E 10° F 20°

Arctic Circle

Reykjavik **ICELAND**

N o r w e g i a n

S e a

Faeroes
(Denmark)

Tromsø

Trondheim

N O R W A Y

S W E D E N

Gulf of Bothnia

Kir

Rockall

Shetland Is.
(U.K.)

Bergen

Sundsvall

Tam

Outer
Hebrides

Orkney Is.

Oslo

Stavanger

Stockholm

Vänern

Ta

SCOTLAND

Glasgow

Edinburgh

N o r t h

Göteborg

Gotland

R

NORTHERN
IRELAND   Belfast

DENMARK

Århus

ATLANTIC

REP. OF
IRELAND

Dublin
(Baile Átha Cliath)

UNITED

S e a

København
(Copenhagen)

Bornholm

Baltic Sea

LIT

WALES

KINGDOM

BIRMINGHAM

Gdańsk

RUSSIA

Wda

Kalinin

OCEAN

Cardiff

ENGLAND

HAMBURG

Hro

LONDON

Amsterdam

BERLIN

**WARSZAWA
(WARSAW)**

Plymouth

Channel Is.

English Channel

Bruxelles
(Brussels)

**NETHER-
LANDS**

Hannover

Odra (Oder)

POLAND

Cabo Fisterra

Channel
Islands

Seine

BELGIUM

Luxembourg

GERMANY

Frankfurt

Rhine

PRAHA
(PRAGUE)

Elbe

Wisla

*Bay
of
Biscay*

PARIS

Loire

LUXEMBOURG

Strasbourg

Danube

CZECH REP.

WIEN
(VIENNA)

SLOVAKIA

Bratislava

FRANCE

Bordeaux

Lyon

Massif

Central

Rhône

Bern

SWITZERLAND

Vaduz

LIECHTENSTEIN

AUSTRIA

HUNGARY

BUDAPEST

PORTUGAL

Andorra
la Vella

Pyrenees

4808
Mt.
Blanc

A l p s

Genova
(Genoa)

MILANO
(MILAN)

Ljubljana

Zagreb

SLOVENIA

CROATIA

Nag

R

LISBOA
(LISBON)

Ebro

MADRID

ANDORRA

Marseille

MONACO

SAN
MARINO

**BOSNIA-
HERZEGOVINA**

Sarajevo

BEOGRAD
(BELGRA

Cabo de
São Vicente

SPAIN

Tajo

BARCELONA

Corse
(Corsica)
(France)

Ajaccio

VATICAN
CITY

ITALY

Adriatic Sea

YUGOSLAVIA

Valencia

*Islas Baleares
(Balearic Islands)*

ROMA
(ROME)

Tiranë
(Tirana)

Skopje

MACEDON

S

Strait of Gibraltar

Gibraltar (U.K.)

Menorca

Eivissa

Mallorca

Sardegna
(Sardinia)
(Italy)

NAPOLI
(NAPLES)

Apennines

ALBANIA

Taranto

Ceuta
(Spain)

Melilla
(Spain)

RABAT

M e d i t e r r a n e a n

Cagliari

Tyrrhenian
Sea

Kerkyra
(Corfu)

GREEC

ALGER
(ALGIERS)

Palermo

Mte. Etna
3340

I o n i a n

Ath
(Ath

Tunis

Sicilia
(Sicily)

S e a

Valletta
MALTA

S e a

Tarābulus
(Tripoli)

A F R I C A

Banghāzī

D 0° E 10° F 20°

© Copyright AND Cartographic Publishers Ltd.

54

Barents Sea

Vorkuta

O. Kolguyev

Vadsø

Murmansk

White
Sea

Arkhangel'sk

Severnaya Dvina

Surgut

Ob'

NOVOSIBIRSK

Ob'

OMSK

Onezhskoye
Ozero
(Lake Onega)

Ladozhskoye
Ozero
(Lake Ladoga)

Vologda

Kirov

PERM'

YEKATERINBURG

CHELYABINSK

Astana

SANKT-PETERBURG
(ST. PETERSBURG)

R U S S I A

Rybinskoye
Vdkhr.

KAZAN'

UFA

NIZHNIY
NOVGOROD

MOSKVA
(MOSCOW)

Volga

SAMARA

MINSK

Dvina

Volga

Aral Sea

LARUS

Prypyats

Don

Khoper

Ural

UKRAINE

KYYIV
(KIEV)

KHARKIV

VOLGOGRAD

Donets

DONETS'K

Don

Astrakhan'

DNIPROPETROVS'K

ROSTOV-NA-DONU

MOLDOVA

Chisinău

Dnipro

Sea of
Azov

Stavropol'

Aktau

ODESA
(ODESSA)

Krym'

Grozhyy

Elbrus
5642

Caspian

Sevastopol'

C a u c a s u s

Ashgabat
(Ashkhabad)

IA

BUCUREŞTI
(BUCHAREST)

B l a c k   S e a

T'BILISI

BAKI
(BAKU)

Sea

MASHHAD

RIA

Burgas

Samsun

YEREVAN

İSTANBUL

Bursa

ANKARA

TEHRĀN
(TEHERAN)

İZMIR

Gaziantep

A   S   I   A

Antalya

Rodos
(Rhodes)
(Greece)

Lefkosía
(Nicosia)

BAGHDĀD

io
on)

BEYROUTH
(BEIRUT)

DIMASHQ
(DAMASCUS)

AMMĀN

Al Kuwayt
(Kuwait)

Persian Gulf

Yerushalayim
(Jerusalem)

EL QÂHIRA
(CAIRO)

Nile

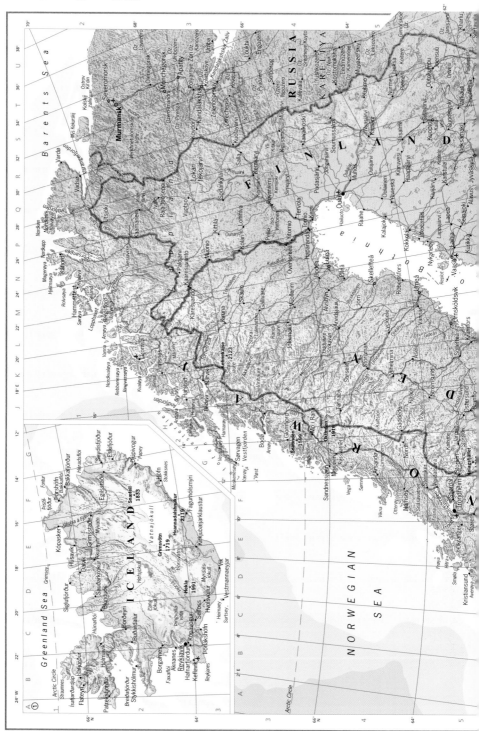

Scandinavia

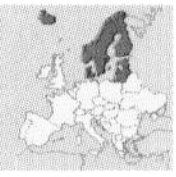

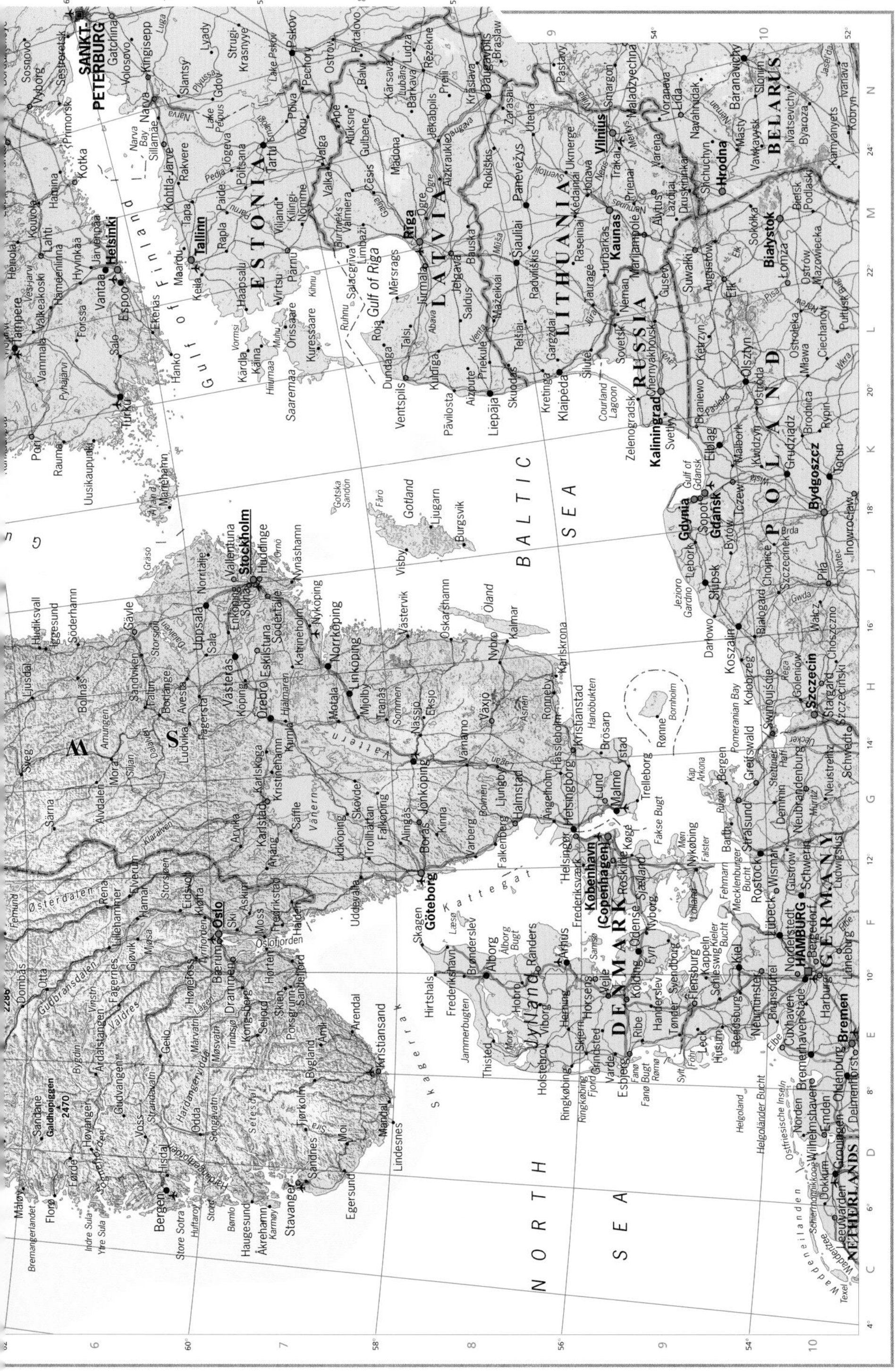

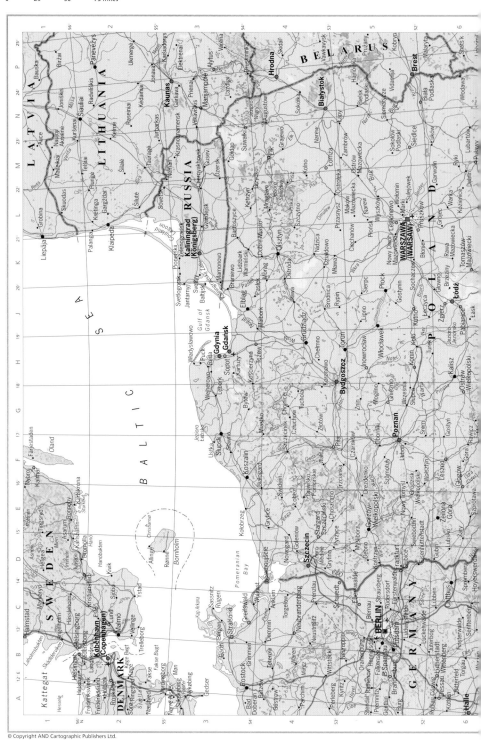

Scale 1 : 4 750 000

0   50   100   150 km
0 25   50   75 miles

58

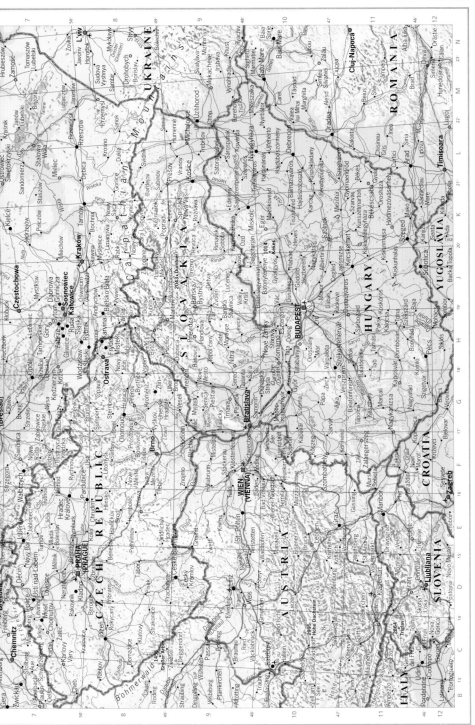

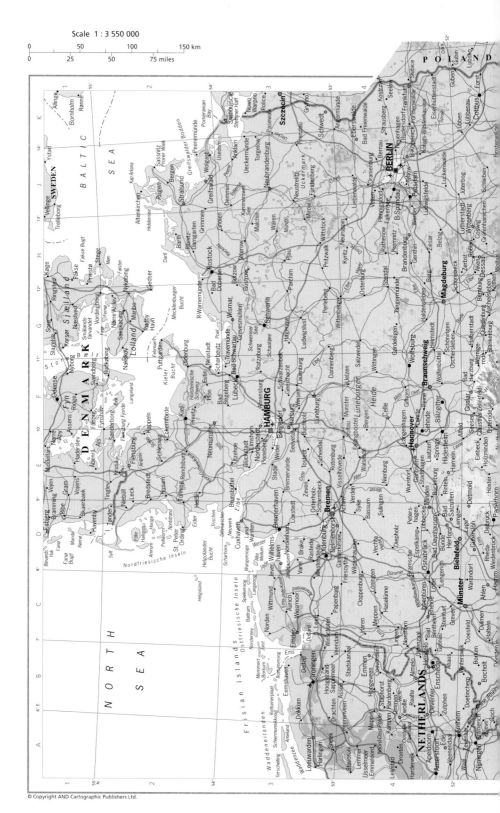

Scale 1 : 3 550 000

0   50   100   150 km
0   25   50   75 miles

POLAND

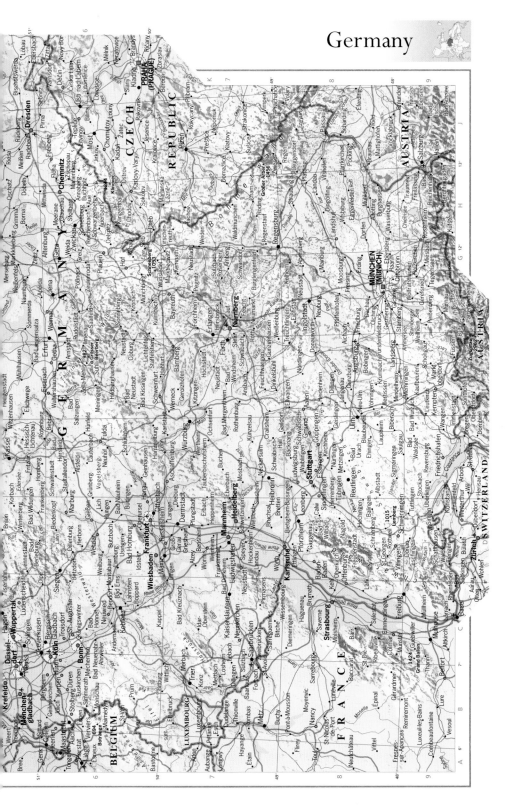

Germany

Scale 1 : 3 150 000

0   50   100   150 km

0   25   50   75 miles

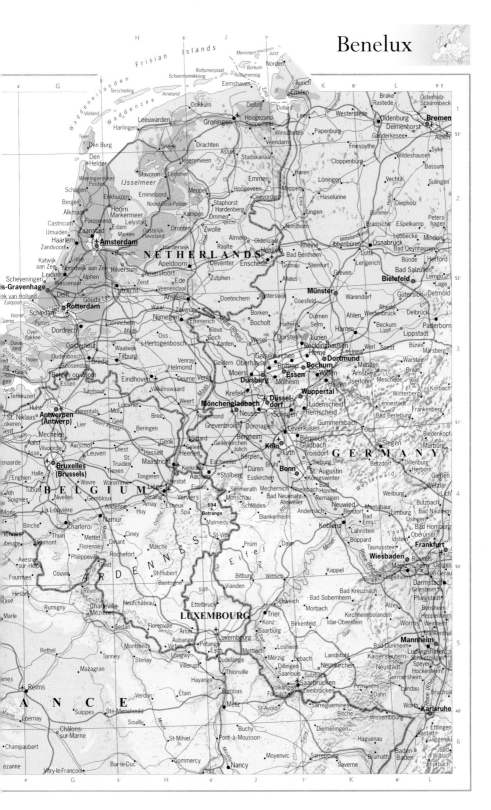

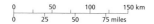

Scale 1 : 4 750 000

| 0 | 50 | 100 | 150 km |
| 0 | 25 | 50 | 75 miles |

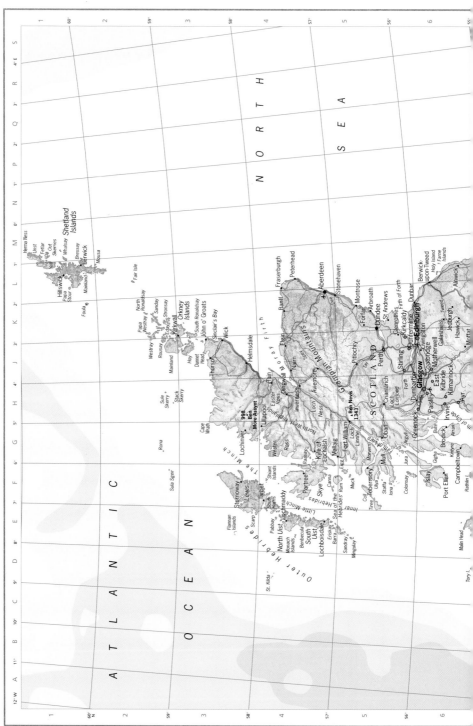

ATLANTIC

OCEAN

NORTH SEA

Shetland Islands

Herma Ness
Unst
Fetlar
Out Skerries
Whalsay
Bressay
Lerwick
Mousa

Hillswick
Papa Stour
Mainland
Foula

Fair Isle

North Ronaldsay
Sanday
Stronsay
Papa Westray
Westray
Rousay
Orkney Islands
Kirkwall
South Ronaldsay
John o' Groats
Eday
Hoy
Mainland
Sinclair's Bay
Wick
Dunnet Head
Thurso
Helmsdale

Sule Skerry
Stack Skerry
Cape Wrath
Rona

Sula Sgeir

Lochinver
The Minch
Ullapool

998 Ben More Assynt

North West Highlands
Easter Ross
Wester Ross
Dingwall
Cromarty
Nain
Elgin
Banff
Fraserburgh
Peterhead
Aberdeen
Stonehaven
Montrose

Moray Firth

Grampian Mountains

Loch Ness
Inverness
Aviemore
Pitlochry
Perth

Ben Nevis 1343

Fort William
Loch Linnhe
Loch Leven
Mallaig
Kyle of Lochalsh

SCOTLAND

Forfar
Arbroath
Dundee
St Andrews
Firth of Tay
Perth
Crianlarich
Stirling
Forth
Dunfermline
Kirkcaldy
Firth of Forth
Edinburgh
Livingston
Glasgow
Coatbridge
Motherwell
East Kilbride
Paisley
Dumbarton
Greenock
Gourock

Firth of Clyde

Flannan Islands
Scarp
Stornoway
Lewis
Tarbet
Harris
Pabbay
Monach Islands
Benbecula
North Uist
Lochmaddy
South Uist
Lochboisdale
Eriskay
Barra
Sandray
Mingulay

Outer Hebrides

St Kilda

Little Minch
Sea of the Hebrides
Shiant Islands
Raasay
Portree
Skye
Rum
Eigg
Muck
Canna

Inner Hebrides

Coll
Tiree
Staffa
Iona
Ulva
Mull
Tobermory
Loch Etive
Oban

Colonsay
Jura
Islay
Port Ellen
Gigha
Kintyre
Campbeltown
Rathlin I.

Firth of Lorn
Arran
Brodick
Ayr
Kilmarnock
Irvine
Kilbride

Berwick-upon-Tweed
Holy Island
Farne Islands
Alnwick
Dunbar
Galashiels
Jedburgh
Hawick
Moffat
Tweed

Main Head

Tory I.

© Copyright AND Cartographic Publishers Ltd.

64

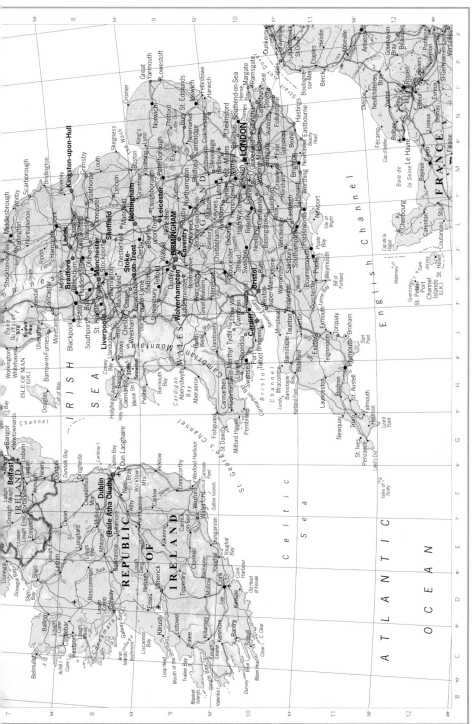

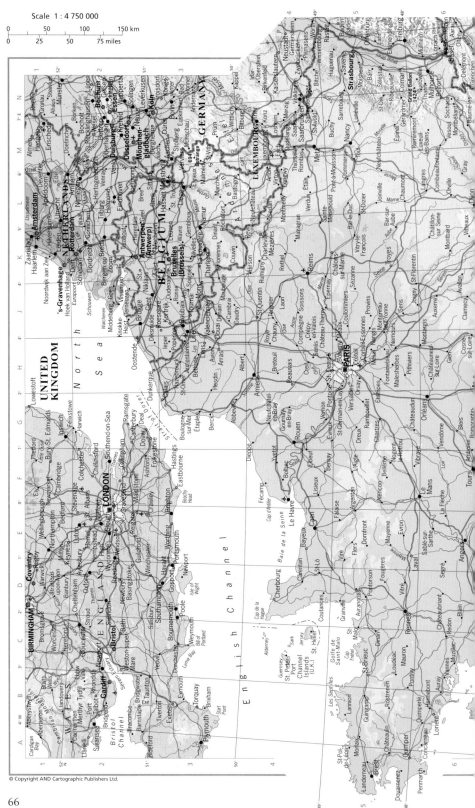

Scale 1 : 4 750 000

0   50   100   150 km
0   25   50   75 miles

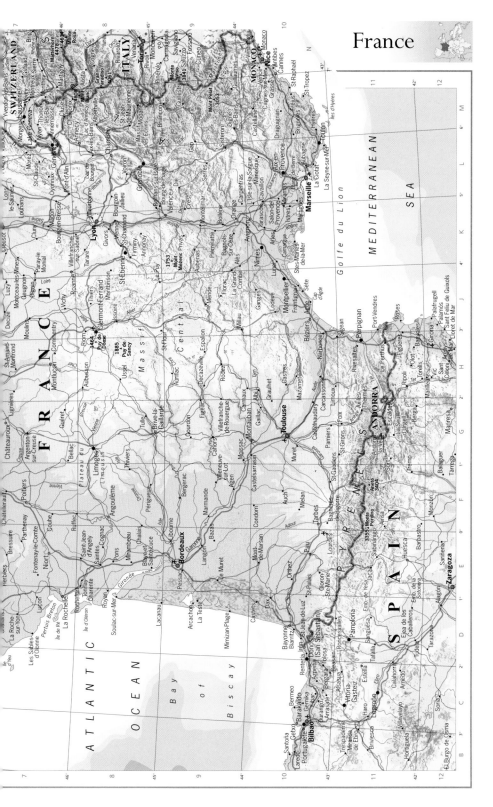

France

Scale 1 : 4 750 000

0   50   100 km
0   25   50 miles

Costa Verde

Bay of Biscay

ATLANTIC OCEAN

Cabo Ortegal
Ortigueira · Cervo
Ferrol · Vivero
As Pontes de · Ribadeo · Luarca · Avilés **Gijón**
A.Coruña · Garcia Rodríguez · Villalba · Tineo · Oviedo · Pola de · Villaviciosa · Santander · Santoña
Carballo · Betanzos · A Fonsagrada · Cangas del · Mieres · (Aller) · Llanes · Laredo · Portugalete · Getxo
Camariñas · Órdes Sta. · Ordes · Lugo · Villablino · Lena · Cabanaquinta · Torrelavega · Embalse · Barakaldo
Cabo Fisterra · Comba · Guitiriz · (Aller) · Reinosa · del Ebro
(Cape Finisterre) · Santiago · Melide · Beberrea · León · Cistierna · Guardo · Sedano · Miranda
Muros · Noia · Teo · Sarria · Ponferrada · Sahagún · Briviesca
Porto do Son · Padrón · Lalín · Astorga · Palencia · Burgos
Cabo Corrubedo · A Estrada · Monforte de · A Bañeza · Villadangos
Sta. Eugenia (Ribeira) · O Grove · Pontevedra · Lemos · O Barco · Benavente · Lerma
Marín · Vilagarcía · Carballino · (Barco de Valdeorras) · Villalpando · Valladolid · Peñafiel · Aranda de Duero
Vigo · Cangas · Redondela · Ourense · Xinzo · A Gudiña · Zamora · Tordesillas · Duero · Cerezo
Porriño · Ponteareas · de Lima · Verín · Bragança · Toro · Medina de Campo · de Abajo
Tui · Caminha · Ponte · Chaves · Miranda · Arévalo · Puerto de Navacerrada
Viana do Castelo · da Barca · Venda Nova · do Douro · Salamanca · Segovia · Colmenar St. Sebastián
Barcelos · Braga · Mirandela · Emb. de · Peñaranda de · Villalba · de los Reyes
Póvoa de · Guimarães · Ricobayo · Bracamonte · Collado · Alcalá de
Varzim · Vila de Conde · Vila Real · Miranda · Fuentesaúco · Ávila · Villalba · MADRID · Henares
Matosinhos · Gondomar · do Douro · Torre de · Emb. de · Alcobendas · Torrejón de
Porto · Espinho · Moncorvo · Almendra · Sta. Teresa · Alcorcón · Getafe
Vila Nova de Gaia · São João · Meda · Lumbrales · Béjar · 2592 · Móstoles · Parla · Valdemoro
de Madeira · Murtosa · Trancoso · Pinhel · Ciudad · Pico · Talavera · Maqueda · Aranjuez
Aveiro · Viseu · Guarda · Rodrigo · Almanzor · de la Reina · Ocaña
Santa · Figueira da Foz · Comba Dão · Emb. de · Navalmoral · Toledo · **SPAI**
Coimbra · Estrela · Gabriel y Galán · de la Mata
Spure · 1993 · Covilhã · Coria · Plasencia · Navahermosa · Madridejos
Leiria · Pombal · Fundão · Emb. de · Cáceres · Navalvillar · Alcázar de S. Juan
Merinha Grande · Serta · Castelo · Alcántara Uno · Trujillo · de Pela · Tomelloso
Nazaré · Bgem. do · Branco · Emb. de · Manzanar
Peniche · Caldas · Castelo de Bode · Nisa · Miajadas · Garcia Sola · Daimiel · La
Cabo Carvoeiro · da Rainha · Abrantes · Valencia · **PORTUGAL** · Alburquerque · Ciudad Real · Valdepe
Torres Vedras · Entroncamento · Tomar · de Alcántara · Cáceres · Emb. de
Vila Franca de Xira · Santarém · Ponte · Portalegre · Navalvillar · la Serena · Almadén · Puertollano
Amadora · de Sor · Montijo · Don · Abenójar
Estoril · **Lisboa (Lisbon)** · Mora · Bgem. do · Monforte · Mérida · Benito · Emb. de · Cabeza · M o r e
Cascais · Almada · Coruche · Maranhão · Elvas · Castuera · del Buey · Puertollano
Costa do Sol · Barreiro · Estremoz · Badajoz · Villanueva · la Serena · Peñarroya · Pozoblanco · La Carolina
Cabo de Espichel · Setúbal · Évora · Almendralejo · de los Barros · Pueblonuevo · Villanueva de · Bailén · Linares
Alcácer do Sal · Zafra · Azuaga · Córdoba · Montoro · Baeza · Úbeda
Grândola · Portel · Jerez de · Emb. del · Andújar · Jódar
Sado · Ardila · los Caballeros · Fregenal · Bembézar · Jaén
Sines · Ferreira · Beja · Moura · de la Sierra · Martos · Alcaudete
do Alentejo · Serpa · Cortegana · Constantina · Montilla · Priego de
Odemira · Castro · Bgem. de Sta. · Valverde · **Córdoba** · Baena · Rute · Córdoba
Verde · Clara · Alcoutim · del Camino · Lora · Palma · Lucena · Alcalá la Real
Aljezur · Portimão · Loulé · Ayamonte · Huelva · del Río · del Río · Écija · Puente-Genil · Archidona · **Granada**
Lagos · Albufeira · Tavira · Almonte · Marchena · Osuna · Antequera · 3482
Cabo de · Faro · Olhão · Dos Hermanas · Alcalá de · Morón de · Mulhacén
S. Vicente · Golfo de · **Sevilla** · Guadaíra · la Frontera · Olvera · Vélez- · Nerja · Almuñécar
Las Cabezas · Utrera · Málaga
Cádiz · Lebrija · de San Juan · Villamartín · Ronda · Alhaurín · **Málaga**
Sanlúcar de Barrameda · Arcos de la Frontera · Ubrique · el Grande · Torremolinos
Jerez de la Frontera · Medina · Marbella · Fuengirola · Estepona · *Costa del Sol*
El Puerto de Sta. María · Sidonia · San Roque
Cádiz · Puerto Real · Barbate · La Línea
San Fernando · Chiclana de la Frontera · Algeciras · Gibraltar (U.K.)
Vejer de la Frontera · Tarifa
Cabo de Trafalgar · Strait of Gibraltar · Isla de Alborán (Spain)
ATLANTIC OCEAN · Cap · Ceuta (Spain)
Spartel · **Tanger** · Cap Negro
El Borj
Tétouan
Asilah · **MOROCCO** · Bou Ahmed

Cordillera Cantábrica

Sierra Nevada
Cordillera

© Copyright AND Cartographic Publishers Ltd.

68

FRANCE
Bayonne
Biarritz
Orthez
Muret
Béziers Agde
Cap d'Agde
Sète
Rentería
Donostia (San
Sebastián)
St-Jean-de-Luz
St-Palais
Pau
Tarbes
Castelnaudary
Aude
Carcassonne
Narbonne
Golfe du Lion
Ispeitia
Alsasua
Beasain
Tolosa
Oloron-Ste-Marie
Lourdes
Bagnères-
de-Bigorre
St-Gaudens
Pamiers
Limoux
Sigean
Estella
Pamplona
Roncesvalles
P Y R E N E E S
St-Girons
Foix
Ax-les-Thermes
Rivesaltes
Perpignan
Port-Vendres
Tafalla
Sanguesa
Jaca
3355 Monte
Perdino
Sabiñanigo
Aneto
3404
ANDORRA
Andorra
la Vella
Les Escales
Le Perthus
Roses
Costa Brava
groño
Alaborra
Arnedo
Tudela
Ejea de los
Caballeros
Emb. de Yesa
Ainsa
Sort
La Seu
d'Urgell
Ripoll
Figueres
Olot
Banyoles
Tarazona
Huesca
Emb. de la
Sotonera
Tremp
Berga
Torelló
Manlleu
Vic
Girona
Palafrugell
Palamós
Sant Feliu
de Guixols
Lloret de Mar
Zaragoza
Alagón
Sariñena
Balaguer
Manresa
Tàrrega
Sant Celoni
Granollers
Arenys de Mar
Mataró
El Burgo
de Ebro
Lleida
Igualada
Sabadell
Badalona
Calatayud
Fraga
Montblanc
Vilafranca
del Penedès
Sants
BARCELONA
Azaila
Caspe
Vilanova
i la Geltrú
Gava
El Prat de Llobregat
Daroca
Alcañiz
Gandesa
Reus
Sitges
Tarragona
Calamocha
Tortosa
Cambrils
Costa Dorada
Monreal
del Campo
Montalbán
Morella
Amposta
Cabo Tortosa
Sant Carlos
de la Rápita
Vinarós
Benicarló
Teruel
Sierra
de Gudar
Torreblanca
Islas Baleares
(Balearic Islands)
Ciutadella
Menorca
Mahón
Cuenca
Onda
Castelló de la Plana
Vila-real
Borriana
La Vall d'Uixo
Islas Columbretes
Pollença
Cap de Formentor
Emb. de
Contreras
Utiel
Sagunt
Golfo de
Sa Dragonera
Sóller
Inca
Sa Pobla
Artà
Manacor
Motilla
del Palancar
Burjassot
Paterna
Torrent
VALENCIA
Valencia
Palma
Llucmajor
Mallorca
Cap de ses
Salines
Cofrentes
Carlet
Algemes
Cullera
Eivissa
(Ibiza)
Cabrera
Albacete
Xàtiva
Gandia
San Antonia Abad
Eivissa (Ibiza)
Chinchilla
de Monte-Aragón
Almansa
Ontinyent
Oliva
Dénia
Xàbia
Cabo de la Nao
Formentera
Yecla
Villena
Alcoi
Benidorm
La Vila
Joiosa
Hellín
Jumilla
Elda
Costa Blanca
Novelda
Aspe
Alicante
Cieza
Crevillent
Elch
Santa Pola
Caravaca
de la Cruz
Molina
de Segura
Orihuela
Torrevieja
Alcantarilla
Murcia
Zarzadilla
de Totana
Alhama
de Murcia
La Union
Cabo de Palos
Lorca
Cartagena
Huercal
Overa
Golfo de
Mazarrón
Aguilas
Albox
Vera
Carboneras
Níjar
Almería
Cabo
de Gata
M e d i t e r r a n e a n
S e a
ALGER
(ALGIERS)
Dellys
Tizi
Ouzou
Ain
Taya
Rouiba
Thenia
Lakhdaria
Boghni
Bou
Ismail
Larba
Ain Bouira
Boufarik
Gouraya
Cherchell
Hadjout
Blida
Béni
Slimane
Sour el
Ghozlane
Ténès
Bouzghaia
Miliana
Médéa
Khemis
Miliana
Berrouaghia
Ech Chélif
ALGERIA
Arzew
Mostaganem
Ain-Tédelès
Bou
Kadir
Bordj
Bou Naam
Theniet
el Had
Ksar el
Boukhari
Ain el
Hadjel
Bouzqoul
Relizane
Atlas
Mountains
Mers el
Kébir
Oran
Gdyel
Oued Tlelat
Mohammadia
Cap Figalo
El Amria
Mascara
Hammam
Bou Hadjar
Beni Saf
Ain Témouchent

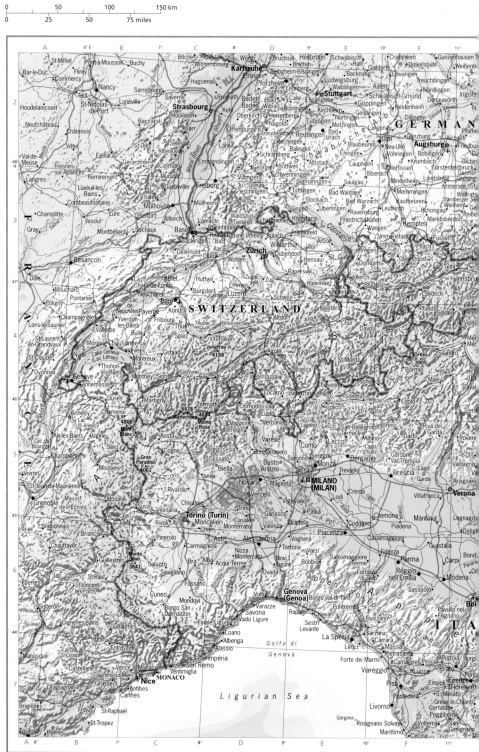

CZECH REPUBLIC

SLOVAKIA

AUSTRIA

HUNGARY

Großglockner
3798

WIEN
(VIENNA)

Bratislava

Salzburg

Linz

Graz

Triglav
2864

Ljubljana

SLOVENIA

Zagreb

CROATIA

Venézia
(Venice)

Gulf
of Venice

Trieste

Snežnik
1796

Rijeka

I s t r a

Pula

Cres

Rab

Pag

Zadar

Vaganski Vrh
1758

BOSNIA-
HERZEGOVINA

D i n a r i c   A l p s

SAN
MARINO

San Marino

A d r i a t i c   S e a

Split

Brač

Hvar

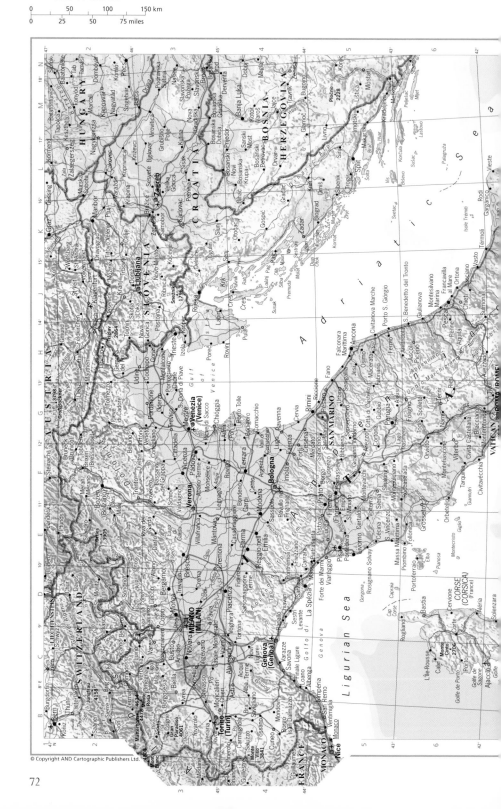

Scale 1 : 4 750 000

0 50 100 150 km
0 25 50 75 miles

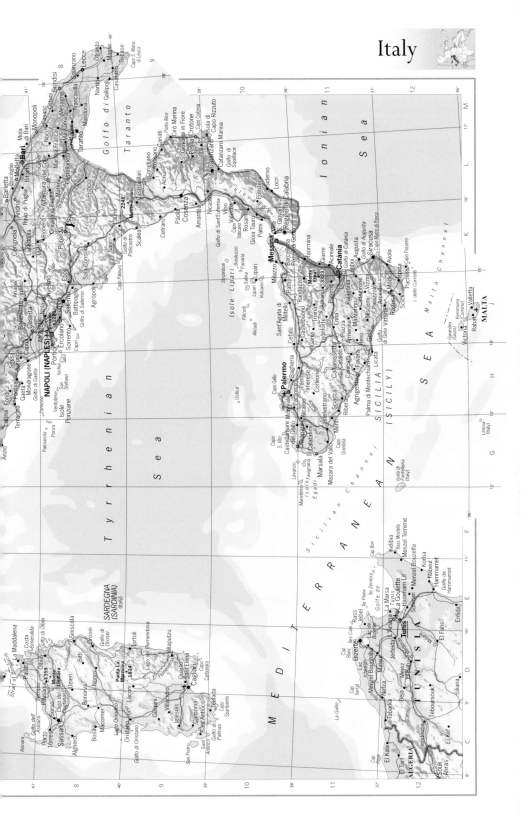

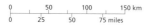

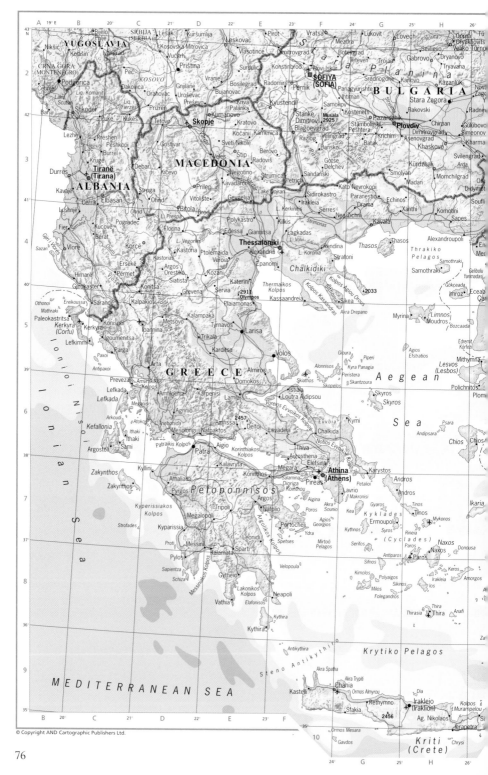

Scale 1 : 14 300 000

0   200   400   600 km
0   100   200   300 miles

A   10° E   65° N   B   15°   C   20°   D   1   25°   E   30°   F   35°   G   40°

Norwegian Sea

Namsos
Kristiansund
Molde
Verdalsøra
Trondheim
2470 Dombås Røros
Galdhøpiggen 1796
Helagsfjället
Østersund
Sundsvall
Fagernes
Lillehammer
Mjøsa Hamar
Hønefoss
Oslo
Borlänge
Arvika
Karlstad
Skövde
Børås
Jönköping
Vänern
Värnamo
Växjö
Karlskrona
Kalmar
Gotland
Öland
Motala
Norrköping
Linköping
Vättern
Nyköping
Västervik
Tärnaby
Jokkmokk
Pello
Sodankylä
Uddjaure
Arvidsjaur
Storuman
Vilhelmina
Åsele
Lycksele
Skellefteå
Åsele
Strömsund
Örnsköldsvik
Umeå
Kramfors
Härnösand
Hudiksvall
Söderhamn
Gävle
Falun
Ludvika
Uppsala
Eskilstuna
Västerås
Södertälje
STOCKHOLM
Norrtälje
Hanko
Espoo
HELSINKI

NORWAY
SWEDEN

Gulf of Bothnia

Haparanda
Luleå
Kemi
Oulu
Pudasjärvi
Kuusamo
Loukhi
Kalevala
Rovaniemi
Kemijärvi Salla
Kandalaksha

FINLAND
KARELIYA

Kokkola
Jakobstad
Vaasa
Seinäjoki
Iisalmi
Kajaani
Jyväskylä
Tampere
Pori
Hämeenlinna
Lahti
Turku
Vantaa
Lappeenranta
Kotka
Mikkeli
Kuopio
Savonlinna

Gulf of Finland

Hiiumaa
Haapsalu
TALLINN
Rakvere
Järve
Kohtla
Narva
Saaremaa
Pärnu
ESTONIA
Viljandi
Tartu
L. Pskov

SANKT-PETERBURG
(ST PETERSBURG)
Gatchina
Pushkin
Sestroretsk
Volkhov
Vyborg

Ladozhskoye Ozero
(Lake Ladoga)
Onezhskoye Ozero

Petrozavodsk
Kondopoga

Segezha
Belomorsk

Beloye More
(White Sea)

Severodvinsk
Novodvinsk
Arkhan

Barents Sea

Kolskiy Poluostrov
Monchegorsk
Apatity
Kandalaksha

BALTIC SEA

Ventspils
Liepāja
Jūrmala
RIGA
Gulf of Riga
Talsi
Valmiera
Valga
Jelgava
Jēkabpils
LATVIA
Šiauliai
Klaipėda
LITHUANIA
Panevėžys
Kėdainiai
Kaunas
VILNIUS
Alytus
Marijampolė

Slupsk
Gdynia
Gdańsk
Kaliningrad
RUSSIA
Chernyakhovsk
Elbląg
Olsztyn
Suwałki
Ełk
POLAND
WARSZAWA
(WARSAW)
Białystok
Łódź
Lublin
Radom
Kielce
Katowice
Kraków

Pskov
Novgorod
Staraya Russa
Valday
Ostrov
Opochka
Velikiye Luki
Nelidovo
Vitsyebsk
Polatsk
Smolensk
Orsha
MAHILYOW
Babruysk
Minsk
Maladzyechna
Barysaw
Baranavichy
Slutsk
BELARUS
Homyel
Mazyr
Navahrudak
Hrodna
Lida

Cherepovets
Rybinsk
Yaroslavl
Kostroma
Ivanovo
Tver'
MOSKVA (MOSCOW)
Vladimir
NIZHN NOVGOR
Dzerzhinsk
Kaluga
Tula
Orel
Bryansk
Lipetsk
Tambov
Voronezh
Kursk
Belgorod

Vologda

Brest
Chernihiv
KYYIV (KIEV)
Zhytomyr
UKRAINE
L'viv
Ternopil'
Rivne
Sumy
Kharkiv
Poltava
Cherkasy
Kremenchuk
Vinnytsya
Kirovohrad
Dniprodzerzhyns'k
DNIPROPETROVS'K
Zaporizhzhya
Kryvyy Rih
Donets'k
Makiyivka
Luhans'k
ROSTOV-NA-DONU
Taganrog
Mariupol'
Kherson
Mykolayiv
ODESA (ODESSA)
Izmayil
Kherson

MOLDOVA
Chisinau
Tiraspol
Bălți

ROMANIA
Cluj-Napoca
Oradea
Târgu Mureş
Braşov
BUCUREŞTI (BUCHAREST)
Constanţa
Craiova
Ploieşti

BULGARIA
Pleven
Ruse
Varna

Sea of Azov
Krym
Simferopol'
Sevastopol'
Yalta

Black Sea

Krasnodar
Stavropol'
Maykop
Novorossiysk

© Copyright AND Cartographic Publishers Ltd.

78

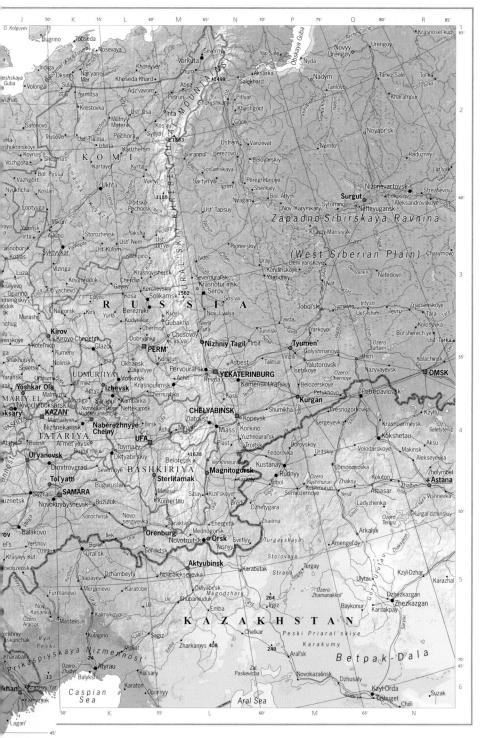

Scale   1 : 45 100 000

| 0 | 500 | 1000 | 1500 | 2000 km |

| 0 | 500 | 1000 miles |

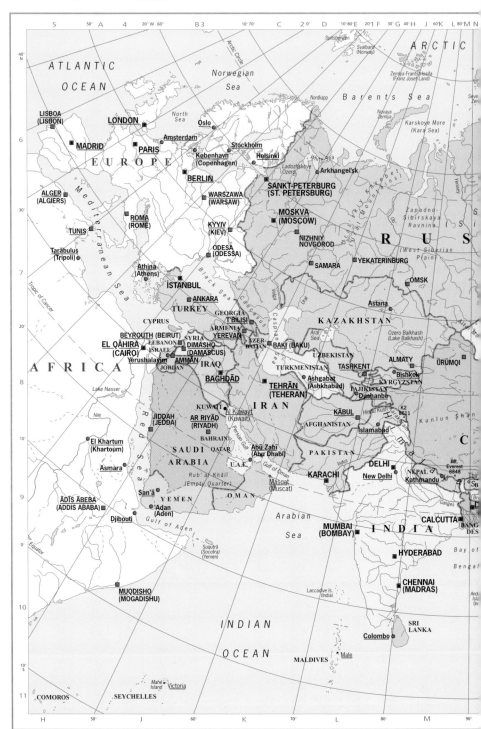

A T L A N T I C
O C E A N

Arctic Circle

Spitsbergen

Svalbard
(Norway)

A R C T I C

Norwegian
Sea

Zemlya Frantsa-Iosifa
(Franz Josef Land)

40°
N

Nordkapp

B a r e n t s   S e a

Seve
Zem

LISBOA
(LISBON)

LONDON

North
Sea

Oslo

Novaya
Zemlya

Karskoye More
(Kara Sea)

6

MADRID

PARIS

Amsterdam

Stockholm

København
(Copenhagen)

Helsinki

White Sea

Ladozhskoye
Ozero

Arkhangel'sk

E U R O P E

BERLIN

SANKT-PETERBURG
(ST. PETERSBURG)

ALGER
(ALGIERS)

WARSZAWA
(WARSAW)

MOSKVA
(MOSCOW)

Zapadno-
Sibirskaya
Ravnina

R   U   S

ROMA
(ROME)

KYYIV
(KIEV)

TUNIS

ODESA
(ODESSA)

NIZHNIY
NOVGOROD

(West Siberian
Plain)

S i

Tarābulus
(Tripoli)

Athina
(Athens)

Black Sea

SAMARA

YEKATERINBURG

OMSK

7

Tropic of Cancer

İSTANBUL

ANKARA

TURKEY

GEORGIA

Caucasus

Volga

Ural

Astana

KAZAKHSTAN

CYPRUS

T'BILISI

ARMENIA

Caspian Sea

Aral
Sea

Ozero Balkhash
(Lake Balkhash)

20°

BEYROUTH (BEIRUT)

SYRIA

YEREVAN

AZER-
BAIJAN

BAKI (BAKU)

ÜRÜMQI

EL QÂHIRA
(CAIRO)

LEBANON
ISRAEL

DIMASHQ
(DAMASCUS)

UZBEKISTAN

TASHKENT

ALMATY

A F R I C A

Yerushalayim
JORDAN

AMMÂN
IRAQ

TURKMENISTAN

Lake Nasser

BAGHDÂD

TEHRÂN
(TEHERAN)

Ashgabat
(Ashkhabad)

TAJIKISTAN

Dushanbe

Bishkek

KYRGYZSTAN

8

Nile

I R A N

KÂBUL

K2
8611

Kunlun Shan

C

KUWAIT
Al Kuwayt
(Kuwait)

Hindu Kush

JIDDAH
(JEDDA)

AR RIYÂD
(RIYADH)

AFGHANISTAN

Islamabad

Red Sea

El Khartum
(Khartoum)

BAHRAIN

QATAR

Abū Zabī
(Abu Dhabi)

PAKISTAN

DELHI

Mt.
Everest
8848

NEPAL

Thir

Asmara

SAUDI
ARABIA

U.A.E.

Gulf of Oman

KARACHI

New Delhi

Kathmandu

SB

Rub' al Khālī
(Empty Quarter)

Maşqaţ
(Muscat)

Ganges

9

San'ā

O M A N

Br

ĀDĪS ĀBEBA
(ADDIS ABABA)

YEMEN

'Adan
(Aden)

CALCUTTA

BANG
DES

Djibouti

Gulf of Aden

Arabian
Sea

MUMBAI
(BOMBAY)

I N D I A

0°

Equator

Suqutrā
(Socotra)
(Yemen)

HYDERABAD

Bay of
Bengal

CHENNAI
(MADRAS)

10

Laccadive Is.
(India)

And
Isla
(In

MUQDISHO
(MOGADISHU)

I N D I A N

O C E A N

SRI
LANKA

Colombo

10°
S

Mahé
Island

Victoria

MALDIVES

Male

11

COMOROS

SEYCHELLES

© Copyright AND Cartographic Publishers Ltd.

80

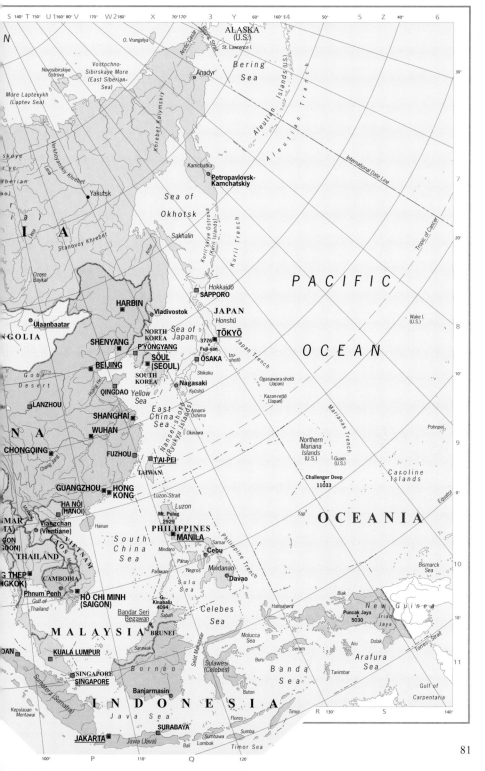

S 140° T 150° U 160° 80° V 170° W 2180° X 70°170° 3 Y 60° 160° E 4 50° 5 Z 40° 6

ALASKA
(U.S.)

O. Vrangelya
St. Lawrence I.

Novosibirskiye
Ostrova

Vostochno-
Sibirskaye More
(East Siberian-
Sea)

Bering
Sea

Aleutian Islands (U.S.)

Anadyr'

More Laptevykh
(Laptev Sea)

Khrebet Kolymskiy

30°

Aleutian Trench

International Date Line

skoye
rye
iberian
r
i a)

Verkhoyanskiy Khrebet

Lena

Yakutsk

Kamchatka

Petropavlovsk-
Kamchatskiy

Sea of

Okhotsk

7

Aleutian Trench

I A

Stanovoy Khrebet

Amur

Sakhalin

Kuril'skiye Ostrova
(Kuril Islands)

Kuril Trench

20°

Tropic of Cancer

Ozero
Baykal

Hokkaido
SAPPORO

PACIFIC

HARBIN

Vladivostok

JAPAN
Honshū

GOLIA

Ulaanbaatar

Sea of
Japan

TŌKYŌ

OCEAN

Wake I.
(U.S.)

8

NORTH
KOREA

SHENYANG

P'YŎNGYANG

3776
Fuji-san

Japan Trench

Gobi
Desert

BEIJING

SŎUL
(SEOUL)

ŌSAKA

Izu-
shotō

10°

SOUTH
KOREA

Shikoku

LANZHOU

QINGDAO

Nagasaki

Kyūshū

Yellow
Sea

Ogasawara-shotō
(Japan)

Kazan-rettō
(Japan)

N A

SHANGHAI

WUHAN

East
China
Sea

Amami-
Ōshima

Marianas Trench

Pohnpei

9

CHONGQING

FUZHOU

Chang Jiang

T'AI-PEI

Nansei-shotō
Ryukyu Islands

Okinawa

Northern
Mariana
Islands
(U.S.)

Guam
(U.S.)

Caroline
Islands

TAIWAN

Hsiang Jiang

GUANGZHOU

HONG
KONG

Luzon Strait

Luzon

Challenger Deep
11033

Equator
0°

MAR
IA)
GON
GON)

HA NÔI
(HANOI)

Yap

OCEANIA

Viangchan
(Vientiane)

Hainan

Mt. Pulog
2929

PHILIPPINES
MANILA

Philippine Trench

THAILAND

South
China
Sea

Mindoro

Samar

Cebu

Bismarck
Sea

10

G THEP
GKOK)

CAMBODIA

Panay

Negros

Mindanao

Davao

Phnum Penh

Sulu
Sea

Palawan

Biak

New Guinea

Gulf of
Thailand

HÔ CHI MINH
(SAIGON)

Kinabalu
4094

Halmahera

Puncak Jaya
5030

Irian
Jaya

10°

Bandar Seri
Begawan

Sabah

Celebes
Sea

Molucca
Sea

DAN

MALAYSIA

BRUNEI

Sarawak

Selat Makasar

Seram

Aru

Dolak

Torres Strait

KUALA LUMPUR

Buru

Banda
Sea

Arafura
Sea

11

SINGAPORE
SINGAPORE

Borneo

Sulawesi
(Celebes)

Tanimbar

Gulf of
Carpentaria

Kepulauan
Mentawai

Banjarmasin

Buton

Sumatera (Sumatra)

I N D O N E S I A

R 130°

S 140°

Java Sea

Jawa (Java)

Flores

Timor

JAKARTA

SURABAYA

Sumbawa

Sumba

Timor Sea

Bali

Lombok

100° P 110° Q 120°

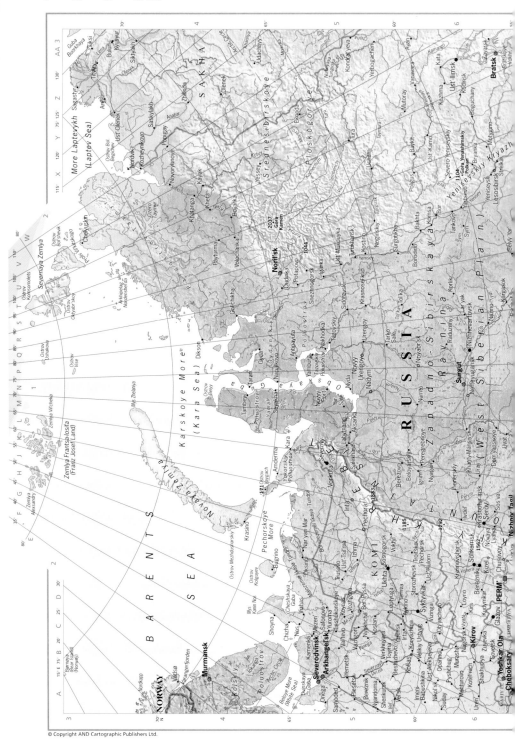

Scale 1 : 18 900 000

0   200   400   600 km
0 100   200   300 miles

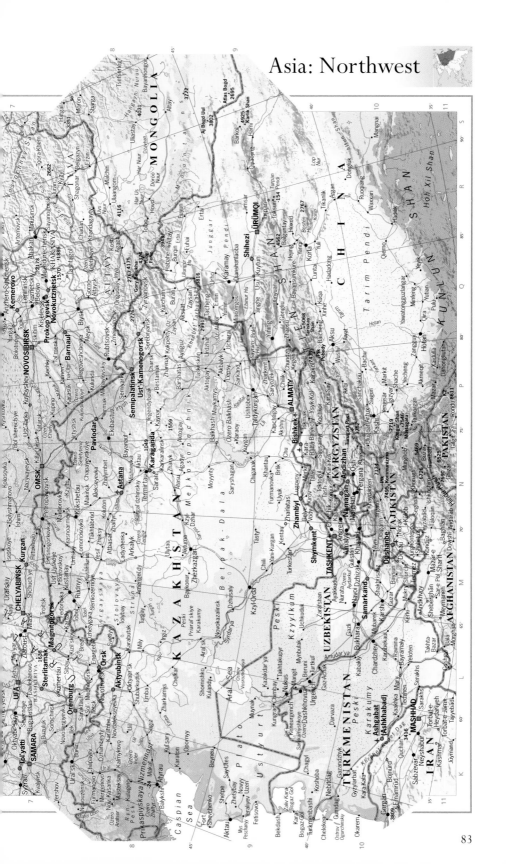

0   200   400   600 km
0   100   200   300 miles

A 75° E 65° B   80°   C 3   85° D 70° 90° E   95° 2 F   100° G   105° H   110° J 115° K 120° L 125° M 1

More
Laptevykh
(Laptev Sea)

75°

Ostrov Bol'shoy
Begichev

Purpe
Tarko
Sale
Urengoy
Sidorovsk
Potapovo
Noril'sk
Dolgany
Volochanka
Kheta
Paylurma
Khatanga
Novorybnoye
Oleneksky
Zaliv

Kharampur
Chaselka
Krasnosel'kup
Khantayka
Ozero
Tama
Aheta
Kheta
Boyarka
Popigay
Ust'-Olenek
Saskylakh
Taymylyr

Raduzhny
Tal'ka
Tol'ka
Khudoseya
Igarka
Snezhnogorsk
2037
Gora
Kamen'
Kureyka
Rassokha
Saskylakh
Bykovskiy
Tiksi

4

Sabun
Ratta
Turukhansk
Koshno
Yessey
Zhilinda
Govorovo
Kyusyur

Vanzhil'kynak
Vereshchagino
Surgutikha
Noginskiy
Bulun
Siktyakh

60°
N
Napas
Lat'yak
Koriki
Kulynigol
Verkhneimbatsk
Bakhta
Tutonchany
S r e d n e s i b i r s k o y e
Olenek
Natara
Dzhardzhan

Belyy Yar
Sym
Bor
Nidym
Tura
P l o s k o g o r ' y e
Udachnyy
Aykhal
Kystatyam
Verkhoy

Ust'-
Ozernoye
Yartsevo
Novonazimovo
Teya
Severo-
Yeniseyskiy
Baykit
Kuyumba
Yukta
Morkoka
Zhigansk
Syalakh
SA

5
Tegul'det
Ust'-Pit'
1104
Gora
Yenashimskiy
Polkan
Chernyshevskiy
Vilyuyskoye
Vodokhranilishche
Vilyuysk
Aryta
Sangar

Yeniseysk
Lesosibirsk
Bogotol
Kazachinskoye
Strelka
Motygino
Mutoray
Vanavara
Mirnyy
Nyurba
Khampa
Batamay

Achinsk
Nazarovo
Balakhta
Boguchany
Kodinsk
Kezhma
Yerbogachen
Preobrazhenka
Suntar
Krestyakh
Ibenge
Ust'-Ta
Namtsy

55°
Krasnoyarsk
Pochet
Zaozernyy
Uyar
Narva
Kansk
Kata
Ust'-Ilimsk
R U S S I A
Lensk
Khamra
Nyuya
Peleduy
Yakutsk
Berdigestyakh
Ytyk-Kyu
Pokrovsk

Bellyk
Artemovsk
Aginskoye
Tayshet
Novaya Igirma
Nepa
Nizhneudinsk
Mama
Turukta
Chapayevo
Olekminsk
Bestyakh
Kachikatsy
Amga

6
Kuragino
Toora-
Khem
2682
TYVA
Tulun
Zima
Bratsk
Bratskoye
Vodokhranilishche
Ust'-Kut
Kirensk
Bodaybo
Chuya
Artemovskiy
S t a n o v o y e
Ulu
Verkhnyaya
Amga
Tommot

Naryn
Orlik
Cheremkhovo
Zalari
Balagansk
Karam
Severobaykal'sk
2287
N a g o r ' y e
Chara
2100

50°
3351
Hövsgöl
Nuur
Mondy
Kyren
Angarsk
Irkutsk
Usol'ye
Pivovarovka
Kushir
Ozero Baykal
Kumurkan
Ust'-Muya
Necyungri

Hatgal
Sharga
Moron
Babushkin
Listvyanka
Turka
Barguzin
B U R Y A T I Y A
2484
Kalakan
Ust'-Nyukzha
Khrebet

Utata
Khamar Daban
Ust'-
Barguzin
Bagdarin
Vitim
Ust'-Urkima
Gonam

7
Horgo
Hutag
Bulgan
Erdenet
Zakamensk
Petropavlovka
Petrovsk
Gusinoozersk
Khorinsk
Y a b l o n o v y y
Ust'-Karenga
Tynda
Zeyskoye
Vodokhranilishche
Borinak

Tsetserleg
Altanbulag
Kyakhta
Krasnyy Chikoy
Maleta
Khilok
Chita
Ksen'yevka
Mogocha
Amazar
Skovorodino
Never
Zeya
Dzhalinda
Magdagachi

Darham
Yamarovka
Tanga
Ingoda
Karymskoye
Shilka
Sretensk
Mohe
Tygda
Chernyayevo

45°
Ulaanbaatar
Bayandelger
2452
Onon
Aksha
Sherlovaya
Borzya
Priargunsk
1501
Qiqian
Argunsk
Zhangling
Oryupino
Hum
Kumara
Mayskiy
Norsk

Arvayheer
Ondorhaan
Kerulen
Javarthushuu
Solov'yevsk
Krasnokamensk
Yitulihe
Tayuan
Orqen
Azzhinji
Aihui
Svobodnyy
Belogorsk

M O N G O L I A
Mandalgovi
Choyr
Choybalsan
Hulun
Nur
Manzhouli
Hailar
D a
H i n g g a n
L i n g
Nenjiang
Sunwu
Blagoveshchensk
Zavitinsk
Raychikhinsk

G o b i
D e s e r t
Buir Nur
Nehe
Oluch'ye
Biro

8
Dalandzadgad
Ergel
Saynshand
Sergelen
Baruun Urt
Tamsagbulag
Bei'an
Yichun
QIQIHAR
Daqing
Anda
Suihua
Hegang
Jiamusi
Shuangyashan

Hongor
Chonogol
Erenhot
Dong
C H I N A
Horqin
Youyi
Qianqi
Zhaodong
HARBIN
Jixi

Urad Houqi
Sonid Zuoqi
Xi Ujimqin Qi
Baicheng
Tuquan
Tao'an
Fuyue
Acheng
Shangzhi
Fangzheng
Mudanjiang

Linhe
Bayan Obo
Wuyuan
Guyang
Qagan Nur
Dalai Nur
Nart
Jarud Qi
Bairin Zuoqi
Tongyu
Taipingchuan
Wuchang
Yabuli
Hulin

40°
Wuhai
Baotou
Hohhot
N E I M O N G O L
(INNER MONGOLIA)
Xilinhot
Habirag
Xianghuang Qi
Bairin
Yuqi
Hexigten Qi
Kar Moron
Jinhe
Tongliao
CHANGCHUN
JILIN
Dongjingcheng
Dunhua

9
Shizuishan
Otog Qi
Dongsheng
Ejin Horo Qi
Zhangjiakou
Jining
Zhangbei
Shangdu
Weichang
Fengning
Chifeng
Naiman Qi
Zhangwu
Siping
Liaoyuan
Huadian
Huinan
Yanji
Tumen
Vladivo

Datong
Xuanhua
Great Wall
Luanping
Chengde
Qingyang
Beipiao
Lingyuan
SHENYANG
Tieling
Hailong
Fusong
N. KOREA
Mys
Povoroty

H   110°   J   115°   K   120°   L   125°   M

Ch'ongjin
Myonggan
Kapsan

130°
N

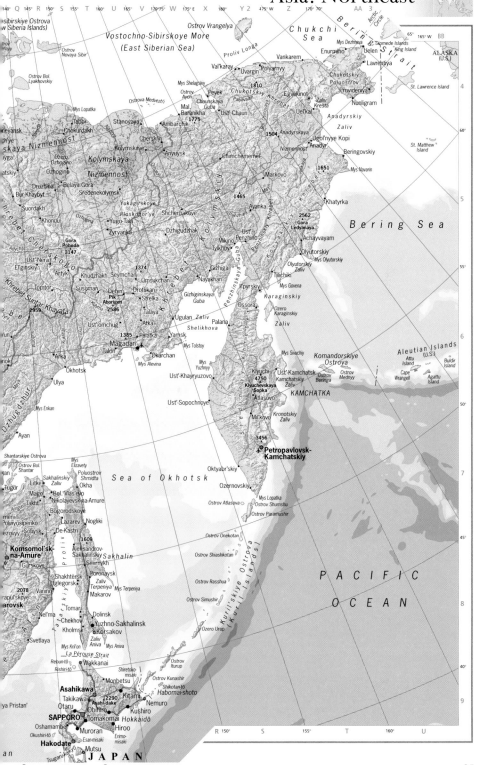

Asia: Northeast

140° Q 145° R 150° S 155° T 160° U 165° V 170°75° W 175° E X 180° Y 2 175° W Z 170° 70° AA 3

ostrirskiye Ostrova
w Siberia Islands)

Ostrov Vrangelya

Chukchi Sea

Berin

Arctic Circle

65° 165° W BB

Vostochno-Sibirskoye More
(East Siberian Sea)

Proliv Longa

Mys Dezhneva

Diomede Islands

ALASKA
(U.S.)

Ostrov
Novaya Sibir

Vankarem

Enurmino

Uelen

Strait

King Island

Val'karay

Uvargin

Polyarnyy

Chukotskiy
Poluostrov

Lavrentiya

St. Lawrence Island

Ostrov Bol.
Lyakhovskiy

Mys Shelagskiy

Pevek

1810

Chukotskiy Khrebet

Egvekinot

Providenrya

Mys Lopatka

Ostrova Medvezh'i

Ostrov
Ayon

Chaunskaya
Guba

Palyavaam

Zaliv
Kresta

Nunligram

Tabor

Mal.
Baranikha

Ust'-Chaun

Uel'kal

Anadyrskiy
Zaliv

60°

ueyansk
rh'ye

Stanovaya

Ambarchik

1775

Chokurdakh

1504

Anadyrskaya

Ugol'nyye Kopi

St. Matthew
Island

skaya Nizmennost'

Chérskiy

Kolymskaye

Anyuysk

Chimchememel'

Nizmennost'

Anadyr'

Beringovskiy

Ozero
Ozhogino

Kolymskaya
Nizmennost'

Markovo

1651

Mys Navarin

5

iyga
atskiy

Druzhina
Belaya Gora

Ozhogino

Khatyrka

Bur-Khaybyt

Sredenekolymsk

1465

Ayanka

2562
Gora
Ledyanaya

Bering Sea

Suordakh

Khonuu

Ozhogina

Yukagirskoye

Ploskozor'ye

Shcherbakove

Ponzhin

Ust'-
Penzhino

Achayvayam

Yugo-Tala

Zyryanka

Dzhigudzhak

Mikino

Tylkhoy

Olyutorskiy

Mys Olyutorskiy

55°

Gora
Pobeda
8147

1374

Gizhiga

Il'pyrskiy

Olyutorskiy
Zaliv

Ust'-Nera
El'ginskiy

Artyk

Khudzhakh

Seymchan

Omsukchan

Nayakhan

Mys Govena

Tomtor

Susuman

Debin

Orotukan

Strelka

Gizhiginskaya
Guba

Ossora

Ozero
Karaginskiy

Karaginskiy

Pik
Aborigen
2586

Talaya

Ugulan Zaliv

Palana

Zaliv

2959

Ust'omchug

Atka

Shelikhova

Patatka

1385

Yamsk

Mys Tolstoy

Magadan
Talon

Okurchan

Arka

Mys Alevina

Mys
Yuzhnyy

Mys Siyuchiy

Komandorskiye
Ostrova

Aleutian Islands
(U.S.)

Okhotsk

Ust'-Khayryuzovo

Klyuchi

4750
Klyuchevskaya
Sopka

Ust'-Kamchatsk

Ostrov
Beringa

Attu
Island

Buldir
Island

Ulya

Ust'-Sopochnoye

Atlasovo

Kamchatskiy
Zaliv

Cape
Wrangell

Agattu
Island

KAMCHATKA

Ayan

Mil'kovo

Kronotskiy
Zaliv

50°

Shantarskiye Ostrova

3456

Petropavlovsk-
Kamchatskiy

Ostrov Bol.
Shantar

Mys
Elizavety

Oktyabr'skiy

Sea of Okhotsk

Tugur

Litke

Sakhalinskiy
Zaliv

Poluostrov
Shmidta

Okha

Ozernovskiy

7

Mago
Takhi

Bel. Vlas'evo

Nikolayevsk-na-Amure

Mys Lopatka

Ostrov Atlasova

Ostrov Shumshu

Bogorodskoye

Lazarev

Ostrov Paramushir

olimyósipenko
ezovyy
Sofiysk

De-Kastri

Nogliki

Komsomol'sk-
na-Amure

1609

Aleksandrov-
Sakhalinskiy

Sakhalin

Ostrov Onekotan

45°

Gurskovo

Smirnykh

Ostrov Shiashkotan

2078
rapul'skoye
arovsk

Shakhtersk
Uglegorsk

Poronaysk

Zaliv
Terpeniya

Mys Terpeniya

Ostrov Rasshua

PACIFIC

Vanino

Makarov

Ostrov Simushir

OCEAN

8

Nel'ma

Tomari

Dolinsk

Ozero Urup

Chekhov

Yuzhno-Sakhalinsk

Svetlaya

Kholmsk

Korsakov

Zaliv
Aniva

Mys Aniva

Mys Kril'on

La Pérouse Strait

Ostrov Iturup

40°

Rebun-tō
Rishiri-tō

Wakkanai

Shiretoko-
misaki

Ostrov Kunashir

Asahikawa

Monbetsu

Shikotan-tō

Takikawa

2290
Asahi-dake

Kitami

Habomai-shoto

Otaru

Obihiro

Nemuro

SAPPORO

Tomakomai

Kushiro

9

Oshamambe

Hokkaidō

Okushiri-tō

Muroran

Hiroo

Esan-misaki

Ermo-misaki

Hakodate

Mutsu

an

JAPAN

Tsugaru

P 140° Q 145°

R 150° S 155° T 160° U

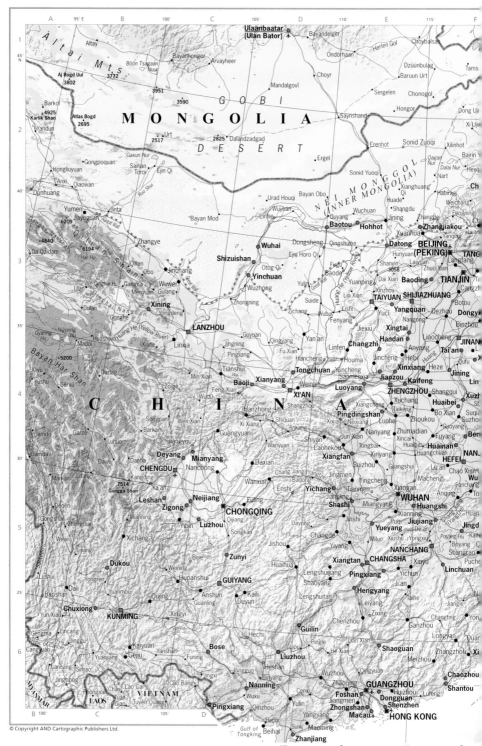

QIQIHAR
Bei'an
Yichun
Hegang
Jiamusi
Suihua
Anda
Daqing
Horqin Youyi Qianqi
Lanxi
Songhua
Bikin
Svetlaya
Mys Krol'on
La Pérouse Strait
Zaliv Aniva
Mys Aniva
Ostrov Iturup

HARBIN
Baicheng
Acheng
Fangzheng
Jixi
Muling
Lesozavodsk
Wakkanai
Rishiri-tō
Rebun-tō
Esashi
Ostrov Kunashir
Shiretoko-misaki

Tao'an
Tuquan
Da an
Zhaodong
Shulan
Yushu
Yilan
Ozero Khanka
Spassk-Dal'niy
Haboro
Nayoro
Monbetsu
Abashiri
Shikotan-tō

Tao'an
Jarud Qi
Jurhe
Tongyu
Taipingchuan
Dongjingcheng
Grodekovo
Takikawa
Asahikawa
2290
Asahi-dake
Kitami
Nemuro

CHANGCHUN
JILIN
Dunhua
Ussuriysk
Rudnaya Pristan'
Oshamambe
Otaru
SAPPORO
Obihiro
Kushiro
HOKKAIDŌ
Hiroo
Enmo-misaki

Tongliao
Shuangliao
Siping
Huadian
Yanji
Tumen
Vladivostok
Nakhodka
Okushiri-tō
Mori
Muroran
Tomakomai
Esan-misaki

Kangping
Liaoyuan
Antu
Najin
Mys Povorotnyy
Matsumae
Hakodate
Tsugaru-kaikyō
Mutsu

Faku
Zhangwu
Tieling
Qingyuan
Hunjiang
Mys Povorotnyy
Aomori
Hachinohe

Fuxin
SHENYANG
FUSHUN
Hyesan
Kilchu
Hiroaki
Ōdate
Morioka
Hanamaki

Jinxi
Liaoyang
Benxi
Kapsan
Kimch'aek
Noshiro
Akita
Ichinoseki
Kamaishi

Jinzhou
ANSHAN
Manp'o
Ch'osan
Pukch'ong
Sakata
Shinjō
Furukawa
Ishinomaki

Yingkou
Haicheng
Sinŭiju
Hamhŭng
Chōngjin
Ryōtsu
Yamagata
Sendai

nhuangdao
Dandong
NORTH
Chŏngju
Sado-shima
Niigata
Fukushima

Wafangdian
Zhuanghe
Korea
Wŏnsan
Suzu-misaki
Ibetsu
Kōriyama

Lüshun
DALIAN
P'YŎNGYANG
Kosŏng
Nanao
Nagano
Iwaki
Utsunomiya

Miaodao
Qundao
Namp'o
Sŏngnim
Sariwŏn
Sŏkch'o
Toyama
Maebashi
Mito
Kashima

Yantai
Haeju
Kaesŏng
SOUL (SEOUL)
Kangnŭng
Tonghae
Ullŭng do
Kanazawa
Matsumoto
Fuji-san 3776
Kōfu
YOKOHAMA

Weihai
Rongcheng
INCH'ŎN
Anyang
Ulchin
Tok-tō
Fukui
Tsuruoka
Gifu
NAGOYA
Shizuoka
Shimoda
Izu-shoto

QINGDAO
Suwŏn
Ch'ŏngju
SOUTH
Andong
Oki-shotō
Dōgo
KYŌTO
Suzuka
Hamamatsu
Miyake-jima

Shandong
Bandao
Kunsan
TAEJŎN
KOREA
P'ohang
Izumo
Yonago
Tottori
OSAKA
KŌBE
Matsusaka
Hachijō-jima

YELLOW SEA
Ch'ŏnju
KWANGJU
PUSAN
Hamada
Okayama
Takamatsu
Wakayama
Tokushima
shotō

Mokp'o
Sunch'ŏn
HIROSHIMA
Hōfu
Matsuyama
Kōchi
Shiono-misaki
Myōjin

Cheju
KITA-KYŪSHŪ
Shimonoseki
Tokushima
SHIKOKU
Sumisu-jima

Yancheng
FUKUOKA
Kurume
Ōita
Nakamura
JAPAN

Xinghua
Taizhou
Cheju do (South Korea)
Gotō-rettō
Saseba
Isahaya
Kumamoto
Nobeoka
Tori-shima

Nantong
Fukue-jima
Nagasaki
Yatsushiro
KYŪSHŪ
Miyazaki

Changzhou
SHANGHAI
Akune
Miyakonojo
Sōfu-gan

ZHOU
Jiaxing
Haining
Kagoshima
Makurazaki
Kanoya

Fenghua
NINGBO
Ōsumi-shotō
Tanega-shima
Yaku-shima

Jinhua
Ninghai
EAST CHINA SEA

Lishui
Linhai
Huangyan
Nansei-shotō (Ryukyu islands)
Amami-Ōshima

Wenzhou
Naze

Fuding
PACIFIC

ZHOU
Naga
Okinawa
OCEAN

Matsu (Taiwan)
Okinawa
Naha

T'ao-yuan
Chi-lung
T'AI-PEI
Hsin-chu
3884
Hsueh-Shan
Sakishima-shotō
Tropic of Cancer

T'ai-chung
3950
Yu Shan
TAIWAN
T'ai-tung

HSIUNG
Ping-tung
Oluan-pi

SEA OF JAPAN
HONSHŪ
CHINA SEA

Scale 1 : 7 900 000

```
0        100        200        300 km
0    50        100        150 miles
```

Sea of Okhotsk

Ostrov Iturup

HOKKAIDŌ

Ostrov Kunashir

Wakkanai
Sōya-misaki
Rebun-tō
Rishiri-tō
Hamatonbetsu
Teshio
Esashi
Otoineppu
Ōmū
Okoppe
Monbetsu
Haboro
Nayoro
Shiretoko-misaki
1819
Shibetsu
Abashiri
Rausu
Yuzhno-Kuril'sk
Rumoi
Kitami
Shibetsu
Shikotan-tō
Asahikawa
Asahi-dake
2290
Kussharo-ko
Shibotsu-jima
Takikawa
Furano
Ikeda
Nemuro
Shakotan-misaki
Ishikari-wan
Iwamizawa
Otaru
Akkeshi
Kamoenai
Kutchan
SAPPORO
Obihiro
Kushiro
Tomakomai
Oshamambe
Shikotsu-ko
Date
Monbetsu
Setana
Uchiura-wan
Hiroo
Okushiri-tō
Yakumo
Mori
Muroran
Urakawa
Erimo-misaki
Kemiso
Esashi
Esan-misaki
Ō-shima
Matsumae
Hakodate
Tsugaru-kaikyō
Ōma
Shiriya-zaki
Kodomari-misaki
Mutsu
Mutsu-wan
Henashi-zaki
Yokohama
Noheji
Aomori
Ajigasawa
Hirosaki
Hachinohe
Ōdate
Ninohe
Noshiro
Kuji
Morioka
Fudai
Miyako
Akita
Honjō
Hanamaki
Yokote
Kamaishi
Kitakami
Sakata
Ichinoseki
Kesennuma
2230
Tsuruoka
Shinjō
Furukawa
Yamagata
Ishinomaki
Kinka-san
Ryōtsu
Shibata
Sendai
Sadoga-shima
Yonezawa
Sōma
Niigata
2105
Suzu-misaki
Sanjō
Fukushima
Haramachi
Nagaoka
Aizu-wakamatsu
Kōriyama
Kashiwazaki
Tajima
Shirakawa
Jōetsu
Nanao
HONSHŪ
Mikuni-sammyaku
Kuroiso
Iwaki
Nagano
Utsunomiya
Hitachi
Toyama
Maebashi
Kiryū
Kanazawa
3180
Takasaki
Oyama
Mito
Matsumoto
Okaya
Tsuchiura
Takayama
Kawagoe
TOKYO
Chōshi
Kōfu
Hachiōji
Funabashi
Inubō-zaki
3192
Iida
Fuji-san
3776
YOKOHAMA
CHIBA
KAWASAKI
3120
NAGOYA
Yokosuka
Katsuura
Toyota
Shizuoka
Sagami-nada
Hamamatsu
Fujieda
Tateyama
Nojima-zaki
Shimoda
Ōmaezaki
Nii-jima
Izu-shotō
Kōzu-shima
Miyakejima
Mikura-jima

JAPAN

PACIFIC OCEAN

Hachijō-jima

Aoga-shima

Sumisu-jima

Tori-shima

Scale 1 : 15 900 000

© Copyright AND Cartographic Publishers Ltd.

90

EAST CHINA
SEA

JAPAN

Nansei-shotō (Ryukyu Islands)

Nago
Okinawa
Naha

Sakishima-shotō

Tropic of Cancer

iangtan CHANGSHA Xinyu
Linchuan Pucheng Wenzhou
Lianyuan Yichun Shangrao
gshuijiang Pingxiang Fuding
ang Hengyang Ji'an Nanping Ningde
uitan Leiyang Taihe Jiangle Matsu
Zixing Changting Yong'an (Taiwan)
A Chenzhou Ganzhou FUZHOU
Shaoguan Longyan Putian
Zhangzhou Quanzhou Chinmen
Meizhou (Taiwan)
Lian Xian Xiamen
le Xian Qingyuan Chaozhou
zhou Huizhou Shantou
GUANGZHOU Lufeng
qing Jiangmen Foshan Dongguan Shanwei
Zhongshan Shenzhen
Macau HONG KONG
Yangxiang
ng

T'ao-yuan Chi-lung
Hsin-chu T'AI-PEI
3884
Hsueh Shan
T'ai-chung
Chang-hua
Chia-i 3950 TAIWAN
Yu Shan
T'ai-nan T'ai-tung
KAO-HSIUNG P'ing-tung
Oluan-pi

Luzon Batan Islands
Strait
Balintang Channel
Babuyan Islands

PACIFIC

OCEAN

Dongsha Qundao
(Pratas)
(China)

Claveria San Vicente
Laoag Aparri
Lal-Lo
Vigan Kabugao Tuguegarao
Bontoc Ilagan
San Fernando Mt. Pulog Santiago
Baguio 2929
Alaminos Dagupan
San Carlos
Tarlac Cabanatuan
Angeles
Olongapo QUEZON CITY
Polillo Is.
MANILA
Pasig Daet
Nasugbu San Pablo Calauag Cantanduanes
Batangas Lucena Lopez Virac
Mamburao Calapan Boac Legaspi
Mindoro 2488 Pinamalayan
Mount Baco Masbate Naasin Catarman
San Pedro Masbate Allen Samar
Calamian Nabas Placer Calbayog
Group Coron Catbalogan
El Nido Kalibo Roxas Ormoc Taclaban
Panay Bogo Leyte
San Jose de Iloilo Bacolod Sogod Libjo
Buenavista Cebu Dinagat
Carcar Tibon
Cauayan Bais Bohol Sungao Dapa
Roxas Negros Madrid
Palawan Puerto Princesa Dumaguete Butuan Tandag
Quezon PHILIPPINES Prosperidad
Dipolog Cagayan de Oro
Brooke's Point Manukan 2560
Liloy Iligan Malaybalay Bislig
Balabac Sibuco Pagadian Mindanao
Balabac Davao
Strait Sibugo Cotabato 2954 Mati
Kudat Zamboanga Mt. Apo
Langkon Isabela Tacurong General Santos
Kota Belud 4094 Jolo Moro Polomoloc
G. Kinabalu Ranau Basilan Gulf Palimbang Glan
Kota Kinabalu Sandakan Pangutaran Jolo Sarangani Is.
Beaufort SABAH Group Sulu Archipelago
Lahad Datu Tomitawi Kepulauan
I A Tungku Bongao Nanusa
Bandar Seri Begawan Semporna Kepulauan
Seria Tawau Karkaralong
BRUNEI Gunung Mulu Kepulauan Talaud
2371 Celebes
Bareo Sea
Bintulu Tarakan Sangir
Belaga 2499 Tanjungselor INDONESIA
Sibu SARAWAK Kepulauan Morotai
Kapit Sangir
gang 2988 KALIMANTAN Sangkulirang Molucca Sea Daruba
Muarawahau

Paracel Islands

S O U T H

C H I N A

S E A

Spratly
Islands

Mindoro Strait

Sulu Sea

Moro
Gulf

Cape San Agustin

INDONESIA

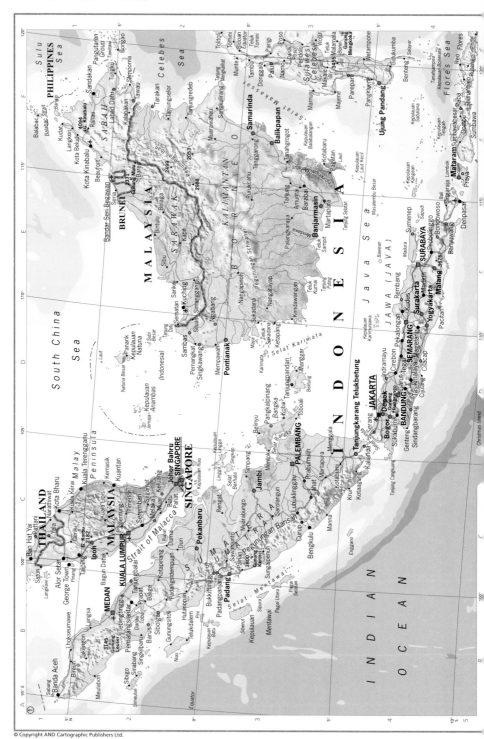

Scale 1 : 15 900 000

0   200   400   600 km
0   100   200   300 miles

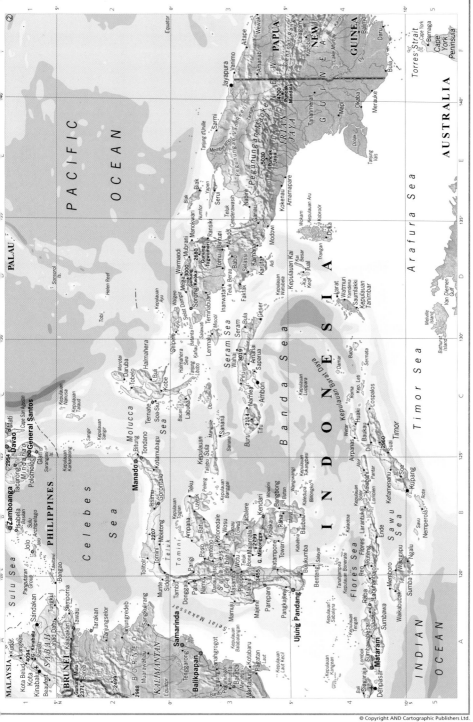

Scale 1 : 15 900 000

| 0 | 200 | 400 | 600 km |

| 0 | 100 | 200 | 300 miles |

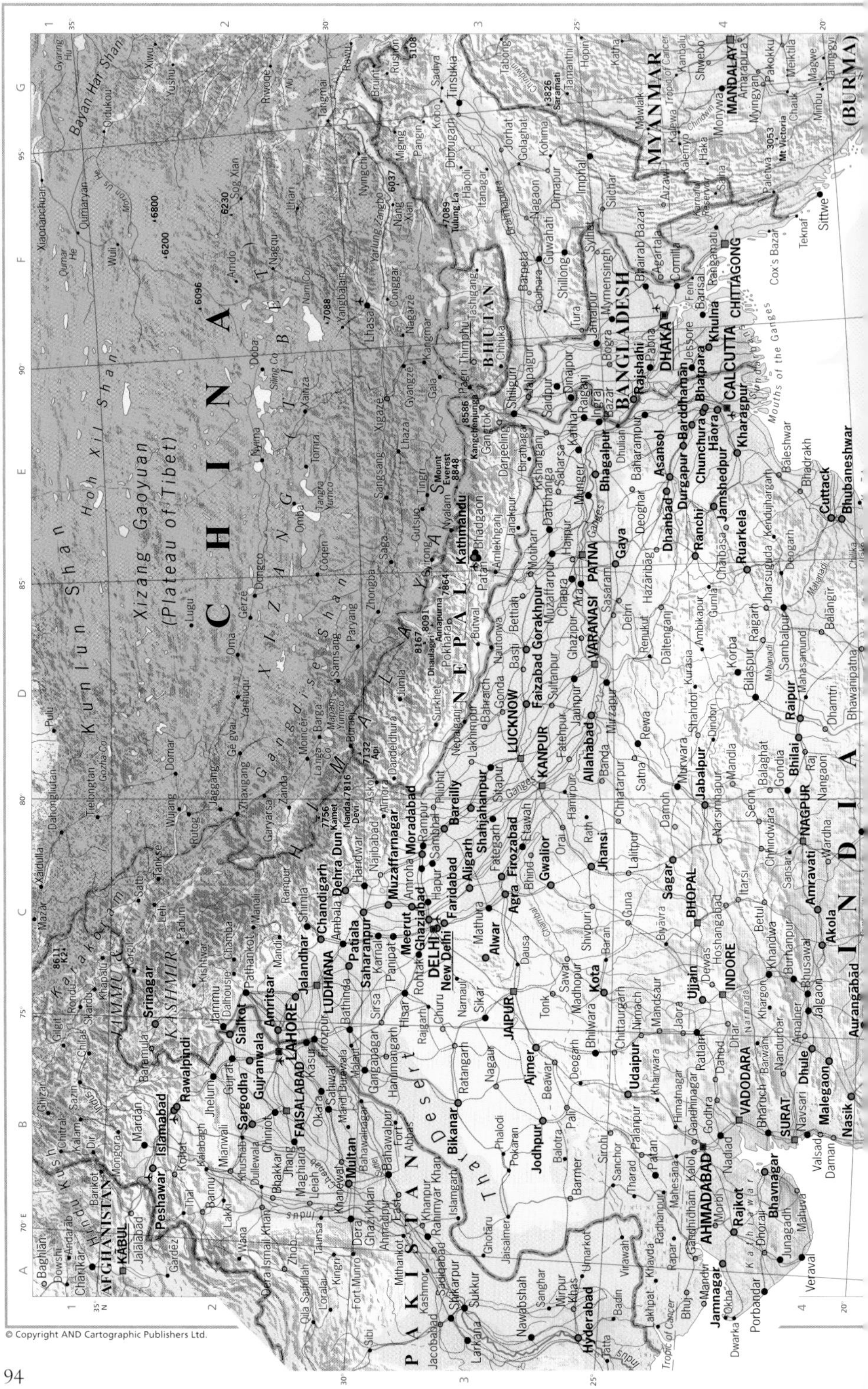

CHINA

XIZANG (TIBET)

Xizang Gaoyuan
(Plateau of Tibet)

Kunlun Shan

Bayan Har Shan

Gangdise Shan

HIMALAYA

KASHMIR

HINDU KUSH

AFGHANISTAN

KABUL

PAKISTAN

Thar Desert

INDIA

NEPAL

Kathmandu

BHUTAN

Thimphu

BANGLADESH

DHAKA

MYANMAR
(BURMA)

Mount Everest 8848

Mouths of the Ganges

Tropic of Cancer

Peshawar Islamabad Rawalpindi Srinagar Jammu
Amritsar LUDHIANA Jalandhar Chandigarh
FAISALABAD LAHORE Gujranwala Sialkot
Multan Bahawalpur
Bikaner DELHI New Delhi Meerut Moradabad
Faridabad Ghaziabad Aligarh Bareilly
JAIPUR Agra Gwalior Firozabad
Ajmer Kota
Jodhpur
AHMADABAD Udaipur BHOPAL Jabalpur
Rajkot VADODARA INDORE NAGPUR Amravati Akola
Bhavnagar SURAT Dhule Malegaon Nasik
Jamnagar
Hyderabad
LUCKNOW KANPUR Allahabad VARANASI PATNA
Gorakhpur Gaya Bhagalpur
Raipur Bhilai
Aurangabad
Ranchi Jamshedpur Asansol Durgapur
CALCUTTA Haora Kharagpur
Bardhaman
Raishahi Khulna CHITTAGONG
Guwahati Shillong Imphal Aizawl MANDALAY
Cuttack Bhubaneshwar
Mt Victoria 3053

© Copyright AND Cartographic Publishers Ltd.

94

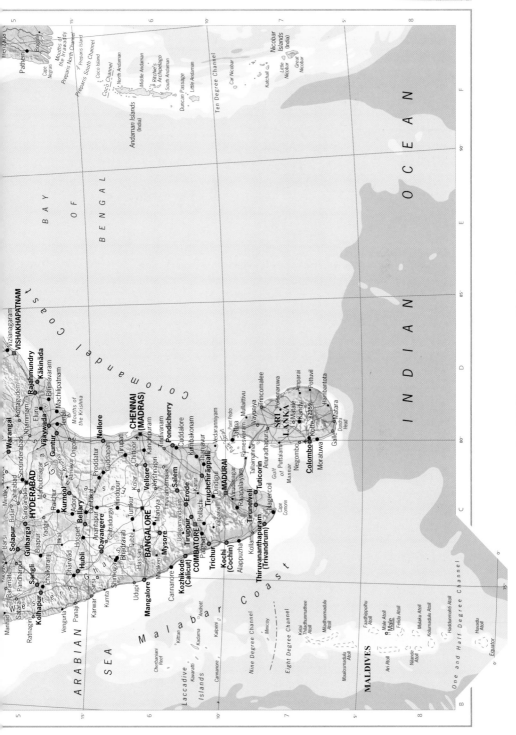

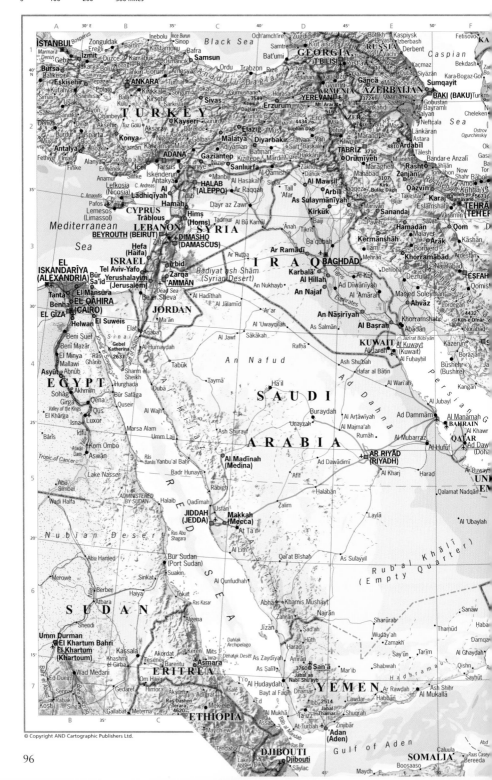

Scale 1 : 17 400 000

```
0        200       400        600 km
0    100     200      300 miles
```

Black Sea

İSTANBUL
Marmara
Denizi   Gebze   İzmit   Düzce   Karrabük   Bartin   İnebolu   İnce Burun   Sinop   Samsun   Och'amch'ire   Zugdidi   Kut'aisi   RUSSIA   Kaspiysk   Izberbash   Fetisovo   KA
Ereğli   Zonguldak   Bafra   Ordu   Trabzon   Rize   Artvin   Samtredia   Bat'umi   Rustayi   GEORGIA   Derbent   Caspian
Bursa   Bolu   Çankırı   Çorum   Amasya   Turhal   T'BILISI   Qubadli   Siyazan   Bekdash
Eskişehir   ANKARA   Kırıkkale   Yozgat   Gümüşhane   3549   Erzurum   Kars   ARMENIA   AZERBAIJAN   Sumqayit   Kara-Bogaz-Gol
Kütahya   Bala   Kırşehir   Sorgun   Tokat   Sivas   YEREVAN   VER   3724   BAKI (BAKU)   Turkm
TURKEY   Kayseri   Gürün   Darende   Elazığ   Muş   Mt. Ararat   Maku   Nakhichevan   Chelekeen
Konya   Aksaray   Niğde   Göksun   Malatya   Diyarbakır   Van   TABRĪZ   Ardabil   Bandar-e Anzali
Karaman   Kahramanmaraş   Adıyaman   Batman   Mardin   Hakkari   Orūmīyeh   Rasht   Amol   Caspian Sea
ADANA   Gaziantep   Kizıltepe   Sanlıurfa   Al Qāmishlī   Zākhō   Dahūk   Mahābād   Zanjan   TEHERÁN
İcel   Tarsus   Antakya   Al Hasakah   Sinjar   Al Mawşil   Arbīl   As Sulaymānīyah   Qazvin   Karaj
HALAB (ALEPPO)   Idlib   Ar Raqqah   Tall 'Afar   Kirkūk   Sanandaj   Qom
Lādhiqīyah   Hamāh   Dayr az Zawr   As Sulaymānīyah   Kermānshāh   Hamadān   Arāk   Kāshān
CYPRUS   Trâblous   Hims (Homs)   Tadmur   Al Bū Kamāl   Bāji   Sāveh   Borūjerd   Khorramābād   Ardestān
LEBANON   Tadmur   SYRIA   'Anah   Tikrīt   Ba'qūbah   Najafābād   ESFAH
BEYROUTH (BEIRUT)   Ar Rutba   I R A Q   BAGHDAD   Dehlorān   Dezfūl   Ahvāz
Hefa (Haïfa)   Ar Ramādī   Karbalā'   Ad Dīwānīyah   Masjed Soleymān
EL ISKANDARÎYA (ALEXANDRIA)   Tel Aviv-Yafo   Yerushalayim (Jerusalem)   'AMMĀN   Al Hillah   An Najaf   Al 'Amārah   Abādān
Tanta   El Mansûra   Bûr Sa'id   ISRAEL   Irbid   Zarqa   An Nukhayb   An Nāsirīyah   Khorramshahr
EL QAHIRA (CAIRO)   Benha   JORDAN   Badiyat ash Shām (Syrian Desert)   As Salmān   Al Başrah   KUWAIT   Al Kuwayt (Kuwait)   Al Fuhayhil   Būshehr (Bushire)
EL GIZA   Helwan   El Suweis   Ma'ān   Al Hadīthah   Al Jālimī   'Ar'ar   Rafhā   Ash Shu'bah   Al Jahrah   Kāzerūn
Beni Suef   Elat   'Aqaba   Al Jawf   Sākākah   Al 'Uwayqīlah   Hafar al Bātin   Al Jubayl   Borāzjān
Beni Mazār   Gebel Katherina 2637   Al Humaydah   Taymā'   An Nafūd   Hā'il   Al Wari'ah   Ad Dammām   Al Manāmah   BAHRAIN   QATAR   Ad Daw (Doha)
El Minya   Sinai   Tabūk   SAUDI   Buraydah   Al Artāwīyah   Al Mubarraz   Al Hufūf   Al Ruways
Mallawi   Sharm el Sheikh   Dubā   'Unayzah   Al Majma'ah   AR RIYĀD (RIYADH)   UNI
Asyūt   Hurghada   Bûr Safāga   Al Wajh   Ash Shurayt   Rumāh   Al Kharj   Harad   Qalamat Nadqān   EM
Sohāg   Akhmīm   Quseir   Umm Lajj   ARABIA   Ad Dawādimī   Afīf   Layla   Al 'Ubaylah
Girga   Qena   Marsa Alam   Rās Bānas   Yanbu'al Bahr   AL MADĪNAH (MEDINA)   Halabān   Zalim
El Khārga   Luxor   Idfu   Kom Ombo   Badr Hunayn   Rub' al Khālī (Empty Quarter)
Aswān Dam   Aswān   Lake Nasser   Rābigh   Qadīmah   Usfān   JIDDAH (JEDDA)   MAKKAH (MECCA)   At Tā'if   As Sulayyil
Abu Simbel   Halaib   Suakin   Al Līth   Qal'at Bīshah
Wadi Halfa   ADMINISTERED BY SUDAN   Ras Abu Shagara   Al Qunfudhah
Nubian Desert   Abu Hamed   Bûr Sudan (Port Sudan)   Abhā   Khamis Mushayt   Sanā
Merowe   Berber   Atbara   Sinkat   Tokar   Ras Kasar   Najrān   Sharūrah   Tharmūd   Haba
SUDAN   Shendi   Haiya   Algena   Jīzān   Sa'dah   Wuday'ah   Zamakh   Tarīm   Al Ghaydah   Damqa
Umm Durman   El Khartum Bahri   Kassala   Akordat   Keren   Harad   Hūth   Sayūn   Qishn
El Khartum (Khartoum)   Khashm el Girba   Tesseney   Barentu   Mar'ib   San'ā   Shabwah   Hadramawt   Sayhūt
Wad Madani   Gedaref   Om Hajer   Dahlak Archipelago   As Zaydīyah   'Amrān   YEMEN   Ar Rawdah   Ash Shihr
Ed Dueim   Aksum   Mekele   Asmara   ERITREA   Al Hudaydah   Nabi Shu'ayb   Dhamār   Lawdar   Habbān   Al Mukallā
Sennar   Rabak   Singa   Gallabat   Metema   Maych'ew   Zinjibār   Ta'izz   Shuqrah   At-Turbah
Kosti   ETHIOPIA   Al Mukhā   Assab   Ibb   Adan (Aden)   Gulf of Aden   SOMALIA
DJIBOUTI   Djibouti   Boosaaso   Bereeda
```

Mediterranean Sea

Tropic of Cancer

R E D   S E A

Persian G
```

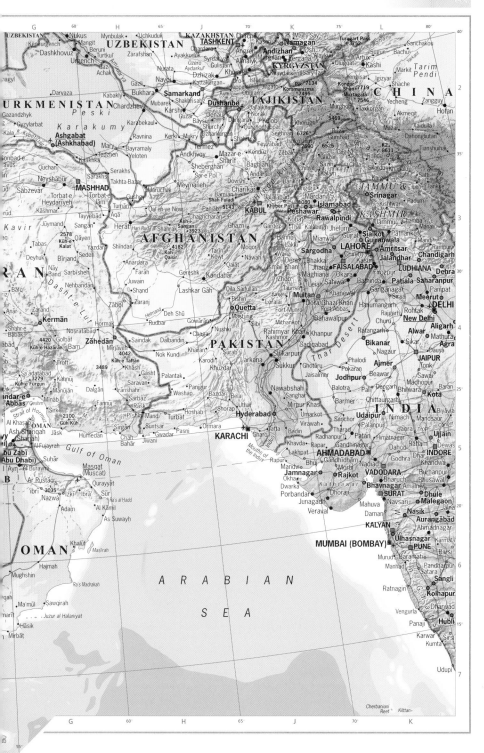

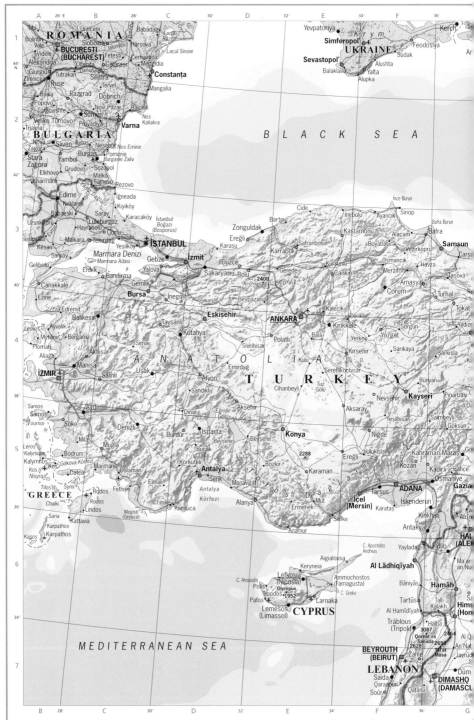

Scale 1 : 7 900 000

0   100   200   300 km

0   50   100   150 km

| A | 26° E | B | 28° | C | 30° | D | 32° | E | 34° | F | 36° |

ROMANIA

Titti
Bolinti
Vale
Videle
Alexandria
Giurgiu
Zirnnicea
Tutrakan
Ruse
Byala
Popovo
Turgovishte
Veliko Turnovo
Traiani
BULGARIA
Nova
Zagora
Sliven
Stara
Zagora
Yambol
Elkhovo
Kharmanli
Turnovo
Rezovo

Urziceni
Slobozia
Ialomita
Cernavoda
BUCUREŞTI
(BUCHAREST)
Oltenita
Fetesti
Calarasi
Medgidia
Danube
Silistra
Razgrad
Dobrich
Novi Pazar
Balchik
Sumen
Provadiya
Aytos
Nesebur
Burgas
Pomorie
Grudovo
Sozopol
Malko

Babadag
Lacul
Razim
Harsova
Lacul Sinoie
Constanţa
Mangalia
Nos
Kaliakra
Varna
Nos Emine
Burgaski Zaliv

Kirklareli
Babaeski
Uzunkopru
Luleburgaz
Hayrabolu
Ipsala
Malkara
Keşan
Sarkoy
Gelibolu
Erdek
Canakkale
Ezine
Edremit
Balikesir

Edirne
Saray
Karacakoy
Kiyikoy
Corlu
Silivri
Tekirdag
Yeşilköy
İSTANBUL
Marmara Denizi
Marmara Adasi
Bandirma
Gebze
Yalova
Gemlik
İznik
İznik Gölü
Bursa
İnegöl

İstanbul
Boğazi
(Bosporus)
İzmit
Düzce
Sakarya
Sakarya
Bolu

BLACK   SEA

Zonguldak
Ereğli
Karasu
Karrabük
Safranbolu
Bartin
Cide
Inebolu
Kastamonu
Boyabat

İnce Burun
Ayancik
Sinop
Alaçam
Bafra Burun
Bafra
Vezirkopru
Samsun
Carsa

Yevpatoriya
Simferopol'
UKRAINE
Sevastopol'
Balaklava
Krym
Alushta
Yalta
Alupka
Kerch
Feodosiya
Sudak
Ar

Lesvos
Mytilini
Ayvalik
Bergama
Aliaga
İZMİR
Manisa
Salihli
Usak

Samos
Samos
Fourni
Soke
Milas
Kalymnos
Kalymnos
Kos
Nisyros
Kos
Gokova Korfezi
Marmaris
Datca
GREECE
Chalki
Rodos
Rodos
Lindos
Kattavia
Saria
Karpathos
Kasos
Karpathos

ANATOLIA
Akhisar
Simav
Tavsanli
Kutahya
Emirdağ
Afyon
Sandikli
Dinar
Eğridir
Gölü
Denizli
Isparta
Burdur
Bucak
Korkuteli
Dalaman
Elmali
Fethiye
Finike
Kumluca

Eskişehir
ANKARA
Polatli
Sivrihisar
Cihanbeyli
Akşehir
Beyşehir
Gölü
Beyşehir
Konya
Bozkir
Karaman
Serik
Antalya
Manavgat
Antalya
Körfezi
Alanya
Ermenek
Anamur

Kalecik
Kirikkale
Bala
Yerkoy
Kirşehir
Şereflikochisar
Tuz
Gölü
Aksaray
TURKEY
Nevşehir
Niğde
Ereğli
Ulukisla
Mut
Silifke
Karatas

Cerikli
Sorgun
Yozgat
Sarikaya
Bunyan
Kayseri
Pinarbaşi
Yeşilhisar
Şambeyli
Göksun
Kahraman Maraş
Kozan
Kadirli
Osmaniye
ADANA
İçel
(Mersin)
Tarsus
İskenderun
Antakya
Kinkhan

Corum
Merzifon
Amasya
Turhal
Tokat
Yildize

MEDITERRANEAN SEA

Aigialousa
Keryneia
Ammochostos
(Famagusta)
Lefkosia
(Nicosia)
Polis
Troodos
Olympus
1952
Pafos
Larnaka
Lemesos
(Limassol)
CYPRUS

C. Apostolos
Andreas
C. Greko
Yayladaġi
Idlib
Al Lādhiqīyah
Bāniyās
Hamāh
Tartūs
Al Hamīdīyah
Tråblous
(Tripoli)
Qornet es
Saouda 3087
BEYROUTH
(BEIRUT)
Saida
Qaraqoun
Soûr
Qatara
Zahle
LEBANON

Gazia
DIMASHQ
(DAMASCU)

| B | 28° | C | 30° | D | 32° | E | 34° | F | 36° | G |

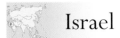

Israel

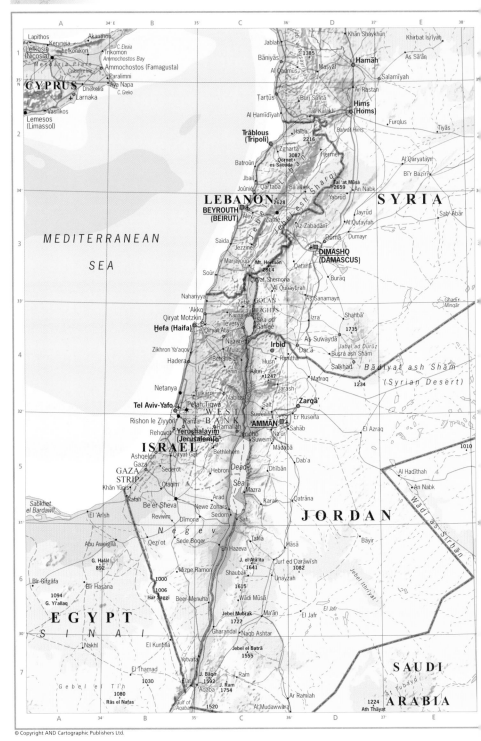

CYPRUS

Lapithos
Akanthou
Keryneia
Lefkosia
(Nicosia)
Lefkonikon
Trikomon
C. Eleaia
Ammochostos Bay
Paralimni
Meseoria Plain
Ceasefire line
Ayia Napa
Dhekelia
C. Greko
Larnaka
Vasilikos
Lemesos
(Limassol)

Jablah
Bāniyās
1385
Khān Shaykhūn
Khirbat Isrīyah
As Sa'ān
Al Qadmūs
Masyāf
Hamāh
Salamīyah
Tartūs
Burj Salītā
Ar Rastan
Al Hamīdīyah
Tall Kalakh
Hims
(Homs)
Furqlus
Trâblous
(Tripoli)
Halba
Bahrat Hims
Tiyās
2216
Zgharta
3087
Hermel
Al Qaryatayn
Batroûn
Qornet
es Saouda
Bi'r Baziri
Jbail
Qartaba
Ba'albek
Tal 'at Mûsa
2659
An Nabk
Joûnie
Yabrūd
LEBANON
2628
SYRIA
BEYROUTH
Aley
(BEIRUT)
Zahlé
Az Zabadāni
Jayrūd
Al Qutayfah
Sab' Ābâr
Saida
Jezzine
Dūmā
Dumayr
Marjayoûn
DIMASHQ
(DAMASCUS)
Soûr
Mt. Hermon
2814
Qatanā
Burāq
Qiryat Shemona
Al Qunaytirah
As Sanamayn
Ghadir
Nahariyya
Minqâr
Zefat
GOLAN
'Akko
HEIGHTS
Izra'
Shahbā'
Qiryat Motzkin
Karmi'el
Teverya
Sea of
Galilee
1735
Hefa (Haifa)
Qiryat Ata
Nazareth
As Suwaydā'
Jabal ad Durūz
Zikhron Ya'aqov
Afula
Dar'a
Busrá ash Sham
Irbid
Hadera
Bet She'an
Husn
Ramtha
Salkhad
Bādiyat ash Shām
Jenin
Ajlun
1247
(Syrian Desert)
Netanya
Jarash
Matraq
1234
Tulkarm
Nablus
Salt
Zarqā'
Tel Aviv-Yafo
Petah Tiqwa
Suweilih
El Ruseifa
Rishon le Ziyyon
WEST
Ramallah
'AMMĀN
El Azraq
Ramla
BANK
Jericho
Na'ur
Rehovot
Yerushalayim
Suweima
Sahāb
(Jerusalem)
ISRAEL
Bethlehem
Mādabā
Dab'a
1010
Ashqelon
Qiryat Gat
Gaza
Sederot
Hebron
Dead
Dhībān
GAZA
STRIP
Ofaqim
Sea
Al Hadīthah
Khān Yūnis
Mazra
An Nabk
Rafah
Arad
Karak
Qatrāna
Sabkhet
Be'er Sheva
Newe Zohar
el Bardawil
Revivim
Sedom
Safi
JORDAN
El 'Arish
Dīmona
Negev
En Hazeva
Abu Aweigila
Qezi'ot
Sede Boger
Tafila
Hāsā
Bāyir
G. Halāl
892
Mizpe Ramon
J. el Atā'ita
1641
Jurf ed Darāwīsh
1082
Bīr Gifgâfa
Bīr Hasana
1000
Shaubak
Unayzah
1006
1615
1094
Har Saggi
Wādī Mūsā
G. Yi'allaq
Beer Menuha
EGYPT
Jebel Mubrak
1727
Ma'ān
El Jafr
SINAI
Gharandal
Nagb Ashtar
Nakhl
El Kuntila
Jebel el Baträ
1555
Yotvata
SAUDI
El Thamad
1030
J. Bāgir
1592
J. Ram
1754
Ram
ARABIA
Gebel el Tih
1080
Elat
Aqaba
Ar Ramlah
1224
Ath Thâyat
Rās el Nafas
Gulf of
(Aqaba)
1520
Al Mudawwara

MEDITERRANEAN

SEA

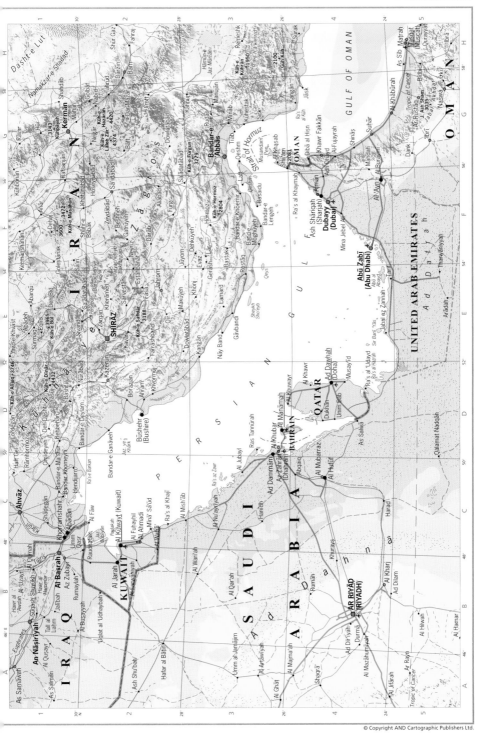

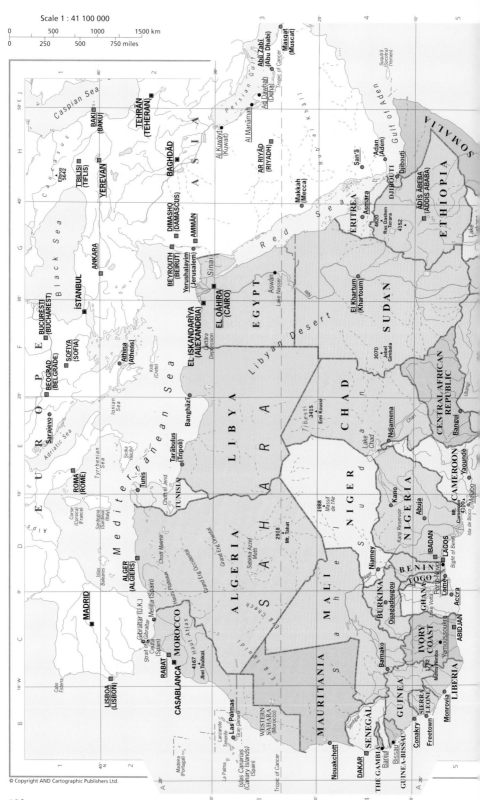

Scale 1 : 41 100 000

0   500   1000   1500 km
0   250   500   750 miles

© Copyright AND Cartographic Publishers Ltd.

102

Scale 1 : 15 900 000

```
0        200      400       600 km
0    100      200      300 miles
```

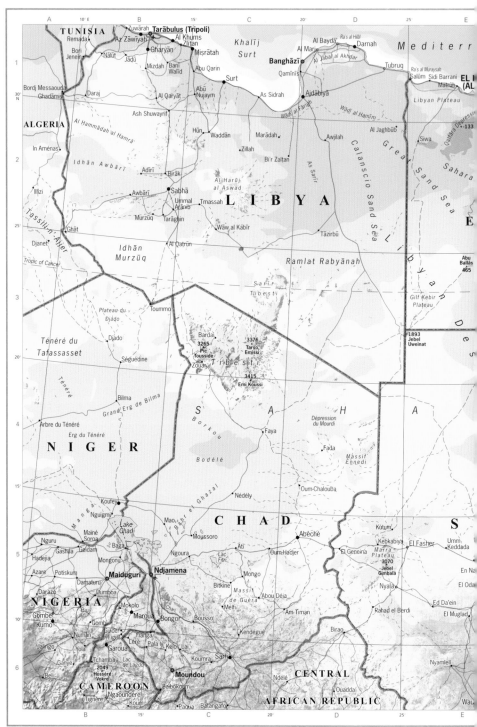

© Copyright AND Cartographic Publishers Ltd.

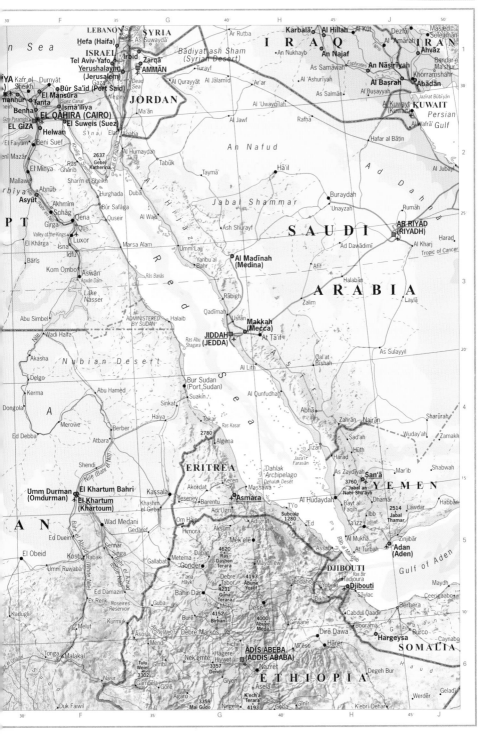

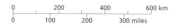

Scale 1 : 15 900 000

© Copyright AND Cartographic Publishers Ltd.

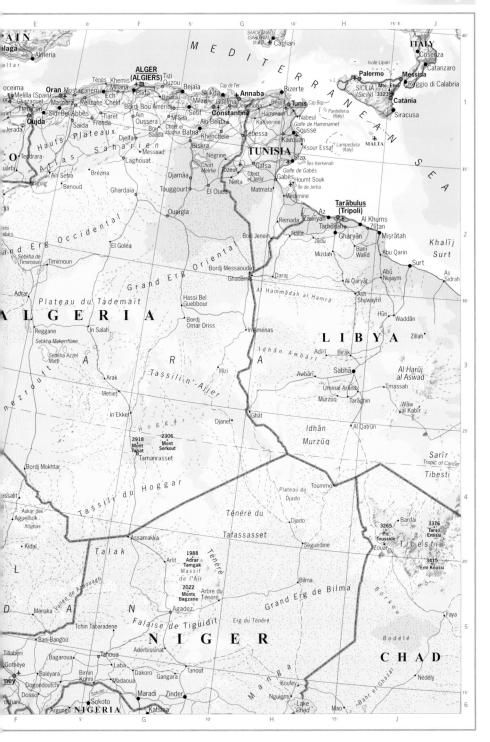

Scale 1 : 15 900 000

| 0 | 200 | 400 | 600 km |

| 0 | 100 | 200 | 300 miles |

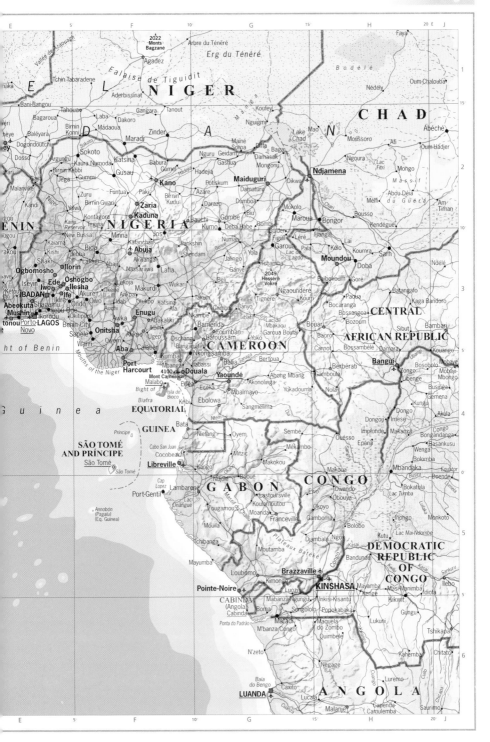

Africa: Central

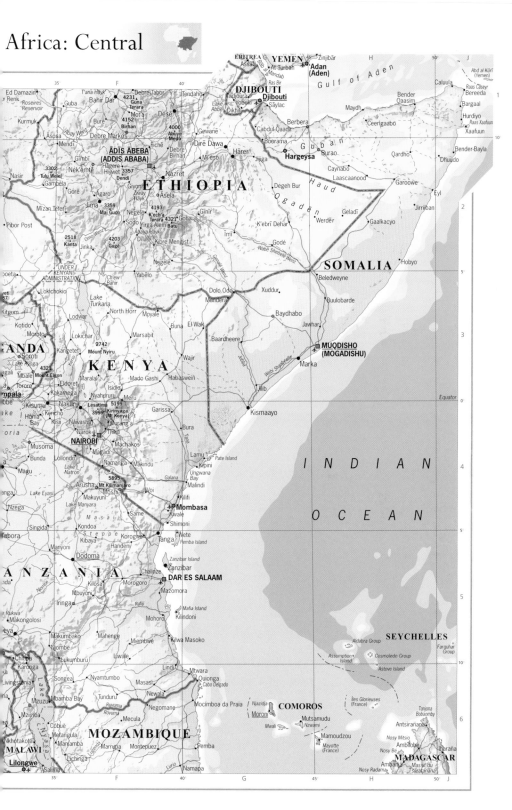

Scale 1 : 15 900 000

0	200	400	600 km
0	100	200	300 miles

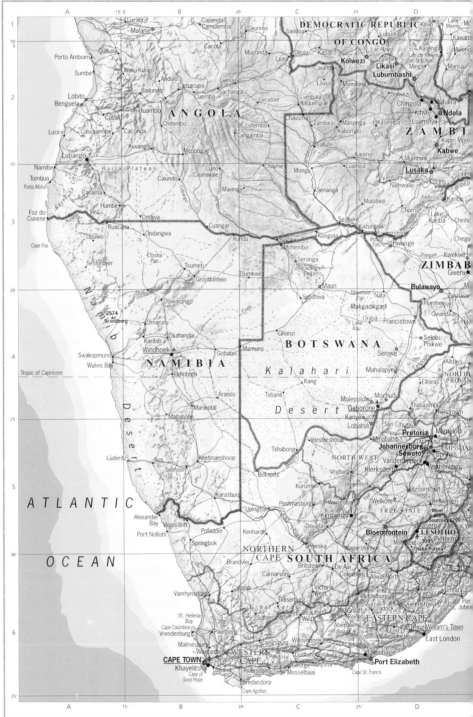

DEMOCRATIC REPUBLIC
OF CONGO

Lucala
Malanje
Quibala
Porto Amboim
Sumbe
Waku-Kungo
Andulo
Camacupa
Bailundo
Lobito
Benguela
Huambo
Kuito
Cuemba
Sachanga
Cubali
Chitembo
Caluquembe
Caconda
Kuvango
Luciria
Menongue
Lubango
Huila Plateau
Namibe
Tombua
Punta Albina
Cahama
Humbe
Foz do
Cunene
Ondjiva
Cuangar
Opuwo
Ruacana
Ondangwa
Rundu
Cape Fria
Etosha
Pan
Sesfontein
Tsumeb
Tsumkwe
Grootfontein
Outjo
Otjiwarongo
2574
Brandberg
Omaruru
Okahandja
Karibib
Windhoek
Gobabis
Swakopmund
Walvis Bay
NAMIBIA
Tropic of Capricorn
Rehoboth
Aranos
Mariental
Maltahöhe
Lüderitz
Aus
Keetmanshoop
Seeheim
Bokspits
Karasburg
ATLANTIC
Alexander
Bay
Vioolsdrift
Port Nolloth
Pofadder
Kenhardt
Springbok
OCEAN
NORTHERN
CAPE
Brandvlei
Carnarvon
Vanrhynsdorp
Calvinia
Fraserburg
St. Helena
Bay
Cape Columbine
Vredenburg
Piketberg
Malmesbury
Worcester
CAPE TOWN
Khayelitsha
Cape of
Good Hope
Strand
WESTERN
CAPE
Riversdale
Mosselbaai
Bredasdorp
Cape Agulhas

Capenda-
Camulemba
Saurimo
Sandoa
Kilwe
Lake
Mweru
Lubudi
Lubudi
Cacola
Muconda
Dilolo
Kasaji
Lac Nzilo
Kasenga
Mwenc
Luau
Caianda
Kolwezi
Tenke
Lufira
Minga
Mansa
Lóvua
Mwinilunga
Likasi
Lubumbashi
Solwezi
Lumbala
Kaquengue
Chingola
Kitwe
Ndola
Manyinga
Kasempa
Luanshya
Luang
Chavuma
Zambezi
Kabompo
Kapiri Mpos
ZAMBI
Lutembo
Cangamba
Lukulu
Kaoma
Kabwe
Chiume
Mongu
Luampa
Lusaka
Cuito
Cuanavale
Mavinga
Senanga
Namwala
Mulobezi
Choma
Lake
Kariba
Chinho
Seronga
Shesheke
Kazungula
Livingstone
Victoria
Falls
Hwange
Shangani
Chegu
Kwekwe
Bagani
Mohembo
Kongola
Seronga
Okavango
Delta
Maun
ZIMBAB
Gweru
Ntwetwe
Pan
Nata
Bulawayo
Plumtree
Zwishavar
Sehithwa
Makgadikgadi
Orapa
Francistown
Gwanda
Ghanzi
Lake
Xau
Selebi-
Phikwe
Alldays
Mamuno
BOTSWANA
Serowe
Kalahari
Mahalapye
NORTH
PROVIN
Kang
Molepolole
Mochudi
Ellisras
Tshane
Gaborone
Thabazimbi
Nylstrom
Vorstershoop
Kanye
Lobatse
Sun City
Mmabatho
Pretoria
Mamelodi
Tshabong
NORTH WEST
Johannesburg
Soweto
Springs
Vryburg
Vanderbijlpark
Vereeniging
Kuruman
Klerksdorp
Bloemhof
Welkom
Kroonstad
Bethlehem
Postmasburg
Warrenton
FREE STATE
Upington
Kimberley
Mont-
aux-
Sources 3299
Maseru
Douglas
Bloemfontein
LESOTHO
3095 Pietermaritz
Jagersfonten
Matatiele
Thaba Putsoa
Prieska
SOUTH AFRICA
De Aar
Coleisberg
Aliwal North
Kok
Britstown
Victoria
West
Middelburg
Elliot
Umtata
Beaufort
West
Graaff-
Reinet
Cradock
Queenstown
Por
St. Johns
Aberdeen
EASTERN CAPE
Fort
Beaufort
King William's Town
East London
Laingsburg
Willowmore
Oudtshoorn
Uitenhage
Touws
River
Little Karoo
Knysna
George
Port Elizabeth
Cape St. Francis

ANGOLA

Namib

Desert

Desert

NORTHERN
CAPE

Great Karoo

E   35°   F   40°   G   45°   H   50°   J

Aldabra Group   **SEYCHELLES**   Farquhar Group

Nakonde   Nombe   1
Lukumburu   Liwale   Assumption Island   Cosmoledo Group
Chitsa   Isoka   Karonga   Livingstonia   Nyamtumbo   Lindi   10°
sama   Isoka   Mtwara   Astove Island
Chama   Songea   Masasi   Quionga
Mzuzu   Mbamba Bay   Tunduru   Newala   Cabo Delgado
pika   Mzimba   Masuguru   Rovuma   Negomane   Mocímboa da Praia   Moroni   **COMOROS**
imba   Lundazi   Cobué   Mecula   Mutsamudu   Njazidja   Tanjona   2
Mfuwe   Metangula   Mutsamudu   Nzwarni   Bobaomby   Antsiranana
Nkhotakota   Maniamba   Lugenda   Marrupa   Mamoudzou   Nosy   Ambilobe   Iharaña
Chipata   **MALAWI**   Lichinga   Montepuez   Pemba   Mayotte   Mitsio   Ambanja
le   Salima   Mandimba   Namapa   (France)   Nosy Be   Massifu   Sambava
auke   **Lilongwe**   Dedza   Nosy Radama   Bealanana   2876   Andapa
Ulongue   Cuamba   Nacala   Analalava   Tsaratanana   Maroantsetra
Bene   Lake Chilwa   Moçambique   Mahajanga   Antalaha
Songo   Lago de   **Zomba**   2419   Nampula   Tanjona Vilanandro   Soalala   Mananara   Tanjona   15°
Cahora Bassa   **Blantyre**   3002   Alto Molócuè   Besalampy   Avaratra   Masoala
Tete   Monte Namuli   Lugela   Ambato Boeny   Soanierana-Ivongo
Changara   Chromo   Mount   Angoche   Maevatanana   Nosy   3
ARE   Mulanje   Mocuba   Moma   Morafenobe   Boraha
ungwiza   **MOZAMBIQUE**   Pebane   Juan de   Maintirano   Farihy Alaotra
Catandica   Caia   Nova   Beravina   Ambatondrazaka
Quelimane   (France)   Nosy Barren   **MADAGASCAR**   Taomasina
Mutare   Chinde   Antsalova   Tsiroanomandidy   **ANTANANARIVO**
Chimoio   Miandrivazo   2643   Moramanga   20°
Castel   Belo Tsiribihina   Tsiafajavona   Vatomandry
Espungabera   Save   Morondava   Antsirabe   Mahanoro
angle   Nova Mambone   Bassas da   Mandabe   Malaimbandy   Fandriana   Marolambo
India   Manja   Ambositra   Nosy-Varika
Mapinhane   (France)   Morombe   Mangoky   Ifanadiana
Chicualacuala   Ilha do Bazaruto   Tanjona   **Fianarantsoa**
Chigubo   Ankaboa   Ankazoabo   Ihosy   Manakara
Massinga   Sakaraha   Vohipeno
Mabalane   Inhambane   Farafangana
porwa   Toliara   Betroka   Vangaindrano   Tropic of Capricorn
Chókwè   Chibuto   Ponta Zavora   Betioky   Onilahy
Macia   Xai-Xai   Bekily   Manantenina
it   **MAPUTO**   Ampanihy   Tôlañaro   25°
ane   Ponta Khehuene   Ambovombe
nzini   Bela Vista   Tanjona
LAND   Vohimena
tte

Mkuze   **I N D I A N**
Lake St. Lucia
Empangeni   **O C E A N**

H   55°   C
Praslin I.   1
Silhouette I.   Victoria
Mahé Island   B   5°

Amirante Is.

Coëtivy I.

I N D I A N   2   INDIAN OCEAN

O C E A N   30°

6   ① A   55° E   B   ② A   50° E   **SEYCHELLES**
20° S   Port Louis
St-Denis   **MAURITIUS**   Aldabra Group   St. Pierre I.   Providence I.
Réunion   **INDIAN**   Assumption Island   Cosmoledo Group
(France)   **OCEAN**   Astove Island   Farquhar Group   Agalega Islands
(Mauritius)

E

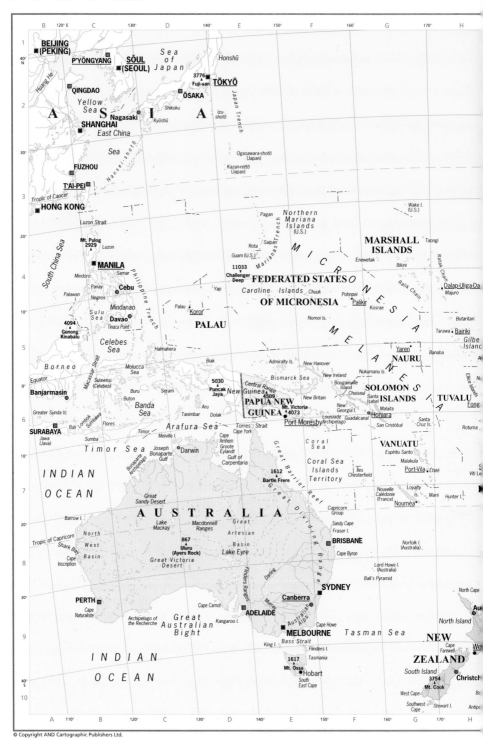

Scale 1 : 55 500 000

0   500   1000   1500   2000 km
0   250   500   750   1000 miles

B   120° E   130°   D   140°   E   150°   F   160°   G   170°   H

1   **BEIJING**
    (PEKING)
                                    S e a   Honshū
40° **P'YŎNGYANG** **SŎUL**   o f
N   **(SEOUL)**   J a p a n   3776▲
                                                 Fuji-san **TŌKYŌ**
    ■**QINGDAO**   **ŌSAKA**
     Yellow   Shikoku
2   A   S   ■■Nagasaki   Izu-
         Sea   shotō
     SHANGHAI   Kyūshū
    ■ East China   A
    ■   Sea   Ogasawara-shotō
30°   (Japan)
    ■**FUZHOU**
                                   Kazan-rettō
                                   (Japan)
    ■**T'AI-PEI**
3   Tropic of Cancer   Wake I.
    ■**HONG KONG**   (U.S.)
                                   Pagan Northern
    Luzon Strait   Mariana
                                         Islands
20°   Mt. Pulog   (U.S.)   **MARSHALL** Taongi
            2929▲ Luzon   Rota Saipan   **ISLANDS**
    ■**MANILA**   Guam (U.S.)   Enewetak   Bikini
    Mindoro Samar   11033   Dalap-Uliga-Da
4   ▲Cebu   **Challenger** Yap **FEDERATED STATES**   Majuro
10° Panay   **Deep**   Caroline Islands Chuuk   Pohnpei
    Palawan Negros   •Palikir
                Mindanao   Palau •Koror   **OF MICRONESIA** Kosrae
    4094   Davao   Nomoi Is.   Butaritari
    ▲Gunong ▲   **PALAU**   Tarawa• Bairiki
    Kinabalu   Gilbe
5   Celebes   Halmahera   Island
     Sea   Yaren• Banaba
    Borneo   Molucca   Biak   Admiralty Is. New Hanover **NAURU**
             Sea   Nukumanu Is.
    Equator Sulawesi   Bismarck Sea New Ireland
    Banjarmasin (Celebes) 5030 New Guinea Bougainville **SOLOMON** S
              Buru Seram   **Puncak** 4509   Island Choiseul **ISLANDS** **TUVALU**
    Banda   Buton   **Jaya**▲ **PAPUA NEW** New Britain New Santa Fong
6   Greater Sunda Is. Aru   Dolak **GUINEA** Mt. Victoria Georgia I. Isabel Honiara
                 Tanimbar   ▲4073 Louisiade Guadalcanal
    SURABAYA Bali Lombok Sumbawa Port Moresby• Archipelago San Cristóbal Santa Rotuma
    Jawa   Flores Torres Strait   Cruz Is.
    (Java)   Sumba   Timor• Cape York
    T i m o r S e a   Cape   C o r a l   **VANUATU**
             Melville I.   Arnhem S e a   Espiritu Santo
10°   Joseph •Darwin Groote   C o r a l S e a Malakula
    I N D I A N Bonaparte   Eylandt Gulf of I s l a n d s Îles **Port-Vila**• Éfaté Viti Le
              Gulf   Carpentaria T e r r i t o r y Chesterfield
    O C E A N Bonaparte
             Archipelago   1612   Nouvelle Loyalty
                             ▲Bartle Frere Calédonie Is.
    Barrow I. Great   (France) Maré Hunter I.
7   Sandy Desert   Capricorn Nouméa•
                                    Group
20° Tropic of Capricorn Lake   G r e a t Sandy Cape Norfolk I.
    Shark Bay North Mackay Macdonnell A r t e s i a n Fraser I. (Australia)
              West   Ranges   **BRISBANE**■
    Cape Basin 867 **A U S T R A L I A** B a s i n Cape Byron
    Inscription   Uluru   Lake Eyre   Lord Howe I.
8   (Ayers Rock)   (Australia)
              Great Victoria   Ball's Pyramid
                 Desert   North Cape
                        Darling **SYDNEY**■
30°   Murray Canberra   North Island Au
    PERTH■   Cape Carnot •**ADELAIDE** Cape Howe
    Cape   Kangaroo I.   Australian   North
    Naturaliste Archipelago of G r e a t Alps **MELBOURNE** T a s m a n S e a
    the Recherche A u s t r a l i a n ■   **NEW**
9   B i g h t King I. Bass Strait Flinders I. ZEALAND Cape
                      Tasmania   Farewell We
    I N D I A N   1617   South Island
                         ▲Mt. Ossa   3754
40° O C E A N   •Hobart   West Cape Mt. Cook Christch
S   South   Southwest Stewart I.
10   East Cape   Cape   Bo
                                                                 Antipc

A   110°   B   120°   C   130°   D   140°   E   150°   F   160°   G   170°   H

© Copyright AND Cartographic Publishers Ltd.

114

J   170°   K   160°   L   150°   M   140°   N   130°   P   120° W   Q

1
40°

**NORTH
AMERICA**

LOS ANGELES ■   2

SAN DIEGO ■

30°

H
a
w
a
ii
an
Is
la
n
d
s

Laysan I.

Necker I.

HAWAII
(U.S.)

P   A   C   I   F   I   C

Guadalupe
(Mexico)

Kauai
Oahu
Honolulu ●   Maui

3

Tropic of Cancer

Hawaii

Johnston I.
(U.S.)

N.
W.
Christmas
Island
Ridge

20°

Is. Revillagigedo
(Mexico)

4

O   C   E   A   N

Palmyra I.
(U.S.)

Tabuaerani

Line

Kiritimati

10°

Howland (U.S.)
Baker (U.S.)

Jarvis
(U.S.)

5

oenix Islands

Birnie   Rawaki
rona   Manra

KIRIBATI

Islands

Malden I.

Equator
0°

Starbuck I.

O   L   Y   N   E   S   I   A

Atafu
Nukunonu   Tokelau
(New Zealand)

Tongareva

Marquesas Islands

6

Swains I.   Danger Is.
Nassau   Manihiki

Vostok I.   Caroline I.

Nuku Hiva

Hiva Oa

SAMOA   American
Savaii   Apia   Samoa
ce)]   Upolu   Tutuila
Tafahi

Flint I.

Iles
Désappointement

10°

Suvorov I.

Rose I.

Cook Islands

Motu One

Iles Palliser

Pukapuka

Archipel des Tuamotu

Raroia

TONGA

Niue   Palmerston I.
(New Zealand)

Aitutaki

Arch.
de la Société   Tahiti

Hao
Iles Duc de
Gloucester

Tonga
Trench

ofa
Ata

Rarotonga

**F r e n c h
P o l y n e s i a**

7

Groupe Actéon

**Horizon Depth
10882**

Mangaia   Iles
Maria

Rurutu

Tubuai   Mururoa

Morane   Gambier
Is.

Tubuai   Islands

Mangareva

20°

Oeno

Tropic of Capricorn

dec.
Is.
land)

Rapa
Marotiri

Henderson I. Ducie I.
Pitcairn Is.
(U.K.)

8

Easter I.
(Chile)

S   o   u   t   h   W   e   s   t

30°

P   a   c   i   f   i   c

B   a   s   i   n

9

n Is.
aland)

40°
10

J   170°   K   160°   L   150°   M   140°   N   130°   P   120°   Q   110°   R

Scale 1 : 18 900 000

0 200 400 600 km
0 100 200 300 miles

INDONESIA

Sumba
Bondokodi
Ngalu Savu Rote
Waingapu *Sawu Sea*
Timor
Kupang

Arafu

Melville Island
Croker Island
Cobou
Cape

Bathurst Island
Van Diemen Gulf
Clarence Strait
Beagle Gulf
Cape Scott
Darwin

Cape Londonderry

Timor Sea

Adelaide River

366
Mou
Evely

INDIAN OCEAN

Sandy I.
Seringapatam Reef
Scott Reef
Bonaparte Port
Warrender
Bonaparte Gulf
Archipelago

Pine Creek
Wingate Mountains
Mataranka
Kather

Wyndham

Drysdale River
Timber Creek
Daly Wate

Collier Bay
Lake Argyle Tourist Village

Sunday Strait
Cape Lévêque
Lombadina
King Sound
Kimberley
Mount Ord 936
Plateau
Halls Creek

Lake Argyle

Newcastle Wate

Kalkaring
Inverway

Lai
Woo

Derby

Rowley Shoals

Broome

Fitzroy Crossing

Tanami De

NO
TER

Sandfire Flat Roadhouse

Tanami

Port Hedland

Great Sandy Desert

Gregory Lake
The Granites

Percival Lakes

Lake Wills
Lake White

AUST R

Monte Bello Is.
Barrow I.

Roebourne

Lake Dora

Lake Mackay

Yuendumu

Mount Ziel 1510

North West Cape
Exmouth

Hamersley Range
Mount Bruce 1235
Wittenoom
Tom Price
1251
Mount Meharry
Newman

Lake Disappointment

Gibson Desert

Lake Macdonald

Mount Liebig 1524

Macdonnell Ran

NO
TER

Minilya Roadhouse
1106 Mount Augustus
Landor

910 Mount Essendon

Lake Hopkins
Lake Neale
Lake Amadeus
Uluru (Ayers Rock) 867

Kulge

North West Basin

Lake Macleod

Carnarvon

Lake Carnegie

WESTERN AUSTRALIA

Mount Aloysius 1085

Musgrave Ranges
1440 Mount Woodroffe

Tropic of Capricorn

Shark Bay
Cape Inscription
Dirk Hartog I.
Useless Loop
Denham
Overlander Roadhouse

Nannine

Wiluna

Yeo Lake

Neale Junction

Great Victoria Deser

SO
AUS

Lake Austin

Leinster

Rason Lake

Lake Maurice

Mount Magnet

Lake Carey

Geraldton

Mullewa

Lake Barlee
Leonora

Payne's Find

Menzies

Nullarbor Plain

Deakin

Wubin

Lake Moore
Coolgardie
Kalgoorlie
Rawlinna

Eucla

Head of Bight

Coo

Badgingarra

Pithara
Bindi Bindi
Southern Cross
Lake Lefroy

Norseman

Twilight Cove

Goomalling
Northam
Merredin
Cunderdin

PERTH
Fremantle
Mandurah
Williams
Lake Grace
Lake Dundas

Point Culver

Great Australian Bigh

Bunbury
Geographe Bay
Cape Naturaliste
Cape Leeuwin
Augusta

Manjimup
Cranbrook
Boxwood Hill
Cheyne Bay

Ravensthorpe
Esperance
Israelite Bay

Cape Arid

Im

Waipole
Point d'Entrecasteaux
Albany
Denmark

Esperance Bay
Archipelago of the Recherche

INDIAN OC

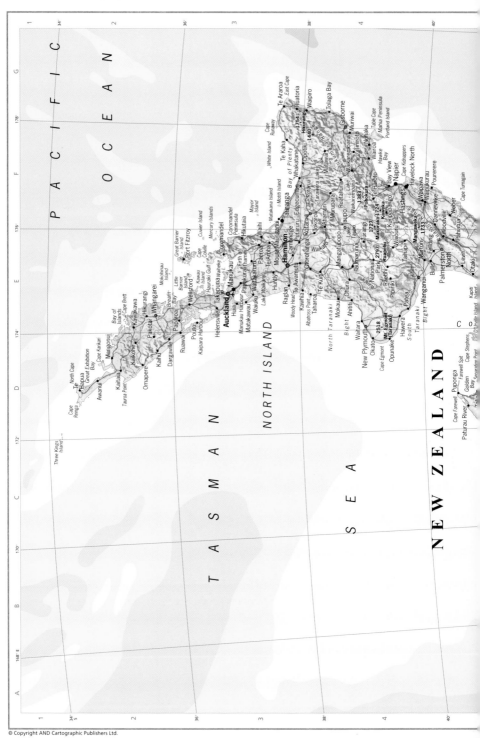

PACIFIC

OCEAN

TASMAN

SEA

NORTH ISLAND

NEW ZEALAND

Three Kings
Island

Cape Reinga
North Cape
Te Hapua
Cape Karikari
Great Exhibition Bay
Awanui
Kaitaia
Tauroa Point
Mangonui
Cape Brett
Bay of Islands
Kaikohe
Kawakawa
Hikurangi
Whangarei
Kaihu
Omapere
Dargaville
Kaipara Harbour
Ruawai
Poutu
Pakotai
Broadwood Bay
Paparoa
Wellsford
Helensville
Huia
Manukau Harbour
Waiuku
Raglan
Kawhia
Tauranga
Woody Head
Albatross Point
Mokau
Waitara
New Plymouth
Okato
Opunake
Cape Egmont
Mt Egmont (Taranaki) 2518
Hawera
Patea
Waverley
Wanganui
Bulls
Marton
Feilding
Palmerston North
Levin
Otaki
Kapiti Island
D'Urville Island
Cape Farewell
Farewell Spit
Golden Bay
Paturau River
Cape Stephens

Little Barrier Island
Great Barrier Island
Port Fitzroy
Kawau Island
Waiheke Island
Mokohinau Island
Cuvier Island
Mercury Islands
Coromandel Peninsula
Coromandel
Mayor Island
Matakana Island
White Island
Waihi
Paeroa
Te Aroha
Thames
Firth of Thames
Hauraki Gulf
Takapuna
Manukau
Auckland
Papakura
Waikato
Huntly
Te Kauwhata
Hamilton
Cambridge
Putaruru
Tokoroa
Mangakino
Taumarunui
Ohakune
Raetihi
Ohura
Te Kuiti
Otorohanga
Te Awamutu
Taupo
Lake Taupo
Turangi
National Park
Ruapehu 2797
Taihape
Tahaenui

Te Araroa
East Cape
Ruatoria
Waipiro
Tolaga Bay
Gisborne
Table Cape
Mahia Peninsula
Portland Island
Wairoa
Hawke Bay
Napier
Hastings
Havelock North
Cape Kidnappers
Waipawa
Waipukurau
Porangahau
Weber
Pahiatua
Woodville
Dannevirke
Cape Turnagain
Cape Runaway
Te Kaha
Bay of Plenty
Whakatane
Opotiki
Te Teko
Kawerau
Rotorua
Lake Rotorua
Lake Rotoiti
Lake Tarawera
Murupara
Rangitaiki
Taupo
Whakatane
1754
Huiarau
1440
Te Puia
Mount Maunganui
Hicks Bay
Tauranga
Katikati
1383
1724
Kaweka
1727
Makorako 1733
Pohokura

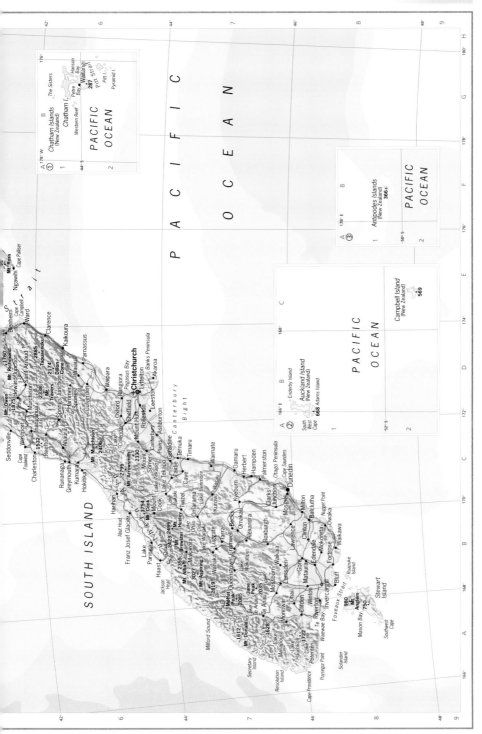

Polar Regions

Glossary

This is a glossary of the geographical terms used in this atlas. The first column shows the local spelling, the second the language of origin, and the third the English translation.

...ıde	Portuguese	reservoir
...ası	Turkish	island
...ra	Greek	peninsula
...en	German	mountains
...es	French	mountains
...i	Italian	mountains
...en	Swedish	river
...hipiélago	Spanish	archipelago
...quipélago	Portuguese	archipelago

...o	Arabic	strait
...hía	Spanish	bay
...hir, bahr	Arabic	bay, lake, river
...a	Portuguese	bay
...e	French	bay
...a	Spanish	lower
...ndar	Arabic, Somalian, Malay, Persian	harbour, port
...raji	Turkish	dam
...rragem	Portuguese	reservoir
...n	Gaelic	mountain
...rg(e)	German	mountain(s)
...ğazı	Turkish	strait
...cht	German	bay
...hayrat	Arabic	lake
...rnu, burun	Turkish	cape

...bo	Spanish	cape
...nal	French, Spanish	canal, channel
...nale	Italian	canal, channel
...rro	Spanish	mountain
...ott	Arabic	marsh, salt lake
...	Tibetan	lake
...llines	French	hills
...rdillera	Spanish	range

...ğ(ı)	Turkish	mountain
...ğlar(ı)	Turkish	mountains
...nau	Indonesian	lake
...ryacheh	Persian	lake
...sht	Persian	desert
...ebel	Arabic	mountain(s)
...o	Korean	island

...balse	Spanish	reservoir
...]	Arabic	sandy desert
...recho	Spanish	strait

...ıg	Chinese	mountain
...ördur	Icelandic	fjord
...ói	Icelandic	bay

...birge	German	range
...lfe	French	bay, gulf

golfo	Italian, Portuguese, Spanish	bay, gulf
göl, gölü	Turkish	lake
gora	Russian	mountain
gory	Russian	mountains
gunong	Malay	mountain
gunung	Indonesian	mountain

H

hai	Chinese	lake, sea
hāmūn	Persian	lake, marsh
hawr	Arabic	lake
hu	Chinese	lake, reservoir

I

île(s)	French	island(s)
ilha(s)	Portuguese	island(s)
isla(s)	Spanish	island(s)

J

jabal	Arabic	mountain(s)
-järvi	Finnish	lake
jaza'ir	Arabic	islands
jazīrat	Arabic	island
jbel	Arabic	mountain
jebel	Arabic	mountain
jezero	Serbo-Croatian	lake
jezioro	Polish	lake
jiang	Chinese	river
-jima	Japanese	island
-joki	Finnish	river
-jökull	Icelandic	glacier

K

kepulauan	Indonesian	islands
khrebet	Russian	mountain range
-ko	Japanese	lake
kolpos	Greek	bay, gulf
körfezi	Turkish	bay, gulf
kryazh	Russian	ridge
küh(ha)	Persian	mountain(s)

L

lac	French	lake
lacul	Romanian	lake
lago	Italian, Portuguese, Spanish	lake
lagoa	Portuguese	lagoon
laguna	Spanish	lagoon, lake
limni	Greek	lake
ling	Chinese	mountain(s), peak
liqeni	Albanian	lake
loch, lough	Gaelic	lake

M

massif	French	mountains
-meer	Dutch	lake, sea
mont	French	mount
monte	Italian, Portuguese, Spanish	mount
montes	Portuguese, Spanish	mountains
monts	French	mountains
muntii	Romanian	mountains
mys	Russian	cape

N

nafud	Arabic	desert
nevado	Spanish	snow-capped mountain
nuruu	Mongolian	mountains
nuur	Mongolian	lake

O

ostrov(a)	Russian	island(s)
ozero	Russian	lake

P

pegunungan	Indonesian	mountains
pelagos	Greek	sea
pendi	Chinese	basin
pesky	Russian	sandy desert
pic	French	peak
pico	Portuguese, Spanish	peak
planalto	Portuguese	plateau
planina	Bulgarian	mountains
poluostrov	Russian	peninsula
puerto	Spanish	harbour, port
puncak	Indonesian	peak
punta	Italian, Spanish	point
puy	French	peak

Q

qundao	Chinese	archipelago

R

ras, rås, ra's	Arabic	cape
represa	Portuguese	dam, reservoir
-rettō	Japanese	archipelago
rio	Portuguese	river
río	Spanish	river

S

sahra	Arabic	desert
salar	Spanish	salt flat
-san	Japanese, Korean	mountain
-sanmaek	Korean	mountains
sebkha	Arabic	salt flat
sebkhet	Arabic	salt marsh
See	German	lake
serra	Portuguese	range
severnaya, severo-	Russian	northern
shan	Chinese	mountain(s)
-shima	Japanese	island
-shotō	Japanese	islands
sierra	Spanish	range

T

tanjona	Malagasy	cape
tanjung	Indonesian	cape
teluk	Indonesian	bay, gulf
ténéré	Berber	desert
-tō	Japanese	island

V

vârful	Romanian	mountain
-vesi	Finnish	lake
vodokhranilishche	Russian	reservoir
volcán	Spanish	volcano

W

wādī	Arabic	watercourse
Wald	German	forest

Z

-zaki	Japanese	cape
zaliv	Russian	bay, gulf

Index

How to use the index

This is an alphabetically arranged index of the places and features that can be found on the maps in this atlas. Each name is generally indexed to the largest scale map on which it appears. If that map covers a double page, the name will always be indexed by the left-hand page number.

Names composed of two or more words are alphabetized as if they were one word.

All names appear in full in the index, except for 'St.' and 'Ste.', which although abbreviated, are indexed as though spelled in full.

Where two or more places have the same name, they can be distinguished from each other by the country or province name which immediately follows the entry. These names are indexed in the alphabetical order of the country or province.

Alternative names, such as English translations, can also be found in the index and are cross-referenced to the map form by the '=' sign. In these cases the names also appear in brackets on the maps.

Settlements are indexed to the position of the symbol, all other features are indexed to the position of the name on the map.

Abbreviations used in this index are explained in the list opposite.

Finding a name on the map

Each index entry contains the name, followed by a page reference and a grid reference. All entries except settlements also contain a symbol indicating the feature type (for example, ocean, river):

Name	Owosso 40 D2
Symbol	Owyhee 38 C2
	Owyhee .... ☑ 38 C2
	Oxford, New Zealand 118 D6
Page reference	Oxford, United Kingdom **62** A3
	Oxnard 44 C2
Grid reference	Oyama 88 K5

The grid reference locates a place or feature within a rectangle formed by the network of lines of longitude and latitude. A name can be found by referring to the red letters and numbers placed around the maps. First find the letter, which appears along the top and bottom of the map, and then the number, down the sides. The name will be found within the rectangle uniquely defined by that letter and number. A number in brackets preceding the grid reference indicates that the name is to be found within an inset map.

Abbreviations

Ak.	Alaska	N.D.	North Dako
Al.	Alabama	Nebr.	Nebras
Ariz.	Arizona	Nev.	Neva
Ark.	Arkansas	Nfld.	Newfoundla
B.C.	British Columbia	N.H.	New Hampshi
Calif.	California	N. Ire.	Northern Irela
Colo.	Colorado	N.J.	New Jers
Conn.	Connecticut	N. Mex.	New Mexi
Del.	Delaware	N.W.T.	Northwest Territor
Dem. Rep. of Congo		N.Y.	New Yo
. Democratic Republic of Congo		Oh.	Ot
Eng.	England	Okla.	Oklahor
Fla.	Florida	Ont.	Onta
Ga.	Georgia	Oreg.	Oreg
Ia.	Iowa	Orkney Is.	Orkney Islan
Id.	Idaho	Pa.	Pennsylvan
Ill.	Illinois	R.G.S.	Rio Grande do S
Ind.	Indiana	R.I.	Rhode Isla
Kans.	Kansas	S.C.	South Caroli
Ky.	Kentucky	Scot.	Scotla
La.	Louisiana	S.D.	South Dako
Man.	Manitoba	Shetland Is.	Shetland Islan
Mass.	Massachusetts	Tenn.	Tenness
Md.	Maryland	Tex.	Tex
Me.	Maine	Ut.	Ut
M.G.	Mato Grosso	Va.	Virgi
Mich.	Michigan	Vt.	Vermc
Minn.	Minnesota	Wash.	Washingt
Miss.	Mississippi	Wis.	Wiscons
Mo.	Missouri	W. Va.	West Virgi
Mont.	Montana	Wyo.	Wyomi
N.B.	New Brunswick	Y.T.	Yukon Territc
N.C.	North Carolina		

Symbols

This is a list of all the symbols used in the index to distinguish between different features. Any entry which has no symbol is a settlement.

A	Country name	☞	Lake, salt lake
a	State or province name	☞	Gulf, strait, bay
■	Country capital	☞	Sea, ocean
▣	State or province capital	☞	Cape, point
▲	Mountain, volcano, peak	☞	Island or island group,
☞	Mountain range		rocky or coral reef
☞	Physical region or feature	✱	Place of interest
☑	River, canal	☞	Historic region

Place	Page	Ref
achen	62	J4
alen	60	F8
alst	62	G4
arau	70	D3
are	70	C3
arschot	62	G4
ba	108	F3
bādān	101	C1
bādeh	101	E1
badla	106	E2
baji	108	F3
bakaliki	108	F3
bakan	82	S7
bancay	50	C6
bano Terme	70	G5
barqū	101	E1
bashiri	88	N1
bava	56	M8
baya Hâyk'	110	F2
bay Wenz	104	G5
bbeville, France	62	D4
bbeville, United States	42	C4
bd al Kūrī	96	F7
bêché	104	D5
bengourou	108	D3
benôjar	68	F6
benrâ	60	E1
bensberg	60	G8
beokuta	108	E3
beraeron	64	H9
berdeen, South Africa	112	C6
berdeen, United Kingdom	64	K4
berdeen, Miss., United States	42	D3
berdeen, S.D., United States	38	G1
berdeen, Wash., United States	38	B1
berdeen Lake	34	M4
berystwyth	64	H9
bez'	78	M1
bhā	104	H4
bhar	98	N5
bidjan	108	D3
bilene	44	G2
biline	32	M6
bingdon, United Kingdom	62	A3
bingdon, United States	42	E2
bnûb	104	F2
boisso	108	D3
bomey	108	E3
bong Mbang	108	G4
bou Déia	104	C5
bqaiq	101	C4
brantes	68	B5
bsaroka Range	38	J4
bū al Abayḍ	101	E4
bu Aweiglia	100	B6
bu Ballâs	104	E3
bu Dhabi = Abū Ẕabī	101	F4
bu Hamed	104	F4
buja	108	F3
bune Yosêf	104	G5
bū Nujaym	104	C1
bu Qarin	104	C1
buro	110	E3
bu Simbel	104	F3
but Head	118	B6
buye Meda	110	F1
bū Ẕabî	101	F4
bu Nujaym	106	J2
caponeta	36	E7
capulco	46	E5
carâ	50	H4
carigua	50	D2
ccra	108	D3
chaguas	46	L7
chayvayam	84	W4
cheng	86	H1
chenkirch	70	G3
chen See	70	G3
chill Island	64	B8
chim	60	E3
chinsk	82	S6
chit	78	L3
ci Göl	76	M7
Cihanbeyli	76	Q6
cireale	72	K11
cklins Island	46	K4
concagua	48	D7
cores	106	(1)B2
Coruña	68	B1
cqui Terme	70	D6
cre	50	C5
cri	72	L9
da	58	K12
da	42	B3
Adak Island	44	(3)C1
Adam	96	G5
Adams Island	118	(2)B1
'Adan	96	E7
Adana	98	F5
Adda	70	E5
Ad Dafrah	101	E5
Ad Dahnä	101	B3
Ad Dakhla	106	B4
Ad Dammâm	101	D3
Ad Dawādimî	96	D5
Ad Dawḫah	101	D4
Ad Dilam	101	B5
Ad Dir'īyah	101	B4
Addis Ababa = Ādīs Ābeba	110	F2
Ad Dîwânîyah	96	D3
Adel	40	B2
Adelaide	16	G6
Adelaide Peninsula	34	M3
Adelaide River	116	F2
Aden = Adan	96	E7
Aderbissinat	108	F1
Adh Dhayd	101	F4
Adi	92	(2)D3
Adige	70	G5
Adigrat	104	G5
Adilabad	94	C5
Adin	38	B2
Adīrî	104	B2
Ādīs Ābeba	110	F2
Adi Ugri	104	G5
Adıyaman	96	C2
Adjud	74	Q3
Adler	98	H2
Admiralty Island	34	E5
Admiralty Islands	114	E6
Adoni	94	C5
Adour	66	F10
Adra	68	H8
Adrano	72	J11
Adrar	106	E3
Adrar des Ifôghas	106	F5
Adrar Tamgak	106	G5
Adria	70	H5
Adriatic Sea	72	H4
Adycha	84	P3
Adygeya	98	J1
Adygeysk	98	H1
Adz'vavom	78	L1
Aegean Sea	76	H5
Afghanistan	96	H3
'Afif	104	H3
Afikpo	108	F3
Afognak Island	44	(1)G4
A Fonsagrada	68	C1
Afragôla	72	J8
'Afrîn	98	G5
Afuá	50	G4
'Afula	100	C4
Afyon	76	N6
Agadez	106	G5
Agadir	106	D2
Agadyr'	82	N8
Agalega Islands	102	J7
Agan	84	B4
Āgaro	110	F2
Agartala	94	F4
Agathonisi	76	J7
Agattu Island	84	W6
Agde	66	J10
Agen	66	F9
Ağın	98	H4
Aginskoye	82	S6
Agios Efstratios	76	H5
Agios Georgios	76	F7
Agios Nikolaos	76	H9
Agnita	74	M4
Agra	94	D3
Agrakhanskiy Poluostrov	98	M2
Agri	72	L8
Ağrı	98	K4
Agrigento	72	H11
Agrinio	76	D6
Agrópoli	72	K8
Agryz	78	K3
Agua Prieta	44	E2
Aguascalientes	46	D4
A Gudiña	68	C2
Aguelhok	106	F5
Águilas	68	J7
Agulhas Negras	50	H8
Ağva	76	M3
Ahar	98	M4
Ahaura	118	C6
Ahaus	62	K2
Ahititi	118	E4
Ahlen	62	K3
Ahmadabad	94	B4
Ahmadnagar	94	B5
Ahmadpur East	94	B3
Ahr	60	B6
Ahram	101	D2
Ahrensburg	60	F3
Ahväz	96	E3
Aichach	60	G8
Aigialousa	98	F6
Aigina	76	F7
Aigio	76	E6
Aigosthena	76	F6
Aihui	84	M6
Aim	84	N5
Ain	66	L7
Aïn Beïda	106	G1
'Aïn Ben Tili	106	D3
Aïn Bessem	68	P8
Aïn el Hadjel	68	P9
Aïn Oussera	106	F1
Ainsa	68	L2
Aïn Sefra	106	E2
Ain Taya	68	P8
Aïn-Tédélès	68	L8
Aïn Témouchent	68	J9
Airão	50	E4
Aire	64	L8
Air Force Island	34	S3
Airolo	70	D4
Airpanas	92	(2)C4
Aisne	62	F5
Aitape	92	(2)F3
Aitkin	40	B1
Aitutaki	114	K7
Aiud	74	L3
Aix-en-Provence	66	L10
Aix-les-Bains	66	L8
Aizawl	94	F4
Aizkraukle	56	N8
Aizpute	56	L8
Aizu-wakamatsu	88	K5
Ajaccio	72	C7
Aj Bogd Uul	86	B2
Ajdābiyā	104	D1
Ajigasawa	88	L3
Ajka	58	G10
Ajlun	100	C4
Ajmän	101	F4
Ajmer	94	B3
Ajo	44	D2
Akanthou	100	A1
Akaroa	118	D6
Akasha	104	F3
Akashi	88	H6
Akbalyk	82	P8
Akçakale	98	H5
Akçakoca	76	P3
Aken	60	H5
Aketi	110	C3
Akhalk'alak'i	98	K3
Akhisar	76	K6
Akhmîm	104	F2
Akhty	98	M3
Akimiski Island	34	Q6
Akita	88	L4
Akjoujt	106	C5
Akka	106	D3
Akkajaure	56	J3
Akkeshi	88	N2
'Akko	100	C4
Akmeqit	96	L2
Aknanes	56	(1)B2
Akobo	110	E2
Akola	94	C4
Akonolinga	108	G4
Akordat	104	G4
Akpatok Island	34	T4
Akqi	82	P9
Akra Drepano	76	G5
Akra Sounio	76	F7
Akra Spatha	76	F9
Akra Trypiti	76	G9
Åkrehamn	56	C7
Akron	40	D2
Aksaray	98	E4
Aksarka	82	M4
Akşehir	76	P6
Akseki	76	P7
Aksha	84	J6
Akshiy	82	P9
Aksu	82	Q9
Aksuat	82	Q8
Aksum	104	G5
Aktau, Kazakhstan	54	K3
Aktau, Kazakhstan	82	N7
Aktogay	82	N8
Aktogay	82	P8
Aktuma	82	M8
Aktyubinsk	78	L4
Akula	110	C3
Akune	88	F8
Akure	108	F3
Akureyri	56	(1)E2
Akwanga	108	F3
Alabama	42	D3
Alaçam	98	F3
Alagoas	50	K5
Alagoinhas	50	K6
Alagón	68	J3
Al Ahmadi	101	C2
Al 'Amârah	96	E3
Alaminos	90	F3
Alamo	38	C3
Alamogordo	44	E2
Alamo Lake	44	D2
Åland	56	K6
Alanya	98	E5
Alappuzha	94	C7
Al Arṭâwîyah	96	E4
Alaşehir	76	L6
Al 'Ashurîyah	104	H1
Alaska	44	(1)F2
Alaska Peninsula	44	(1)E4
Alaska Range	44	(1)G3
Alassio	70	D6
Alatri	72	H7
Alatyr'	78	J4
Alaverdi	98	L3
Alavus	56	M5
Alaykuu	82	N9
Al 'Ayn	101	F4
Alazeya	84	S2
Alba, Italy	70	D6
Alba, Spain	68	E4
Alba Iulia	74	L3
Albania	76	B3
Albania	34	Q6
Albany, Australia	116	C6
Albany, Ga., United States	42	E3
Albany, Ky., United States	42	E2
Albany, N.Y., United States	40	F2
Albany, Oreg., United States	38	B2
Albardão do João Maria	52	L4
Al Başrah	96	E3
Albatross Bay	116	H2
Albatross Point	118	E4
Al Baydâ'	104	D1
Albenga	70	D6
Albert	62	E4
Alberta	34	H6
Albertirsa	58	J10
Albert Kanaal	62	G3
Albert Lea	40	B2
Albert Nile	110	E3
Albertville	66	M8
Albi	66	H10
Albina	50	G2
Albino	70	E5
Albion	38	F1
Ålborg	56	E8
Ålborg Bugt	56	F8
Albox	68	H7
Albstadt	60	E8
Albufeira	68	B7
Al Bū Kamâl	98	J6
Albuquerque	44	E1
Alburquerque	68	D5
Albury	116	J7
Al Buṣayyah	101	B1
Alcácer do Sal	68	B6
Alcala de Guadaira	68	E7
Alcala de Henares	68	G4
Alcalá la Real	68	G7
Alcamo	72	G11
Alcanar	68	K3
Alcantarilla	68	J7
Alcaraz	68	H6
Alcaudete	68	G7
Alcazar de San Juan	68	G5
Alcobendas	68	G4
Alcoi	68	K6
Alcolea del Pinar	68	H3
Alcorcón	68	G4
Alcoutim	68	C7
Aldabra Group	112	(2)A2
Aldan	84	M5
Aldan	84	N5
Aldeburgh	64	J2
Alderney	66	C4
Aldershot	62	B3
Aleg	106	C5
Aleksandrov-Sakhalinskiy	84	Q6
Aleksandrovskiy Zavod	84	K6
Aleksandrovskoye	78	Q2
Alekseyevka	82	N7
Aleksinac	74	J6
Alençon	66	F5
Aleppo = Ḥalab	98	G5
Alès	66	K9
Aleşd	58	M10
Alessándria	70	D6
Ålesund	56	D5

123

Aleutian Islands	▨ 44	(3)B1	Alma, *Canada*	40	F1	Amadjuak Lake	▨ 34	S4	Analalava	112
Aleutian Range	◣ 44	(1)F4	Alma, *Nebr.*,			Amadora	68	A6	Anamur	98
Aleutian Trench	◪ 80	W5	*United States*	38	G2	Amahai	92	(2)C3	Anan	88
Alexander Archipelago	▨ 44	(1)K4	Alma, *Wis., United States*	40	B2	Amakusa-Shimo-shima	◈ 88	E7	Anantapur	94
Alexander Bay	112	B5	Almada	68	A6	Amaliada	76	D7	Anan'yiv	74
Alexander City	42	D3	Almadén	68	F6	Amalner	94	C4	Anapa	98
Alexandra	118	B7	Al Madînah	104	G3	Amamapare	92	(2)E3	Anápolis	50
Alexandreia	76	E4	Al Majma'ah	96	E4	Amami-Ōshima	◈ 80	S7	Anär	101
Alexandria =			Almalyk	82	M9	Amanab	92	(2)F3	Anārak	96
El Iskandarîya,			Al Manâmah	◼ 101	D3	Amándola	72	H6	Anardara	96
Egypt	104	E1	Almansa	68	J6	Amantéa	72	L9	Anatolia	◈ 76
Alexandria, *Romania*	74	N6	Al Marj	104	D1	Amapá	◼ 50	G3	Añatuya	52
Alexandria, *La.*,			Almaty	82	P9	Amapá	50	G3	Anchorage	44 (1
United States	42	C3	Al Mawṣil	98	K5	Amarante	50	J5	Ancona	72
Alexandria, *Minn.*,			Al Mazâḩumīyah	101	B4	Amarapura	90	B2	Ancud	52
United States	40	A1	Almazán	68	H3	Amarillo	44	F1	Anda	86
Alexandria, *Va.*,			Almeirim	50	G4	Amasya	98	F3	Andalgalá	52
United States	40	E3	Almelo	62	J2	Amay	62	H4	Åndalsnes	56
Alexandroupoli	76	H4	Almendralejo	68	D6	Amazar	84	L6	Andalusia	42
Alexis Creek	34	G6	Almería	68	H8	Amazon = Amazonas	▨ 48	F4	Andaman Islands	◈ 90
'Aley	100	C3	Al'met'yevsk	82	J7	Amazonas	◼ 50	D4	Andaman Sea	◣ 90
Aley	▨ 82	Q7	Almiros	76	E5	Amazonas	▨ 50	E4	Andapa	112
Aleysk	82	Q7	Al Mish'āb	101	C2	Ambala	94	C2	Andaräb	96
Al Farwâniyah	101	B2	Almonte	68	D7	Ambanjä	112	H2	Andenne	62
Al Fâw	101	C2	Almora	94	C3	Ambarchik	84	U3	Andernach	62
Alfeld	60	E5	Almosa	38	E3	Ambato	50	B4	Anderson	▨ 34
Alföld	◈ 74	H2	Al Mubarraz	101	C4	Ambato Boeny	112	H3	Anderson	42
Alfonsine	70	H6	Al Mudawwara	100	D7	Ambatondrazaka	112	H3	Andes	◣ 48
Alfreton	62	A1	Al Mukallā	96	E7	Amberg	60	G7	Andfjorden	◣ 56
Al Fuḩayḩil	101	C2	Al Mukhā	104	H5	Ambikapur	94	D4	Andipsara	▨ 76
Al-Fujayrah	101	G4	Almuñécar	68	G8	Ambilobe	112	H2	Andizhan	82
Algeciras	68	E8	Al Muqdādīyah	98	L7	Amboise	66	G6	Andkhvoy	96
Algemes	68	K5	Al Nu'ayrīyah	101	C3	Ambon	92	(2)C3	Andoas	50
Algena	104	G4	Alnwick	64	L6	Ambositra	112	H4	Andong	88
Alger	◼ 106	F1	Alonnisos	▨ 76	F5	Ambovombe	112	H5	Andorra	◪ 68
Algeria	◮ 106	E3	Alor	◈ 92	(2)B4	Amchitka Island	▨ 44	(3)B1	Andorra la Vella	◼ 68
Al Ghāṭ	101	A3	Alor Setar	90	C5	Amderma	82	L4	Andover	62
Al Ghaydah	96	F6	Alotau	116	K2	Amdo	94	F2	Andøya	◪ 56
Alghero	72	C8	Alpena	40	D1	Ameland	◪ 62	H1	Andradina	52
Algiers = Alger	◼ 106	F1	Alphen	62	G2	Amengel'dy	82	M7	Andreanof Islands	◈ 44 (3
Algona	40	B2	Alpi Lepontine	◣ 70	D4	American Falls	38	D2	Andrews	44
Al Hadīthah	100	E5	Alpine	44	E2	American Samoa	◈ 114	J7	Andria	72
Alhama de Murcia	68	J7	Alpi Orobie	◣ 70	E4	Americus	42	E3	Andros	76
Al Ḩamar	101	B5	Alps	◣ 70	B5	Amersfoort	62	H2	Andros, *Greece*	◈ 76
Al Ḩamīdīyah	100	C2	Al Qadmūs	100	D1	Amery	34	N5	Andros, *The Bahamas*	◈ 42
Al Ḩammādah al Ḩamrā'	◼ 106	G3	Al Qāmishlī	98	J5	Amery Ice Shelf	◈ 120	(2)M2	Andros Town	42
Al Harūj al Aswad	◪ 104	C2	Al Qar'ah	101	B3	Ames	40	B2	Andrott	◈ 94
Al Ḩasakah	98	J5	Al Qaryah	104	B1	Amfilochia	76	D6	Andrychów	58
Alhaurmín el Grande	68	F8	Al Qaryatayn	100	E2	Amfissa	76	E6	Andújar	68
Al Ḩijāz	◪ 104	G2	Al Qaṭrūn	104	B3	Amga	▨ 84	L5	Andulo	112
Al Ḩillah	96	D3	Al Qunayṭirah	100	C3	Amga	84	N4	Aneto	◣ 68
Al Ḩilwah	101	B5	Al Qunfudhah	104	H4	Amgun'	84	P6	Angara	▨ 84
Al Hoceima	106	E1	Al Qurayyāt	104	G1	Amherst	34	U7	Angarsk	84
Al Ḩudaydah	104	H5	Al Qurnah	101	B1	Amiens	62	E5	Ånge	56
Al Ḩufūf	101	C4	Al Quṣayr	101	A1	Amirante Islands	◈ 112	(2)H2	Angel de la Guarda	◈ 44
Al Ḩumaydah	96	C4	Al Quṭayfah	100	D3	Amistad Reservoir	▨ 44	F3	Angeles	92
Aliabad	101	F2	Als	◪ 60	E1	Amlekhganj	94	D3	Ångelholm	56
Aliağa	76	J6	Alsask	34	K6	Âmli	56	E7	Angeln	◪ 60
Aliakmonas	▨ 76	E4	Alsasua	68	H2	'Ammân	◼ 100	C5	Angermünde	60
Âli Bayramlı	98	N4	Alsfeld	60	E6	Ammerland	▨ 62	K1	Angern	60
Alicante	68	K6	Altaelva	▨ 56	M2	Ammersee	▨ 70	F2	Angers	66
Alice	42	B4	Altai Mountains	◣ 86	A1	Ammochostos	98	E6	Anglesey	◪ 64
Alice Springs	116	F4	Altamira	50	G4	Ammochostos Bay	◼ 100	A1	Angmagssalik = Tasiilaq	34
Alicudi	◈ 72	J10	Altamura	72	L8	Amo	▨ 90	C2	Ango	110
Aligarh	94	C3	Altanbulag	84	H6	Amol	96	F2	Angoche	112
Alindao	110	C2	Altay	◈ 82	R7	Amorgós	◈ 76	H8	Angol	52
Alingås	56	G8	Altay, *China*	86	B1	Amos	40	E1	Angola	◮ 102
Alisos	▨ 44	D2	Altay, *Mongolia*	70	D4	Ampana	92	(2)B3	Angola	40
Aliwal North	112	D6	Altdorf	70	D4	Ampanihy	112	G4	Angostura Reservoir	▨ 38
Al Jabal al Akhḍar	◣ 104	D1	Alte Mellum	◪ 60	D3	Amparai	94	D7	Angoulême	66
Al Jaghbūb	104	D2	Altenburg	60	H4	Ampezzo	70	H4	Angren	82
Al Jālamīd	104	G1	Altenkirchen	60	J2	Amposta	68	L4	Anguilla	◪ 46 (1
Al Jarah	101	B2	Altkirch	70	C3	Amrān	96	D6	Aniak	44 (1
Al Jawf	104	G2	Alto Garças	50	G7	Amravati	94	C4	Anina	74
Aljezur	68	B7	Alto Molócuè	112	F3	Amritsar	94	B2	Anıyaman	98
Al Jifārah	101	A5	Alton, *United Kingdom*	62	B3	Amroha	94	C3	Ankang	86
Al Jubayl	101	C3	Alton, *United States*	40	B3	Amrum	◪ 60	D2	Ankara	◼ 98
Aljustrel	68	B7	Altoona	40	G2	Amsterdam, *Netherlands*	◼ 62	G2	Ankazoabo	112
Al Kāmil	96	G5	Alto Parnaíba	50	H5	Amsterdam,			Anklam	60
Al Khābūrah	101	G5	Altötting	70	H2	*United States*	40	F2	Ankpa	108
Al Kharj	101	B4	Altun Shan	◈ 82	S10	Amstetten	70	K2	Ånn	▨ 56
Al Khaṣab	101	G3	Alturas	38	B2	Am Timan	104	D5	Anna	78
Al Khawr	101	D4	Altus	42	B3	Amudar'ya	▨ 82	L9	Annaba	106
Al Khubar	101	D3	Al 'Ubaylah	96	F5	Amundsen Gulf	◣ 34	G2	Annaberg-Buchholz	60
Al Khums	106	H2	Alüksne	56	H6	Amundsen Sea	◣ 120	(2)GG3	An Nabk, *Saudi Arabia*	100
Al Khuwayr	101	D3	Alupka	98	E1	Amungen	◪ 56	H6	An Nabk, *Syria*	100
Alkmaar	62	G2	Alushta	98	F1	Amuntai	92	(1)F3	An Nafud	◈ 104
Al Kūt	96	E3	Al 'Uwayqīlah	104	H1	Amur	▨ 84	P6	An Nā'irīyah	96
Al Kuwayt	◼ 101	C2	Al 'Uzayr	101	B1	Amursk	84	P6	An Najaf	96
Al Lādhiqīyah	98	F6	Alva	42	B2	Amvrakikos Kolpos	▨ 76	C6	Annapolis	◼ 40
Allahabad	94	D3	Alvarães	50	E4	Anabar	▨ 84	J2	Annapurna	▲ 94
Allakh-Yun'	84	P4	Ålvdalen	56	H6	Anaconda	38	D1	Ann Arbor	40
Alldays	112	D6	Älvsbyn	56	L4	Anacortes	38	B1	An Nāşirīyah	104
Allen	90	G4	Al Wafrā'	101	B2	Anadarko	42	B3	Annecy	70
Allendale	42	E3	Al Wajh	104	G2	Anadolu Dağları	◣ 98	H3	Annemasse	70
Allentown	40	E2	Alwar	94	C3	Anadyr'	84	X4	Anniston	42
Aller	▨ 60	E4	Al Wari'ah	101	B3	Anadyrskaya Nizmennost'	◣ 84	X3	Annobón	◈ 108
Aller = Cabañiquinta	68	E1	Alytus	58	P3	Anadyrskiy Zaliv	◣ 84	Y3	Annonay	66
Alliance	38	F2	Alzira	68	K5	Anafi	◈ 76	H8	An Nukhayb	100
Allier	▨ 66	J8	Alzey	60	D7	'Anah	98	K5	Anqing	86
Allinge	58	D2	Amadi	110	D3	Anaheim	44	C2	Ansbach	60
Al Lith	104	H3	Amādīyah	98	K5	Anáhuac	44	F3	Anshan	88

Atoka — 42 B3
Atokos — 76 C6
Atol das Rocas — 50 L4
Aţ Ţā'if — 96 D5
Attapu — 90 D4
Attawapiskat — 34 Q6
Attersee — 70 J3
Attica — 40 C2
Attu Island — 44 (3)A1
Attu Island — 120 (1)KK4
At Turbah — 104 H5
Atyrau — 78 K5
Aubagne — 66 L10
Aubange — 62 H5
Aube — 66 K5
Aubenas — 66 K9
Aubry Lake — 34 F3
Auburn, Al.,
  United States — 42 D3
Auburn, Calif.,
  United States — 38 B3
Auburn, Nebr.,
  United States — 38 G2
Auburn, Wash.,
  United States — 38 B1
Aubusson — 66 H8
Auce — 58 M1
Auch — 66 F10
Auchi — 108 F3
Auckland — 118 E3
Auckland Island — 118 (2)B1
Aude — 66 H10
Aue — 60 H6
Auerbach — 60 H6
Augathella — 116 J5
Augsburg — 70 F2
Augusta, Australia — 116 C6
Augusta, Italy — 72 K11
Augusta, Ga.,
  United States — 42 E3
Augusta, Me.,
  United States — 40 G2
Augustów — 58 M4
Aulla — 70 E6
Aurangābād — 94 C5
Auray — 66 C6
Aurich — 62 K1
Aurillac — 66 H9
Aurora, Colo.,
  United States — 38 F3
Aurora, Ill.,
  United States — 40 C2
Aurora, Mo.,
  United States — 42 C2
Aurukun — 116 H2
Aus — 112 B5
Auschwitz = Oświęcim — 58 J7
Austin, Minn.,
  United States — 40 B2
Austin, Nev.,
  United States — 38 C3
Austin, Tex.,
  United States — 42 B3
Australia — 116 E4
Australian Alps — 114 E9
Australian Capital
  Territory — 116 J7
Austria — 70 J3
Autun — 66 K7
Auxerre — 66 J6
Avallon — 66 J6
Avam — 84 E2
Āvārsin — 98 M4
Aveiro — 68 B4
Avellino — 72 J8
Averøya — 56 D5
Avesnes-sur-Helpe — 62 F4
Avesta — 56 J6
Avezzano — 72 H6
Aviemore — 64 J4
Avignon — 66 K10
Ávila — 68 F4
Avilés — 68 E1
Avion — 62 E4
Avola — 72 K12
Avon, United Kingdom — 62 A2
Avon, United Kingdom — 62 A3
Avranches — 66 D5
Avrig — 74 M4
Awaji-shima — 88 H6
Awanui — 118 D2
Awat — 82 Q9
Awatere — 118 D5
Awbārī — 104 B2
Awjilah — 104 D2
Awka — 108 F3
Ax-les-Thermes — 66 G11
Ayacucho — 50 C6
Ayaguz — 82 Q8
Ayakkuduk — 82 M9
Ayamonte — 68 C7
Ayan — 84 E3

Ayan — 84 P5
Aya Napa — 100 A2
Ayancık — 98 F3
Ayanka — 84 V4
Ayaviri — 50 C6
Aydın — 98 B5
Aydıncık — 76 R8
Ayers Rock = Uluru — 116 F5
Aykhal — 84 J3
Aykino — 82 H5
Aylesbury — 62 B3
Aylmer Lake — 34 K4
Ayni — 96 J2
Ayní — 82 M10
Ayon 'Isá — 98 H5
Ayoûn el 'Atroûs — 106 D5
Ayr, Australia — 116 J3
Ayr, United Kingdom — 64 H6
Aytos — 74 Q7
Ayutthaya — 90 C4
Ayvalik — 76 J5
Azaila — 68 K3
Azaouâd — 106 E5
Āzarān — 98 M5
Azare — 108 G2
A'zāz — 98 G5
Azdavay — 76 R3
Azerbaijan — 98 M3
Azogues — 50 B4
Azores = Açores — 106 (1)B2
Azov — 78 G5
Azpeitia — 68 H1
Azrou — 106 D2
Aztec — 38 E3
Azuaga — 68 E6
Azul — 52 K6
Az Zabadānī — 100 D3
Aż Żahrān — 101 D3
Az Zāwiyah — 104 B1
Az Zubayr — 101 B1

B

Ba'albek — 100 D2
Baardheere — 110 G3
Babadag — 74 R5
Babaeski — 76 K3
Bāb al Mandab — 96 F7
Babanusa — 110 D1
Babar — 92 (2)C4
Babayevo — 78 G3
Babayurt — 98 M2
Babo — 92 (2)D3
Bābol — 96 F2
Babruysk — 78 E4
Babura — 108 F2
Babushkin — 84 H6
Babuyan Islands — 90 G3
Bacabal — 50 J4
Bacan — 92 (2)C3
Bacău — 74 P3
Baccarat — 70 B2
Bachu — 96 L2
Back — 34 M3
Bačka Palanka — 74 G4
Bačka Topola — 74 G4
Backnang — 70 E2
Bac Liêu — 90 D5
Bacolod — 90 G4
Badajós — 50 H4
Badajoz — 68 D6
Bad al Milḩ — 98 K7
Badalona — 68 N3
Bad Ausee — 70 J3
Bad Bentheim — 62 K2
Bad Berleburg — 60 D5
Bad Doberan — 60 G2
Bad Dürkheim — 60 D7
Bad Ems — 62 K4
Baden — 58 F9
Baden-Baden — 70 D2
Bad Freienwalde — 60 K4
Badgastein — 70 J3
Badgingarra — 116 C6
Bad Harzburg — 60 F5
Bad Hersfeld — 60 E6
Bad Homburg — 60 D6
Bad Honnef — 62 K4
Badin — 94 A4
Bad Ischl — 70 J3
Bādiyat ash Shām — 100 D4
Bad Kissingen — 60 F6
Bad Kreuznach — 62 K5
Bad Langensalza — 60 F5
Bad Lauterberg — 60 F5
Bad Liebenwerda — 60 J5
Bad Mergentheim — 60 E7
Bad Nauheim — 60 D6
Bad Neuenahr-Ahrweiler — 62 K4
Bad Neustadt — 60 F6
Bad Oeynhausen — 60 D4

Badong — 86 E4
Bad Reichenhall — 70 H3
Bad Säckingen — 60 C9
Bad Salzuflen — 60 D4
Bad Salzungen — 60 F6
Bad Schwartau — 60 F3
Bad Segeberg — 60 F3
Bad Sobernheim — 62 K5
Bad Urach — 70 E2
Bad Vöslau — 74 D2
Bad Waldsee — 70 E3
Bad Wilbad — 70 D2
Bad Wildungen — 60 E5
Bad Windsheim — 60 F7
Bad Wurzach — 70 E3
Baena — 68 F7
Bærum — 56 F7
Baeza — 68 G6
Baffin Bay — 32 J2
Baffin Island — 34 R2
Bafia — 108 G4
Bafoulabé — 108 B2
Bafoussam — 108 G3
Bāfq — 96 G3
Bafra — 98 F3
Bafra Burun — 98 G3
Bāft — 101 G2
Bafwasende — 110 D3
Baga — 104 B5
Bagani — 112 C3
Bagaroua — 108 E2
Bagdad — 44 D2
Bagdarin — 84 J6
Bagé — 52 L5
Baggs — 38 E2
Baghdād — 96 D3
Bagheria — 72 H10
Baghlān — 96 J2
Bagnères-de-Bigorre — 66 F10
Bagno di Romagna — 70 G7
Bagnols-sur-Cèze — 66 K9
Baguio — 90 G3
Bagun Datuk — 92 (1)C2
Baharampur — 94 E4
Bahawalnagar — 94 B3
Bahawalpur — 94 B3
Bahçe — 98 G5
Bahia — 50 J6
Bahía Blanca — 52 J6
Bahía Blanca — 52 J6
Bahía de Banderas — 46 C4
Bahía de Campeche — 46 F4
Bahía de Manta — 50 A4
Bahía de Petacalco — 46 D5
Bahía de Pisco — 50 B6
Bahía de Santa Elena — 50 A4
Bahía de Sechura — 50 A5
Bahía Grande — 52 H9
Bahía Kino — 36 D6
Bahía Kino — 46 B3
Bahía Negra — 52 K3
Bahía Samborombón — 52 K6
Bahir Dar — 104 G5
Bahrain — 94 D3
Bahrain — 101 D4
Baḩrat Ḩimş — 100 D2
Bahr el Abiad — 104 F5
Bahr el Azraq — 104 F5
Bahr el Ghazal — 104 C5
Bahr el Ghazal — 110 C2
Bahr el Jebe — 110 E2
Bahr el Nîl = Nile — 104 F4
Baía de Marajó — 50 H4
Baía de Todos os Santos — 50 K6
Baía do Bengo — 108 H6
Baia Mare — 74 L2
Baião — 50 H4
Baia Sprie — 74 L2
Baïbokoum — 110 B2
Baicheng, China — 82 Q9
Baicheng, China — 86 G1
Baie Comeau — 40 G1
Baie de la Seine — 62 B5
Baie de la Somme — 62 D4
Baie du Poste — 34 S6
Baie St. Paul — 40 F1
Baiji — 94 K6
Baile Átha Cliath = Dublin — 64 F8
Bailén — 68 G6
Bailleul — 62 E4
Bailundo — 112 B2
Bainbridge — 42 E3
Bairiki — 114 H5
Bairin Yuoqi — 86 F2
Bairin Zuoqi — 86 F2
Bairnsdale — 116 J7
Bais — 90 G5
Baja — 74 F3
Baja California — 36 C5
Bakchar — 82 Q6
Bakel — 108 B2
Baker — 114 J5

Baker, Calif.,
  United States — 38
Baker, Mont.,
  United States — 38
Baker, Oreg.,
  United States — 38
Baker Lake — 34
Baker Lake — 34
Bakersfield — 44
Bakhta — 84
Baki — 96
Bakkafjörður — 56 (1)
Bakkaflói — 56 (1)
Baku = Baki — 96
Balā — 90
Balabac — 90
Balabac Strait — 90
Balagansk — 84
Balaghat — 94
Balaguer — 68
Balakhta — 82
Balaklava — 98
Balakovo — 78
Bālā Morghāb — 82
Bālan — 74
Balāngīr — 94
Balashov — 78
Balassagyarmat — 74
Balaton — 74
Balatonfüred — 74
Balatonlelle — 74
Balchik — 98
Balclutha — 118
Bald Knob — 40
Baldwin — 42
Balearic Islands =
  Islas Baleares — 68
Bāleshwar — 94
Baley — 84
Baléyara — 108
Balguntay — 82
Bali — 92 (1)
Balige — 92 (1)
Balıkesir — 76
Balıkpapan — 92 (1)
Balimo — 92 (2)
Balingen — 70
Balintang Channel — 90
Balkhash — 82
Ballarat — 116
Balleny Island — 120 (2)
Ballina, Australia — 116
Ballina,
  Republic of Ireland — 64
Ballinasloe — 64
Ballinger — 44
Ball's Pyramid — 116
Ballymena — 64
Balmazújváros — 74
Balotra — 94
Balranald — 116
Balş — 74
Balsas — 46
Balsas — 50
Balta — 74
Bălţi — 74
Baltic Sea — 56
Baltijsk — 58
Baltimore — 40
Baltrum — 60
Balvi — 56
Balykchy — 78
Balykshi — 78
Bam — 96
Bamaga — 116
Bamako — 108
Bamba — 106
Bambari — 110
Bamberg — 60
Bambesa — 110
Bambouk — 106
Bambouk Kaarta — 108
Bamda — 86
Bamenda — 108
Bāmiān — 96
Banaba — 114
Bañados del Izozog — 50
Banalia — 110
Banana, Australia — 116
Banana,
  Dem. Rep. of Congo — 110
Banaz — 76
Ban Ban — 90
Banbury — 64
Banda — 94
Banda Aceh — 92
Bandama — 108
Bandar-e 'Abbās — 101
Bandar-e Anzalī — 101
Bandar-e Deylam — 101
Bandar-e Ganāveh — 101
Bandar-e Khomeir — 101

Name	Page	Grid
ndar-e Lengeh	101	F3
ndar-e Ma'shur	101	C1
ndar-e Torkeman	96	F2
ndar Khomeynï	101	C1
ndar Seri Begawan	■ 92	(1)E2
nda Sea	⊟ 92	(2)C3
nd-e Moghüyeh	101	F3
ndirma	76	K4
ndundu	110	B4
ndung	92	(1)D4
neasa	74	Q5
ndee	98	L6
ff, Canada	34	H6
ff, United Kingdom	64	K4
ngalore	94	C6
ngangté	108	G3
ngassou	110	C3
ngbong	92	(2)B3
nggi	⊟ 92	(1)F1
nghâzî	104	D1
ngka	⊟ 92	(1)D3
ngkok = Krung Thep	■ 90	C4
ngladesh	A 94	E4
ngor, N.Ire., United Kingdom	64	G7
ngor, Wales, United Kingdom	64	H8
ngor, United States	40	G2
ng Saphan Yai	90	B4
ngui	■ 110	B3
n Hat Yai	90	C5
n Hua Hin	90	B4
ni-Bangou	108	E1
nī Walīd	106	H2
niyâs	98	F6
nja Luka	74	E5
njarmasin	92	(1)E3
njul	■ 108	A2
n Khemmarat	90	D3
nks Island = Moa, Australia	⊟116	H2
nks Island, B.C., Canada	⊟ 34	G1
nks Island, N.W.T., Canada	⊟ 34	G2
nks Lake	⊿ 38	C1
nks Peninsula	⊟118	D6
nks Strait	►116	J8
nnerman Town	42	F5
nnu	94	B2
novce	58	H9
nská	58	J9
nská Štiavnica	58	H9
nsko	76	F3
ntry	64	C10
nyo	108	G3
nyoles	68	N2
nyuwangi	92	(1)E4
nde	86	E3
nding	86	F3
nji	86	D4
n Lôc	90	D4
nro	110	B2
nshan	90	B1
naume	86	E2
nying	86	F4
naume	62	E4
nqûbah	96	D3
nuedano	52	H3
	74	G7
nbai	92	(1)F3
nboo	40	C2
nkaldo	68	H1
namati	94	B5
namula	94	B2
nan	78	E4
nanavichy	74	N3
naolt	74	F1
nbados	A 50	F1
nbastro	68	L2
nbate	68	E8
nbuda	⊟ 46	M5
ncaldine	116	J4
ncău	⊿ 74	K2
ncellona Pozzo di Gotto	72	K10
ncelona, Spain	68	N3
ncelona, Venezuela	46	M6
ncelos, Brazil	50	E4
ncelos, Spain	68	B3
nco de Valdeorras = O Barco	68	D2
ncs	74	E4
ndâ	98	M3
ndai	104	C3
nddhamãn	94	E4
ndejov	58	L8
nreilly	94	C3
nents Sea	⊿ 82	E3
nentu	104	G4
neo	92	(1)F2
nga	94	D2
ngaal	110	J1
Barguzin	84	H6
Bar Harbor	40	G2
Bari	72	L7
Barikot	94	B1
Barinas	50	C2
Bârîs	104	F3
Barisal	94	F4
Barito	∠ 92	(2)A3
Barkam	86	C4
Barkava	56	P8
Barkly Tableland	⊟116	F3
Barkol	82	S9
Bârlad	74	Q3
Bârlad	∠ 74	Q3
Bar-le-Duc	62	H6
Barletta	72	L7
Barmer	94	B3
Barmouth Bay	►► 64	H9
Barnaul	82	Q7
Barnsley	64	L8
Barnstaple	64	H10
Barnstaple Bay	►► 64	H10
Barpeta	94	F3
Barquisimeto	50	D1
Barr	70	C2
Barra, Brazil	50	J6
Barra, United Kingdom	⊟ 64	E4
Barracão do Barreto	50	G5
Barra do Bugres	50	F7
Barra do Corda	50	H5
Barra do Garças	50	G7
Barra do São Manuel	50	G5
Barragem de Santa Clara	⊿ 68	B7
Barragem de Sobradinho	⊿ 50	J5
Barragem do Castelo de Bode	⊿ 68	B5
Barragem do Maranhão	⊿ 68	C6
Barranca, Peru	50	B3
Barranca, Peru	50	B6
Barranquilla	46	K6
Barreiras	50	H6
Barreiro	68	A6
Barretos	50	H8
Barrie	40	E2
Barron	40	B1
Barrow	44	(1)F1
Barrow-in-Furness	64	J7
Barrow Island	⊟116	B4
Barrow Strait	►► 34	N2
Barshatas	82	P8
Barsi	94	C5
Barstow	44	C2
Bar-sur-Aube	66	K5
Barth	60	H2
Bartin	98	E3
Bartle Frere	⊟114	E7
Bartlesville	42	B2
Bartlett	38	G2
Bartoszyce	58	K3
Barus	92	(1)B2
Baruun Urt	86	E1
Barwani	94	B4
Barysaw	78	E4
Basaidu	101	F3
Basankusu	110	B3
Basarabeasca	74	R3
Basarabi	74	R5
Basca	72	C2
Basel	70	C3
Bashkiriya	■ 78	K4
Bâsht	101	D1
Basilan	⊟ 92	(2)B1
Basildon	62	C3
Basiluzzo	⊟ 72	K10
Basingstoke	64	L10
Başkale	98	K4
Basoko	110	C3
Bassano	36	D1
Bassano del Grappa	70	G5
Bassar	108	E3
Bassas da India	⊟112	F4
Basse Santa Su	106	C6
Basse Terre	46	M5
Bassett	38	G2
Bass Strait	►►116	H7
Bassum	60	D4
Bastak	101	F3
Bastānābād	98	M5
Basti	94	D3
Bastia	72	D6
Bastogne	62	H4
Bastrop, La., United States	42	C3
Bastrop, Tex., United States	42	B3
Bata	108	F4
Batagay	84	N3
Batak	76	G3
Batamay	84	M4
Batangas	90	G4
Batan Islands	⊟ 90	G2
Batanta	⊟ 92	(2)C3
Batemans Bay	116	K7
Batesville	42	D3
Bath, United Kingdom	64	K10
Bath, United States	40	E2
Bathinda	94	B2
Bathurst, Australia	116	J6
Bathurst, Canada	34	T7
Bathurst Inlet	34	K3
Bathurst Island, Australia	⊟116	E2
Bathurst Island, Canada	⊟ 34	M1
Batman	96	D2
Batna	106	G1
Baton Rouge	■ 42	C3
Bátonyterenye	74	G2
Batroûn	100	C2
Battipaglia	72	J8
Battle	∠ 34	J6
Battle Creek	40	C2
Battle Harbour	34	V6
Battle Mountain	38	C2
Batu	▲110	F2
Batui	92	(2)B3
Bat'umi	98	J3
Batu Pahat	92	(1)C2
Baturino	82	R6
Baubau	92	(2)B4
Bauchi	108	F2
Baudette	40	B1
Baukau	92	(2)C4
Baume-les-Dames	66	M6
Bauru	52	M3
Bauska	56	N8
Bautzen	58	D6
Bawean	⊟ 92	(1)E4
Bawiti	104	E2
Bawku	108	D2
Bayamo	46	J4
Bayanaul	82	P7
Bayandelger	84	H7
Bayan Har Shan	■ 86	B4
Bayanhongor	86	C1
Bayan Mod	86	D2
Bayan Obo	86	D2
Bayansumküre	82	Q9
Bayburt	98	J3
Bay City, Mich., United States	40	D2
Bay City, Tex., United States	42	B4
Baydhabo	110	G3
Bayerische Alpen	■ 70	G3
Bayeux	62	B5
Bayfield	40	B1
Bayindir	76	K6
Bâyir	100	D6
Baykit	82	T5
Baykonur	82	M8
Bay Minette	42	D3
Bay of Bengal	►► 94	E5
Bay of Biscay	►► 66	C3
Bay of Fundy	►► 34	T8
Bay of Islands	►►118	C2
Bay of Plenty	►►118	F3
Bayonne	66	D10
Bayramaly	96	H2
Bayramiç	76	J5
Bayreuth	60	G7
Baysun	96	J2
Bayt al Faqïh	104	H5
Bay View	118	F4
Baza	68	H7
Bazas	66	E9
Bazdar	96	J4
Beach	38	F1
Beachy Head	⊟ 62	C4
Beagle Gulf	⊟116	E2
Bealanana	112	H2
Bear Island	⊟ 64	B10
Bear Island = Bjørnøya	⊟ 82	B3
Bear Lake	⊿ 38	D2
Beasain	68	H1
Beas de Segura	68	H6
Beatrice	42	B1
Beatty	44	C1
Beaufort, Malaysia	92	(1)F1
Beaufort, N.C., United States	42	F3
Beaufort, S.C., United States	42	E3
Beaufort Sea	⊿ 32	Q2
Beaufort West	112	C6
Beaumont	42	C3
Beaune	66	K6
Beauvais	62	E5
Beaver	38	D3
Beaver Creek	44	(1)J3
Beaver Dam	40	C3
Beaver Falls	40	D2
Beawar	94	B3
Beazley	52	H5
Bebra	60	E6
Bečej	74	H4
Béchar	106	E2
Beckley	42	E2
Becks	118	B7
Beckum	62	L3
Beclean	74	M2
Bedford, United Kingdom	64	M9
Bedford, United States	42	D2
Bedworth	62	A2
Beenleigh	116	K5
Beer Menuha	100	C6
Be'ér Sheva'	100	B5
Beeville	42	B4
Behbehän	101	D1
Bei'an	84	M7
Beihai	90	D2
Beijing	■ 86	F3
Beipan	∠ 86	D5
Beipiao	86	G2
Beira	112	E3
Beirut = Beyrouth	■100	C3
Beiuş	74	K3
Beizhen	88	A3
Bēja	106	G1
Beja	106	G1
Bejaïa	106	G1
Béjar	68	E4
Bekdash	96	F1
Békés	58	L11
Békéscsaba	74	J3
Bekily	112	H4
Bela	96	J4
Bela Crkva	74	J5
Belaga	92	(1)E2
Belarus	A 54	G2
Bela Vista	112	E5
Belaya	∠ 78	K3
Belaya Gora	84	R3
Belchatów	58	J6
Belcher Islands	⊟ 34	Q5
Beledweyne	110	H3
Belém	■ 50	H4
Belen	46	C2
Belfast	⊟ 64	G7
Belfield	38	F1
Belfort	70	B3
Belgazyn	82	T7
Belgium	A 62	G4
Belgorod	78	G4
Belgrade = Beograd	■ 74	H5
Beli	108	G3
Belice	∠ 72	H11
Belinyu	74	F4
Belitung	92	(1)D3
Belize	⊟ 92	(1)D3
Belize	A 46	G5
Belize	46	G5
Beliac	66	G7
Bella Coola	34	F6
Bellary	94	C5
Bellefontaine	40	D2
Belle Fourche	38	F2
Belle Glade	42	E4
Belle Île	⊟ 66	B6
Belle Isle	⊟ 34	V6
Bellême	66	F5
Belieterre	40	E1
Belleville, Canada	40	E2
Belleville, United States	42	B2
Bellingham	38	B1
Bellingshausen Sea	⊿120	(2)JJ4
Bellinzona	70	E4
Bello	50	B2
Belluno	70	H4
Bellyk	84	E6
Belmont	40	E2
Belmonte, Brazil	50	K7
Belmonte, Spain	68	H5
Belmopan	■ 46	G5
Belmullet	64	B7
Belogorsk	84	M6
Belogradchik	74	K6
Belo Horizonte	⊟ 50	J7
Beloit, Kans., United States	42	B2
Beloit, Wis., United States	40	C2
Belomorsk	78	F2
Belorechensk	98	H1
Beloretsk	78	L4
Belo Tsiribihina	112	G3
Belovo	82	R7
Beloyarskiy	82	M5
Beloye More	⊿ 78	G1
Belozersk	78	G3
Belozerskoye	78	N3
Belye Vody	82	M9
Bely Yar	82	Q6
Belzig	60	H4
Bembibre	68	D2
Bemidji	40	A1
Bena Dibele	110	C4
Benavente	68	E3
Benbecula	⊟ 64	E4

Name	Page	Grid
Bend	38	B2
Bender-Bayla	110	J2
Bender Qaasim	110	H1
Bendorf	62	K4
Bene	112	E3
Benešov	58	D8
Benevento	72	J7
Bengbu	86	F4
Bengkulu	92	(1)C3
Benguela	112	A2
Benguerir	106	D2
Benha	104	F1
Beni	110	D3
Beni	◪50	D6
Beni Abbès	106	E2
Benicarló	68	L4
Benidorm	68	K6
Benī Mazâr	104	F2
Beni Mellal	106	D2
Benin	▲108	E2
Benin City	108	F3
Beni Saf	68	J9
Beni Slimane	68	P8
Beni Suef	104	F2
Benito Juaréz	52	K6
Benjamin Constant	50	D4
Benkelman	38	F2
Benkovac	70	L6
Ben More Assynt	▲64	H3
Ben Nevis	▲64	H5
Bennington	40	F2
Benoud	106	F2
Bensheim	60	D7
Benson, Ariz., United States	44	D2
Benson, Minn., United States	36	G2
Benteng	92	(2)B4
Bentinck Island	⊠116	G3
Bentonville	42	C2
Bentung	92	(1)C2
Benue	◪108	G3
Benxi	86	G2
Beograd	■74	H5
Bepazarı	98	D3
Berat	76	B4
Beravina	112	H3
Berber	104	F4
Berbera	104	H5
Berbérati	110	B3
Berchtesgaden	70	J3
Berck	62	D4
Berdigestyakh	84	M4
Berdyans'k	78	G5
Berdychiv	78	E5
Bereeda	110	J1
Berehove	74	K1
Bererreá	68	C2
Berettyóújfalu	74	J2
Berettys	◪58	L10
Bereznik	78	H2
Berezniki	78	L3
Berezovo	78	N2
Berezovyy	84	P6
Berga	68	M2
Bergama	76	K5
Bérgamo	70	E5
Bergara	68	H1
Bergedorf	60	F3
Bergen, Netherlands	62	G2
Bergen, Norway	56	C6
Bergen, Germany	60	J2
Bergen, Germany	60	E4
Bergen op Zoom	62	G3
Bergerac	66	F9
Bergheim	62	J4
Bergisch Gladbach	60	C6
Bergsfjordhalvøya	◙56	L1
Beringen	62	H3
Beringovskiy	84	X4
Bering Sea	◪44	(1)C4
Bering Strait	◄44	(1)C2
Berkeley	44	B1
Berkner Island	⊠120	(2)A2
Berkovitsa	74	L6
Berlin, Germany	■60	J4
Berlin, United States	40	F2
Bermejillo	44	F3
Bermejo	◪52	K4
Bermeo	68	H1
Bermuda	⊠32	H6
Bern	■70	C4
Bernado	44	E2
Bernau	60	J4
Bernay	62	C5
Bernburg	60	G5
Berner Alpen	▲70	C4
Beroun	58	D8
Berounka	◪60	J7
Berovo	76	E3
Berrouaghia	68	N8
Berry Islands	⊠42	F4

Name	Page	Grid
Bertoua	108	G4
Bertram	40	D1
Beruni	82	L9
Berwick-upon-Tweed	64	L6
Besalampy	112	G3
Besançon	66	M6
Beshneh	101	F2
Bessemer	42	D3
Bestamak	82	P8
Bestuzhevo	78	H2
Bestyakh, Russia	84	L3
Bestyakh, Russia	84	M4
Betanzos	68	B1
Bêtdâmbâng	90	C4
Bethany	40	B2
Bethel, Ak., United States	44	(1)E3
Bethel, Pa., United States	40	F2
Bethlehem, Israel	100	C5
Bethlehem, South Africa	112	D5
Béthune	62	E4
Betioky	112	G4
Betoota	116	H5
Betpak-Dala	◙82	M8
Betroka	112	H4
Bet-She'an	100	C4
Bettiah	94	D3
Betul	94	C4
Betzdorf	60	C6
Beulah	40	C2
Beverley	64	M8
Beverungen	60	E5
Bexhill	62	C4
Bey Dağları	◪76	M8
Beyla	108	C3
Beyneu	82	J8
Beypazarı	76	P4
Beyrouth	■100	C3
Beyşehir	76	P7
Beyşehir Gölü	◪76	P7
Bezhetsk	78	G3
Béziers	66	J10
Bhadgaon	94	E4
Bhadrakh	94	E4
Bhadravati	94	C6
Bhagalpur	94	E3
Bhairab Bazar	94	F4
Bhakkar	94	B2
Bhamo	90	B2
Bharuch	94	B4
Bhatpara	94	E4
Bhavnagar	94	B4
Bhawanipatna	94	D5
Bhilai	94	D4
Bhilwara	94	B3
Bhīmavaram	94	D5
Bhind	94	C3
Bhiwandi	94	B5
Bhopal	94	C4
Bhubaneshwar	94	E4
Bhuj	94	A4
Bhusawal	94	C4
Bhutan	▲94	E3
Biak	92	(2)E3
Biak	◙92	(2)E3
Biała	◪58	K8
Biała Podlaska	58	N5
Białogard	58	F3
Białystok	58	N4
Biarritz	66	D10
Biasca	70	D4
Bibbiena	70	F6
Biberach	70	E2
Bicaz	74	P3
Bickerton Island	⊠116	G2
Bicske	74	F2
Bida	108	F3
Bidar	94	C5
Bidbid	101	H5
Biddeford	40	F2
Bideford	64	H10
Biedenkopf	60	D6
Biel	70	C3
Bielefeld	60	D4
Biella	70	D5
Bielsko-Biała	58	J8
Bielsk Podlaski	58	N5
Biên Hoa	90	D4
Bietigheim-Bissingen	70	E2
Big	◪34	G2
Biga	76	K4
Bigadiç	76	L5
Big Desert	◙116	H7
Big Falls	40	B1
Bighorn	◪36	E2
Bighorn Lake	◪38	E1
Bighorn Mountains	▲38	E2
Bight of Bangkok	◄90	C4
Bight of Benin	◄108	E3
Bight of Biafra	◄108	F4
Big Lake	44	(1)H2

Name	Page	Grid
Bignona	106	B6
Big Pine	42	E5
Big Rapids	40	C2
Big River	34	K6
Big Sandy	38	D1
Big Sioux	◪38	G2
Big Spring	44	F2
Big Sur	44	B1
Big Trout Lake	◪34	P6
Bihać	70	L6
Bijapur	94	C5
Bijar	98	M6
Bijeljina	74	G5
Bijelo Polje	74	G6
Bijie	86	D5
Bikaner	94	B3
Bikin	84	N7
Bikini	⊠114	G4
Bilaspur	94	D4
Biläsuvar	98	N4
Bila Tserkva	78	F5
Bilbao	68	H1
Bileća	74	F7
Bilecik	76	M4
Bilečko Jezero	◪74	F7
Biled	74	H4
Biłgoraj	58	M7
Bilhorod-Dnistrovs'kyy	78	F5
Bilina	60	J6
Billings	38	D1
Bill of Portland	◄64	K11
Bilma	104	B4
Biloxi	42	D3
Bimini Islands	⊠42	F4
Binche	62	G4
Bindi Bindi	116	C6
Bindura	112	E3
Bingen	60	C7
Binghamton	40	E2
Bingöl	98	J4
Binongko	◙92	(2)B4
Bintulu	92	(1)E2
Bintuni	92	(2)D3
Binyang	90	D2
Binzhou	86	F3
Biograd	70	L7
Birāk	106	H3
Birao	104	D5
Biratnagar	94	E3
Bi'r Baẕīrī	100	E2
Birdsville	116	G5
Bireun	92	(1)B1
Bīr Gifgâfa	100	A6
Birhan	▲104	A6
Bīr Hasana	100	A6
Bīrjand	96	G3
Birkenfeld	62	K5
Birmingham, United Kingdom	64	L9
Birmingham, United States	42	D3
Bir Mogrein	106	C3
Birnie	⊠114	J6
Birnin-Gwari	108	F2
Birnin Kebbi	108	E2
Birnin Konni	108	F2
Birnin Kudu	108	F2
Birobidzhan	84	N7
Birsk	78	L3
Biržai	58	P7
Bi'r Zaltan	104	C2
Bisbee	44	E2
Biscéglie	72	L7
Bischofshofen	70	J3
Bischofswerda	58	D6
Biševo	◙72	L6
Bishkek	■82	N9
Bishop	38	C3
Bishop Auckland	64	L7
Bishop's Stortford	62	C3
Biskra	106	G2
Bislig	90	H5
Bismarck	■36	F2
Bismarck Sea	◙114	E6
Bissau	■106	B6
Bistcho Lake	◪34	H5
Bistrița	74	M2
Bistrița	◪74	P3
Bitburg	62	J5
Bitche	60	C7
Bitkine	104	C5
Bitlis	98	K4
Bitola	76	D3
Bitonto	72	L7
Bitterfeld	60	H5
Bitterroot Range	▲38	C1
Bitti	72	D8
Bitung	92	(2)C2
Biu	108	G2
Biwa-ko	◙88	H6
Bixby	40	B3
Biyävra	94	C4

Name	Page
Biysk	82
Bizerte	106
Bjelovar	74
Bjørnøya	⊠82
B-Köpenick	60
Blackburn	64
Blackfoot	38
Blackfoot Reservoir	◪38
Black Hills	▲38
Blackpool	64
Black Range	▲44
Black River Falls	40
Black Rock Desert	◙38
Blacksburg	40
Black Sea	◙98
Blacks Harbour	40
Black Sugarloaf	▲116
Black Volta	◪108
Blackwater	◪64
Blagny-sur-Bresle	62
Blagodarnyy	98
Blagoevgrad	76
Blagoveshchenka	82
Blagoveshchensk	84
Blain	66
Blair	38
Blairsden	38
Blairsville	42
Błaj	74
Blakely	42
Blanco	◪50
Blanding	44
Blankenberge	62
Blankenburg	60
Blankenheim	62
Blantyre	112
Blasket Islands	⊠64
Blaubeuren	70
Blaye-et-Sainte-Luce	66
Bled	70
Blenheim	118
Blevands Huk	⊠60
Blida	106
Blind River	36
Bloemfontein	▢12
Bloemhof	112
Blois	66
Blönduós	56 (1
Błonie	58
Bloomfield	42
Bloomington, Ill., United States	40
Bloomington, Ind., United States	40
Bludenz	70
Blue Earth	40
Bluefield	40
Bluefields	46
Blue Mountain Lake	40
Blue Mountains	▲38
Blue Nile = Bahr el Azraq	◪104
Bluenose Lake	◪34
Bluff, New Zealand	118
Bluff, United States	44
Blumenau	52
Blythe	44
Blytheville	42
Bo	108
Boac	90
Boa Vista, Brazil	◙50
Boa Vista, Cape Verde Islands	▢108 (1
Bobbili	94
Bóbbio	70
Bobigny	62
Boblingen	70
Bobo Dioulasso	108
Bobr	◪58
Bobrov	78
Bôca do Acre	50
Boca Grande	◙46
Boca Grande	◙48
Bocaiúva	50
Bocaranga	110
Bochart	40
Bochnia	58
Bocholt	60
Bochum	60
Bodaybo	84
Bode	◪60
Bodélé	◪104
Boden	56
Bodham	94
Bodmin	64
Bodø	56
Bodrog	◪58
Bodrum	76
Boe	▲38
Boende	110
Bogale	90
Bogalusa	42

gabilla	116	K5
hni	68	P8
nor Regis	62	B4
o	90	G4
or	92	(1)D4
orodskoye	84	Q6
otá	50	C3
otol	82	R6
ra	94	E4
uchany	84	F5
ué	106	C5
Hai	86	F3
merwald	60	H7
ol	90	G5
umin	58	H8
açu	50	E4
se	38	C2
se City	44	F1
nürd	82	K10
atola	110	B4
é	108	B2
spits	112	C5
ungu	110	C4
pec	62	C5
e, China	82	Q9
e, Ghana	108	D3
chiv	58	N8
asławiec	58	E6
gatanga	108	D2
rad	74	R4
ntin-Vale	74	N5
var	40	B3
via	50	D7
ène	66	K9
nås	56	J6
men	56	G8
nisi	98	L3
obo	108	H5
ogna	70	G6
ognesi	50	C5
omba	108	H4
otnoye	82	Q6
shaya Pyssa	78	J2
sherech'ye	78	P3
shezemel'skaya Tundra	82	J4
Shirta	84	C4
shoy Atlym	78	N2
shoy Osinovaya	84	W3
shoy Vlas'evo	84	Q6
shoy Yuga	78	P2
sover	62	A1
on	64	K8
J	98	D3
vadin	76	P6
rano = Bozen	70	G4
na	108	G6
nbala	116	J7
nbay = Mumbai	94	B5
nili	110	D3
n Jesus da Lapa	50	J6
nlo	56	C7
nnak	84	M6
náb	98	M5
aaparte Archipelago	116	B2
avista Bay	34	W7
adeno	70	G6
ido	110	C3
ndokodi	116	C1
ndoukou	108	D3
adowoso	92	(1)E4
ngandanga	110	C3
ngao	92	(2)A1
gor	108	H2
ifacio	72	D7
n	60	C6
ners Ferry	38	C1
orva	72	C8
the	108	B3
toc	90	G3
yhád	74	F3
ne	40	D3
nville	42	C2
rama	110	G2
saaso	96	E7
thia Peninsula	34	M2
ué	108	G5
pard	60	C6
, Russia	84	D4
, Sudan	110	E2
, Turkey	76	S7
, Yugoslavia	74	K5
ah Peak	38	C3
ås	56	G8
äzjän	101	D2
deaux	66	E9
den Peninsula	34	Q2
der Town	116	H7
dj Bou Arréridj	106	F1
dj Bounaam	68	M9
dj Flye Sante Marie	106	E3
dj Messaouda	106	G2

Bordj Mokhtar	106	F4
Bordj Omar Driss	106	G3
Borgarnes	56	(1)C2
Borger	44	F1
Borgomanero	70	D5
Borgo San Dalmazzo	70	C6
Borgo San Lorenzo	70	G7
Borgosésia	70	D5
Borgo Val di Taro	70	E6
Bori Jenein	106	H2
Borislav	58	N8
Borisoglebsk	78	H4
Borjomi	98	K3
Borken	62	J3
Borkou	104	C4
Borkum	62	J1
Borlänge	56	H6
Bórmida	70	D6
Bórmio	70	F4
Borna	60	H5
Borneo	92	(1)E3
Bornholm	56	H9
Borodino	82	R5
Borodinskoye	56	Q6
Boromo	108	D2
Borovichi	78	F3
Borovskoy	78	M4
Borriana	68	K5
Borroloola	116	G3
Borşa	74	M2
Borshchiv	74	P1
Borshchovochnyy Khrebet	84	J7
Bordêyri	56	(1)C2
Borüjerd	96	E3
Borzya	84	K6
Bosa	72	C8
Bosanska Dubica	74	D4
Bosanska Gradiška	74	E4
Bosanska Kostajnica	70	M5
Bosanska Krupa	74	D5
Bosanski Brod	74	F4
Bosanski Novi	74	D4
Bosanski Petrovac	74	D5
Bosansko Grahovo	70	M6
Boşca	74	J4
Bose	90	D2
Bosilegrad	74	K7
Boskovice	58	F8
Bosna	74	E5
Bosnia-Herzegovina	74	E5
Bosobolo	110	B3
Bosporus = İstanbul Boğazı	76	M3
Bosporus	96	A1
Bossambélé	110	B2
Bossangoa	110	B2
Bossier City	42	C3
Bosten Hu	82	R9
Boston, United Kingdom	64	M9
Boston, United States	40	F2
Botevgrad	74	L7
Botlikh	96	E1
Botna	74	R3
Botoşani	74	P2
Botou	86	F3
Botrange	62	J4
Botswana	112	C4
Bottrop	62	J3
Bou Ahmed	68	F9
Bouaké	108	C3
Bouar	110	B2
Bouârfa	106	E2
Boufarik	68	N8
Bougainville Island	114	F6
Bougainville Reef	115	J3
Bougouni	108	C2
Bougzoul	68	N9
Bouira	106	F1
Bou Ismaïl	68	N8
Bou Izakarn	106	D3
Boujdour	106	C3
Bou Kadir	68	M8
Boulder	38	E2
Boulder City	44	D1
Boulia	116	G4
Boulogne-sur-Mer	62	D4
Bounty Islands	114	H10
Bourem	106	E5
Bourg-de-Piage	66	L9
Bourg-en-Bresse	66	L7
Bourges	66	H6
Bourgoin-Jallieu	66	L8
Bournemouth	64	L11
Bou Saâda	106	F1
Boussu	62	F4
Boutilimit	106	C5
Bouzghaïa	68	M8
Bowbells	38	F1
Bowen	116	J4

Bowie, Ariz., United States	44	E2
Bowie, Tex., United States	44	G2
Bowkan	98	M5
Bowling Green, Fla., United States	42	E4
Bowling Green, Ky., United States	42	D2
Bowling Green, Mo., United States	42	C2
Bowman	38	F1
Bowman Bay	34	R3
Bo Xian	86	F4
Boxwood Hill	116	C6
Boyabat	98	F3
Boyang	86	F5
Boyarka	84	F2
Boysen Reservoir	38	E2
Boyuibe	52	J3
Bozcaada	76	H5
Boz Dağ	76	M7
Bozeman	38	D1
Bozen	70	G4
Bozkır	76	Q7
Bozoum	110	B2
Bozüyük	76	N5
Bra	70	C6
Brač	74	D6
Bracciano	72	G6
Bräcke	56	H5
Brad	74	K3
Brádano	72	L8
Bradford	64	L8
Brady	42	B3
Braga	68	B3
Bragança, Brazil	50	H4
Bragança, Portugal	68	D3
Brahmapur	94	D5
Brahmaputra	94	F3
Bräila	74	Q4
Brainerd	40	B1
Braintree	62	C3
Brake	60	D3
Bramming	60	D1
Brampton	40	E2
Bramsche	60	H4
Branco	50	E3
Brandberg	112	A4
Brandenburg	60	H4
Brandenton	42	E4
Brandon	34	M7
Brandvlei	112	C5
Brandýs	58	D7
Braniewo	58	J3
Brasileia	50	D6
Brasília	50	H7
Braslaw	56	P9
Braşov	74	N4
Bratislava	58	G9
Bratsk	84	G5
Bratskoye Vodokhranilishche	84	G5
Brattleboro	40	F2
Braţul	74	R4
Braunau	70	J2
Braunschweig	60	F4
Brawley	44	C2
Bray	64	F8
Brazil	48	G4
Brazzaville	110	B4
Brčko	74	F5
Brda	58	G4
Bream Bay	118	E2
Breckenridge	44	G2
Břeclav	58	F9
Breda	62	G3
Bredasdorp	112	C6
Bredstedt	60	E2
Bredy	78	M4
Bree	62	H3
Bregenz	70	E3
Breiðafjörður	56	(1)A2
Bremangerlandet	56	B6
Bremen, Germany	60	D3
Bremen, United States	42	D3
Bremerhaven	60	D3
Bremerton	38	B1
Bremervörde	60	E3
Brenham	42	B3
Brennero	70	G4
Brenner	70	G4
Brentwood	62	C3
Brescia	70	F5
Breslau = Wrocław	58	G6
Bressanone = Brixen	72	F2
Bressay	64	M1
Bressuire	66	E7
Brest, Belarus	78	D4
Brest, France	66	A5
Breteuil	62	E5
Bretten	60	D7

Breves	50	G4
Brewarrina	116	J5
Brewton	42	D3
Brežice	74	C4
Brézina	106	F2
Brezno	58	J9
Bria	110	C2
Briançon	70	B6
Briceni	74	Q1
Bridgend	64	J10
Bridgeport, Calif., United States	44	C1
Bridgeport, Conn., United States	40	F2
Bridgeport, Nebr., United States	38	F2
Bridgetown	50	F1
Bridgewater	34	U8
Bridgwater	64	J10
Bridlington	64	M7
Brienzer See	70	D4
Brig	70	C4
Brigham City	38	D2
Brighton, United Kingdom	62	B4
Brighton, United States	38	F3
Brignoles	70	B7
Brikama	108	A2
Brilon	60	D5
Brindisi	72	M8
Brinkley	42	C3
Brisbane	16	K5
Bristol, United Kingdom	64	K10
Bristol, United States	42	E2
Bristol Bay	44	(1)E4
Bristol Channel	64	H10
British Columbia	34	F5
Britstown	112	C6
Brive-la-Gaillarde	66	G8
Briviesca	68	G2
Brixen	70	G4
Brixham	64	J11
Brlik	82	N9
Brno	58	F8
Broad Sound	116	J4
Broadus	38	E1
Brockton	40	F2
Brockville	40	E2
Brod	74	J9
Brodeur Peninsula	34	P2
Brodick	64	G6
Brodnica	58	J4
Broken Arrow	46	E1
Broken Bow	42	C3
Broken Hill	116	H6
Brokopondo	50	F2
Bromölla	58	D1
Bromsgrove	64	K9
Brønderslev	56	E8
Brooke's Point	90	F5
Brookhaven	36	H5
Brookhaven	42	C3
Brookhaven	46	F2
Brookings, Oreg., United States	38	B2
Brookings, S.D., United States	38	G2
Brooks	34	J6
Brooks Range	44	(1)F2
Brooksville	42	E4
Broome	116	D3
Brösarp	56	H9
Brovary	78	F4
Brownfield	44	F2
Browning	38	D1
Brownsville, Tenn., United States	42	D2
Brownsville, Tex., United States	42	B4
Brownwood	42	B3
Bruchsal	60	D7
Bruck, Austria	70	L3
Bruck, Austria	70	M2
Bruck an der Mur	74	C2
Brugge	62	F3
Brühl	62	J4
Bruint	94	G3
Brumado	50	J6
Brumath	62	C2
Bruneau	38	C2
Bruneck	70	G4
Brunei	92	(1)E2
Brunflo	56	H5
Brunico = Bruneck	72	F2
Brunsbüttel	60	E3
Brunswick, Ga., United States	42	E3
Brunswick, Me., United States	40	G2
Bruntal	58	G8
Brush	38	F2
Brussels = Bruxelles	62	G4
Bruxelles	62	G4

Bryan	42	B3	Burglengenfeld	60	H7	Cabezas	50	E7	Caldwell, Id.,		
Bryanka	82	S6	Burgos	68	G2	Cabimas	50	C1	*United States*	38	
Bryansk	78	F4	Burgsvik	56	K8	Cabinda	▣08	G6	Caldwell, Kans.,		
Brzeg	58	G7	Burhaniye	76	K5	Cabinda	▣108	G6	*United States*	42	
Brzeg Dolny	58	F6	Burhanpur	94	C4	Cabo Bascuñán	⊟52	G4	Calf of Man	⊟64	
Brzeziny	58	J6	Burjassot	68	K5	Cabo Beata	⊟46	K5	Calgary	34	
B-Spandau	58	C5	Burj Sāfītā	100	D2	Cabo Camarón	⊟46	G5	Calhoun	42	
Bubi	⊿112	E4	Burketown	116	G3	Cabo Carvoeiro	⊟68	A5	Calhoun City	42	
Bucak	98	D5	Burkeville	40	E3	Cabo Catoche	⊟46	G4	Calhoun Falls	42	
Bucaramanga	50	C2	Bur-Khaybyt	84	P3	Cabo Corrientes,			Cali	50	
Buchanan	108	B3	Burkina	▲108	D2	*Colombia*	⊟50	B2	Calicut = Kozhikode	94	
Buchan Gulf	⊟34	S2	Burlin	78	K4	Cabo Corrientes, *Mexico*	⊟46	C4	Caliente	38	
Bucharest = Bucureşti	■74	P5	Burlington, *Colo.*,			Cabo Corrubedo	⊟68	A2	California	■36	
Buchen	60	E7	*United States*	44	F1	Cabo Cruz	⊟46	J5	Calilabad	98	
Buchholz	60	E3	Burlington, *Ia.*,			Cabo de Espichel	⊟68	A6	Callao	50	
Buchy	66	M5	*United States*	40	B2	Cabo de Gata	⊟68	H8	Caloundra	116	
Bückeburg	60	E4	Burlington, *Vt.*,			Cabo de Hornos	⊟52	H10	Caltagirone	72	
Bucureşti	■74	P5	*United States*	40	F2	Cabo de la Nao	⊟68	L6	Caltanissetta	72	
Budapest	■74	G2	Burma = Myanmar	▲90	B2	Cabo Delgado	⊟112	G2	Caluquembe	112	
Budennovsk	98	L1	Burnet	42	B3	Cabo de Palos	⊟68	K7	Caluula	110	
Büdingen	60	E6	Burney	38	B2	Cabo de São Roque	⊟50	K5	Calvi	72	
Budrio	70	G6	Burnie	116	J8	Cabo de Sao Tomé	⊟52	N3	Calvin	42	
Buenaventura, *Colombia*	50	B3	Burns	38	C2	Cabo de São Vicente	⊟68	A7	Calvinia	112	
Buenaventura, *Mexico*	44	E3	Burns Junction	38	C2	Cabo de Trafalgar	⊟68	D8	Calw	70	
Buena Vista	38	E3	Burns Lake	34	F6	Cabo dos Bahías	⊟52	H8	Camaçari	50	
Buenos Aires	■52	K5	Burqin	82	R8	Cabo Fisterra	⊟68	A2	Camacupa	112	
Buffalo, *Okla.*,			Burra	116	G6	Cabo Frio	⊟52	N3	Camagüey	46	
United States	42	B2	Burrel	76	C3	Cabo Gracias á Dios	⊟46	H6	Camaiore	70	
Buffalo, *N.Y.*,			Bursa	76	M4	Cabo Mondego	⊟68	A4	Camana	50	
United States	40	E2	Bür Safāga	104	F2	Cabo Norte	⊟50	H3	Camargue	▣66	
Buffalo, *S.D.*,			Bür Sa'īd	104	F1	Cabo Orange	⊟50	G3	Camariñas	68	
United States	38	F1	Bur Sudan	104	G4	Cabo Ortegal	⊟68	B1	Camarones	52	
Buffalo, *Tex.*,			Burtnieks	⊟56	N8	Cabo Peñas	⊟68	E1	Ca Mau	90	
United States	42	B3	Burton-upon-Trent	64	L9	Caborca	44	D2	Camberley	64	
Buffalo, *Wyo.*,			Buru	⊡92	(2)C3	Cabo Rojo	⊟46	E4	Cambodia	▲90	
United States	38	E2	Burundi	▲110	D4	Cabo Roxo	⊟108	A2	Cambrai	62	
Buffalo Lake	⊿34	J4	Bururi	110	D4	Cabo San Diego	⊟52	H9	Cambria	38	
Buffalo Narrows	34	K5	Burwell	38	G2	Cabo San Francisco de			Cambrian Mountains	◣64	
Buftea	74	N5	Buryatiya	■84	J6	Paula	⊟52	H8	Cambridge, *New Zealand*	118	
Bug	⊿58	L5	Bury St. Edmunds	62	C2	Cabo San Juan	⊟108	F4	Cambridge,		
Bugojno	74	E5	Büshehr	101	D2	Cabo San Lucas	⊟36	D7	*United Kingdom*	64	
Bugrino	82	H4	Bushire = Büshehr	101	D2	Cabo Santa Elena	⊟46	J7	Cambridge, *Md.*,		
Bugul'ma	78	K4	Businga	110	C3	Cabo Tortosa	⊟68	L4	*United States*	40	
Buguruslan	78	K4	Busira	⊿110	C4	Cabo Tres Puntas	⊟52	H8	Cambridge, *Mass.*,		
Buḩayrat al Asad	⊿98	H5	Buşrá ash Shām	100	D4	Cabot Strait	⊟34	U7	*United States*	40	
Buḩayrat ath Tharthār	⊿98	K6	Bussum	62	H2	Cabrera	⊟68	N5	Cambridge, *Oh.*,		
Buhuşi	74	P3	Busto Arsizio	70	D5	Čačak	74	H6	*United States*	40	
Builth Wells	64	J9	Buta	110	D3	Cáceres, *Brazil*	50	F7	Cambridge Bay	34	
Buinsk	78	J3	Butare	110	D4	Cáceres, *Spain*	68	D5	Cambrils	68	
Buir Nur	⊟86	F1	Butaritari	⊡114	H9	Cachimbo	50	G5	Camden, *Ark.*,		
Bujanovac	74	J7	Bute	⊡64	G6	Cachoeira do Sul	52	L4	*United States*	42	
Buje	70	J5	Butembo	110	D3	Cachoeiro de Itapemirim	50	J8	Camden, *S.C.*,		
Bujumbura	■110	D4	Buðardalur	56	(1)C2	Cacola	112	B2	*United States*	42	
Bukachacha	84	K6	Buton	⊡92	(2)B3	Caconda	112	B2	Cameron, *La.*,		
Bukavu	110	D4	Butte, *Mont.*,			Čadca	58	H8	*United States*	42	
Bukhara	96	H2	*United States*	38	D1	Cadillac, *Mich.*,			Cameron, *Mo.*,		
Bukkittinggi	92	(1)C3	Butte, *Nebr.*,			*United States*	40	C2	*United States*	42	
Bukoba	110	E4	*United States*	38	G2	Cadillac, *Mont.*,			Cameron, *Tex.*,		
Bula, *Indonesia*	92	(2)D3	Butuan	90	H5	*United States*	36	E2	*United States*	42	
Bula, *Papua New Guinea*	92	(2)F4	Butwal	94	D3	Cádiz	68	D8	Cameroon	▲108	
Bülach	70	D3	Butzbach	60	D6	Caen	62	B5	Cametá	50	
Bulawayo	112	D4	Bützow	60	G3	Caernarfon	64	H8	Çamiçigölü	⊿76	
Buldir Island	⊡84	X6	Buulobarde	110	H3	Cagayan de Oro	90	G5	Caminha	68	
Bulgan	84	G7	Buxton	62	A1	Cagli	70	H7	Camiranga	50	
Bulgaria	▲74	M7	Buy	78	H3	Cagliari	72	D9	Camocim	50	
Buli	92	(2)C2	Buynaksk	98	M2	Cagnes-sur-Mer	70	C7	Camooweal	116	
Bulle	70	C4	Büyükada	⊟76	L4	Caguas	46	L5	Camopi	50	
Bullhead City	44	D1	Büyükçekmece	76	L4	Cahama	112	A3	Campbell Island	⊡118	(2)
Bulls	118	E5	Buzai Gumbad	96	K2	Cahors	66	G9	Campbell River	34	
Bulukumba	92	(2)B4	Buzançais	66	G7	Cahuapanas	50	B5	Campbellsville	40	
Bulun	84	M2	Buzău	74	P4	Cahul	74	R4	Campbellton	40	
Bumba	110	C3	Buzău	⊿74	Q4	Caia	112	F3	Campbeltown	64	
Bumbeşti Jiu	74	L4	Buzuluk	78	K4	Caianda	112	C2	Campeche	46	
Buna	110	F3	Byala	74	N6	Caicos Islands	⊟46	K4	Câmpeni	74	
Bunbury	116	C6	Byala Slatina	74	L6	Cairns	116	J3	Câmpia Turzii	74	
Buncrana	64	E6	Byam Martin Island	⊡34	L2	Cairo = El Qâhira	■104	F1	Campina Grande	50	
Bunda	110	E4	Byaroza	56	N10	Cairo	42	D2	Campinas	50	
Bundaberg	116	K4	Bydgoszcz	58	H4	Caiundo	112	B3	Campobasso	72	
Bünde	60	D4	Bygdin	⊿56	D6	Cajamarca	50	B5	Campo de Criptana	68	
Bungunya	116	J5	Bygland	56	D7	Cakovec	74	D3	Campo de Diauarum	50	
Bunia	110	E3	Bykovskiy	84	M2	Calabar	108	F3	Campo Gallo	52	
Bunkie	42	C3	Bylot Island	⊡34	R2	Calabozo	50	D2	Campo Grande	▣52	
Bunnell	42	E4	Byskeälven	⊿56	L4	Calafat	74	K6	Campo Maior	50	
Bünyan	98	F4	Bystrīce	58	G8	Calahorra	68	J2	Campo Mourão	52	
Buôn Mê Thuột	90	D4	Bystrzyca Kłodzka	58	F7	Calais	62	D4	Campos	52	
Buotama	⊿84	M4	Bytatay	⊿84	N3	Calais	40	H3	Câmpulung	74	
Bura	110	F4	Bytča	58	H8	Calamar	50	C3	Câmpulung Moldovenesc	74	
Buran	82	R8	Bytom	58	H7	Calamian Group	⊟90	F4	Cam Ranh	90	
Buranj	94	D2	Bytów	58	G3	Calamocha	68	J4	Çan	76	
Burao	110	H2	Bzura	⊿58	J5	Cālan	74	L4	Canada	▲32	
Burāq	100	D3				Calanscio Sand Sea	▣104	D2	Canadian	44	
Buraydah	96	D4	**C**			Calapan	90	G4	Canadian	⊿44	
Burco	104	J6				Călăraşi, *Moldova*	74	R2	Çanakkale	76	
Burdur	98	D5	Caaguazú	52	K4	Călăraşi, *Romania*	74	Q5	Çanakkale Boğazı	⊟76	
Burdur Gölü	⊟76	N7	Caaballococha	50	C5	Calatafim	72	G11	Canal de Panamá	⊟46	
Burē	104	G5	Caballo Reservoir	⊿44	E2	Calatayud	68	J3	Cananea	44	
Büren	62	L3	Cabanatuan	90	G3	Calauag	90	G4	Canary Islands =		
Burg	60	G4	Cabano	40	G1	Calbayog	90	G4	Islas Canarias	⊡102	
Burgas	74	Q7	Cabañaquinta	68	E1	Calçoene	50	G3	Canary Islands =		
Burgaski Zaliv	⊟74	Q7	Cabdul Qaadir	104	H5	Calcutta	94	K4	Islas Canarias	▣106	
Burgdorf	70	C3	Cabeza del Buey	68	E6	Caldas da Rainha	68	A5	Cañaveras	68	
Burghausen	70	H2				Caldera	52	G4			

Name	Page	Grid
nberra	■116	J7
ncún	46	G4
ndarli Körfezi	◄76	J6
ndelaro	Z74	C8
ndlemas Island	48	J9
ngamba	112	B2
ngas	68	B2
ngas de Narcea	68	D1
nguyuan	90	B2
ngzhou	86	F3
nicatti	72	H11
nindé	50	K4
nkiri	98	E3
nna	64	F4
nnanore	94	B6
nnanore	94	C6
nnes	70	C7
nnock	62	A2
non City	44	E1
ntanduanes	90	G4
nterbury	62	D3
nterbury Bight	◄118	C7
nterbury Plains	118	C6
n Tho	90	D5
nton, *Miss.*, United States	42	D3
nton, *Oh.*, United States	42	E1
nton, *S.D.*, United States	38	G2
numã	50	F4
numã	Z50	F5
nutama	50	E5
nyon	44	F1
nyon Ferry Lake	38	D1
o Bǎng	90	D2
orle	70	H5
o Blanc	72	D11
o Bon	►106	H1
o Corse	72	D5
o d'Agde	66	J10
o d'Antifer	62	C5
o de Fer	106	G1
o de Formentor	68	P5
o de la Hague	66	D4
o-de-la-Madeleine	40	F1
o de Nouvelle-France	34	S4
o de ses Salines	68	P5
o des Trois Fourches	68	H9
oe Agulhas	112	C6
oe Alexandra	52	P9
oe Andreas	96	B2
oe Apostolos Andreas	98	F6
oe Arid	116	D6
oe Arnaoutis	98	D6
oe Arnhem	116	G2
oe Barren Island	116	J8
oe Bauld	34	V6
oe Blanco	38	B2
oe Borda	116	G7
oe Breton Island	34	U7
oe Brett	118	E2
oe Byron	116	K5
oe Campbell	118	E5
oe Canaveral	42	E4
oe Canaveral	42	E4
oe Carnot	116	F6
oe Charles	40	E3
oe Chidley	34	U4
oe Christian	34	T2
oe Churchill	34	N5
oe Clear	64	C10
oe Cleare	44	(1)H4
oe Coast	108	D3
oe Cod	40	G2
oe Columbine	112	B6
oe Colville	118	E3
oe Comorin	94	C7
oe Constantine	44	(1)E4
oe Coral	42	E4
oe Crawford	116	G3
oe Croker	116	F2
oe Dalhousie	44	(1)L1
oe Direction	116	H2
oe Disappointment	52	P9
oe Dominion	34	R3
oe Dorchester	34	Q3
oe Dorset	34	R4
oe Dyer	34	U3
oe Egmont	118	D4
oe Eleaia	100	B1
oe Farewell, *Greenland*	32	F4
oe Farewell, *New Zealand*	118	D5
oe Fear	42	F3
oe Finisterre = Cabo Fisterra	68	A2
oe Flattery, *Australia*	116	J2
oe Flattery, *United States*	38	A1
oe Forestier	116	J8
Cape Foulwind	118	C5
Cape Fría	112	A3
Cape Girardeau	40	C3
Cape Greko	98	F6
Cape Grenville	116	H2
Cape Grim	116	H8
Cape Harrison	34	V6
Cape Hatteras	42	F2
Cape Henrietta Maria	34	Q5
Cape Horn = Cabo de Hornos	52	H10
Cape Howe	116	K7
Cape Inscription	116	B5
Cape Jaffa	116	G7
Cape Karikari	118	D2
Cape Kellett	34	F2
Cape Kidnappers	118	F4
Cape Leeuwin	116	B6
Cape Lévêque	116	D3
Cape Londonderry	116	E2
Cape Lookout	46	J2
Cape May	40	F3
Cape Mendenhall	44	(1)D4
Cape Mendocino	38	A2
Cape Mercy	34	U4
Cape Meredith	52	J9
Cape Naturaliste	116	B6
Capenda-Camulemba	112	B1
Cape Negrais	90	A3
Cape Nelson	116	H7
Cape Newenham	44	(1)E4
Cape of Good Hope	112	B6
Cape Palliser	118	E5
Cape Palmas	108	C4
Cape Parry	34	G2
Cape Providence	118	A8
Cape Race	32	G5
Cape Ray	34	V7
Cape Reinga	118	D2
Cape Romanzof	44	(1)D3
Cape Runaway	118	G3
Cape Sable	34	T8
Cape St. Elias	44	(1)J4
Cape St. Francis	112	C6
Cape San Agustin	90	H5
Cape San Blas	42	D4
Cape Saunders	118	C7
Cape Scott	116	E1
Cape Stephens	118	D5
Cape Terawhiti	118	E5
Cape Three Points	108	D4
Cape Town	■112	B6
Cape Turnagain	118	F5
Cape Verde	▲108	(1)B2
Cape Wessel	116	G2
Cape Wrangell	84	W6
Cape Wrath	64	G3
Cape York	116	H1
Cape York Peninsula	116	H2
Cap Figalo	68	J9
Cap Fréhel	66	C5
Cap Gris-Nez	62	E4
Cap-Haïtien	46	K5
Cap Juby	106	C3
Cap Lopez	108	F5
Cap Negro	68	E9
Capo Carbonara	72	D10
Capo Colonna	72	M9
Capo Gallo	72	H10
Capo Granitola	72	G11
Capo Murro di Porco	72	K11
Capo Palinuro	72	J8
Capo Passero	72	K12
Capo Santa Maria di Leuca	72	N9
Capo San Vito	72	G10
Capo Spartivento	72	G10
Capo Vaticano	72	K10
Capraia	72	D5
Cap Rhir	106	C2
Capri	72	J8
Capricorn Group	116	K4
Cap Rosa	72	C11
Cap Serrat	72	D11
Cap Spartel	68	E9
Cap Timiris	106	B5
Capua	72	J7
Cap Verga	108	B2
Cap Vert	108	A2
Caquetá	Z50	C2
Caracal	74	M5
Caracarai	50	E3
Caracas	■50	D1
Caransebeş	74	K4
Carauari	50	D4
Caravaca de la Cruz	68	J6
Caravelas	50	K7
Carazinho	52	L4
Carballiño	68	B2
Carballo	68	B1
Carbondale, *Ill.*, United States	42	D2
Carbondale, *Pa.*, United States	42	F1
Carboneras	68	J7
Carbónia	72	C9
Carcar	90	G4
Carcassonne	66	H10
Cardiff	◎64	J10
Cardigan Bay	◄64	H9
Cardston	38	D1
Carei	74	K2
Carentan	66	D4
Cariacica	52	N3
Cariati	72	L9
Caribbean Sea	■46	J6
Carlet	68	K5
Carleton Place	40	E1
Carlisle, *United Kingdom*	64	K7
Carlisle, *United States*	40	E2
Carlow	64	F9
Carlsbad	44	F2
Carlyle	38	F1
Carmacks	34	D4
Carmagnola	70	C6
Carmarthen	64	H10
Carmarthen Bay	◄64	G10
Carmaux	66	H9
Carmen	■46	B3
Carmona	68	E7
Carnarvon, *Australia*	116	B4
Carnarvon, *South Africa*	112	C6
Car Nicobar	94	F7
Carnot	110	B2
Carnsore Point	64	F9
Carolina	50	H5
Caroline Beach	42	F3
Caroline Island	114	L6
Caroline Islands	114	E5
Carpathian Mountains	▲58	J8
Carpatii Meridionali	▲74	K3
Carpentras	66	L9
Carpi	70	F6
Carrabelle	42	E4
Carrara	70	F6
Carrickfergus	64	G7
Carrick-on-Suir	64	E9
Carrington	38	G1
Carrizozo	44	E2
Carroll	40	B2
Carrollton, *Ky.*, United States	40	D3
Carrollton, *Mo.*, United States	42	C1
Çarşamba	98	G3
Carson City	◎38	C3
Cartagena, *Colombia*	50	B1
Cartagena, *Spain*	68	K7
Carthage	42	C3
Cartwright	34	V6
Caruarú	50	K5
Carúpano	50	E1
Casablanca	106	D2
Casa Grande	44	D2
Casale Monferrato	70	D5
Casalmaggiore	70	F6
Casarano	72	N9
Cascade, *Id.*, United States	38	C2
Cascade, *Mont.*, United States	38	C1
Cascade Range	▲38	B2
Cascade Reservoir	☑38	C2
Cascais	68	A6
Cascavel	52	L3
Cáscara	72	J7
Cashel	112	E3
Casino	116	K5
Cásma	50	M5
Casper	38	E2
Caspian Sea	◄54	J3
Cassiar	34	F5
Cassino	72	H7
Castanhal	50	H4
Castelbuono	72	J11
Castel di Sango	72	J7
Castellammare del Golio	72	G10
Castellane	70	B7
Castellaneta	72	L8
Castelli	52	J4
Castelló de la Plana	68	K5
Castelnaudary	66	G10
Castelo Branco	68	C5
Castelsarrasin	66	G10
Castelvetrano	72	G11
Castets	66	D10
Castiglion Fiorentino	70	G7
Castilla	72	J6
Castlebar	64	C8
Castleford	64	L8
Castle Point	118	F5
Castres	66	H10
Castricum	■46	G2
Castries	■46	M6
Castro	52	M3
Castro Verde	68	B7
Castrovíllari	72	L9
Castuera	68	E6
Catamarca	52	H4
Catandica	112	E3
Catánia	72	K11
Catanzaro	72	L10
Catanzaro Marina	72	L10
Catarman	90	G4
Catbalogan	90	H4
Cat Island	42	F5
Cat Lake	34	N6
Cato Island	116	L4
Catriló	52	J6
Catskill Mountains	▲36	M3
Cattólica	70	H7
Cauayan	90	G5
Cauca	Z50	C2
Caucaia	50	K4
Caucasia	50	B2
Caucasus	▲98	K2
Caudry	62	F4
Cauquenes	52	G6
Caura	Z50	E2
Causapscal	40	G1
Cǎuşeni	74	S3
Cavaillon	66	L10
Cavalese	70	G4
Cavan	64	E8
Cavárzere	70	H5
Cave	118	C7
Cavinas	50	D6
Cavtat	74	F7
Caxias	50	J4
Caxias do Sul	52	L4
Caxito	108	G6
Çay	76	P6
Cayce	42	E3
Çaycuma	76	Q3
Cayenne	◎50	G3
Cayman Islands	46	H5
Caynabo	110	H2
Cayos Miskitos	46	H6
Cay Sal Bank	42	E5
Cazorla	68	H7
Ceanannus Mor	64	F8
Ceará	■50	J4
Cebu	90	G4
Cebu	90	G4
Cécina	70	F7
Cedar City	38	D3
Cedar Falls	40	B2
Cedar Lake	34	L6
Cedar Rapids	40	B2
Cedros	36	C6
Ceduna	116	F6
Ceerigaabo	110	H1
Cefalù	72	J10
Cegléd	74	G2
Celaya	46	D4
Celebes = Sulawesi	92	(2)A3
Celebes Sea	92	(2)B2
Celje	74	C3
Celldömölk	74	E2
Celle	60	F4
Celtic Sea	■64	E10
Centerville	40	B2
Cento	70	G6
Central African Republic	▲110	C2
Central City	38	G2
Centralia, *Ill.*, United States	40	C3
Centralia, *Wash.*, United States	38	B1
Central Range	▲92	(2)F3
Central Siberian Plateau = Srednesibirskoye Ploskogor'ye	80	N2
Cenxi	90	E2
Ceres, *Argentina*	52	J4
Ceres, *Brazil*	50	H7
Cerezo de Abajo	68	G3
Cerignola	72	K7
Çerikli	98	E4
Çerkes	76	Q4
Çerkezköy	76	K3
Cernavodǎ	74	R5
Cero Champaqui	▲52	J5
Cerralvo	36	E7
Cěrrik	76	C3
Cerritos	44	F4
Cerro Aconcagua	▲52	G5
Cerro Bonete	▲52	H4
Cerro de la Encantada	▲36	C5
Cerro de Pasco	50	B6
Cerro Huehuento	▲46	C4
Cerro Las Tórtolas	▲52	H5
Cerro Marahuaca	▲50	D3
Cerro Mercedario	▲52	G5
Cerro Murallón	▲52	G8
Cerro Nevado	▲52	H6

131

Cerro Pena Nevade ▲ 46 D4
Cerro San Lorenzo ▲ 52 G8
Cerro San Valentín ▲ 52 G8
Cerros de Bala ▲ 50 D6
Cerro Tres Picos ▲ 52 J6
Cerro Tupungato ▲ 52 H5
Cerro Yaví ▲ 50 D2
Cerro Yogan ▲ 52 H9
Certaldo 70 G7
Cervaro ◪ 72 K7
Cervia 70 H6
Cervionne 72 D6
Cervo 68 C1
Cesena 70 H6
Cesenático 70 H6
Cēsis 56 N8
Česká Lípa 60 K6
České Budějovice 70 K2
Český Krumlov 70 K2
Çeşme 76 J6
Česna ◪ 70 M5
Cessano ◪ 70 J7
Cessnock 116 K6
Cetate 74 L5
Cetinje 74 F7
Cetraro 72 K9
Ceuta 106 D1
Cevizli 76 P7
Chachapoyas 50 B5
Chaco Boreal ▣ 52 K3
Chad ▲ 104 C5
Chadan 82 S7
Chadron 38 F2
Chagai 96 H4
Chagda 84 N5
Chaghcharān 96 J3
Chagyl 96 G1
Chāh Bahār 96 H4
Chāībāsa 94 E4
Chainat 90 C3
Chaiyaphum 90 C3
Chalais 66 F8
Chalhuanca 50 C6
Chalinze 110 F5
Chalki ▣ 76 K8
Chalkida 76 F6
Chalkidiki ▣ 76 F4
Challans 66 D7
Challapata 50 D7
Challenger Deep ▣ 114 E4
Challis 38 D2
Châlons-sur-Marne 62 G6
Chalon-sur-Saône 62 K7
Cham 60 H7
Chama 112 E2
Chamba 94 C2
Chambal ◪ 94 C3
Chamberlain 38 G2
Chambersburg 40 E3
Chambéry 70 A5
Chambly 62 E5
Chamonix 70 B5
Champagnole 70 A4
Champaign 40 C2
Champaubert 62 F6
Champlitte 70 A3
Chañaral 52 G4
Chandalar ◪ 34 B3
Chandeleur Islands ▲ 46 G3
Chandigarh 94 C2
Chandler 44 D2
Chandrapur 94 C5
Changane ◪ 112 E4
Changara 112 E3
Changchun 88 C2
Changde 86 E5
Chang-hua 86 G6
Chang Jiang ◪ 86 D4
Changsha 86 E5
Changshu 86 G4
Changting 86 F5
Changzhi 86 E3
Changzhou 86 F4
Chania 76 G9
Channel Islands, United Kingdom ▣ 64 K12
Channel Islands, United States ▣ 36 C5
Channel-Port aux Basques 34 V7
Chanthaburi 90 C4
Chantilly 62 E5
Chanute 42 B2
Chao Phraya ◪ 90 C4
Chaouèn 106 D1
Chao Xian 86 F4
Chaoyang 86 G2
Chaozhou 86 F6
Chapada Diamantina ▲ 50 J6
Chapais 40 F1
Chapayev 78 K4
Chapayevo 84 K4

Chapayevskoye 82 N7
Chapecó 52 L4
Chapleau 40 D1
Chapra 94 D3
Chara 84 K5
Charcas 44 F4
Chard 34 J5
Chardara 96 J1
Chardzhev 96 H2
Chari ◪ 104 C5
Chārīkār 96 J2
Charleroi 62 G4
Charlesbourg 40 F1
Charleston, New Zealand 118 C5
Charleston, S.C., United States 42 F3
Charleston, W.Va., United States ▣ 42 E2
Charlestown 42 D2
Charleville 116 J5
Charleville-Mézières 62 G5
Charlevoix 40 C1
Charlotte, Mich., United States 40 D2
Charlotte, N.C., United States 42 E2
Charlottesville 42 F2
Charlottetown ▣ 34 U7
Charlton Island ▣ 34 Q6
Charsk 82 Q8
Charters Towers 116 J4
Chartres 66 G5
Charymovo 78 Q3
Chasel'ka 84 C3
Chastyye 78 K3
Châteauguay 40 F1
Châteaubriant 66 D6
Châteaudun 66 G5
Châteaulin 66 A5
Châteauneuf-sur-Loire 66 H5
Châteauroux 66 G7
Château-Thierry 62 F5
Châtellerault 66 F7
Châtenois 70 A2
Chatham 40 D2
Chatham Island ▣ 118 (1)B1
Chatham Islands ▣ 118 (1)B1
Châtillon-sur-Seine 66 K6
Chattanooga 36 J4
Chauffayer 70 B6
Chauk 94 F4
Chaumont 66 L5
Chaunskaya Guba ◪ 84 V3
Chauny 62 F5
Chaves, Brazil 50 G4
Chaves, Portugal 68 C3
Chavuma 112 C2
Cheb 60 H6
Cheboksary 78 J3
Chechnya ▣ 98 L2
Cheduba Island ▣ 94 F5
Cheektowaga 40 E2
Chegdomyn 84 N6
Chegutu 112 E3
Chehalis 38 B1
Cheju 88 D7
Cheju do ▣ 88 D7
Chekhov 84 Q7
Chelan 38 C1
Cheleken 96 F2
Chélif ◪ 68 L8
Chelkar 82 K8
Chełm 58 N6
Chełmno 58 H4
Chelmsford 62 C3
Cheltenham 64 L10
Chelyabinsk 78 M3
Chelyuskin 82 U2
Chemnitz 60 H6
Chenab ◪ 94 B2
Cheney Reservoir ◪ 42 B2
Chengde 86 F2
Chengdu 86 C4
Chengshan Jiao ▣ 88 B5
Chennai 94 D6
Chenzhou 86 E5
Chepes 52 H5
Cher ◪ 66 G6
Cheraw 42 F3
Cherbaniani Reef ▣ 94 B6
Cherbourg 66 D4
Cherchell 68 N8
Cherdyn 78 L2
Cheremkhovo 84 G6
Cherepovets 78 G3
Cherkasy 78 F5
Cherkessk ▣ 98 K1
Chermoz 78 L3
Chernihiv 78 F4
Chernivtsi 78 E5
Chernushka 78 L3
Chernyakhovsk 58 L3

Chernyayevo 84 M6
Chernyshevsk 84 K6
Chernyshevskiy 84 J4
Chernyye Zemli ▣ 78 J5
Cherokee 40 A2
Cherskiy 84 U3
Cherven Bryag 74 M6
Chervonohrad 78 D4
Chesapeake 42 F2
Cheshskaya Guba ◪ 78 J1
Cheshunt 62 C3
Chester, United Kingdom 64 K8
Chester, Calif., United States 38 B2
Chester, Mont., United States 38 D1
Chesterfield 64 L8
Chesterfield Inlet 34 N4
Chetumal 46 G5
Chetwynd 34 G5
Ch'ew Bahir ◪ 110 F3
Cheyenne ◪ 38 F2
Cheyenne ▣ 38 F2
Cheyenne Wells 44 F1
Cheyne Bay ◪ 116 C6
Chhatarpur 94 C4
Chhindwara 94 C4
Chhuka 94 E3
Chia-i 86 G6
Chiang Khan 90 C3
Chiang-Mai 90 B3
Chiang Rai 90 B3
Chiavari 70 E6
Chiavenna 70 E4
Chiba 88 L6
Chibougamau 34 S6
Chibuto 112 E4
Chicago 40 C2
Chicapa ◪ 110 C5
Chichagof Island ▣ 44 (1)K4
Chichaoua 106 D2
Chichester 62 B4
Chichester 42 B3
Chiclana de la Frontera 68 D8
Chiclayo 50 B5
Chico 52 H8
Chico ◪ 40 F2
Chicoutimi 34 S7
Chicualacuala 112 E4
Chiemsee ◪ 70 H3
Chieri 70 C5
Chiese ◪ 70 F5
Chieti 72 J6
Chifeng 86 F2
Chiganak 82 N8
Chigubo 112 E4
Chihuahua 44 E3
Chiili 82 M9
Chikwa 112 E2
Chilas 94 B1
Childress 44 F2
Chile ▲ 48 E2
Chile Chico 52 G8
Chilik 82 P9
Chilika Lake ◪ 94 D4
Chillán 52 G6
Chillicothe, Mo., United States 40 B3
Chillicothe, Oh., United States 40 D3
Chilliwack 38 B1
Chiloquin 38 B2
Chilpancingo 46 E5
Chi-lung 86 G5
Chimbay 82 K9
Chimborazo ▲ 50 B4
Chimbote 50 B5
Chimchememel' 84 V3
Chimec 74 J1
Chimoio 112 E3
China ▲ 80 N6
Chincha Alta 50 B6
Chincilla de Monte-Aragón 68 J6
Chin do ▣ 88 C6
Chindwin ◪ 90 A2
Chingola 112 D2
Chinhoyi 112 E3
Chiniot 94 B2
Chinju 88 E6
Chinmen ▣ 90 F2
Chinnur 94 C5
Chióggia 70 H5
Chios 76 H6
Chios ▣ 76 J6
Chipata 112 E2
Chippewa Falls 40 B2
Chipping Norton 62 A3
Chirchik 82 M9
Chirikof Island ▣ 44 (1)F5
Chiromo 112 F3
Chirpan 76 H2

Chirripo ▲ 46
Chişinău ▣ 74
Chişineu-Criş 74
Chita 84
Chitato 110
Chitembo 112
Chitipa 110
Chitradurga 94
Chitral 94
Chitré 46
Chittagong 94
Chittaurgarh 94
Chittoor 94
Chitungwiza 112
Chiume 112
Chivasso 70
Chizha 78
Chodov 60
Choiseul ▣ 114
Chojnice 58
Chokurdakh 84
Chōkwé 112
Cholet 66
Choma 112
Chomutov 58
Chona ◪ 84
Chonan 88
Chone 50
Ch'ŏngjin 88
Ch'ŏngju 88
Chŏngp'yŏng 88
Chongqing 88
Chŏngŭp 88
Ch'ŏnju 88
Chonogol 86
Chon Thanh 90
Chop 58
Chornobyl' 78
Chornomors'ke 78
Ch'osan 88
Chōshi 88
Choszczno 58
Choteau 38
Chott el Hodna ◪ 106
Chott el Jerid ◪ 106
Chott Melrhir ◪ 106
Choybalsan 84
Choyr 86
Chre ◪ 66
Christchurch 118
Christiansburg 40
Christiansø ▣ 58
Christmas Island ▣ 92 (1
Chrudim 58
Chrysi ▣ 76 H
Chu 82
Chubut ◪ 52
Chugach Mountains ▲ 34
Chūgoku-sanchi ▲ 86
Chugwater 38
Chukchi Sea ◪ 44 (1
Chukotskiy Khrebet 84
Chukotskiy Poluostrov ◪ 84
Chula Vista 44
Chulucanas 50
Chulym ◪ 82
Chum 78
Chumikan 84
Chum Phae 90
Chumphon 90
Chunchura 94
Chundzha 82
Ch'ungju 88
Chur 70
Churapcha 84
Churchill 34
Churchill, Man., Canada ◪ 34
Churchill, Nfld., Canada ◪ 34
Churchill Falls 34
Churchill Peak ▲ 34
Churu 94
Chuska Mountains ▲ 44
Chusovoy 78
Chute des Passes 34
Chuuk ▣ 114
Chuvashiya ▣ 78
Chuxiong 90
Chuya ◪ 84
Ciadır-Lunga 74
Cide 98
Ciechanów 58
Ciego de Avila 46
Cienfuegos 46
Cieza 68
Cihanbeyli 98
Cijulang 92 (1
Cilacap 92 (1
Cili 86
Cimarron ◪ 42
Cimişlia 74
Cîmpeni 58

Name	Ref	Grid
inca	✓ 68	L3
incinnati	40	D3
ine	76	L7
iney	62	H4
intalapa	46	F5
ircle, Ak., United States	44	(1)J2
ircle, Mont., United States	38	E1
ircleville	40	D3
rebon	92	(1)D4
rò Marina	72	M9
sco	42	B3
stierna	68	E2
tronelle	42	D3
ttadella	70	G5
tta di Castello	70	H7
ucea	74	K3
udad Acuña	44	F3
udad Bolívar	50	E2
udad Camargo	44	E3
udad del Carmen	46	F5
udad del Este	52	L4
udad Delicias	44	E3
udad del Maíz	44	G4
udad de México	■ 46	E5
udad de Valles	46	E4
udad Guayana	50	E2
udad Juárez	44	E2
udad Madero	44	G4
udad Mante	46	E4
udad Obregón	46	C3
udad Real	68	G6
udad-Rodrigo	68	D4
udad Valles	44	G4
udad Victoria	36	G7
utadella	68	P4
vidale del Friuli	70	J4
vita Castellana	72	G6
vitanova Marche	72	H5
vitavécchia	72	F6
zre	98	K5
acton-on-Sea	62	D3
air Engle Lake	☑ 38	B2
airview	116	J4
amecy	66	J6
are Island	⊠ 64	B8
arence	118	D6
arence Strait	⊟116	E2
arendon	44	F2
arkdale	44	D2
arksburg	42	E2
arksdale	42	C3
arks Junction	118	C7
arkston	38	C1
arksville, Ark., United States	42	C2
arksville, Tenn., United States	42	D2
aro	☑ 50	G7
austhal-Zellerfeld	60	F5
averia	90	G3
ayton	44	F1
ear Island	⊠ 64	C10
ear Lake	40	B2
ear Lake Reservoir	☑ 38	B2
earwater	☑ 38	C1
earwater	42	E4
earwater Mountains	▲ 38	C1
eburne	42	B3
ermont, Australia	116	J4
ermont, France	62	E5
ermont-Ferrand	66	J8
es	70	F4
eveland, Oh., United States	40	D2
eveland, Tenn., United States	42	E2
eveland, Tex., United States	42	B3
lifden	118	A7
lifton	44	E2
imax	38	E1
ines Corners	44	E2
inton, Canada	34	G6
inton, New Zealand	118	B8
inton, Ark., United States	40	B3
inton, Ia., United States	36	H3
inton, Miss., United States	42	C3
inton, Mo., United States	40	B3
inton, N.C., United States	42	F3
inton, Okla., United States	42	B2
ipperton Island	⊠ 46	C6
onmel	64	E9
oppenburg	60	D4
loquet	40	B1
loud Peak	▲ 38	E2
Clovis, Calif., United States	38	C3
Clovis, N.Mex., United States	44	F2
Cluj-Napoca	74	L3
Cluny	66	K7
Cluses	70	B4
Clyde	✓ 64	H6
Clyde River	34	T2
Coaldale	38	C3
Coalville	38	C2
Coari	50	E4
Coast Mountains	▲ 34	E5
Coast Range	■ 38	B3
Coatbridge	64	J6
Coats Island	⊠ 34	Q4
Coatzacoalcos	46	F5
Cobalt	34	R7
Cobán	46	F5
Cobija	50	D6
Cobourg	36	L3
Cobourg Peninsula	⊟116	F2
Cóbuè	112	E2
Coburg	60	F6
Cochabamba	50	D7
Cochin = Kochi	94	C7
Cochrane	40	D1
Cockburn Town	42	G5
Coco	✓ 46	H6
Cocoa	42	E4
Cocobeach	108	F4
Coco Channel	⊟ 90	A4
Coco Island	⊠ 90	A4
Codajás	50	E4
Codigoro	70	H6
Cod Island	⊠ 34	U5
Codlea	74	N4
Codó	50	J4
Codogno	70	E5
Codroipo	70	J5
Cody	38	E2
Coesfeld	60	C5
Coëtivy Island	⊠102	J6
Coeur d'Alene	38	C1
Coeur d'Alene Lake	⊠ 38	C1
Coevorden	62	J2
Coffs Harbour	116	K6
Cofrents	68	J5
Cognac	66	E8
Cogne	70	C5
Coiba	⊠ 48	C3
Coihaique	52	G8
Coimbatore	94	C6
Coimbra	68	B4
Colchester	62	C3
Colebrook	40	F1
Coleman	42	B3
Coleraine	64	F6
Colesberg	112	D6
Colfax	38	C1
Colibaşi	74	M5
Colico	70	E4
Coll	⊠ 64	F5
Collado-Villalba	68	F4
College Station	42	B3
Collier Bay	⊟116	D3
Collingwood	40	E2
Collins	42	D3
Colmar	70	C2
Colmenar Viejo	68	G4
Colombia	▲ 50	C3
Colombo	94	C7
Colonia Las Heras	52	H8
Colonial Heights	40	E3
Colonsay	⊠ 64	F5
Colorado	■ 38	E3
Colorado, Colo., United States	✓ 44	E1
Colorado, Tex., United States	✓ 44	G4
Colorado Plateau	⊠ 44	D1
Colorado Springs	38	F3
Columbia	✓ 38	C1
Columbia, La., United States	42	C3
Columbia, Md., United States	42	F2
Columbia, Mo., United States	42	C2
Columbia, S.C., United States	⊡ 42	E3
Columbia, Tenn., United States	42	D2
Columbia Mountains	■ 34	G6
Columbus, Ga., United States	42	E3
Columbus, Ind., United States	42	D2
Columbus, Miss., United States	42	D3
Columbus, Mont., United States	38	E1
Columbus, Nebr., United States	38	G2
Columbus, N.Mex., United States	44	E2
Columbus, Oh., United States	⊡ 42	E1
Columbus, Tex., United States	42	B4
Colville	✓ 44	(1)G2
Colville Lake	44	(1)M2
Comacchio	70	H6
Comăneşti	74	P3
Comarnic	74	N4
Combarbalá	52	G5
Combeaufontaine	66	M6
Comilla	90	A2
Comino = Kemmuna	⊠ 72	J12
Commentry	66	H7
Commercy	62	H6
Como	70	E5
Comoé	✓108	D3
Comondú	36	D6
Comoros	▲112	G2
Compiègne	62	E5
Comrat	74	R3
Comstock	44	F3
Conakry	■ 108	B3
Concarneau	66	B6
Conceição do Araguaia	50	H5
Concepción, Bolivia	50	E7
Concepción, Chile	52	G6
Conches-en-Ouche	62	C6
Concho	✓ 46	C3
Concord, Calif., United States	44	B1
Concord, N.H., United States	⊡ 40	F2
Concord, N.C., United States	42	E2
Concordia, Argentina	52	K5
Concordia, United States	42	B2
Condé-sur-Noireau	62	B6
Condobolin	116	J6
Condom	66	F10
Conegliano	70	H5
Conggar	94	F3
Congo	▲102	E6
Congo	▲108	G5
Connecticut	⊡ 40	F2
Connemara	⊠ 64	C8
Conrad	38	D1
Côn Son	⊠ 90	D5
Constanţa	98	C1
Constantina	68	E7
Constantine	106	G1
Consul	38	E1
Contact	38	D2
Contamana	50	B5
Contwoyto Lake	⊠ 34	J3
Conway	42	F3
Conway	42	C2
Conwy	64	J8
Conwy Bay	⊟ 64	H8
Coober Pedy	116	F5
Cookeville	40	C3
Cook Inlet	⊟ 44	(1)G4
Cook Islands	⊠114	K7
Cook Strait	⊟118	E5
Cooktown	116	J3
Coolabah	116	J6
Coolgardie	116	D6
Cooma	116	J7
Coonabarabran	116	J6
Coon Rapids	40	B1
Coopers Town	42	F4
Coorabie	116	F6
Coos Bay	38	B2
Cootamundra	116	J6
Copenhagen = København	⊡ 56	G9
Copiapó	52	G4
Copper Harbor	40	C1
Côqen	94	E2
Coquille	38	B2
Coquimbo	52	G4
Corabia	74	M6
Coral	36	K1
Coral Sea	⊟116	K2
Coral Sea Islands Territory	⊡114	F7
Coral Sea Islands Territory	⊟116	J2
Coral Springs	42	E4
Corantijn	✓ 50	F3
Corbeil-Essonnes	66	H5
Corbigny	66	J6
Corby	62	B2
Cordele	42	E3
Cordillera Cantábrica	■ 68	D2
Cordillera Central	■ 48	E5
Cordillera del Condor	■ 50	B5
Cordillera de Mérida	■ 48	D5
Cordillera de Oliva	■ 52	G4
Cordillera Isabella	■ 46	G6
Cordillera Occidental	■ 48	E5
Cordillera Oriental	■ 48	D5
Cordillera Penibética	■ 68	F8
Cordillera Vilcabamba	■ 50	C6
Córdoba, Argentina	52	J5
Córdoba, Spain	68	F7
Corfu = Kerkyra	⊠ 76	B5
Coria	68	D5
Corigliano	72	L9
Corinth	42	D3
Corinto	50	H7
Cork	64	D10
Cork Harbour	⊟ 64	D10
Corleone	72	H11
Corn Islands	⊠ 48	C2
Cornwall	36	M2
Cornwallis Island	⊠ 34	M2
Coro	50	D1
Corocoro	50	D7
Coromandel	118	E3
Coromandel Coast	⊠ 94	D6
Coromandel Peninsula	⊡118	E3
Coron	90	G4
Coronation Gulf	⊟ 34	J3
Coronel Oviedo	52	K4
Coronel Pringles	52	J6
Coronel Suárez	52	J6
Corpus Christi	42	B4
Corrientes	52	K4
Corrigan	42	C3
Corriverton	50	F2
Corse	72	D6
Corsica = Corse	⊠ 72	D6
Corsicana	42	B3
Corte	72	D6
Cortegana	68	D7
Cortez	44	E1
Cortina d'Ampezzo	70	H4
Cortland	40	E2
Cortona	72	F5
Coruche	68	B6
Çorum	98	F3
Corumbá	50	F7
Corvallis	38	B2
Corvo	⊠106	(1)A2
Cosenza	72	L9
Cosmoledo Group	⊠112	(2)A2
Cosne-sur-Loire	66	H6
Cossato	70	D5
Costa Blanca	⊟ 68	K7
Costa Brava	⊟ 68	P3
Costa del Sol	⊟ 68	G8
Costa de Mosquitos	⊟ 46	H6
Costa Dorada	⊟ 68	M4
Costa do Sol	⊟ 68	A6
Costa Rica	▲ 46	G7
Costa Smeralda	⊟ 72	D7
Costa Verde	⊟ 68	D1
Costeşti	74	M5
Coswig	60	H5
Cotabato	90	G5
Cotonou	108	E3
Cottage Grove	38	B2
Cottbus	58	D6
Cotulla	42	B4
Couhe	66	F7
Coulommiers	62	F6
Council Bluffs	38	F2
Courland Lagoon	⊟ 58	L2
Courtacon	62	F6
Courtenay	36	B2
Coushatta	42	C3
Coutances	66	D4
Couvin	62	G4
Covasna	74	P4
Coventry	64	L9
Covilhã	68	C4
Covington, Ga., United States	42	E3
Covington, Ky., United States	42	E2
Covington, Va., United States	40	D3
Cowell	116	G6
Cowes	62	A4
Cowra	116	J6
Çox's Bazar	94	F4
Cradock	112	D6
Craig	38	E2
Crailsheim	60	F7
Craiova	74	L5
Cranbrook, Australia	116	C6
Cranbrook, United States	36	C6
Crater Lake	☑ 38	B2
Crato	50	K5
Crawford	38	F2
Crawfordsville	40	C2
Crawley	62	B3
Cree Lake	⊠ 34	K5
Creil	62	E5
Crema	70	E5
Cremona	70	F5

Index

Crépy-en-Valois ... 62 E5
Cres ... 70 K6
Cres ... 70 K6
Crescent City ... 38 B2
Crest ... 66 L9
Creston ... 40 B2
Crestview ... 36 J5
Crestview ... 46 G2
Crete = Kriti ... 76 H10
Créteil ... 62 E6
Creuse ... 66 G7
Crevillent ... 68 K6
Crewe ... 64 K8
Crianlarich ... 64 H5
Criciúma ... 52 M4
Cristalina ... 50 H7
Cristóbal Colón ... 32 J8
Crna Gora ... 74 F7
Croatia ... 74 C4
Crockett ... 42 B3
Croker Island ... 116 F2
Cromer ... 64 P9
Cromwell ... 118 B7
Crooked Island ... 46 K4
Crookston ... 36 G2
Cross City ... 42 E3
Cross Lake ... 34 M6
Crossville ... 40 C3
Crotone ... 72 M9
Crowley ... 42 C3
Crownest Pass ... 36 D2
Crown Point ... 40 C2
Cruz Alta ... 52 L4
Cruz del Eje ... 52 J5
Cruzeiro do Sul ... 50 C5
Crvenka ... 74 G4
Crystal City ... 42 B4
Crystal Falls ... 40 C1
Crystal River ... 42 E4
Crystal Springs ... 42 C3
Csorna ... 74 E2
Csurgó ... 70 N4
Cuamba ... 112 F2
Cuando ... 112 C3
Cuangar ... 112 B3
Cuango ... 110 B5
Cuanza ... 110 B5
Cuatro Ciénegas ... 44 F3
Cuauhtémoc ... 44 E3
Cuba ... 38 E3
Cuba ... 46 H4
Cubal ... 110 A6
Cubali ... 112 A2
Cubango ... 112 B3
Çubuk ... 76 R4
Cucuí ... 50 D3
Cúcuta ... 50 C2
Cuddalore ... 94 C6
Cuddapah ... 94 C6
Cuemba ... 112 B2
Cuenca, Ecuador ... 50 B4
Cuenca, Spain ... 68 H4
Cuernavaca ... 46 E5
Cuero ... 42 B4
Cuiabá ... 50 F7
Cuilo ... 110 B5
Cuito ... 112 B3
Cuito Cuanavale ... 112 B3
Culbertson ... 38 E1
Culfa ... 98 L4
Culiacán ... 46 C4
Cullera ... 68 K5
Cullman ... 42 D3
Culpepper ... 50 (1)A1
Culuene ... 50 G6
Culverden ... 118 D6
Cumaná ... 50 E1
Cumberland ... 40 E3
Cumberland Peninsula ... 34 T3
Cumberland Sound ... 34 T3
Cummings ... 38 B3
Cumpas ... 44 E2
Çumra ... 76 Q7
Cunderdin ... 116 C6
Cunene ... 112 A3
Cuneo ... 70 C6
Cunnamulla ... 116 J5
Čuprija ... 74 J6
Cure ... 66 J6
Curicó ... 52 G5
Curitiba ... 52 M4
Currais Novos ... 50 K5
Curral Velho ... 108 (1)B1
Currie ... 116 H7
Curtea de Argeş ... 74 M4
Curtici ... 74 J3
Curtis Island ... 116 K4
Curuá ... 50 G5
Curup ... 92 (1)C3
Curuzú Cuatiá ... 52 K4
Curvelo ... 50 J7
Cusco ... 50 C6

Cuthbert ... 42 E3
Cutro ... 72 L9
Cuttack ... 94 E4
Cuvier Island ... 118 E3
Cuxhaven ... 60 D3
Cuya ... 50 C7
Cuyuni ... 50 F2
Cwmbran ... 64 J10
Cyclades = Kyklades ... 76 G7
Cypress Hills ... 36 D2
Cyprus ... 98 E6
Czarnków ... 58 F5
Czech Republic ... 58 C8
Częstochowa ... 58 J7
Człuchów ... 58 G4

D

Da'an ... 86 G1
Daaquam ... 40 F1
Dab'a ... 100 D5
Dabas ... 74 G2
Dabat ... 104 G5
Dabola ... 108 B2
Dąbrowa Górnicza ... 58 J7
Dąbuleni ... 74 M6
Dachau ... 70 G2
Daet ... 90 G4
Dagana ... 106 B5
Dagestan ... 98 M2
Dagua ... 90 G3
Da Hinggan Ling ... 86 G1
Dahlak Archipelago ... 104 H4
Dahlonega ... 42 E3
Dahn ... 62 K5
Dahod ... 94 B4
Dahongliutan ... 96 L2
Dahūk ... 98 K5
Daimiel ... 68 G5
Dai Xian ... 86 E3
Dakar ... 108 A2
Dakoro ... 108 F2
Dakota City ... 38 G2
Dakovica ... 74 H7
Dakovo ... 74 F4
Dalai Nur ... 86 F2
Dalälven ... 56 J5
Dalaman ... 98 C5
Dalandzadgad ... 86 C2
Dalap-Uliga-Darrit ... 114 H5
Da Lat ... 90 D4
Dalbandin ... 96 H4
Dalby ... 116 K5
Dalgān ... 96 G4
Dalhart ... 44 F1
Dalhousie ... 94 C2
Dali ... 90 C1
Dalian ... 86 G3
Dalizi ... 88 D3
Dallas ... 42 B3
Dalloa ... 108 C3
Dalry ... 64 H6
Dältenganj ... 94 D4
Dalton ... 42 E3
Dalvík ... 56 (1)D2
Daly Waters ... 116 F3
Daman ... 94 B4
Damanhûr ... 104 F1
Damar ... 92 (2)C4
Damara ... 108 H3
Damasak ... 108 G2
Damascus = Dimashq ... 100 D3
Damaturu ... 108 G2
Damoh ... 94 C4
Damqawt ... 96 F6
Danau Poso ... 92 (2)A3
Danau Toba ... 92 (1)B2
Danau Towuti ... 92 (2)B3
Danba ... 86 C4
Dandeldhura ... 94 D3
Dandong ... 88 C3
Da Nĕng ... 90 D3
Dangara ... 96 J2
Danger Islands ... 114 K7
Danghe Nanshan ... 86 B3
Daniel ... 38 D1
Danilov ... 78 H3
Dank ... 101 G5
Dankov ... 78 G4
Dannenberg ... 60 G3
Dannevirke ... 118 F5
Dansville ... 40 E2
Danube ... 54 F3
Danville, Ill.,
  United States ... 42 D1
Danville, Ky.,
  United States ... 42 E2
Danville, Va.,
  United States ... 42 F2
Dan Xian ... 90 D3
Dao Phu Quôc ... 90 C4

Dapa ... 90 H5
Dapaong ... 108 E2
Da Qaidam ... 86 B3
Daqing ... 84 M7
Dar'ā ... 100 D4
Dārāb ... 101 F2
Darabani ... 74 P1
Daraj ... 104 B1
Darazo ... 108 G2
Darbhanga ... 94 E3
Dardanelles = Çanakkale
  Boğazı ... 76 J4
Darende ... 98 G4
Dar es Salaam ... 110 F5
Darfo ... 70 F5
Dargaville ... 118 D2
Darham ... 84 H7
Darjeeling ... 94 E3
Darling ... 116 H6
Darlington ... 64 L7
Darłowo ... 56 J9
Dărmăneşti ... 74 P3
Dar Mazār ... 101 G2
Darmstadt ... 60 D7
Darnah ... 104 D1
Darnley Bay ... 34 G3
Daroca ... 68 J3
Darß ... 60 H2
Dartmouth ... 34 U8
Daru ... 92 (2)F4
Daruba ... 92 (2)C2
Daruvar ... 70 N5
Darvaza ... 82 K9
Darwin ... 16 F2
Daryacheh-ye
  Bakhtegan ... 101 E2
Daryācheh-ye Orūmīyeh ... 98 L5
Daryācheh-ye Tashk ... 101 E2
Dārzīn ... 101 H2
Dashkhovuz ... 82 K9
Dasht-e Kavir ... 96 F3
Dasht-e Lut ... 101 H1
Datça ... 76 K8
Date ... 88 L2
Datong ... 86 C3
Datong ... 86 E2
Daugava ... 78 E3
Daugavpils ... 78 E3
Daun ... 62 J4
Dauphin ... 34 M6
Dausa ... 94 C3
Dāvāci ... 98 N3
Davangere ... 94 C6
Davao ... 90 H5
Davenport ... 40 B2
Daventry ... 62 A2
David ... 46 H7
Davis Sea ... 120 (2)Q3
Davis Strait ... 34 V3
Davlekanovo ... 82 J7
Davos ... 70 E4
Dawa ... 86 G2
Dawqah ... 96 F6
Dawson ... 44 (1)K3
Dawson Creek, B.C.,
  Canada ... 34 G5
Dawson Creek, Y.T.,
  Canada ... 34 G4
Dawu ... 86 C4
Dax ... 66 D10
Daxian ... 86 D4
Dayong ... 86 E5
Dayr az Zawr ... 98 J6
Dayton, Oh.,
  United States ... 40 D2
Dayton, Tenn.,
  United States ... 40 C3
Dayton, Tex.,
  United States ... 42 C4
Dayton, Wash.,
  United States ... 38 C1
Daytona Beach ... 42 E4
De Aar ... 112 C6
Dead Sea ... 100 C5
Deakin ... 116 E6
Deal ... 62 D3
De'an ... 86 F5
Deán Funes ... 52 J5
Dease Lake ... 44 (1)M4
Dease Strait ... 34 J3
Death Valley ... 38 C3
Deba Habe ... 108 G2
Debar ... 76 C3
Debin ... 84 S4
Dęblin ... 58 L6
Dębno ... 58 D5
Debre Birhan ... 110 F2
Debrecen ... 74 J2
Debre Markos ... 104 G5
Debre Tabor ... 104 G5

Decatur, Al.,
  United States ... 40 C
Decatur, Ill., United States ... 40 C
Decazeville ... 66 H
Deccan ... 94 C
Děčín ... 58 D
Decize ... 66
Decorah ... 40
Dedoplis ... 98 N
Dédougou ... 108 D
Dedza ... 112
Deering ... 44 (1)
Deer Lake ... 34
Deer Lodge ... 38 D
Deer Park ... 38 D
Dee, Scot.,
  United Kingdom ... 64 H
Dee, Wales,
  United Kingdom ... 64
De Funiak Springs ... 42
Degeh Bur ... 110
Deggendorf ... 70
Dehaj ... 101
Dehalak Desēt ... 96
Deh Bid ... 101
Deh-Dasht ... 101
Dehküyeh ... 101
Dehlonān ... 96
Dehra ... 96
Dehra Dun ... 94
Dehri ... 94
Deh Shū ... 96
Deinze ... 62
Dej ... 74
De Kalb ... 42
De-Kastri ... 84
Dekese ... 110
Delano ... 44
Delaware ... 40
Delaware ... 42
Delbrück ... 60
Delémont ... 70
Delfoi ... 76
Delft ... 62
Deltzijl ... 62
Delgo ... 104
Delhi, India ... 94
Delhi, United States ... 40
Delitzsch ... 60
Dellys ... 68
Delmenhorst ... 60
Delnice ... 70
Delray Beach ... 42
Del Rio ... 44
Delta, Colo.,
  United States ... 38
Delta, Ut., United States ... 38
Delta del Orinoco ... 50
Delta Junction ... 44 (1)
Deming ... 44
Demirci ... 76
Demmin ... 60
Democratic Republic of
  Congo ... 110
Demopolis ... 42
Demyanka ... 78
Dem'yanskoye ... 78
Denain ... 62
Denau ... 96
Denbigh ... 62
Den Burg ... 62
Dender ... 62
Dendi ... 110
Denham ... 116
Den Helder ... 62
Dénia ... 68
Deniliquin ... 116
Denio ... 38
Denison, Ia.,
  United States ... 38
Denison, Tex.,
  United States ... 42
Denizli ... 98
Denmark ... 54
Denmark ... 116
Denmark Strait ... 32
Denpasar ... 92 (1)
Denton ... 44
D'Entrecasteaux Islands ... 116
Denver ... 38
Deogarh, India ... 94
Deogarh, India ... 94
Deoghar ... 94
De Panne ... 62
Depok ... 92 (1)
Dépression du Mourdi ... 104
Deputatskiy ... 84
Dêqên ... 90
Dera Ghazi Khan ... 96
Dera Ismail Khan ... 96
Derbent ... 98
Derby, Australia ... 116

Name	Page	Ref
erby, *United Kingdom* ...	64	L9
e Ridder ...	42	C3
ermott ...	42	C3
ervenia ...	74	E5
esё ...	104	G5
nseado ...	52	H8
nseado ...	◪52	H8
nsert Center ...	44	C2
ns Moines, *Ia., United States* ...	▣36	H3
ns Moines, *N.Mex., United States* ...	44	F1
nsna ...	◪78	F4
nssau ...	60	H5
nsvres ...	62	D4
nta ...	74	J4
ntmold ...	60	D5
ntroit ...	36	K3
ntroit Lakes ...	40	A1
nt Udom ...	90	C4
ntva ...	58	J9
nurne ...	62	H3
nva ...	74	K4
nventer ...	62	J2
nvil's Lake ...	◪34	L7
nvils Lake ...	38	G1
nvil's Point ...	42	F5
nvnya ...	74	Q6
nvon Island ...	◪34	P1
nvonport ...	116	J8
nwas ...	94	C4
nyang ...	86	C4
nyhuk ...	96	G3
nzfül ...	96	E3
nzhou ...	86	F3
nahran = Aẓ Ẓahrān ...	101	D3
naka ...	◪94	F4
namār ...	104	H5
namtri ...	94	D4
nanbad ...	94	E4
nar ...	94	C4
nārwād ...	94	B5
naulagiri ...	▲94	D3
nekelia ...	100	A2
nibān ...	100	C5
noraji ...	94	B4
nule ...	94	B4
nulian ...	94	E4
nuudo ...	110	J2
na ...	▣76	H9
namantina ...	50	H7
namantino ...	50	F6
namond Islets ...	▣116	K3
nane Bank ...	▣116	J3
nanópolis ...	50	H6
nbā al Ḥiṣn ...	101	G4
nbbiena ...	72	F5
nbrugarh ...	94	F3
nckens ...	44	F2
nckinson ...	38	F1
nckson ...	42	D2
ndiéni ...	108	C2
ndymoteicho ...	66	L9
ne ...	66	L9
nébougou ...	108	D2
neburg ...	60	D7
néma ...	108	C2
nemel ...	◪60	E5
nemeringen ...	60	C8
nepholz ...	60	D4
neppe ...	62	D5
nest ...	62	H4
nffa ...	108	G2
ngne-les-Bains ...	70	B6
ngoin ...	66	J7
njon ...	66	L6
nkhil ...	104	H5
nkili ...	76	J5
nklosmta ...	▲98	L2
nksmuide ...	62	E3
nkson ...	82	Q3
nkwa ...	108	G2
nla ...	110	F2
nli ...	92	(2)C4
nlijan ...	98	L3
nlenburg ...	60	D6
nlingen, *Germany* ...	60	F8
nlingen, *Germany* ...	60	B7
nllingham ...	44	(1)F4
nllion ...	36	D2
nllon ...	38	D1
nllon Cone ...	▲118	D6
nolo ...	112	C2
nmapur ...	94	F3
nmashq ...	■100	D3
nmitrovgrad, *Bulgaria* ...	74	N7
nmitrovgrad, *Russia* ...	78	J4
nmitrovgrad, *Yugoslavia* ...	74	K7
nmona ...	100	C5
nnagat ...	▣90	H4
nnajpur ...	94	E3
nnan ...	66	C5
Dinant ...	62	G4
Dinar ...	98	D4
Dinaric Alps ...	◪70	L6
Dindigul ...	94	C6
Dindori ...	94	D4
Dingle Bay ...	◪64	B9
Dingolfing ...	70	H2
Dinguiraye ...	108	B2
Dingwall ...	64	H4
Dinkelsbühl ...	60	F7
Dinosaur ...	38	E2
Diomede Islands ...	▣84	AA3
Dioriga Kointhou ...	◪76	F7
Diourbel ...	106	B6
Dipolog ...	90	G5
Dir ...	94	B1
Dirē Dawa ...	110	G2
Dirk Hartog Island ...	▣116	B5
Dirranbandi ...	116	J5
Disko = Qeqertarsuatsiaq ...	▣34	V2
Disko Bugt = Qeqertarsuup Tunua ...	◪34	V3
Diss ...	62	D2
Distrito Federal ...	▣50	H7
Dithmarschen ...	▣60	D2
Dīvāndarreh ...	98	M6
Divinópolis ...	52	N3
Divo ...	108	C3
Divriği ...	98	H4
Dixon ...	40	C2
Dixon Entrance ...	◪44	(1)L5
Diyarbakır ...	98	J5
Dja ...	◪108	G4
Djado ...	106	H4
Djamâa ...	106	G1
Djambala ...	108	G5
Djanet ...	106	G4
Djelfa ...	106	F2
Djéma ...	110	D2
Djibo ...	108	D2
Djibouti ...	▲104	H5
Djibouti ...	■104	H5
Djolu ...	110	C3
Djougou ...	108	E3
Djúpivogur ...	56	(1)F2
Dnieper ...	◪78	F5
Dniester ...	◪74	Q1
Dnipro ...	◪54	H3
Dniprodzerzhyns'k ...	78	F5
Dnipropetrovs'k ...	78	F5
Dnister ...	◪54	G3
Dno ...	78	E3
Doba, *Chad* ...	110	B2
Doba, *China* ...	94	E2
Döbeln ...	60	J5
Doboj ...	74	F5
Dobre Miasto ...	58	K4
Dobrich ...	74	Q6
Dobryanka ...	78	L3
Doctor Arroyo ...	44	F4
Dodecanese = Dodekanisos ...	▣76	J8
Dodge City ...	38	F3
Dodoma ...	■110	F5
Doetinchem ...	62	J3
Doğanşehir ...	98	G4
Dôgo ...	▣88	G5
Dogondoutchi ...	108	E2
Doha = Ad Dawḥah ...	■101	D4
Doka ...	92	(2)D4
Dokkum ...	62	J1
Dolak ...	▣92	(2)E4
Dolbeau ...	40	F1
Dole ...	70	A3
Dolgany ...	84	E2
Dolinsk ...	84	Q7
Dollard ...	◪60	C3
Dolný Kubrin ...	58	J8
Dolomiti ...	◪70	G4
Dolo Odo ...	110	G3
Dolores ...	52	K6
Dolphin and Union Strait ...	◪34	H3
Domar ...	94	D2
Domažlice ...	60	H7
Dombås ...	56	E5
Dombóvár ...	74	F3
Domfront ...	66	E5
Dominica ...	▲48	E2
Dominican Republic ...	▲48	D1
Domodóssola ...	70	D4
Domokos ...	76	L5
Dompu ...	92	(2)A4
Domžale ...	70	K4
Don ...	◪54	H2
Donau = Danube ...	◪70	H2
Donaueschingen ...	70	D3
Donauwörth ...	60	F8
Don Benito ...	68	E6
Doncaster ...	64	L8
Dondra Head ...	▷94	D7
Donegal ...	64	D7
Donegal Bay ...	◪64	D7
Donets ...	◪54	H3
Donets'k ...	78	G5
Dongco ...	94	D2
Dongfang ...	90	D3
Donggala ...	92	(2)A3
Donggou ...	88	C4
Dongguan ...	90	E2
Dông Hôi ...	90	D3
Dongjingcheng ...	88	E1
Donglük ...	82	R10
Dongning ...	88	F2
Dongo ...	108	H4
Dongola ...	104	F4
Dongou ...	108	H4
Dongsha Qundao ...	▣90	F2
Dongsheng ...	86	E3
Dong Ujimqin Qi ...	86	F1
Dongying ...	86	F3
Donji Vakuf ...	42	C2
Donner Pass ...	70	N6
Donostia ...	◪38	B3
Donostia ...	68	J1
Donousa ...	◪76	H7
Dora ...	◪70	C5
Dorchester ...	64	K11
Dordrecht ...	62	G3
Dorfen ...	70	H2
Dori ...	108	D2
Doring ...	◪112	B6
Dorion ...	40	C1
Dormagen ...	62	J3
Dornbirn ...	70	E3
Dorog ...	58	H10
Dorohoi ...	74	P2
Döröö Nuur ...	◪82	S8
Dorsten ...	62	J3
Dortmund ...	60	C5
Dos Hermanas ...	68	E7
Dosse ...	◪60	H4
Dosso ...	108	E2
Dothan ...	42	D3
Douai ...	62	F4
Douala ...	108	F4
Douarnenez ...	66	A5
Doubs ...	◪70	B3
Douentza ...	108	C2
Douglas, *South Africa* ...	112	C5
Douglas, *United Kingdom* ...	64	H7
Douglas, *Ariz., United States* ...	44	E2
Douglas, *Ga., United States* ...	42	E3
Douglas, *Wyo., United States* ...	38	E2
Doullens ...	62	E4
Dourados ...	52	L3
Douro ...	◪68	B3
Dover, *United Kingdom* ...	62	D3
Dover, *United States* ...	▣42	F2
Dover, *Australia* ...	116	J8
Dover-Foxcroft ...	40	G1
Dowlatābād, *Iran* ...	101	E2
Dowlatābād, *Iran* ...	101	G2
Dowshī ...	96	J2
Drac ...	◪70	B6
Drachten ...	62	J1
Dragan ...	◪56	H4
Drăgănești-Olt ...	74	M5
Drăgășani ...	74	M5
Draguignan ...	70	B7
Drakensberg ...	◪112	D6
Drake Passage ...	◪52	G10
Drama ...	76	G3
Drammen ...	56	F7
Drasenhofen ...	70	M2
Drau ...	◪70	J4
Drava ...	◪74	E4
Dravograd ...	72	K2
Drawsko Pomorskie ...	58	E4
Dresden ...	60	J5
Dreux ...	62	D6
Drezdenko ...	58	E5
Drina ...	◪74	G5
Driva ...	◪56	E5
Drniš ...	74	D6
Drobeta-Turnu Severin ...	74	K5
Drochia ...	74	Q1
Drogheda ...	64	F8
Drohobych ...	58	N8
Drôme ...	◪66	K9
Dronne ...	◪66	E6
Dronning Maud Land ...	▣120	(2)F2
Dronten ...	62	H2
Drummondville ...	40	F1
Druskininkai ...	56	M9
Druzhina ...	84	Q3
Drvar ...	74	D5
Dryanovo ...	74	N7
Dryden ...	36	H2
Drysdale River ...	116	E3
Dschang ...	108	G3
Ḍubā ...	104	G2
Dubai = Dubayy ...	101	F4
Dubăsari ...	74	S2
Dubawnt Lake ...	◪34	L4
Dubayy ...	101	F4
Dubbo ...	116	J6
Dübendorf ...	70	D3
Dublin, *Republic of Ireland* ...	64	F8
Dublin, *United States* ...	42	E3
Dublin Bay ...	◪64	F8
Dubna ...	78	G3
Dubnica ...	58	H9
Du Bois ...	40	E2
Dubois, *Id., United States* ...	38	D2
Dubois, *Wyo., United States* ...	38	E2
Dubovskoye ...	78	H5
Dubreka ...	108	B3
Dubrovnik ...	74	F7
Dubuque ...	40	B2
Duchesne ...	38	D2
Ducie Island ...	▣114	P8
Dudelange ...	62	J5
Duderstadt ...	60	F5
Dudinka ...	82	R4
Dudley ...	64	K9
Duero ...	◪68	F3
Dugi Otok ...	▣74	B6
Duifken Point ...	▷116	H2
Duisburg ...	62	J3
Duiveland ...	◪62	F3
Duk Faiwil ...	110	E2
Dukhān ...	101	D4
Dukla ...	58	L8
Dukou ...	86	C5
Dulan ...	86	B3
Dulce ...	44	E1
Dulce ...	◪52	J4
Dul'Durga ...	84	J6
Dullewala ...	94	B2
Dülmen ...	60	C5
Dulovo ...	74	Q6
Duluth ...	40	B1
Dūmā ...	100	D3
Dumaguete ...	90	G5
Dumai ...	92	(1)C2
Dumas, *Ark., United States* ...	42	C3
Dumas, *Tex., United States* ...	38	F3
Ḍumayr ...	100	D3
Dumbarton ...	64	H5
Dúmbier ...	▲58	J9
Dumboa ...	108	G2
Dumfries ...	64	J6
Dümmer ...	◪60	D4
Dumont d'Urville Sea ...	◪120	(2)U3
Dumyât ...	104	F1
Duna = Danube ...	◪74	E2
Dunaj = Danube ...	◪58	G10
Dunajská Streda ...	74	E2
Dunakeszi ...	74	G2
Dunărea = Danube ...	◪74	K5
Dunaújváros ...	74	F3
Dunav = Danube ...	◪74	J5
Dunayivtsi ...	78	E2
Dunbar, *Australia* ...	116	H3
Dunbar, *United Kingdom* ...	64	K6
Duncan ...	38	B1
Duncan Passage ...	◪90	A4
Dundaga ...	56	M8
Dundalk ...	64	F7
Dundalk Bay ...	◪64	F8
Dundee, *South Africa* ...	112	E5
Dundee, *United Kingdom* ...	64	K5
Dunedin ...	118	C7
Dunfermline ...	64	J5
Dungarvan ...	64	E9
Dungeness ...	▷62	C4
Dungu ...	110	D3
Dungun ...	90	C6
Dunhua ...	88	E2
Dunhuang ...	86	A2
Dunkerque ...	62	E3
Dunkirk ...	40	E2
Dún Laoghaire ...	64	F8
Dunnet Head ...	▷64	J3
Dunseith ...	38	G1
Dunsmuir ...	38	B2
Duque de Caxias ...	52	N3
Du Quoin ...	42	D2
Durance ...	◪66	L10
Durango, *Mexico* ...	44	F4
Durango, *Spain* ...	68	H1
Durango, *United States* ...	38	E3
Durant ...	42	B3
Durazno ...	52	K5
Durban ...	112	E5
Düren ...	62	J4

Durgapur 94 E4
Durham, *Canada* 40 D2
Durham, *United Kingdom* . . 64 L7
Durham, *United States* . . . 42 F2
Duri . . . . 92 (1)C2
Durmå 101 B4
Durmanec 74 C3
Durmitor . . . . ▲74 G6
Durrës 76 B3
Dursey . . . . ▣64 B10
Dursunbey 76 L5
D'Urville Island . . . . ▣118 D5
Dushanbe . . . . ▣96 J2
Düsseldorf 62 J3
Duvno 70 N7
Duyun 86 D5
Düzce 76 P4
Dvina . . . . ▨54 H2
Dvinskaya Guba . . . . ▶78 G1
Dwarka 94 A4
Dworshak Reservoir . . . . ▨38 C1
Dyat'kovo 78 F4
Dyersburg 42 D2
Dyje . . . . ▨70 M2
Dzavhan . . . . ▨82 S8
Dzerzhinsk 78 H3
Dzhalinda 84 L6
Dzhambeyty 78 K4
Dzhankoy 78 F5
Dzhardzhan 84 L3
Dzharkurgan 96 J2
Dzhetygara 78 M4
Dzhezkazgan 78 N5
Dzhigudzhak 84 T4
Dzhizak 82 M9
Dzhusaly 78 M5
Działdowo 58 K4
Dzüünbulag 86 F1

E

Eads 38 F3
Eagle . . . . 44 (1)J3
Eagle Lake . . . . ▨38 B2
Eagle Pass 44 F3
East Antarctica . . . . ▣120 (2)P2
Eastbourne 62 C4
East Cape . . . . ▨118 G3
East China Sea . . . . ▨86 H4
East Dereham 62 C2
Easter Island . . . . ▣114 Q8
Eastern Cape . . . . ▣112 D6
Eastern Ghats . . . . ▨94 C6
Easter Ross . . . . ▣64 H4
East Falkland . . . . ▣52 K9
East Grinstead 62 C3
East Kilbride 64 H6
Eastleigh 62 A4
East Liverpool 42 E1
East London 112 D6
Eastmain 34 R6
Eastmain . . . . ▨34 S6
East Point 42 E3
East Retford 62 B1
East St. Louis 40 B3
East Siberian Sea =
    Vostochno-
    Sibirskoye More . . . . ▨84 U2
Eatonton 42 E3
Eau Claire 40 B2
Ebbw Vale 64 J10
Ebensee 70 J3
Eberbach 60 D7
Ebersbach 58 D6
Ebersberg 70 G2
Eberswalde 60 J4
Ebinur Hu . . . . ▨82 Q9
Éboli 72 K8
Ebolowa 108 G4
Ebro . . . . ▨68 K3
Eceabat 76 J4
Ech Chélif 106 F1
Echinos 76 G3
Echo Bay 34 H3
Écija 68 E7
Eckernförde 60 E2
Ecuador . . . . ▲50 B4
Ed 104 H5
Edam 62 H2
Eday . . . . ▣64 K2
Ed Da'ein 104 E5
Ed Damazin 104 F5
Ed Debba 104 F4
Ed Dueim 104 F5
Ede, *Netherlands* 62 H2
Ede, *Nigeria* 108 E3
Edéa 108 G4
Edelény 58 K9
Eden, *Australia* 116 J7
Eden, *United States* . . . 44 G2
Edendale 118 B8

Eder . . . . ▨60 D5
Edersee . . . . ▨60 E5
Edessa 76 E4
Edgecumbe 118 F3
Edinburgh . . . . ▣64 J6
Edineţ 74 Q1
Edirne 76 J3
Edmonds 38 B1
Edmonton . . . . ▣34 J6
Edmundson 36 N2
Edmundston 40 G1
Edolo 70 F4
Edremit 76 J5
Edremit Körfezi . . . . ▨76 H5
Edwards 44 C2
Edwards Plateau . . . . . . ▣44 F2
Eemshaven 62 J1
Éfaté . . . . ▣114 G7
Eferding 58 D9
Effingham 42 D2
Eganville 40 E1
Eger . . . . ▨60 G6
Eger 74 H2
Egersund 56 D7
Eggenfelden 70 H2
Egilsstaðir . . . . 56 (1)F2
Eğridir 76 N7
Eğridir Gölü . . . . ▨76 N6
Egvekinot 84 Y3
Egypt . . . . ▲104 E2
Ehingen 70 E2
Eibar 68 H1
Eichstätt 70 G2
Eider . . . . ▶60 D2
Eidsvold 116 K5
Eidsvoll 56 F6
Eifel . . . . ▨62 J4
Eigg . . . . ▣64 F5
Eight Degree Channel . . . ▶94 B7
Eilenburg 60 H5
Einbeck 60 E5
Eindhoven 62 H3
Eirunepé 50 D5
Eiseb . . . . ▨112 C4
Eisenach 60 F6
Eisenerz 70 K3
Eisenhüttenstadt 58 D5
Eisenstadt 70 M3
Eisleben 60 G5
Eivissa 68 M5
Eivissa . . . . ▣68 M6
Ejea de los Caballeros . . . 68 J2
Ejido Insurgentes 36 D6
Ejin Horo Qi 86 D3
Ejin Qi 86 C2
Ejmiadzin 98 L3
Ekalaka 38 F1
Ekenäs 56 M7
Ekibastuz 82 P7
Ekimchan 84 N6
Ekonda 82 V4
Eksjo 56 H8
Ekwan . . . . ▨34 Q6
El Aaiún . . . . ▣106 C3
Elafonisos . . . . ▣76 E8
El 'Alamein 104 E1
El Amria 68 J9
El 'Arîsh 100 A5
Elat 100 A6
Elazığ 98 H4
El Azraq 100 D5
Elba . . . . ▣72 E6
El Banco 50 C2
Elbasan 76 C3
El Baúl 50 D2
Elbe . . . . ▨60 F3
Elbeuf 62 D5
Elbistan 98 G4
Elblag 58 J3
El Borj 68 E9
Elbow 36 E1
Elbrus . . . . ▲98 K2
El Burgo de Ebro 68 K3
El Burgo de Osma 68 G3
El Cajon 44 C2
El Callao 50 E2
El Campo 42 B4
El Centro 44 C2
El Cerro 50 E7
Elch 68 K6
Elda 68 K6
El'dikan 84 P4
Eldorado 52 L4
El Dorado, *Mexico* 36 E7
El Dorado, *Ark.,*
    United States 42 C3
El Dorado, *Kans.,*
    United States 42 B2
El Dorado, *Venezuela* . . 50 E2
Eldoret 110 F3
Elefsina 76 F6
Elektrėnai 58 P3

El Encanto 50 C4
Elephant Butte Reservoir . . ▨44 E2
Eleuthera . . . . ▣36 L6
El Fahs 72 D12
El Faiyûm 104 F2
El Fasher 104 E5
El Geneina 104 D5
Elgin, *United Kingdom* . . 64 J4
Elgin, *Ill., United States* . . 40 C2
Elgin, *N.D., United States* . . 38 F1
El'ginskiy 84 Q4
El Gîza 104 F1
El Goléa 106 F2
El Iskandarîya 104 E1
Elista . . . . ▣78 H5
Elizabeth 40 F2
Elizabeth City 42 F2
Elizabethton 42 E2
El Jadida 106 D2
El Jafr 100 D6
El Jafr . . . . ▨100 D6
Elk 58 M4
Elk . . . . ▨58 M4
El Kala 72 C12
Elk City 44 G1
El Kef 72 C12
El Kelaâ des Srarhna . . . 106 D2
El Khârga 104 F2
Elkhart, *Ind.,*
    United States 40 C2
Elkhart, *Kans.,*
    United States 42 A2
El Khartum . . . . ▲104 F4
El Khartum Bahri 104 F4
Elkhorn . . . . ▨38 G2
Elkhorn 40 C2
Elkhovo 76 J2
Elkins 40 E3
Elko, *Canada* 38 C1
Elko, *United States* 38 C2
Elk River 40 B1
El Kuntilla 100 B7
Ellendale 36 G2
Ellensburg 38 B1
Ellesmere Island . . . . . . ▣32 K1
Ellice Islands . . . . ▣114 H6
Elliot 112 D6
Ellis 34 J8
Ellisras 112 D4
Elliston 116 F6
Ellsworth 40 G2
Ellwangen 70 F2
Elmadağ 76 R5
Elmali 76 M8
El Mansûra 104 F1
El Minya 104 F2
Elmira 40 E2
Elmshorn 60 E3
El Muglad 104 E5
El Nido 90 F4
El Obeid 104 F5
El Odaiya 104 E5
El Oued 106 G2
El Paso 44 E2
El Portal 44 C1
El Potosi 44 F4
El Prat de Llobregat 68 N3
El Puerto de Santa María . . 68 D8
El Qâhira . . . . ▣104 F1
El Reno 42 B2
El Sahuaro 44 D2
El Salvador . . . . ▲46 F6
Elster . . . . ▨60 H5
Elsterwerda 60 J5
El Sueco 44 E3
El Suweis 104 F2
Eltanin Bay . . . . ▶120 (2)JJ2
El Tarf 72 C12
El Thamad 100 B7
El Tigre 50 E2
El Turbio 52 G9
Eluru 94 D5
Elvas 68 C6
Elverum 56 F6
Elvira 50 C5
Ely, *United Kingdom* . . . 64 N9
Ely, *United States* 38 D3
Emajõgi . . . . ▨56 P7
Emämrüd 96 F2
Emba 78 L5
Emba . . . . ▨78 L5
Embalse de Alarcon . . . . ▨68 H5
Embalse de Alcántara Uno . . ▨68 D5
Embalse de Almendra . . . ▨68 D3
Embalse de Contreras . . . ▨68 J5
Embalse de Gabriel y
    Galán . . . . ▨68 D4
Embalse de Garcia Sola . . ▨68 E5
Embalse de Guadalhorce . . ▨68 F8
Embalse de Guadalmena . . ▨68 G6
Embalse de Guri . . . . . . ▨50 E2

Embalse de la Serena . . . ▨68
Embalse de la Sotonera . . ▨68
Embalse del Bembézar . . ▨68
Embalse del Ebro . . . . . ▨68
Embalse del Río Negro . . ▨48
Embalse de Negratmn . . . ▨68
Embalse de Ricobayo . . . ▨68
Embalse de Santa Teresa . . ▨68
Embalse de Yesa . . . . . . ▨68
Embalse Toekomstig . . . . ▨50
Embarcación 52
Emden 60
Emerald 116
Emi Koussi . . . . ▲104
Emin 82
Emirdağ 76
Emmeloord 62
Emmen 62
Emmendingen 70
Emmerich 62
Emory Peak . . . . ▲44
Empalme 44
Empangeni 112
Empoli 70
Emporia 42
Empty Quarter =
    Rub' al Khâlî . . . . . . ▣96
Ems . . . . ▣62
Ems-Jade-Kanal . . . . . . ▨60
Enafors 78
Encarnación 52
Encs 74
Ende 92 (2)
Enderby Island . . . . ▣118 (2)
Energetik 78
Enewetak . . . . ▣114
Enez 76
Enfida . . . . 72 E
Engel's 78
Enggano . . . . ▣92 (1)
Enghien 62
England . . . . ▣64
English Channel . . . . . . ▶64
Engozero 56
'En Hazeva 100
Enid 42
Enkhuizen 62
Enköping 56
Enna 72
En Nahud 104
Enngonia 116
Ennis,
    Republic of Ireland . . 64
Ennis, *United States* . . . 38
Enniscorthy 64
Enniskillen 64
Enns 70
Enns . . . . ▨70
Enschede 62
Ensenada 44
Enshi 86
Entebbe 110
Enterprise 38
Entrevaux 70
Entroncamento 68
Enugu 108
Enurmino 84
Envira 50
Enz . . . . ▨70
Enza . . . . ▨70
Epanomi 76
Épéna 110
Épernay 66
Épinal 70
Epsom 62
Eqlid 101
Equatorial Guinea . . . . . ▲108
Erbach 60
Erçek 98
Erciş 98
Ercolano 72
Érd 74
Erdek 76
Erdemli 76
Erdenet 84
Erding 70
Erechim 52
Ereğli, *Turkey* 98
Ereğli, *Turkey* 98
Ereikoussa . . . . ▣76
Erenhot 86
Erfurt 60
Ergani 98
Erg Chech . . . . ▣106
Erg du Ténéré . . . . ▣106
Ergel 86
Erg Iguidi . . . . ▣106
Erie 40
Erimo-misaki . . . . ▶64
Eriskay . . . . ▣64
Eritrea . . . . ▲104
Erlangen 60

Forssa 56 M6
Forst 60 K5
Forsyth 38 E1
Fort Abbas 94 B3
Fortaleza 50 K4
Fort Bayne 40 C4
Fort Beaufort 112 D6
Fort Benton 38 D1
Fort Bragg 44 B1
Fort Chipewyan 34 J5
Fort Cobb Reservoir 42 B2
Fort Collins 38 E2
Fort-de-France 46 M6
Fort Dodge 40 B2
Forte dei Marmi 70 F7
Fort Frances 40 B1
Fort George 34 R6
Fort Gibson Lake 42 B2
Fort Good Hope 34 F3
Forth 64 H5
Fort Hope 34 P6
Fortín Coronel Eugenio
Garay 52 J3
Fort Kent 40 G1
Fort Lauderdale 42 E4
Fort Liard 34 G4
Fort Mackay 34 J5
Fort Macleod 38 D1
Fort McMurray 34 J5
Fort McPherson 44 (1)L2
Fort Munro 96 J4
Fort Myers 42 E4
Fort Nelson 34 G5
Fort Norman 44 (1)M3
Fort Payne 42 D3
Fort Peck Reservoir 38 E1
Fort Pierce 42 E4
Fort Pierre 38 F2
Fort Portal 110 E3
Fort Providence 34 H4
Fortrose 118 B8
Fort Rupert 34 R6
Fort St. John 34 G5
Fort Saint Lucie 42 E4
Fort Scott 42 C2
Fort Severn 34 P5
Fort Shevchenko 82 J9
Fort Simpson 34 G4
Fort Smith, Canada 34 J4
Fort Smith, United States 42 C2
Fort Stockton 44 F2
Fort Summer 44 F2
Fortuna 38 F1
Fortune Bay 34 V7
Fort Vermilion 34 H5
Fort Wayne 42 D1
Fort William 64 G5
Fort Worth 42 B3
Fort Yates 38 F1
Foshan 90 E2
Fosna 56 F5
Fossano 70 C6
Fossombrone 70 H7
Fougamou 108 G5
Fougères 66 D5
Foula 64 K1
Foulness 62 C3
Foumban 108 G3
Fourmies 62 G4
Fournoi 76 J7
Fouta Djallon 108 B2
Foveaux Strait 118 A8
Foxe Basin 34 R3
Foxe Channel 34 R4
Foxe Peninsula 34 R4
Fox Islands 44 (1)D5
Foz do Cunene 112 A3
Foz do Iguaçu 52 L4
Fraga 68 L3
Franca 52 M3
Francavilla 72 M8
Francavilla al Mare 72 J6
France 66 G7
Franceville 108 G5
Francisco I. Madero 44 F4
Francistown 112 D4
Francs Peak 38 E2
Frankenberg 60 D5
Frankenthal 60 D7
Frankfort, Ind.,
United States 42 D1
Frankfort, Ky.,
United States 42 E2
Frankfurt, Germany 60 K4
Frankfurt, Germany 60 D6
Franklin, N.C.,
United States 40 D3
Franklin, Tenn.,
United States 40 C3
Franklin Bay 34 F2
Franklin D. Roosevelt
Lake 38 C1

Franklin Mountains 34 F3
Franklin Strait 34 M2
Franz Josef Glacier 118 C6
Franz Josef Land =
Zemlya
Frantsa-Iosifa 82 J2
Fraser 34 G6
Fraserburg 112 C6
Fraserburgh 64 L4
Fraser Island 116 K5
Frater 40 D1
Frauenfeld 70 D3
Fredensborg 58 B2
Frederick, Md.,
United States 40 E3
Frederick, Okla.,
United States 42 B3
Fredericksburg, Tex.,
United States 42 B3
Fredericksburg, Va.,
United States 40 E3
Fredericktown 40 B3
Fredericton 34 T7
Frederikshåb = Paamiut 34 X4
Frederikshavn 56 F8
Frederikssund 58 B2
Frederiksværk 56 G9
Fredrikstad 56 F7
Freeport, Ill.,
United States 40 C2
Freeport, Tex.,
United States 42 B4
Freeport City 42 F4
Freer 42 B4
Free State 112 D3
Freetown 108 B3
Fregenal de la Sierre 68 D6
Freiberg 60 J6
Freiburg 70 C3
Freilassing 70 H3
Freising 70 G2
Freistadt 70 K2
Fréjus 66 M10
Fremantle 116 C6
Fremont, Calif.,
United States 44 B1
Fremont, Nebr.,
United States 36 G3
Frenchglen 38 C2
French Guiana 50 G3
French Polynesia 114 L7
Frenda 106 F1
Fresnes-sur-Apances 70 A3
Fresnillo 46 D4
Fresno 44 C1
Fresno Reservoir 38 E1
Freudenstadt 70 D2
Freyung 60 J8
Frias 52 H4
Fribourg 70 C4
Friedburg 70 G2
Friedrichshafen 70 E3
Friesach 70 K4
Friesoythe 60 C3
Frisian Islands 62 H1
Fritzlar 60 E5
Frobisher Bay 34 T4
Frolovo 78 H5
Frome 64 K10
Frontera 46 F5
Frontignan 66 J10
Frosinone 72 H7
Frøya 56 D5
Fruges 62 E4
Frýdek Mistek 58 H8
Fudai 88 L4
Fuding 86 G5
Fuengirola 68 F8
Fuentesauco 68 E3
Fuerteventura 106 C3
Fugu 86 E3
Fuhai 82 R8
Fujieda 88 K6
Fujin 84 N7
Fuji-san 88 K6
Fukuchiyama 88 H6
Fukue 88 E7
Fukue-jima 88 E7
Fukui 88 J5
Fukuoka 88 F7
Fukushima 88 L5
Fukuyama 88 G6
Fulda 60 E6
Fulda 60 E6
Fuling 86 D5
Fulton 42 D2
Funabashi 88 L6
Funafuti 114 H6
Funchal 106 B2
Fundão 68 C4
Funing 90 D2
Funtua 108 F2

Furano 88 M2
Fürg 101 F2
Furmanovka 82 N9
Furmanovo 78 J5
Furneaux Group 116 J8
Furqlus 100 E2
Fürstenberg 60 J3
Fürstenfeldbruck 70 G2
Fürstenwalde 60 K4
Fürth 60 F7
Furukawa 88 L4
Fushun 88 B3
Fusong 88 D2
Füssen 70 F3
Futog 74 G4
Fuxhou 86 F5
Fu Xian 86 D3
Fuxin 86 G2
Fuyang 86 F4
Fuyu 86 G1
Fuyun 82 R8
Fuzhou 90 F1
Fyn 60 F1
Fynshav 60 F2

G

Gaalkacyo 110 H2
Gabès 106 H2
Gabon 108 G5
Gaborone 112 D4
Gabrovo 74 N7
Gacé 62 C6
Gacko 74 F6
Gäddede 56 H4
Gadsden 42 D3
Gâeşti 74 N5
Gaeta 72 H7
Gafsa 106 G2
Gaggenau 70 D2
Gagnoa 108 C3
Gagra 98 J2
Gaildorf 70 E2
Gaillac 66 G10
Gainesville, Fla.,
United States 42 E4
Gainesville, Ga.,
United States 42 E3
Gainesville, Mo.,
United States 42 C2
Gainesville, Tex.,
United States 42 B3
Gai Xian 88 B3
Gala 94 E3
Galana 110 F4
Galanta 70 N2
Galapagos Islands = Islas
Galápagos 50 (1)B1
Galashiels 64 K6
Galaţi 74 P4
Galdhøpiggen 56 D6
Galena 44 (1)F3
Galesburg 40 B2
Galich 78 H3
Gallabat 104 G5
Galle 94 D7
Gallipoli 72 N8
Gallipolis 42 E2
Gállivare 56 L3
Gallup 44 E1
Galtat Zemmour 106 C3
Galveston Bay 36 G6
Galway 64 C8
Galway Bay 64 C8
Gambèla 110 E2
Gambier Islands 114 N8
Gamboma 110 B4
Gamboula 110 B3
Gan 84 L7
Ganado 44 E1
Gâncă 104 M3
Gandajika 110 C5
Gander 34 W7
Ganderkesee 60 D3
Gandesa 68 L3
Gândhidhâm 94 B4
Gandhinagar 94 B4
Gandia 68 K6
Gandu 50 K6
Ganganagar 94 B3
Gangara 108 F2
Gangdise Shan 94 D2
Ganges 66 J10
Ganges 94 E3
Gangi 72 J11
Gangtok 94 E3
Gannett Peak 38 E2
Ganta 108 C3
Ganye 108 G3
Ganzhou 86 E5
Gao 106 E5

Gaoual 106 C
Gap 70 B
Garanhuns 50 K
Garbsen 60 E
Gardelegen 60 G
Garden City 38 F
Gardëz 96 J
Gardone Val Trómpia 70 F
Gargždai 58 L
Gariau 92 (2)D
Garissa 110 F
Garland 42 B
Garlasco 70 D
Garliava 58 N
Garmisch-Partenkirchen 70 G
Garnett 42 B
Garonne 66 E
Garoowe 110 H
Garoua 108 G
Garoua Boulaï 108 G
Garry Lake 34 L
Garut 92 (1)D
Garwolin 58 L
Gary 36 J
Garyarsa 94 D
Garzê 86 B
Gasan Kuli 96 F
Gasht 96 H
Gashua 108 G
Gastonia 42 E
Gastre 52 H
Gatchina 78 F
Gateshead 64 L
Gatesville 42 B
Gatineau 40 E
Gatrüyeh 101 F
Gauja 56 N
Gaula 56 F
Gauteng 112 D
Gava 68 N
Gävbandī 101 E
Gavdos 76 G1
Gävle 56 J
Gawler 116 G
Gawler Ranges 116 G
Gaxun Nur 86 C
Gaya, India 94 E
Gaya, Niger 108 E
Gaylord 40 D
Gayndah 116 K
Gayny 78 K
Gaza 100 B
Gaz-Achak 82 L
Gazandzhyk 82 K10
Gaza Strip 100 B
Gaziantep 98 G
Gazipaşa 76 Q
Gazli 82 L
Gbaaka 108 C
Gbarnga 108 C
Gdańsk 58 H
Gdov 56 P
Gdyel 68 K
Gdynia 58 H
Gebel at Tîh 100 A
Gebel Halâl 100 A
Gebel Katherina 104 F
Gebel Yi'allaq 100 A
Gebze 76 M
Gedaref 104 G
Gediz 76 E
Gediz 76 M
Gedser 60 G
Geel 62 H
Geelong 116 H
Geesthacht 60 F
Geidam 108 G
Geilenkirchen 62 J
Geilo 56 E
Geinhausen 60 E
Geislingen 70 E
Geita 110 E
Gejiu 90 C
Gela 72 J11
Geladi 110 H
Geldern 62 J
Geleen 62 H
Gelendzhik 98 H
Gelibolu 76 J
Gelibolu Yarimadasi 76 J
Gelsenkirchen 62 K
Gembloux 62 G
Gembu 108 G
Gemena 110 B
Gemlik 76 M
Gemlik Körfezi 76 L
Gemona del Friuli 70 J
Genalē Wenz 110 H
General Acha 52 J
General Alvear 52 H
General Pico 52 J

eneral Pinedo	52	J4	Gilgit	96	K2	Gökçeada	⊡ 76	H4	Gora Ledyanaya	▲ 84	W4
eneral Roca	52	H6	Gilgit	94	B1	Gökova Körfezi	► 76	K8	Gora Pobeda	▲ 84	R4
eneral Santos	90	H5	Gillam	34	N5	Göksun	98	G5	Gora Yenashimskiy		
eneva	40	E2	Gillette	38	E2	Golaghat	94	F3	Polkan	▲ 82	S6
enève	70	B4	Gillingham	62	C3	Golan Heights	▣ 100	C3	Goražde	74	F6
engma	90	B2	Gills Rock	40	C1	Golbāf	101	G2	Gorbitsa	84	K6
enil	⊿ 68	F7	Gilroy	38	B3	Gólbasi	98	G5	Goré	108	H3
enk	62	H4	Gimbī	110	F2	Gol'chikha	82	Q3	Gorë	110	F2
enoa = Genova	70	D6	Gimli	34	M6	Gölcük	76	K5	Gore	118	B8
enova	70	D6	Gimol'skoe Ozero	⊿ 56	R5	Gołdap	58	M3	Gorgān	96	F2
ent	62	F3	Gīnīr	110	G2	Gold Coast	116	K5	Gorgona	► 70	E7
enteng	92	(1)D4	Gióia del Colle	72	L8	Golden Bay	► 118	D5	Gori	98	L2
enthin	60	H4	Gióia Tauro	72	K10	Goldendale	38	B1	Gorinchem	62	H3
eographe Bay	► 116	B6	Gioura	⊡ 76	F5	Golden Gate	► 44	B1	Goris	98	M4
eorge	112	C6	Giresun	98	H3	Goldfield	38	C3	Gorizia	70	J5
eorge	⊿ 34	T5	Girga	104	F2	Goldsboro	40	E3	Gorki	78	N1
eorge Town, Australia	116	J8	Girona	68	N3	Gôle	98	K3	Gorlice	58	L8
eorge Town, Malaysia	92	(1)C1	Gironde	⊿ 66	E8	Goleniów	58	D4	Görlitz	58	D6
eorge Town, United States	42	F5	Girvan	64	H6	Golestānak	101	F1	Gorna Oryakhovitsa	74	N6
eorgetown, Gambia	108	B2	Gisborne	118	G4	Golfe d'Ajaccio	► 72	C7	Gornji Milanovac	74	H5
eorgetown, Guyana	■ 50	F2	Gisenyi	110	D4	Golfe de Gabès	► 106	H2	Gorno-Altaysk	⊙ 82	R7
eorgetown, Ky., United States	42	E2	Gitega	110	D4	Golfe de Hammamet	► 106	H1	Gorno Oryakhovitsa	76	H1
eorgetown, S.C., United States	42	F3	Giurgiu	74	N6	Golfe de Porto	► 72	C6	Gorodets	78	H3
eorgetown, Tex., United States	42	B3	Givet	62	G4	Golfe de Sagone	► 72	C6	Gorontalo	92	(2)B2
eorge West	42	B4	Givors	66	K8	Golfe de Saint-Malo	► 66	C5	Goryachiy Klyuch	98	H1
eorgia	▲ 98	K2	Giyon	110	F2	Golfe de Tunis	► 72	E11	Gory Belukha	▲ 82	R8
eorgia	â 42	E3	Gizhiga	84	U4	Golfe de Valinco	► 72	C7	Gory Ulutau	▲ 78	N5
eorgian Bay	► 40	D1	Gizhiginskaya Guba	► 84	T4	Golfe du Lion	► 66	J10	Gorzów Wielkopolski	58	E5
era	60	H6	Giżycko	58	L3	Golfo de Almería	► 68	H8	Goslar	60	F5
eraldine	118	C7	Gjiri i Vlorës	► 76	B4	Golfo de Batabanó	► 46	H4	Gospić	72	K4
eraldton, Australia	116	B5	Gjirokaster	76	C4	Golfo de Cádiz	► 68	C7	Gosport	66	D3
eraldton, Canada	36	J2	Gjøvik	56	F6	Golfo de California	► 46	B3	Gostivar	76	C3
erardmer	70	B2	Glacier Peak	▲ 38	B1	Golfo de Chiriquí	► 46	H7	Gostyń	58	G6
eräsh	101	F3	Gladstone	116	K4	Golfo de Corcovado	► 52	F7	Gostynin	58	J5
erede	98	E3	Glamoč	74	D5	Golfo de Cupica	► 50	B2	Göteborg	56	F8
erefsried	70	G3	Glan	⊿ 60	C7	Golfo de Fonseca	► 46	G6	Gotha	60	F6
ereshk	96	H3	Glan	92	(2)C1	Golfo de Guayaquil	► 50	A4	Gothèye	108	E2
ergal	68	H7	Glarner Alpen	► 70	D4	Golfo de Honduras	► 46	G5	Gotland	⊡ 56	K8
erik	90	C5	Glasgow, United Kingdom	64	H6	Golfo del Darién	► 50	B2	Gotō-rettō	⊡ 88	E7
erlach	38	C2	Glasgow, Ky., United States	40	C3	Golfo dell' Asinara	► 72	C7	Gotse Delchev	76	F3
ermantown	40	C3	Glasgow, Mont., United States	38	E1	Golfo de los Mosquitos	► 50	A2	Gotska Sandön	⊡ 56	K7
ermany	▲ 60	E6	Glauchau	60	H6	Golfo de Mazarrón	► 68	J7	Göttingen	60	E5
ermencik	76	K7	Glazov	82	J6	Golfo de Morrosquillo	► 50	B1	Gouda	62	G2
ermering	70	G2	Gleisdorf	70	L3	Golfo de Panamá	► 46	J7	Gough Island	⊡ 102	B10
ermersheim	62	L5	Glendale, Ariz., United States	44	D2	Golfo de Penas	► 52	F8	Goundam	106	E5
ernika	68	H1	Glendale, Calif., United States	44	C2	Golfo de San Jorge	► 52	H8	Gouraya	68	M8
erolzhofen	60	F7	Glendambo	116	G6	Golfo de Santa Clara	44	D2	Gourdon	66	G9
erzë	94	D2	Glendive	38	F1	Golfo de Tehuantepec	► 46	E5	Gournay-en-Bray	62	D5
eser	92	(2)D3	Glennallen	44	(1)H3	Golfo de Venezuela	► 50	C1	Governador Valadares	50	J7
etafe	68	G4	Glenn Innes	116	K5	Golfo di Augusta	► 72	K11	Governor's Harbour	42	F4
ettysburg	38	F2	Glenrothes	64	J5	Golfo di Catánia	► 72	K11	Govorovo	84	M3
etxo	68	H1	Glens Falls	40	F2	Golfo di Gaeta	► 72	H7	Gowârân	96	J4
eugnon	66	K7	Glenwood, Ark., United States	40	B4	Golfo di Gela	► 72	J11	Goya	52	K4
evaş	98	K4	Glenwood, Minn., United States	40	A1	Golfo di Génova	► 72	C4	Gozha Co	⊿ 94	D1
evgelija	76	E3	Glenwood, N.Mex., United States	44	E2	Golfo di Manfredonia	► 72	L7	Gozo = Gwardex	⊡ 72	J12
ewanë	104	H5	Glenwood Springs	38	E3	Golfo di Òlbia	► 72	D8	Graaff-Reinet	112	C6
eyik Dağ	▲ 76	G8	Glidden	40	B1	Golfo di Oristano	► 72	C9	Grabovica	74	K5
eyser	38	D1	Glina	70	M5	Golfo di Orosei	► 72	D8	Gračac	70	L6
eyve	76	N4	Gliwice	58	H7	Golfo di Palmas	► 72	C10	Gračanica	74	F5
hadāmis	106	G2	Głogów	58	F6	Golfo di Policastro	► 72	K9	Gradačac	74	F5
hadir Mingār	Ⓟ 100	E3	Glomfjord	56	H3	Golfo di Salerno	► 72	J8	Grafton, Australia	116	K5
hana	▲ 108	D3	Glomma	⊿ 56	F5	Golfo di Sant'Eufemia	► 72	K10	Grafton, United States	38	G1
hanzi	112	C4	Glorieuses	⊡ 102	H7	Golfo di Squillace	► 72	L10	Graham Island	► 44	(1)L5
harandal	100	C6	Gloucester, United Kingdom	64	K10	Golfo di Taranto	► 72	L8	Grajaú	50	H5
hardaïa	106	F2	Gloucester, United States	40	F2	Golfo di Trieste	► 70	J5	Grajewo	58	M4
haro	96	J5	Głowno	58	J6	Golfo di San Matías	► 52	J6	Gram	60	E1
haryān	106	H2	Głuchołazy	58	G7	Gölhisar	76	M8	Grampian Mountains	▲ 64	H5
hāt	104	B2	Glückstadt	60	E3	Golin Baixing	88	A1	Granada, Nicaragua	46	G6
hazaouet	106	E1	Gmünd, Austria	70	J4	Gölköy	98	G3	Granada, Spain	68	G7
haziabad	94	C3	Gmünd, Austria	70	L2	Gölmarmara	76	K6	Granby	40	F1
hazipur	94	D3	Gmunden	70	J3	Golyshmanovo	82	M6	Gran Canaria	⊡ 106	B3
hazn	96	J3	Gniezno	58	G5	Goma	110	D4	Grand Bahama	⊡ 42	F4
heorgheni	74	N3	Gnjilane	76	D2	Gombe	108	G2	Grand Ballon	▲ 66	N6
herla	74	L2	Gnoien	60	H3	Gombi	108	G2	Grand Bank	34	V7
hizar	94	B1	Goalpara	94	F3	Gomera	⊡ 106	B3	Grand Canyon	⊙ 38	D3
hotāru	94	B3	Goba	110	F2	Gómez Palacio	44	F3	Grande, Bolivia	⊿ 50	E7
iannitsa	76	E4	Gobabis	112	B4	Gonam	⊿ 84	M5	Grande, Brazil	⊿ 50	J6
iannutri	⊡ 72	F6	Gobernador Gregores	52	G8	Gonbad-e Kavus	96	G2	Grande Cache	34	H6
iarre	72	K11	Gobi Desert	⊙ 86	C2	Gonda	94	D3	Grande Prairie	34	H5
ibraltar	68	E8	Gobustan	96	E1	Gonder	104	G5	Grand Erg de Bilma	⊙ 106	H5
ibson Desert	▨ 116	D4	Goch	62	J3	Gondia	94	D4	Grand Erg Occidental	⊙ 106	F3
iideän	⊿ 56	K5	Godbout	40	G1	Gondomar	68	B3	Grand Erg Oriental	⊙ 106	F3
iien	66	H6	Godé	110	G2	Gönen	76	K4	Grand Falls, N.B., Canada	40	G1
ießen	60	D6	Goderich	40	D2	Gongga Shan	▲ 86	C5	Grand Falls, Nfld., Canada	34	V7
ifhorn	60	F4	Godhra	94	B4	Gonghe	86	C3	Grand Forks, Canada	36	C2
ifu	88	J4	Gödöllő	74	G2	Gongliu	82	Q9	Grand Forks, United States	38	G1
igha	⊡ 64	G6	Gods Lake	⊿ 34	N6	Gongpoquan	86	B2	Grand Haven	40	C2
iglio	⊡ 72	E6	Godthåb = Nuuk	⊙ 34	W4	Gongshan	90	B1	Grand Island	38	G2
ijón	68	E1	Goeree	⊡ 62	F3	Gonzáles	36	G7	Grand Junction	38	E3
ila	⊿ 44	E2	Goes	62	F3	Gonzales	42	B4	Grand Marais, Mich., United States	40	C1
ila Bend	44	D2	Gogama	40	D1	González	44	G4	Grand Marais, Minn., United States	40	B1
ilan Garb	98	L6	Goiânia	⊙ 50	H7	Goodland	38	F3	Grand-Mère	40	F1
ilazi	98	N3	Goiás	⊙ 50	G6	Goolgowi	116	J6	Grândola	68	B6
ilbert Islands	⊡ 114	H5	Goiás	50	G7	Goomalling	116	C6	Grand Portage	40	C1
ilbués	50	H5				Goondiwindi	116	K5	Grand Rapids, Canada	34	M6
iilching	70	G2				Goose Lake	⊿ 38	B2	Grand Rapids, Mich., United States	40	C2
iilf Kebir Plateau	▨ 104	E3				Göppingen	70	E2			
iilgandra	116	J6				Góra	58	F6			
						Gora Bazardyuzi	▲ 98	M3			
						Gora Kamen	▲ 82	S4			
						Gorakhpur	94	D3			

139

Grand Rapids, Minn., United States	40	B1
Grand Teton	38	D2
Grangeville	38	C1
Granite Falls	40	A2
Granollers	68	N3
Gran Paradiso	70	C5
Grantham	64	M9
Grants	44	E1
Grants Pass	38	B2
Granville	66	D5
Granville Lake	34	M5
Gräsö	56	K6
Grasse	70	B7
Grassrange	38	E1
Grass Valley	38	B3
Graulhet	66	G10
Gravelines	62	E3
Gravenhurst	40	E2
Gravesend	62	C3
Gravina in Puglia	72	L8
Gray	66	L6
Grayling	40	D2
Grays	62	C3
Grays Lake	38	D2
Grayville	40	C3
Graz	70	L3
Great Abaco	42	F4
Great Artesian Basin	116	H4
Great Australian Bight	116	E6
Great Bahama Bank	46	J4
Great Barrier Island	118	E3
Great Barrier Reef	116	J2
Great Basin	38	C3
Great Bear Lake	44	(1)M2
Great Bend	44	G1
Great Dividing Range	116	J4
Greater Antilles	46	J5
Greater Sunda Islands	114	B6
Great Exhibition Bay	118	E3
Great Exuma	36	L7
Great Falls	38	D1
Great Inagua	46	K4
Great Karoo	112	C6
Great Malvern	64	K9
Great Nicobar	94	F7
Great Ouse	64	N9
Great Plains	38	F2
Great Rift Valley	110	E5
Great Salt Lake	38	D2
Great Salt Lake Desert	38	D2
Great Sand Sea	104	D2
Great Sandy Desert	116	D4
Great Slave Lake	32	N3
Great Victoria Desert	116	E5
Great Wall	86	C3
Great Yarmouth	64	P9
Greece	76	D5
Greeley	38	F2
Green	38	D3
Green Bay	40	C2
Greenfield	42	D2
Greenland	32	G2
Greenland Sea	32	B2
Greenock	64	H6
Green River, Wyo., United States	38	E2
Green River, Ut., United States	38	D3
Greensboro	42	F2
Greensburg, Ind., United States	42	D2
Greensburg, Pa., United States	40	E2
Greenvale	116	J3
Green Valley	46	B2
Greenville, Liberia	108	C3
Greenville, Al., United States	42	D3
Greenville, Fla., United States	42	E3
Greenville, Miss., United States	42	C3
Greenville, N.C., United States	40	E3
Greenville, S.C., United States	42	E3
Greenwood, Miss., United States	42	C3
Greenwood, S.C., United States	42	E3
Gregory	38	G2
Gregory Lake	116	E4
Greifswald	60	J2
Greifswalder Bodden	60	J2
Greiz	60	H6
Grenada	36	J5
Grenada	50	A50
Grenchen	70	C3
Grenoble	66	L8
Gretna	42	C4
Greve in Chianti	70	G7

Greven	62	K2
Grevena	76	D4
Grevenbroich	62	J3
Grevesmühlen	60	G3
Greybull	38	E2
Greymouth	118	C6
Grey Range	116	H5
Griesheim	60	D7
Grieskirchen	70	J2
Grigoriopol	74	S2
Grimma	60	H5
Grimmen	60	J2
Grimsby	64	M8
Grimsey	56	(1)D1
Grimstadir	56	(1)E2
Grímsvötn	56	(1)E2
Grindsted	56	E9
Grobina	58	L1
Gröbming	70	J3
Grodekovo	86	J2
Grodzisk Wielkopolski	58	F5
Grójec	58	K6
Gronau	60	C4
Groningen	60	B3
Groote Eylandt	116	G2
Grootfontein	112	B3
Großenhain	60	J5
Großer Arber	60	J7
Grosser Beerberg	60	F6
Grosseto	72	F6
Groß-Gerau	60	D7
Großglockner	70	H3
Groswater Bay	34	V6
Grottaglie	72	M8
Groupe Actéon	114	N8
Grove Hill	42	D3
Groznyy	98	L2
Grubišno Polje	74	E4
Grudovo	76	K2
Grudziądz	58	H4
Grünberg	60	D6
Gryazi	78	G4
Gryazovets	78	H3
Gryfice	58	E4
Gryfino	60	K3
Grytøya	56	J2
Grytviken	52	P9
Gstaad	70	C4
Guadalajara, Mexico	46	D4
Guadalajara, Spain	68	G4
Guadalcanal	114	F7
Guadalquivir	68	E7
Guadalupe	46	A3
Guadalupe	46	E3
Guadeloupe	48	E2
Guadiana	68	C7
Guadix	68	G7
Guaíra	52	L3
Guajará Mirim	50	D6
Guam	114	E4
Guanambi	50	J6
Guanare	50	D2
Guane	46	H4
Guangshui	86	D4
Guangyuan	86	D4
Guangzhou	90	E2
Guanipa	50	E2
Guanling	86	D5
Guantánamo	46	J4
Guanyun	86	F3
Guaporé	50	E6
Guaqui	50	D7
Guarabira	50	K5
Guarda	68	C4
Guardo	68	F2
Guasave	36	E4
Guastalla	70	F6
Guatemala	46	F6
Guatemala	46	F6
Guaviare	50	D3
Guayaquil	50	B4
Guayaramerín	50	D6
Guaymas	44	D3
Guba, Democratic Republic of Congo	110	D6
Guba, Ethiopia	104	G5
Guba Buorkhaya	84	N2
Gubakha	78	L3
Guban	110	G2
Gubbi	94	C6
Gúbbio	70	H7
Guben	60	K5
Gubin	58	D6
Gudaut'a	98	J2
Gudbransdalen	56	E6
Gudermes	98	M2
Gudvangen	56	D6
Guebwiller	60	C9
Guéckédou	108	B3
Guelma	106	G1
Guelph	40	D2
Guéret	66	B7

Guernsey	66	C4
Guernsey	38	F2
Guerrero Negro	44	D3
Gugë	110	F2
Güh Küh	96	G4
Guiana	46	L7
Guiana Highlands	50	F3
Guider	108	G3
Guiglo	108	C3
Guildford	64	M10
Guilianova	72	H6
Guilin	90	E1
Guillaumes	70	B6
Guillestre	70	B6
Guimarães	68	B3
Guinea	108	B2
Guinea-Bissau	108	A2
Güines	46	H4
Guingamp	66	B5
Güiria	50	E1
Guise	62	F5
Guitiriz	68	C1
Guiyang	86	D5
Gujranwala	94	B2
Gujrat	94	B2
Gulang	86	C3
Gulbarga	94	C5
Gulbene	56	P8
Gulf of Aden	96	E7
Gulf of Alaska	44	(1)H4
Gulf of Aqaba	96	B4
Gulf of Boothia	34	N2
Gulf of Bothnia	56	K6
Gulf of Carpentaria	116	G2
Gulf of Finland	56	M7
Gulf of Gdansk	58	J3
Gulf of Guinea	108	D4
Gulf of Mannar	94	C7
Gulf of Martaban	90	B3
Gulf of Mexico	46	F3
Gulf of Oman	101	G4
Gulf of Riga	56	M8
Gulf of St. Lawrence	34	U7
Gulf of Santa Catalina	44	C2
Gulf of Thailand	90	C4
Gulf of Tongking	90	D3
Gulf of Venice	70	H5
Gulfport	42	D3
Gulistan	82	M9
Gülşehir	76	S6
Gulu	110	E3
Gölübovo	76	H2
Gumdag	96	F2
Gumel	108	F2
Gumla	94	D4
Gummersbach	62	K3
Gummi	108	F2
Gümüşhane	98	H3
Guna	94	C4
Guna Terara	104	G5
Gungu	110	B5
Gunib	98	M2
Gunnbjørns Fjeld	120	(1)U2
Gunnedah	116	K6
Gunnison, Colo., United States	38	E3
Gunnison, Ut., United States	38	D3
Gunong Kinabalu	92	(1)F1
Guntakal	94	C5
Guntur	94	D5
Gunung Kerinci	92	(1)C3
Gunung Korbu	92	(1)C2
Gunung Kwoka	92	(2)D3
Gunung Leuser	92	(1)B2
Gunung Mekongga	92	(2)B3
Gunung Mulu	92	(1)E2
Gunung Pangrango	92	(1)C4
Gunungsitoli	92	(1)B2
Gunung Togwomeri	92	(2)D3
Günzburg	70	F2
Gunzenhausen	60	F7
Guoyang	86	F4
Gura Humorului	74	N2
Gurk	70	K4
Gurskoye	84	P6
Gürün	98	G4
Gurupi	50	H4
Gusau	108	F2
Gusev	58	M3
Gushgy	96	H2
Gusinoozersk	84	H6
Güspini	72	C9
Güssing	70	M3
Güstrow	60	H3
Gütersloh	60	D5
Guthrie, Okla., United States	38	G3
Guthrie, Tex., United States	44	F2
Gutsuo	94	E3
Guttenberg	40	B2

Guwahati	94	
Guyana	50	
Guyang	86	
Guymon	44	
Guyuan	86	
Guzar	96	
Gvardejsk	58	
Gwadar	96	
Gwalior	94	
Gwanda	112	
Gwardex	72	J
Gwda	58	
Gweebarra Bay	64	
Gweru	112	
Gyangzê	94	
Gyaring Hu	86	
Gyaros	76	
Gyda	82	
Gydanskiy Poluostrov	82	
Gyirong	94	
Gyldenløues Fjord	34	
Gympie	116	
Gyomaendröd	74	
Gyöngyös	74	
Györ	74	
Gypsumville	34	
Gytheio	76	
Gyula	74	
Gyumri	98	
Gyzylarbat	96	

H

Haapajärvi	56	
Haapsalu	56	
Haar	70	
Haarlem	62	
Haast	118	
Habahe	82	
Habarüt	96	
Habaswein	110	
Habbän	96	
Habbānīyah	98	
Habirag	86	
Habomai-Shoto	84	
Haboro	88	
Hachijō-jima	88	
Hachinohe	88	
Hachiōji	88	
Hadadong	82	
Haddunmahti Atoll	94	
Hadejia	108	
Hadejia	108	
Hadera	100	
Haderslev	60	
Ḩaḑramaut	96	
Hadilik	82	R
Hadjout	68	
Haeju	88	
Haenam	88	
Ḩafar al Bāṭin	101	
Hafnarfjördur	56	(1)
Haft Gel	101	
Hagen	62	
Hagenow	60	
Ḩägere Hiywet	110	
Hagerstown	40	
Haguenau	62	
Haicheng	88	
Haifa = Ḥefa	100	
Haikou	90	
Ha'il	96	
Hailar	84	
Hailey	38	
Hailong	88	
Hailuoto	56	
Hainan	90	
Haines Junction	44	(1)
Haining	86	
Hai Phong	90	
Haiti	46	
Haiya	104	
Hajdúböszörmény	74	
Hajdúhadház	58	L
Hajdúnánás	58	L
Hajdúszoboszló	58	L
Hajipur	94	
Hajmah	96	
Hajnówka	58	
Haka	94	
Hakkâri	98	
Hakodate	88	
Ḩalabān	104	
Ḩalabja	98	
Halaib	104	
Halba	100	
Halberstadt	60	
Halden	56	
Haldensleben	60	
Halifax	34	

Name		Page	Ref
ifax Bay	◳	116	J3
l		70	G3
l Beach		34	Q3
le		62	G4
lein		70	J3
ligen	◳	60	D2
lock		38	G1
l Peninsula	◳	34	T4
ls Creek		116	E3
ɪmahera	◳	92	(2)C2
ɪmahera Sea	◳	92	(2)C3
ɪmstad		58	B1
tern		62	K3
mada		88	G6
madān		96	E3
māh		98	G6
mamatsu		88	J6
mar		56	F6
marøy	◳	56	H2
matonbetsu		88	M1
mbantota		94	D7
mburg, Germany		60	E3
mburg, Ark., United States		42	C3
mburg, N.Y., United States		40	E2
meenlinna		56	N6
meln		60	E4
mersley Range	◳	116	C4
mhüng		88	D3
mi		82	S9
milton, Australia		116	H7
milton, Bermuda		46	M2
milton, Canada		40	E2
milton, New Zealand		118	E3
milton, Al., United States		42	D3
milton, Mont., United States		38	D1
milton, Oh., United States		40	D3
mina		56	P6
mirpur		94	D3
mm		60	C5
mmada du Drâa	◳	106	D3
mmam Bou Hadjar		68	K9
mmamet		72	E12
mmam Lif		106	H1
mmelburg		60	E6
mmerfest		56	M1
mmer Springs		118	D6
mpden		118	C7
mūn-e Jaz Mūrīān	◳	101	H3
namaki		88	L4
nau		60	D6
ncești		74	R3
ncheng		86	E3
ncock		40	C1
ndan		86	E3
ndeni		110	F5
nderslev		56	E9
ndlová		58	H9
nford		44	C1
ngayn Nuruu	◳	82	T8
ngu		86	F3
ngzhou		86	F4
nidh		101	C3
nko		56	M7
nksville		38	D3
nna		34	K6
nnibal		42	C2
nnover		60	E4
nö	◳	58	D2
nöbukten	◳	58	D2
Nõi	◳	90	D2
noi = Ha Nõi	◳	90	D2
nover		40	F2
n Shui	◳	86	D4
nson Bay	◳	118	(1)B1
numangarh		94	B3
nzhong		86	D4
o	◳	114	M7
ora		94	E4
paranda		56	N4
poli		94	F3
pur		94	C3
raq, Saudi Arabia		96	E5
raq, Yemen		104	H4
ramachi		88	L5
rare	◳	112	E3
rbin		86	H1
rbour Breton		34	V7
rburg		60	F3
rdangerfjorden	◳	56	C7
rdangervidda	◳	56	D6
rdenberg		62	J2
rderwijk		62	H2
rdin		38	E1
rdy		42	C2
ren		62	K2
rer		110	G2
rgeysa		110	G2

Name		Page	Ref
Har Hu	◿	86	B3
Haridwar		94	C3
Harihari		118	C6
Harima-nada	◳	88	H6
Hari Rud	◿	96	H3
Harlan		40	A2
Hārlāu		74	P2
Harlem		38	E1
Harlingen, Netherlands		62	H1
Harlingen, United States		42	B4
Harlow		64	N10
Harlowtown		38	E1
Harney Basin	◳	36	B3
Harney Lake	◿	38	C2
Härnösand		56	J5
Har Nuur	◿	82	S8
Haro		68	H2
Harricanaw	◿	34	R6
HHarrisburg, Ill., United States		40	C3
Harrisburg, Pa., United States	◱	42	F1
Harrison		40	B3
Harrison Bay	◣	44	(1)G1
Harrisville		40	D2
Harrogate		64	L8
Har Saggi	▲	100	B6
Harsin		98	M6
Hârşova		74	Q5
Harstad		56	J2
Hartberg		70	L3
Hartford	◱	40	F2
Hartland Point	◿	64	H10
Hartlepool		64	L7
Har Us Nuur	◿	82	S8
Harvey		38	G1
Harwich		62	D3
Harz	◿	60	F5
Häsä		100	C6
Haselünne		60	C4
Hashtpar		98	N5
Häsik		96	G6
Haskell		42	B3
Haslemere		62	B3
Hassan		94	C6
Hasselfelde		60	F5
Hasselt		62	H4
Haßfurt		60	F4
Hassi Bel Guebbour		106	G3
Hässleholm		56	G8
Hastings, New Zealand		118	F4
Hastings, United Kingdom		62	C4
Hastings, Minn., United States		40	B2
Hastings, Nebr., United States		38	G2
Hateg		74	K4
Hatgal		84	G6
Ha Tinh		90	D3
Hatteras		42	F2
Hattiesburg		42	D3
Hatvan		74	G2
Haud	◳	104	H6
Haud Ogadēn	◳	110	G2/H2
Haugesund		56	C7
Hauraki Gulf	◳	118	E3
Haut Atlas	◳	106	D2
Hauts Plateaux	◳	106	E2
Havana		42	C1
Havana = La Habana	◳	46	H4
Havant		64	M11
Havel	◿	58	C5
Havelock, New Zealand		118	D5
Havelock, United States		42	F3
Havelock North		118	F4
Havenby		60	D1
Haverfordwest		64	H10
Havlíčkův Brod		58	E8
Havre		38	E1
Havre-St-Pierre		34	U6
Havrylivtsi		74	P1
Havza		98	F3
Hawaii	◳	44	(2)E2
Hawaii	◳	44	(2)E4
Hawaiian Islands	◳	114	J3
Hawera		118	E4
Hawi		44	(2)F3
Hawick		64	K6
Hawke Bay	◳	118	F4
Hawker		116	G6
Hawr al'Awdah	◿	101	B1
Hawr al Hammar	◿	101	B1
Hawthorne		38	C3
Hay		116	H6
Hay	◿	34	H5
Hayange		68	J5
Haydarābād		98	L5
Hayden		44	D2
Hayrabolu		76	K3
Hay River		34	H4
Hays		42	B2
Hazard		40	D3

Name		Page	Ref
Hazāribāg		94	E4
Hazebrouck		62	E4
Hazelton, Canada		34	F5
Hazelton, United States		40	E2
Head of Bight	◳	116	F6
Hearne		42	B3
Hearst		40	D1
Hebbronville		44	G3
Hebgen Lake	◿	38	D2
Hebi		86	E3
Hebron, Canada		34	U5
Hebron, Israel		100	C5
Hebron, Nebr., United States		38	G2
Hebron, N.D., United States		38	F1
Hecate Strait	◳	34	E6
Hechi		90	D2
Hechingen		70	D2
Hede		56	G5
Heerenveen		62	H2
Heerlen		62	J4
Hefa		100	B4
Hefei		86	F4
Hegang		86	J1
Hegura-jima	◳	88	J5
Hegyfalu		70	M3
Heide		60	E2
Heidelberg		60	D7
Heidenheim		70	F2
Heilbad Heiligenstadt		60	F5
Heilbronn		60	E7
Heilmaey	◳	56	(1)C3
Heinola		56	N6
Hejing		82	R9
Hekla	◳	56	(1)D3
Helagsfjället	◣	56	G5
Helena, Ark., United States		42	C3
Helena, Mont., United States	◱	38	D1
Helen Reef	◳	92	(2)D2
Helensville		118	E3
Helgea		58	D1
Helgoland	◿	60	C2
Helgoländer Bucht	◿	60	D2
Hellín		68	J6
Helmand	◿	96	H3
Helmond		62	H3
Helmsdale		64	J3
Helmstedt		60	G4
Helodrano Antongila	◳	112	H3
Helong		88	E2
Helsingborg		56	G8
Helsinge		58	B1
Helsingør		56	G8
Helsinki	◳	56	N6
Helston		64	G11
Helwan		104	F2
Hemel Hempstead		64	M10
Henashi-zaki	◳	88	K3
Henderson, Ky., United States		40	C3
Henderson, Nev., United States		38	D3
Henderson, N.C. United States		42	F2
Henderson Island	◳	114	P8
Hendersonville		40	C3
Hendijarn		101	C1
Hengelo		62	J2
Hengyang		86	E5
Henichesk		78	F5
Henin-Beaumont		62	E4
Hennebont		66	B6
Henningsdorf		60	J4
Henryetta		40	A3
Henzada		90	B3
Heppenheim		60	E3
Heppner		38	C1
Hepu		90	D2
Hérádsflói	◳	56	(1)F2
Herald Cays	◳	116	J3
Herat		96	H3
Herbert		118	C7
Herborn		60	D6
Herceg-Novi		74	F7
Hereford, United Kingdom		64	K9
Hereford, United States		46	D2
Herentals		62	G3
Herford		60	D4
Herisau		70	E3
Herlen Gol	◿	86	E1
Hermagor		70	J4
Herma Ness	◿	64	M1
Hermel		100	D2
Hermiston		38	C1
Hermosillo		36	D6
Hernád	◿	58	L9
Herne		60	C5
Herne Bay		60	D3

Name		Page	Ref
Herning		56	E8
Herrenberg		70	D2
Hersbruck		60	G7
Herstat		62	H4
Hertlay		62	E6
Hervey Bay		116	K5
Herzberg		60	F5
Hesdin		62	E4
Heshan		90	D2
Hesselø	◳	58	A1
Hessisch-Lichtenau		60	E5
Hettstedt Lutherstadt		60	G5
Heves		58	K10
He Xian		90	E2
Hexigten Qi		85	F2
Heze		86	F3
Hialeah		42	E4
Hiawatha		42	B2
Hibbing		40	B1
Hickory		40	D3
Hidaka-sammyaku	◳	88	M2
Hidalgo del Parral		46	C3
Hiddensee	◳	60	H2
Hierro	◳	106	B3
Higashi-suidō	◳	88	E7
High Point		40	E3
High Wycombe		62	B3
Hiiumaa	◳	56	M7
Hikurangi		118	E2
Hikurangi	▲	118	G3
Hikutaia		118	E3
Hildburghausen		60	F6
Hildesheim		60	E4
Hillsboro, Oh., United States		42	C2
Hillsboro, Oreg., United States		38	B1
Hillsboro, Tex., United States		44	G2
Hillsville		40	D3
Hillswick		64	L1
Hilo		44	(2)F4
Hilton Head Island		42	E3
Hilva		98	H5
Hilversum		62	H2
Himalayas	◣	80	L6
Himarë		76	B4
Himatnagar		94	B4
Himeji		88	H6
Himora		104	G5
Ḥimş		100	D2
Hindu Kush	◣	94	A1
Hindupur		94	C6
Hinesville		42	E3
Hingoli		94	C5
Hinnøya	◳	56	H2
Hino		88	M2
Hirosaki		88	L3
Hiroshima		88	G6
Hirson		62	G5
Hirtshals		56	E8
Hisar		94	C3
Hisdal		56	C6
Hispaniola	◳	48	D2
Hitachi		88	L5
Hitoyoshi		88	F7
Hitra	◳	56	D5
Hiuchi-nada	◳	88	G6
Hiva Oa	◳	114	M6
Hjälmaren	◳	56	H7
Hjalmar Lake	◣	34	K4
Hjelmsøya	◳	56	M1
Hlinsko		58	E8
Hlohovec		70	N2
Hlyboka		74	N1
Hlybokaye		78	E2
Ho		108	E3
Hobart, Australia	◳	116	J8
Hobart, United States		44	G1
Hobbs		44	F2
Hobro		56	E8
Hobyo		110	H3
Hồ Chi Minh		90	D4
Höchstadt		60	F7
Hockenheim		60	D7
Hódmezővásárhely		74	H3
Hodonin		58	G9
Hoek van Holland		62	G3
Hoeryŏng		88	E2
Hof		60	G6
Hofgeismar		60	E5
Höfn	◳	56	(1)F2
Hofsjökull	◳	56	(1)D2
Höfu		88	F6
Hohe Dachstein	◣	58	C10
Hohe Tauern	◣	72	B3
Hohhot		86	E2
Hoh Xil Shan	◣	82	E1
Hội An		90	D3
Hoima		110	E3
Hokitika		118	C6

INDEX

Entry		Page	Grid
Hokkaidō	☒	88	N2
Holbæk		58	A2
Holbrook		44	D2
Holdrege		38	G2
Holguín		46	J4
Holič		70	N2
Hollabrunn		70	M2
Holland		40	C2
Hollis		44	G2
Hollywood		42	E4
Holman		34	H2
Hólmavík		56	(1)C2
Holmes Reefs	☒	116	J3
Holstebro		56	E8
Holsteinische Schweiz	☑	60	F2
Holsteinsborg = Sisimiut		34	W3
Holton		42	B2
Holyhead		64	H8
Holy Island, Eng., United Kingdom	☒	64	L6
Holy Island, Wales, United Kingdom	☒	64	H8
Holyoke		38	F2
Holzkirchen		70	E5
Holzminden		60	E5
Homa Bay		110	E4
Homberg		60	E5
Hombori		106	E5
Home Bay	◄	34	T3
Homestead		42	E4
Homewood		42	D3
Homs = Ḩimş		100	D2
Homyel'		78	F4
Hondo, N.Mex., United States		44	E2
Hondo, Tex., United States		44	G3
Honduras	▲	46	G6
Hønefoss		56	F6
Honey Lake	☑	38	B2
Honfleur		62	C5
Hon Gai		90	D2
Hong Kong		90	E2
Hongliuyuan		86	B2
Hongor		86	E1
Honiara	☒	114	F6
Honjō		88	K4
Honokaa		44	(2)F3
Honolulu	☒	44	(2)D2
Honshū	☒	88	L5
Hooge	☒	60	D2
Hoogeveen		62	J2
Hoogezand-Sappemeer		62	J1
Hooper Bay		44	(1)D3
Hoorn		62	H2
Hoorn Islands	☒	114	H7
Hopa		98	J3
Hope, Canada		38	B1
Hope, Ak., United States		34	B4
Hope, Ark., United States		42	C3
Hopedale		34	U5
Hopetoun		116	H7
Hopin		94	G4
Hopkinsville		40	C3
Hoquiam		38	B1
Horadiz		98	M4
Horasan		98	K3
Horgo		84	F7
Horizon Depth	☒	114	D7
Hormak		96	H4
Hormoz		101	F3
Horn		70	L2
Hornavan	☑	56	J3
Horncastle		62	B1
Horodenka		74	N1
Horodok		58	N8
Horqin Youyi Qianqi		84	L7
Horsens		56	E9
Horsham, Australia		116	H7
Horsham, United Kingdom		62	B3
Horten		56	F7
Hortiguela		68	G2
Horton	☑	44	(1)N2
Ḩoseynābād		101	N2
Hoshab		96	H4
Hoshangabad		94	C4
Hospet		94	C5
Hosséré Vokre	▲	108	G3
Hotan		82	Q10
Hotan	☑	82	Q10
Hot Springs, Ark., United States		40	B4
Hot Springs, N.C., United States		40	D3
Hottah Lake	☑	34	H3
Houdan		62	D6
Houdelaincourt		70	A2
Houghton		40	C1
Houlton		40	G1
Houma, China		86	E3
Houma, United States		36	H6
Houmt Souk		106	H2
Houston		36	G6
Hovd		82	S8
Hövsgöl Nuur	☑	84	F6
Howard Junction		118	D5
Howland	☒	114	J5
Hoxie		42	C2
Höxter		60	E5
Hoxud		82	R9
Hoy	☒	64	J3
Høyanger		56	D6
Hoyerswerda		60	K5
Hradeç Králové		58	E7
Hranice		58	G8
Hrazdan		98	L3
Hrodna		58	N4
Hron	☑	58	H9
Hrubieszów		58	N7
Hsin-chu		90	G2
Hsueh-Shan	▲	90	G2
Hsweni		90	B2
Huacho		50	B6
Huade		86	E2
Huadian		88	D2
Huaibei		86	F4
Huaibin		86	F4
Huaihua		86	D5
Huainan		86	F4
Huaiyin		86	F4
Huaki		92	(2)C4
Huallaga	☑	50	B5
Huambo		112	B2
Huancavelica		50	B6
Huancayo		50	B6
Huang	☑	84	H4
Huangchuan		86	F4
Huang He	☑	86	F3
Huangshan		86	F5
Huangshi		86	F4
Huang Xian		86	G3
Huangyan		86	G5
Huanren		88	C3
Huanuco		50	B5
Huaráz		50	B5
Huarmey		50	B6
Huasco		52	G4
Huashixia		86	B3
Huatabampo		36	E6
Hubli		94	C5
Huch'ang		88	D3
Huddersfield		64	L8
Huddinge		56	K7
Hudiksvall		56	J6
Hudson		40	F2
Hudson	☑	40	F2
Hudson Bay		34	L6
Hudson Bay	◄	34	P5
Hudson Strait	◄	34	S4
Huê		90	D3
Huelva		68	D7
Huercal Overa		68	J7
Huesca		68	K2
Huéscar		68	H7
Huftaroy	☒	56	C6
Hugo		42	B3
Hugo Lake	☑	42	B3
Huia		118	E3
Huich'ōn		88	D3
Huila Plateau	☒	112	A3
Huinan		88	C2
Huinca Renancó		52	J5
Huizhou		90	E2
Hulin		84	N7
Hull		40	E1
Hulst		62	G3
Hulun Nur	☑	84	K7
Huma		84	M6
Huma	☑	84	M6
Humaitá		50	E5
Humbe		112	A3
Humboldt		34	L6
Humboldt	☑	38	C2
Hümedān		96	G4
Humenné		58	L9
Humphrey		38	D2
Humpolec		58	E8
Hün		104	C2
Hünaflói	◄	56	(1)C2
Hunchun		88	F2
Hunedoara		74	K4
Hünfeld		60	E6
Hungary	▲	74	F3
Hungen		60	D6
Hungerford		116	H5
Hŭngnam		88	D4
Hunjiang		88	D3
Hunsrück	☒	60	B7
Hunstanton		62	C2
Hunte	☑	60	D4
Hunter Island	☒	114	H8
Huntingburg		42	D2
Huntingdon, United Kingdom		62	B2
Huntingdon, United States		42	E2
Huntington		42	D1
Huntington Beach		44	C2
Huntly		118	E3
Huntsville, Canada		40	E1
Huntsville, Al., United States		42	D3
Huntsville, Tex., United States		46	E2
Hunyuan		86	E3
Ḩür		101	G1
Hurdiyo		110	J1
Hurghada		104	F2
Huron		38	G2
Hürth		62	J4
Húsavík		56	(1)E1
Huşi		74	R3
Huslia		44	(1)F2
Husn		100	C4
Husum		60	E2
Hutag		84	G7
Hutanopan		92	(1)B2
Hutchinson		44	G1
Ḩūth		104	H4
Huttwil		70	C3
Huvadu Atoll	☒	94	B8
Huy		62	H4
Huzou		86	G4
Hvannadalshnúkur	▲	56	(1)E2
Hvar		74	D6
Hvar	☒	74	D6
Hvolsvöllur		56	(1)C3
Hwange		112	D3
Hyak		38	B1
Hyannis		38	F2
Hyderabad, India		94	C5
Hyderabad, Pakistan		96	J4
Hyères		66	M10
Hyesan		88	E3
Hyndam Peak	▲	38	D2
Hyūga		88	F7
Hyvinkää		56	N6
Iaco	☑	50	D6
Ialomița	☑	74	P5
Ianca		74	Q4
Iaşi		74	Q2
Ibadan		108	E3
Ibagué		50	B3
Ibar	☑	74	H6
Ibb		104	H5
Ibbenbüren		60	C4
Iberia		50	C5
Ibiza = Eivissa		68	M5
Ibiza = Eivissa	☒	68	M6
Ibotirama		50	J6
Ibrā'		96	G5
'Ibrī		101	G5
Ica		50	B6
İçel		98	F5
Iceland	▲	54	C1
Ichalkaranji		94	B5
Ichinoseki		88	L4
Idabel		42	C3
Ida Grove		40	A2
Idah		108	F3
Idaho	▣	38	D2
Idaho Falls		38	D2
Idar-Oberstein		60	C7
Idfu		104	F3
Idhān Awbārī	☒	106	H3
Idhan Murzūq	☒	106	H4
Idiofa		110	C4
Idlib		98	G6
Ieper		62	E4
Ierapetra		76	H9
Ifanadiana		112	H4
Ife		108	E3
Igarka		82	R4
Iggesund		56	J6
Igizyar		96	L2
Iglésias		72	C9
Igloolik		34	Q3
Ignace		40	B1
Iğneada		76	K3
Igoumenitsa		76	C5
Igra		78	M2
Igrim		78	M3
Igualada		68	M3
Iguatu		50	K5
Iharaña		112	H2
Ihosy		112	H4
Ihtiman		76	F2
Iida		88	J6
Iim	☑	70	
Iisalmi		56	
Iiulissat		34	
Ijebu Ode		108	
IJmuiden		62	
IJssel	☑	62	
IJsselmeer	☑	62	
Ikaria	☒	76	
Ikeda		88	
Ikela		110	
Ikhtiman		74	
Iki	☒	88	
Ikire		108	
Ikom		108	
Ikopa	☑	112	
Ikorodu		108	
Ilagan		90	
Ilām		96	
Iława		58	
Ilbenge		84	
Ilebo		110	
Île d'Anticosti	☒	34	
Île de Jerba	☒	106	
Île de la Gonâve	☒	46	
Île de Noirmoutier	☒	66	
Île de Ré	☒	66	
Île d'Oléron	☒	66	
Île d'Yeu	☒	66	
Île Europa	☒	112	
Ilek		78	
Ilek	☑	78	
Île Plane	☒	72	
Îles Cani	☒	72	
Îles Chesterfield	☒	114	
Îles Crozet	☒	102	
Îles de la Madeleine	☒	34	
Îles Désappointement	☒	114	
Îles d'Hyères	☒	66	
Îles Duc de Gloucester	☒	114	
Îles Glorieuses	☒	112	
Ilesha		108	
Îles Kerkenah	☒	106	
Îles Maria	☒	114	
Îles Palliser	☒	114	
Île Tidra	☒	106	
Île Zembra	☒	72	
Ilfracombe		64	
Ilha da Trindade	☒	48	
Ilha de Marajó	☒	50	
Ilha de São Luís	☒	50	
Ilha do Bazaruto	☒	112	
Ilha Fernando de Noronha	☒	50	
Ilha Grande de Gurupa	☒	50	
Ilhas Martin Vaz	☒	52	
Ilhéus		50	
Iliamna Volcano	▲	44	(1)
Iligan		90	
Ilkal		94	
Iller	☑	70	
Illertissen		70	
Illichivs'k		70	
Illinois	▣	36	
Illinois	☑	40	
Illizi		106	
Ilmenau		60	
Ilo		50	
Iloilo		90	
Ilorin		108	
Ilovlya		78	
Il'pyrskiy		84	
Ilwaco		38	
Ilych	☑	78	
Imabari		88	
Imatra		56	
Imeni-Babushkina		82	
Imeni Polinyosipenko		84	
Imese		110	
Imī		110	
Imişli		98	
Immenstadt		70	
Imola		70	
Imotski		74	
Imperatriz		50	
Impéria		72	
Imperial		38	
Impfondo		110	
Imphal		94	
Imrali Adasi	☒	76	
Imroz		76	
Imst	☑	50	
In Aménas		106	
Inangahua		118	
Inanwatan		92	(2)
Iñapari		50	
Inarijärvi	☑	56	
Inca		68	
Ince Burun	⊵	98	
Inch'ŏn		88	
Incirlova		76	
Indalsälven	☑	56	

dependence, Kans.,
  United States 42 B2
dependence, Mo.,
  United States 40 B3
dia .... ▲94 C4
diana .... ▣36 J3
diana 40 E2
dianapolis .... ◘42 D2
dian Ocean .... ◙94 D8
dianola 40 B2
dian Springs 38 C3
diga 78 J1
dio 44 C2
donesia .... ▲92 (1)D3
dore 94 C4
dramayu .... 92 (1)D4
dre .... ◙66 G6
dre Sula .... ◙56 C6
dus .... ◙96 K3
ebolu 98 E3
ecik 76 K4
egöl 98 C3
Ekker 106 G4
eu 74 J3
elheim 62 L5
geniero Jacobacci . 52 H7
gham 116 J3
goda .... ◙84 J6
golstadt 70 G2
gráj Bāzār 94 E3
gushetiya .... ◙98 L2
hambane 112 F4
irida .... ◙50 D3
ishmore .... ◘64 B8
kisi-Kisantu 108 H6
n .... ◙70 H2
ner Hebrides ..... ◙64 F5
ner Mongolia =
  Nei Monggol .... ◙86 E2
neston 116 G7
nisfail 116 J3
nsbruck 70 G3
ongo 110 B4
owrocław 58 H5
  Salah 106 F3
sein 90 B3
ta 82 K4
terlaken 70 C4
ternational Falls . 40 B1
tsy 78 H1
ubō-zaki .... ◘88 L6
ukjuak 34 R5
uvik .... 44 (1)L2
vercargill 118 B8
verness 64 H4
verway 116 E3
vestigator Group .. ◙116 F6
vestigator Strait . ◙116 G7
ya 82 R7
ya .... ◙84 R4
annina 76 C5
kanga .... ◙82 F4
la 42 B2
na .... ◙64 F5
nian Sea .... ◙76 B6
nioi Nisoi .... ◙76 B5
s .... ◙76 H8
wa .... ◙36 H3
wa City 40 B2
wa Falls 40 B2
ameri 50 H7
atinga 72 N2
atovo 78 H5
iales 50 B3
iaŭ 50 K6
oh .... 92 (1)C2
orá 50 G7
py 110 C2
sala 76 J4
swich 64 P9
aluit .... ◘34 T4
uique 52 G3
uitos 50 C4
acoubo 50 G2
akleia 76 F3
akleia .... ◙76 H8
akleio 76 H9
aklion = Irakleio . 54 G4
an .... ▲96 F3
inshahr 96 H4
apuato 46 D4
aq .... ▲96 D3
oid 100 C4
oit 78 M3
ecê 50 J6
giz 78 M5
giz .... ◙78 M5
nil M'Goun .... ▲106 D2
an Jaya .... ◙92 (2)E3
nga 110 F5
ri .... ◙50 G4
sh Sea .... ◙64 G8

Irkutsk 84 G6
Iron Mountain 40 C1
Ironton 42 E2
Ironwood 40 B1
Irrawaddy .... ◙94 F5
Irshava 74 L1
Irta 78 J2
Irtysh .... ◙78 P3
Irtyshsk 82 P7
Irumu 110 D3
Irún 68 J1
Irvine 64 H6
Irving 44 G2
Isabela .... 92 (2)B1
Isabella 40 B1
Isabella Lake .... ◙44 C1
Ísafjarðardjúp ... ◙56 (1)A1
Ísafjörður .... ◙56 (1)B1
Isahaya 86 J4
Isar .... ◙70 G3
Ischia .... ◙72 H8
Ise 88 J6
Isel .... ◙70 H4
Isère .... ◙70 B5
Iserlohn 62 K3
Isérnia 72 J7
Isetskoye 78 N3
Iseyin 108 E3
Isfana 96 J2
Ishikari-wan ..... ◙88 L2
Ishim 78 N3
Ishim .... ◙78 N4
Ishinomaki 88 L4
Ishkoshim 96 K2
Isiolo 110 F3
Isiro 110 D3
Iskär .... ◙74 M6
Iskenderun 98 G5
Iskitim 82 Q7
Isla Alejandro Selkirk ◙52 E5
Isla Campana ..... ◙52 F8
Isla Clarence .... ◙52 G9
Isla Clarión ..... ◙46 B5
Isla Coiba .... ◙46 H7
Isla Contreras ... ◙52 F9
Isla de Alborán .. ◙68 G9
Isla de Bioco .... ◙108 F4
Isla de Chiloé ... ◙52 G7
Isla de Coco ..... ◙46 G7
Isla de Cozumel .. ◙46 G4
Isla de la Juventud ◙46 H4
Isla de los Estados ◙52 J9
Isla de Malpelo .. ◙50 A3
Isla de Margarita . ◙50 E1
Isla de Providencia ◙46 H6
Isla de San Andrés ◙46 H6
Isla de São Francisco ◙52 M4
Isla de São Sebastião ◙52 M3
Isla Desolación .. ◙52 F9
Isla Española .... ◙50 (1)B2
Isla Fernandina .. ◙50 (1)A2
Isla Gorgona ..... ◙50 B3
Isla Grande ...... ◙52 N3
Isla Grande de Tierra del
  Fuego .... ◙52 H9
Isla Guafo .... ◙52 F7
Isla Hoste .... ◙52 G10
Isla Isabela ..... ◙50 (1)A2
Isla La Tortuga .. ◙50 D1
Isla Londonderry . ◙52 G9
Islamabad .... ◙94 B2
Isla Madre de Dios ◙52 F8/9
Isla Marchena .... ◙50 (1)A1
Islamgarh 94 B3
Islamorada 42 E5
Isla Navarino .... ◙52 H10
Island Lake ...... ◙34 M6
Islands of the Four
  Mountains ...... ◙44 (1)C5
Isla Pinta .... ◙50 (1)A1
Isla Puná .... ◙50 A4
Isla Riesco ...... ◙52 G9
Isla Robinson Crusoe ◙52 E5
Isla San Benedicto ◙46 B5
Isla San Cristóbal ◙50 (1)B2
Isla San Salvador . ◙50 (1)A2
Isla Santa Cruz .. ◙50 (1)A2
Isla Santa Inés .. ◙52 F9
Isla Santa María . ◙50 (1)A2
Islas Baleares ... ◙68 N5
Islas Canarias ... ◙102 A3
Islas Canarias ... ◙106 B3
Islas Columbretes . ◙68 L5
Islas de la Bahía . ◙46 G5
Islas de los
  Desventurados .. ◙52 E4
Islas Galápagos .. ◙50 (1)B1
Islas Juan Fernández ◙52 E5
Islas Los Roques . ◙50 D1
Islas Marías ..... ◙46 C4
Islas Socorro .... ◙46 B5
Islas Revillagigedo ◙46 B5

Islas Wollaston .. ◙52 H10
Isla Wellington .. ◙52 F8
Islay .... ◙64 F6
Isle .... ◙66 F8
Isle of Man ...... ◙64 H7
Isle of Wight .... ◙64 L11
Isle Royale ...... ◙40 C1
Isles of Scilly .. ◙64 F12
Ismâ'îlîya 104 F1
İsmayıllı 98 N3
Isna 104 F2
Isoka 112 E2
Isola delle Correnti ◙72 J12
Isola di Capo Rizzuto 72 M10
Isola di Pantelleria ◙72 G12
Isole Égadi ...... ◙72 F11
Isole Lipari ..... ◙72 J10
Isole Ponziane ... ◙72 H8
Isole Trémiti .... ◙72 K6
Iso-Vietonen ..... ◙56 N3
Isparta 76 N7
Íspica 72 J12
Israel .... ▲100 B5
Israelite Bay .... ◙116 D6
Issia 108 C3
Issimu .... 92 (2)B2
Issoire 66 J8
Issoudun 66 H7
İstanbul 98 C3
İstanbul Boğazı .. ◙98 C3
Istiaia 76 F6
Istmo de Tehauntepec ◙46 F5
Istra .... ◙70 J3
Istres 66 K10
Itaberaba 50 J6
Itabira 50 J7
Itabuna 50 K6
Itacoatiara 50 F4
Itaituba 50 F4
Itajaí 52 M4
Italy .... ▲72 E4
Itambacuri 50 J7
Itanagar 94 F3
Itapebi 50 K7
Itapetinga 50 J7
Itapicuru .... ◙50 K6
Itapicuru Mirim .. 50 J4
Itapipoca 50 K4
Itarsi 94 C4
Ithaca 40 C2
Ithaki 76 C6
Ithaki .... ◙76 C6
Itiquira .... ◙50 F/G7
Itu .... ◙50 C5
Ituiutaba 50 H7
Itumbiara 50 H7
Ituni 50 F2
Ituri .... ◙110 C3
Ituxi .... ◙50 D5
Itzehoe 60 E3
Ivalo 56 P2
Ivanava 56 N10
Ivangrad 74 G7
Ivanhoe, Australia 116 H6
Ivanhoe, United States 40 A2
Ivano-Frankivs'k . 78 D5
Ivanovo 78 H3
Ivatsevichy 56 N10
Ivdel' 78 M2
Ivittuut 34 X4
Ivory Coast ...... ▲108 C3
Ivosjön .... ◙58 D1
Ivrea 70 C5
Ivujivik 34 R4
Iwaki 88 L5
Iwamizawa 88 L2
Iwo 108 E3
Iyo-nadā .... ◙88 G7
Izberbash 98 M2
Izegem 62 F4
Izhevsk .... ◙78 K3
Izhma 78 K1
Izhma .... ◙78 K2
Izk 96 G5
Izki 101 G5
Izmayil 74 R4
İzmir 98 B3
İzmir Körfezi .... ◙76 J6
İzmit 98 C3
İznik 98 C3
İznik Gölü .... ◙98 C3
Izra 70 J5
Izra' 100 C3
Izumo 88 J6
Izu-shotō .... ◙88 K6

J

Jabal ad Durûz ... ▲100 D4
Jabal Akhḍar ..... ▲101 G5

Jabal al Nuṣayrīyah ◙100 D1
Jabal an Nabī Shu'ayb ▲104 H4
Jabal Ash Sham ... ▲101 G5
Jabal aẓ Ẕannah .. 101 E4
Jabalpur 94 C4
Jabal Shammar .... ◙104 G2
Jabal Thamar ..... ▲104 J5
Jabiru 116 F2
Jablah 100 C1
Jablonec 58 E7
Jablunkov 58 H8
Jaboatão 50 K5
Jaca 68 K2
Jacareacanga 50 G5
Jackman 40 F1
Jacksboro 42 B3
Jackson, Calif.,
  United States .. 38 B3
Jackson, Minn.,
  United States .. 40 B2
Jackson, Miss.,
  United States .. ◘42 C3
Jackson, Oh.,
  United States .. 42 E2
Jackson, Tenn.,
  United States .. 42 D2
Jackson Head ..... ◙118 B6
Jackson Lake ..... ◙38 D2
Jacksonville, Fla.,
  United States .. 42 E3
Jacksonville, Ill.,
  United States .. 40 B3
Jacksonville, N.C.,
  United States .. 42 F3
Jacksonville, Tex.,
  United States .. 42 B3
Jacmel 46 K5
Jacobabad 94 A3
Jacobina 50 J6
Jacunda 50 H4
Jacupiranga 52 M3
Jade .... ◙60 D3
Jadebusen .... ◙60 D3
Jādū 106 H2
Jaén 68 G7
Jaen 50 B5
Jaffna 94 D7
Jagdalpur 94 D5
Jagersfontein 112 D5
Jaggang 94 C2
Jagst .... ◙60 E7
Jahrom 101 E2
Jaipur 94 C3
Jaisalmer 94 B3
Jajce 74 E5
Jakarta .... ◙92 (1)D4
Jakobshavn = Iiulissat 34 W3
Jakobstad 56 M5
Jalālābād 94 B2
Jalandhar 94 C2
Jalapa Enríquez .. 46 E5
Jalgaon 94 C4
Jālibah 101 B1
Jalingo 108 G3
Jalna 94 C5
Jalón .... ◙68 J3
Jalpaiguri 94 E3
Jalūlā 98 L6
Jamaica .... ▲46 H5
Jamalpur 94 E3
Jambi .... 92 (1)C3
James .... ◙38 G2
James .... ◙34 Q6
Jamestown, N.Y.,
  United States .. 40 E2
Jamestown, N.D.,
  United States .. 38 G1
Jammerbugten ..... ◙56 E3
Jammu 94 B2
Jammu and Kashmir ◙94 B2
Jamnagar 94 B4
Jämsä 56 N6
Jamshedpur 94 E4
Janakpur 94 E3
Janaúba 50 J7
Jandaq 96 F3
Jandongi 110 C3
Jane Peak .... ▲118 B7
Janesville 40 C2
Jan Mayen .... ◙32 C2
Janos 44 E2
Jánossomorja 70 N3
Janów Lubelski ... 58 M7
Jantarnyj 58 J2
Januária 50 J7
Jaora 94 C4
Japan .... ▲88 L5
Japan Trench ..... ◙114 E2
Japurá .... ◙50 D4
Jarābulus 98 H5
Jaramillo 52 H8
Jarash 100 C4

Jardim 52 K3
Jarosław 58 M7
Järpen 56 G5
Jarud Qi 86 G2
Järvenpää 56 N6
Jarvis 114 K6
Jasel'da 56 N10
Jäsk 101 G4
Jason Islands 52 J9
Jasper, Al., United States 42 D3
Jasper, Fla.,
  United States 42 E3
Jasper, Tex.,
  United States 42 C3
Jastrebarsko 70 L5
Jászberény 74 G2
Jataí 50 G7
Jatapu 50 F4
Jaunpur 94 D3
Java = Jawa 92 (1)E4
Javarthushuu 84 J7
Java Sea 92 (1)E4
Javoriv 58 N8
Jawa 92 (1)E4
Jawhar 110 H3
Jayapura 92 (2)F3
Jayrūd 100 D3
Jaza'ir Farasān 104 H4
Jazīrat Būbīyān 101 C2
Jazīrat-ye Khārk 101 D2
Jbail 100 C2
Jbel Ayachi 106 E2
Jbel Bou Naceur 106 E2
Jbel Toubkal 106 D2
Jean 38 C3
Jebba 108 E3
Jebel Bāqir 100 C7
Jebel el Atā'ita 100 C6
Jebel el Batrā 100 C7
Jebel-esh Sharqi 100 C3
Jebel Gimbala 104 D5
Jebel Ithrīyat 100 D6
Jebel Liban 100 C3
Jebel Mubrak 100 C6
Jebel Ram 100 C7
Jebel Uweinat 104 E3
Jedburgh 64 K6
Jedda = Jiddah 96 C5
Jedeida 72 D12
Jędrzejów 58 K7
Jefferson 40 B2
Jefferson City, Mo.,
  United States 40 B3
Jefferson City, Tenn.,
  United States 42 E2
Jeffersonville 40 C3
Jega 108 E2
Jēkabpils 56 N8
Jelgava 56 M8
Jemaja 92 (1)D2
Jena 60 G6
Jendouba 106 G1
Jenin 100 C4
Jenkins 40 D3
Jequié 50 J6
Jequitinhonha 50 J7
Jerada 106 E2
Jeremoabo 50 K6
Jerez 44 F4
Jerez de la Frontera 68 D8
Jerez de los Caballeros 68 D6
Jericho, Australia 116 J4
Jericho, Israel 100 C5
Jersey 66 C4
Jersey City 42 G1
Jerusalem =
  Yerushalayim 100 C5
Jesenice 74 B3
Jesenik 58 G7
Jesi 70 J7
Jésolo 70 H5
Jessore 94 E4
Jesup 42 E3
Jeumont 62 G4
Jever 60 C3
Jeypore 94 D5
Jezioro 58 D4
Jezioro Gardno 56 J9
Jezioro Jeziorsko 58 H6
Jezioro Łebsko 58 F3
Jezioro Śniardwy 58 L4
Jezioro Wigry 58 N2
Jezzine 100 C3
Jhang Maghiana 94 B2
Jhansi 94 C3
Jharsuguda 94 D4
Jhelum 94 B2
Jialing Jiang 86 D4
Jiamusi 86 J1
Ji'an 86 E5
Jiangle 86 F5
Jiangling 86 E4

Jiangmen 86 E6
Jiangyou 86 C4
Jiaonan 86 F3
Jiaozou 86 E3
Jiaxing 86 G4
Jiayuguan 86 B3
Jibou 74 L2
Jičín 58 E7
Jiddah 96 C5
Jiesjavrre 56 N2
Jiexiu 86 E3
Jihlava 58 E8
Jijia 74 Q2
Jijiga 110 G2
Jilib 110 G3
Jilin 88 D2
Jima 110 F2
Jimbolia 74 H4
Jiménez 44 F3
Jimsar 82 R9
Jinan 86 F3
Jinapo Hu 88 E3
Jinchang 86 C3
Jincheng 86 E3
Jindřichův Hradec 58 E8
Jingdezhen 86 F5
Jinggu 86 C6
Jinghe 82 Q9
Jinghong 86 C6
Jingmen 86 E4
Jingning 86 D3
Jingxi 86 D6
Jinhua 86 F5
Jining, China 86 E2
Jining, China 86 F3
Jinja 110 E3
Jinka 110 F2
Jinsha 86 C5
Jinshi 86 E5
Jinta 86 B2
Jinxi 86 G2
Jinzhou 86 G2
Jirgatol 96 K2
Jirkov 60 J6
Jīroft 101 G2
Jirriiban 110 H2
Jishou 86 D5
Jiu 74 L4
Jiujiang 86 F5
Jiwani 96 H4
Jixi 88 F1
Jīzān 104 H4
Jizera 58 D7
J. J. Castelli 50 D4
Joal-Fadiout 106 B6
João Pessoa 50 L5
Jódar 68 G7
Jodhpur 94 B3
Joensuu 78 E2
Jõetsu 88 K5
Jõgeva 56 P7
Johannesburg,
  South Africa 112 D5
Johannesburg,
  United States 44 C1
John Day 38 C2
John o' Groats 64 J3
John Redmond
  Reservoir 42 B2
Johnson 42 A2
Johnson City 40 D3
Johnson's Crossing 44 (1)L3
Johnston Island 114 J4
Johnstown 40 E2
Johor Bahru 92 (1)C2
Joigny 66 J5
Joinville, Brazil 52 M4
Joinville, France 66 L5
Jokkmokk 56 K3
Jökulsá á Fjöllum 56 (1)E1
Jolfa 98 L4
Joliet 36 J3
Joliette 40 F1
Jolo 92 (2)B1
Jolo 92 (2)B1
Jonava 58 P2
Jonesboro 40 B3
Jones Sound 34 P1
Jonesville 42 C3
Jonglei Canal 110 E2
Jongunjärvi 56 P4
Joniškis 58 N1
Jönköping 56 H8
Jonquière 40 F1
Joplin 42 C2
Jordan 100 D5
Jordan 38 E1
Jordan Valley 38 C2
Jorhat 94 F3
Jörn 56 L4
Jos 108 F3
José de San Martín 52 G7

Joseph Bonaparte Gulf 116 E2
Joûnié 100 C2
Juan de Nova 112 G3
Juàzeiro 50 J5
Juàzeiro do Norte 50 K5
Juba 110 E3
Jubba 110 G3
Júcar 68 J5
Juchitán 46 F5
Judenburg 70 K3
Juhre 84 L8
Juist 60 B3
Juiz de Fora 52 N3
Julesburg 38 F2
Juli 50 C7
Juliaca 50 C7
Juliana Top 50 F3
Jülich 62 J4
Jumilla 68 J6
Jumla 94 D3
Junagadh 94 B4
Junction 42 B3
Junction City 42 B2
Jundah 116 H4
Juneau 44 (1)L4
Jungfrau 70 C4
Junggar Pendi 82 R8
Jun Xian 86 E4
Jūra 58 M2
Jura 64 G5
Jura 70 B4
Jurbarkas 58 M2
Jurf ed Darāwīsh 100 C6
Jurhe 86 G2
Jūrmala 56 M8
Jūrmala 78 D3
Juruá 50 D4
Juruena 50 F5
Juruena 50 F6
Justo Daract 52 H5
Jutaí 50 D5
Jüterbog 60 J5
Juwain 96 H3
Ju Xian 86 F3
Jūymand 96 G3
Jūyom 101 F2
Juzur al Halaniyat 96 G6
Jylland 56 E8
Jyväskylä 78 E2
Jyväskylä 56 N5

K

K2 94 C1
Kaakhka 96 G2
Kaamanen 56 P2
Kaaresuvanto 56 M2
Kaarta 106 C6
Kabaena 92 (2)B4
Kabakly 96 H2
Kabala 108 B3
Kabale 110 E4
Kabalo 110 D5
Kabardino-Balkariya 98 K2
Kabompo 112 D2
Kabongo 110 D5
Kabugao 90 G3
Kābul 96 J3
Kabwe 112 D2
Kachikattsy 84 M4
Kachug 84 H6
Kadama 94 B6
Kadañ 58 C7
Kadinhani 76 Q6
Kadirli 98 G5
Kadoka 38 F2
Kadoma 112 D3
Kadugli 104 E5
Kaduna 108 F2
Kadzherom 78 L2
Kaédi 106 C5
Kaesŏng 88 D5
Kafanchan 108 F3
Kaffrine 108 A2
Kafiau 92 (2)C3
Kāfjord 56 N1
Kafr el Sheikh 104 F1
Kafue 112 D3
Kaga 88 J5
Kaga Bandoro 110 B2
Kagoshima 88 F8
Kahemba 110 B5
Kahnūj 101 G3
Kahraman Maraş 98 G5
Kahurangi Point 118 C5
Kaiama 108 E3
Kai Besar 92 (2)D4
Kaifeng 86 E4
Kaihu 118 D2
Kaihua 86 F5
Kai Kecil 92 (2)D4

Kaikohe 118 D
Kaikoura 118 D
Kaili 86 D
Kailua 44 (2)D
Kailua Kona 44 (2)E
Kaimana 92 (2)D
Käina 56 M
Kainji Reservoir 108 E
Kaipara Harbour 118 D
Kairouan 106 H
Kaiserslautern 60 C
Kaišiadorys 58 F
Kaitaia 118 C
Kaiyuan 90 C
Kajaani 56 P
Kakamega 110 E
Kakata 108 B
Kakhovs'ke
  Vodoskhovyshche 78
Käkinäda 94 D
Kaktovik 44 (1)J
Kalabagh 94 B
Kalabahi 92 (2)B
Kalabakan 92 (1)K
Kalach 78 H
Kalachinsk 78 H
Kalach-na-Donu 78 H
Kaladar 40 E
Ka Lae 44 (2)F
Kalahari Desert 112 C
Kalajoki 56 M
Kalakan 84 H
Kalam 94 H
Kalamata 76 E
Kalamazoo 40 C
Kalampaka 76 C
Kalaotoa 92 (2)B
Kalapana 44 (2)G
Kalaupapa 44 (2)H
Kalavryta 76 E
Kale 76 L
Kalecik 98 E
Kaledupa 92 (2)B
Kalemie 110 D
Kalemyo 94 F
Kalevala 56 F
Kalewa 94 F
Kalgoorlie 116 D
Kalianda 92 (1)C
Kalibo 90 G
Kalima 110 D
Kalimantan 92 (1)E
Kaliningrad 58 H
Kaliningradskij Zaliv 58
Kalispell 38 D
Kalisz 58 H
Kalixälven 56 M
Kalkan 76 M
Kalkaring 116 E
Kalkaska 40 C
Kallavesi 56 P
Kallsjön 56 G
Kalmar 56 J
Kalmykiya 98 M
Kalmykovo 78 K
Kalocsa 74 G
Kalol 94 B
Kalpakio 76 C
Kalpeni 94 B
Kaltag 44 (1)F
Kaluga 78 G
Kalyan 94 B
Kalymnos 76 J
Kalymnos 76 J
Kama 54 J
Kama 110 D
Kamaishi 88 L
Kamande 110 D
Kamango 82 H
Kambarka 78 K
Kambo Ho 88
Kamchatka 84 T
Kamchatskiy Zaliv 84 V
Kamenica 76 H
Kamenka, Russia 76 H
Kamenka, Russia 78
Kamen'-na-Obi 82
Kamen'-Rybolov 88 G
Kamensk-Shakhtinsky 78 H
Kamensk-Ural'skiy 78 M
Kamenz 58
Kamet 94 C
Kamiiso 88 L
Kamina 110 D
Kamituga 110 D
Kamiyaku 88 F
Kamloops 34 H
Kamoenai 88 L
Kampala 110 E
Kampen 62 J
Kampong Cham 90
Kam''yanets'-Podil's'kyy 78 N

Name	Pg	Grid
myanyets	56	M10
myshin	78	J4
myzyak	78	J5
nab	44	D1
nanga	110	C5
nazawa	88	J5
nbalu	94	G4
nchipuram	94	C6
ndahār	96	J3
ndalaksha	56	S3
ndalakshskiy Zaliv	► 78	F1
ndi	108	E2
ndira	76	N3
ndy	94	D7
ne	40	E2
neohe	44	(2)D2
ng	112	C4
ngaatsiaq	34	W3
ngal	98	G4
ngān, *Iran*	101	E3
ngān, *Iran*	101	G4
ngaroo Island	⊠116	G7
ngchenjunga	▲ 94	E3
ngding	86	C4
ngeq	⊟ 34	Y4
ngerluarsoruseq	34	W4
ngersuatsiaq	34	W2
ngetet	110	F3
ngiqsualujjuaq	34	T5
ngmar	94	E3
ngnüng	88	E5
ngo	108	G4
ngping	86	G2
niama	110	C5
nji Reservoir	◪102	D4
njiža	74	H3
nkaanpää	56	M6
nkakee	40	C2
nkan	108	C2
nkossa	106	C5
nnapolis	42	E2
no	108	F2
noya	88	F8
npur	94	D3
nsas	◪ 42	A2
nsas	↗ 42	B2
nsas City, *Kans.*, United States	42	C2
nsas City, *Mo.*, United States	42	C2
nsk	82	T6
nta	▲110	F2
ntchari	108	E2
ntemirovka	78	G5
nye	112	C4
o-Hsiung	86	G6
olack	106	B6
oma	112	C2
panga	110	C5
p Arkona	⊟ 58	C3
pchagay	82	P9
p Cort Adelaer = Kangeq	⊟ 34	Y4
p Farvel = Uummannarsuaq	⊟ 34	Y5
pfenberg	70	L3
pidağı Yarimadası	⊠ 76	K4
piri Mposhi	112	D2
pit	92	(1)E2
piti Island	⊠118	E5
plice	70	K2
poeta	110	E3
posvár	74	E3
ppel	60	C6
ppeln	60	E2
ppl	70	F3
psan	88	E3
puskasing	36	K2
puvár	74	E2
ra	↗ 82	M4
ra, *Russia*	82	M4
ra, *Togo*	108	E3
ra Ada	⊠ 76	K8
ra-Balta	82	N9
rabekaul	96	H2
ra-Bogaz-Gol	96	F1
rabutak	78	M5
racabey	76	L4
racaköy	76	L3
racal Tepe	▲ 76	Q8
rachayevo-Cherkesiya	◪ 98	J2
rachayevsk	98	J2
rachi	96	J5
raganda	82	N8
raginskiy Zaliv	► 84	V5
raj	96	F2
rak	100	C5
ra-Kala	96	G2
ra-Köl	82	N9
rakol	82	P9
rakoram	► 80	L6
raksar	84	K6

Name	Pg	Grid
Karam	84	H5
Karaman	98	E5
Karamay	82	R8
Karamea	118	D5
Karamea Bight	►118	C5
Karamürsel	76	M4
Karaoy	82	N8
Karapınar	76	R7
Kara-Say	82	P9
Karasburg	112	B5
Kara Sea = Karskoye More	◪ 82	L3
Karasu	98	D3
Karasuk	82	P7
Karasuk	↗ 82	P7
Karatal	↗ 82	P8
Karataş	98	F5
Karatobe	78	K5
Karaton	78	K5
Karatsu	88	E7
Karazhal	78	P5
Karbalā'	96	D3
Karcag	74	H2
Karditsa	76	D5
Kärdla	56	M7
Kareliya	◪ 56	R4
Karepino	78	L2
Karesuando	56	M2
Kargalinskaya	98	M2
Kargasok	82	Q6
Kargat	↗ 82	P6
Kargil	94	C2
Kargopol'	78	G2
Kariba	112	D3
Kariba Dam	⊠112	D3
Karibib	112	B4
Karimata	⊠ 92	(1)D3
Karimnagar	94	C5
Karkaralinsk	82	P8
Karkinits'ka Zatoka	► 78	F5
Karlik Shan	▲ 86	A2
Karlovac	74	C4
Karlovasi	76	J7
Karlovo	76	G2
Karlovy Vary	60	H6
Karlshamn	58	D1
Karlskoga	56	H7
Karlskrona	56	H8
Karlsruhe	60	D8
Karlstad, *Norway*	56	G7
Karlstad, *United States*	40	A1
Karlstadt	60	E7
Karmala	94	C5
Karmi'el	100	C4
Karmøy	56	C7
Karnafuli Reservoir	↗ 94	F4
Karnal	94	C3
Karnische Alpen	▲ 70	H4
Karnobat	76	J2
Karodi	96	J4
Karonga	110	E5
Karpathos	76	K9
Karpathos	⊠ 76	K9
Karpenisi	76	D6
Karpogory	78	H2
Karrabük	98	E3
Kars	98	K3
Karsakpay	78	N5
Kärsava	56	P8
Karshi	96	J2
Karskoye More	◪ 82	L3
Karslyaka	76	K6
Karstula	56	N5
Kartaly	78	M4
Kartayel'	78	K2
Kartuzy	58	H3
Karufa	92	(2)D3
Karumba	116	H3
Karur	94	C6
Karvina	58	H8
Karwar	94	B6
Karystos	76	G6
Kasai	↗110	B4
Kasaji	112	C2
Kasama	112	E2
Kasansay	82	N9
Kasba Lake	↗ 34	L4
Kasempa	112	D2
Kasenga	112	D2
Kāshān	96	F3
Kashi	96	L2
Kashima	86	L3
Kashiwazaki	88	K5
Käshmar	96	H2
Kashmor	96	J4
Kasimov	78	H4
Kasli	78	M3
Kasongo	110	D4
Kasos	⊠ 76	K9
Kaspi	98	L3
Kaspiysk	98	M2
Kassala	104	G4

Name	Pg	Grid
Kassandreia	76	F4
Kassel	60	E5
Kasserine	106	G1
Kastamonu	98	E3
Kastelli	76	F9
Kastoria	76	D4
Kasulu	110	E4
Kasumkent	98	N3
Kasur	94	B2
Kata	84	G5
Katchall	◪ 94	F7
Katerini	76	E4
Katete	112	E2
Katha	94	G4
Katherine	116	F2
Kathiawar	◪ 96	K5
Kathmandu	◪ 94	E3
Kati	108	C2
Katihar	94	E3
Katiola	108	C3
Kato Nevrokopi	76	F3
Katonga	↗110	E3
Katoomba	116	K6
Katowice	58	J7
Katrineholm	56	J7
Katsina	108	F2
Katsina-Ala	108	F3
Katsuura	88	L6
Kattakurgan	96	J2
Kattavia	76	K9
Kattegat	► 56	F8
Katun'	↗ 82	R7
Katwijkaan Zee	62	G2
Kauai	⊠ 44	(2)B1
Kaufbeuren	70	F3
Kauhajoki	56	M5
Kaunas	58	N3
Kauno	↗ 58	P3
Kaunus	54	G2
Kaura Namoda	108	F2
Kavadarci	76	D3
Kavala	76	B3
Kavajë	76	G4
Kavaratti	◪ 94	B6
Kavarna	74	R6
Kawagoe	88	K6
Kawakawa	118	G2
Kawambwa	110	D5
Kawasaki	88	K6
Kawau Island	⊠118	E3
Kaweka	▲118	F4
Kawhia	118	E4
Kawkareik	90	B3
Kawthaung	90	B4
Kaya	108	D2
Kayak	82	U3
Kaycee	38	E2
Kayenta	44	D1
Kayes	108	B2
Kaynar	76	P5
Kaynar	82	P8
Kayseri	98	F4
Kazachinskoye	84	E5
Kazach'ye	84	P2
Kazakdar'ya	82	K9
Kazakhstan	◪ 82	L8
Kazan'	► 78	J3
Kazan	↗ 34	M4
Kazan	76	H2
Kazan-rettō	⊠114	E3
Kazbek	▲ 98	L2
Kăzerün	101	D2
Kazincbarcika	74	H1
Kazungula	112	D3
Kea	⊠ 76	G7
Kearney	36	G3
Keban Baraji	↗ 98	H4
Kébémér	106	B5
Kebkabiya	104	D5
Kebnekajse	▲ 56	K3
K'ebrī Dehar	110	G2
K'ech'a Terara	▲110	F2
Keçiborlu	76	N7
Kecskemet	74	G2
Kédainiai	58	N2
Kedgwick	40	G1
Kedougou	108	B2
Kędzierzyn-Koźle	58	H7
Keele	↗ 44	(1)M3
Keene	40	F2
Keetmanshoop	112	B5
Keewatin	40	B1
Kefallonia	⊠ 76	C6
Kefamenanu	92	(2)B4
Keflavík	56	(1)B2
Kegen'	82	P9
Keg River	34	H5
Kehl	70	C2
Keitele	↗ 56	N5
Kékes	▲ 74	H2

Name	Pg	Grid
Kelai Thiladhunmathee Atoll	⊠ 94	B7
Kelheim	70	G2
Kelibia	72	F12
Kelkit	↗ 98	G3
Kelmě	58	M2
Kélo	108	H3
Kelowna	34	H7
Kelso	38	B1
Keluang	92	(1)C2
Kem'	78	F2
Kemalpaşa	76	K6
Kemasik	92	(1)C2
Kemer, *Turkey*	76	M8
Kemer, *Turkey*	76	N8
Kemerovo	82	R6
Kemi	56	N4
Kemijärvi	56	P3
Kemijärvi	↗ 56	P3
Kemijoki	↗ 56	P3
Kemmerer	38	D3
Kemmuna	⊠ 72	J12
Kemnath	60	G7
Kemp's Bay	42	F5
Kempten	70	F3
Kendal	64	K7
Kendall	42	E4
Kendari	92	(2)B3
Kendawangan	92	(1)E3
Kendégué	108	H2
Kendujhargarh	94	E4
Kenedy	42	B4
Kenema	108	B3
Keneurgench	96	G1
Kenge	110	B4
Kengtung	90	B2
Kenhardt	112	C5
Kénitra	106	D2
Kenmore	64	C10
Kennett	42	D2
Kennewick	38	C1
Keno Hill	44	(1)K3
Kenora	36	H2
Kenosha	40	C2
Kentau	82	M9
Kentucky	◪ 36	J4
Kentwood	42	C3
Kenya	▲102	G5
Keokuk	40	B2
Kepno	58	H6
Kepulauan Anambas	⊠ 92	(1)D2
Kepulauan Aru	⊠ 92	(2)E4
Kepulauan Ayu	⊠ 92	(2)D2
Kepulauan Balabalangan	⊠ 92	(1)F3
Kepulauan Banggai	⊠ 92	(2)B3
Kepulauan Barat Daya	⊠ 92	(2)C4
Kepulauan Batu	⊠ 92	(1)B3
Kepulauan Bonerate	⊠ 92	(2)A4
Kepulauan Kai	⊠ 92	(2)D4
Kepulauan Kangean	⊠ 92	(1)F4
Kepulauan Karimunjawa	⊠ 92	(1)D4
Kepulauan Karkaralong	⊠ 92	(2)B2
Kepulauan Laut Kecil	⊠ 92	(1)F3
Kepulauan Leti	⊠ 92	(2)C4
Kepulauan Lingga	⊠ 92	(1)C3
Kepulauan Lucipara	⊠ 92	(2)C4
Kepulauan Mentawai	⊠ 92	(1)B3
Kepulauan Nanusa	⊠ 92	(2)C2
Kepulauan Natuna	⊠ 92	(1)D2
Kepulauan Riau	⊠ 92	(1)C2
Kepulauan Sabalana	⊠ 92	(1)F4
Kepulauan Sangir	⊠ 92	(2)C2
Kepulauan Solor	⊠ 92	(2)B4
Kepulauan Sula	⊠ 92	(2)B3
Kepulauan Talaud	⊠ 92	(2)C2
Kepulauan Tanimbar	⊠ 92	(2)D4
Kepulauan Tengah	⊠ 92	(1)F4
Kepulauan Togian	⊠ 92	(2)B3
Kepulauan Tukangbesi	⊠ 92	(2)B4
Kepulauan Watubela	⊠ 92	(2)D3
Kerch	98	G1
Kerchevskiy	78	L3
Kerempe Burnu	⊟ 76	R2
Keren	104	G4
Kericho	110	F4
Kerio	↗110	F3
Kerki	96	J2
Kerkrade	62	J4
Kerkyra	76	B5
Kerkyra	⊠ 76	B5
Kerma	104	F4
Kermadec Islands	⊠114	H8
Kermadec Trench	◪114	J9
Kerman	101	G1
Kermānshāh	96	E3
Kermānshāhān	101	F1
Keros	⊠ 76	H8
Kerpen	62	J4
Kerrville	42	B3
Kerulen	↗ 84	J7
Keryneia	98	E6
Keşan	76	J4

INDEX

Kesennuma	88	L4
Keşiş Dağları	▲96	C2
Keszthely	74	E3
Keta	108	E3
Ketapang	92	(1)D3
Ketchikan	44	(1)L4
Kētou	108	E3
Ķetrzyn	58	L3
Kettering	64	M9
Kettle Falls	36	C2
Kewanee	40	C2
Keweenaw Peninsula	⊟40	C1
Key Largo	42	E4
Keystone Lake	▣42	B2
Key West	42	E5
Kezhma	84	G5
Kežmarok	58	K8
Khabarovsk	84	P7
Khadyzhensk	98	H1
Khakasiya	▣82	R7
Khairwāra	94	B4
Khalig el Suweis	⇒104	F2
Khalīj Surt	⇒104	C1
Khalūf	96	G5
Khamis Mushay	96	D6
Khamkkeut	90	C3
Khampa	84	L4
Khamrā	84	J4
Khān al Baghdād	98	K7
Khandagayty	82	S7
Khandwa	94	C4
Khanewal	94	B2
Khannya	☑82	X4
Khanpur	94	B3
Khān Shaykhūn	100	D1
Khantau	82	N9
Khantayka	84	D3
Khanty-Mansiysk	78	N2
Khān Yūnis	100	B5
Khapalu	94	C1
Kharabali	78	J5
Kharagpur	94	E4
Kharampur	84	B4
Kharan	96	J4
Khargon	94	C4
Kharkiv	78	G5
Kharlu	56	R6
Kharmanli	76	H3
Kharnmam	94	D5
Kharovsk	78	H3
Khartoum = El Khartum ..	▣104	F4
Khasavyurt	98	M2
Khāsh	96	H4
Khashgort	78	N1
Khashm el Girba	104	G4
Khashuri	98	K3
Khaskovo	76	H3
Khatanga	84	G2
Khātūnābād	101	F1
Khatyrka	84	X4
Khavda	96	J5
Khawr Fakkān	101	G4
Khaydarken	96	K2
Khayelitsha	112	B6
Khemis Miliana	106	F1
Khemisset	106	D2
Khenchela	106	G1
Kherāmeh	101	E2
Kherson	78	F5
Kheta	82	T3
Kheta	☑82	T3
Kheygiyakha	☑78	P2
Khilok	82	J6
Khirbat Isrīyah	100	E1
Khīyāv	98	M4
Khmel'nyts'kyy	78	E5
Khodā Afarīn	98	M4
Kholmsk	84	Q7
Khonj	101	E3
Khon Kaen	90	C3
Khonuu	84	Q3
Khoper	☑78	H4
Khor	84	P7
Khor	☑84	P7
Khoreyver	78	L1
Khorinsk	84	H6
Khorramābād	96	E3
Khorramshahr	101	C1
Khorugh	96	K2
Khoseda Khard	78	L1
Khouribga	106	D2
Khrebet Cherskogo	▬84	P3
Khrebet Dzhagdy	▬84	N6
Khrebet Dzhugdzhur	▬84	N5
Khrebet Khamar Daban	▬84	G6
Khrebet Kolymskiy	▬80	U3
Khrebet Kopet Dag	▬96	G2
Khrebet Suntar Khayata ..	▬84	P4
Khrebet Tarbagatay	▬82	Q8
Khroma	☑84	Q2
Khudoseya	84	C3
Khudzhakh	84	R4
Khujand	96	J1
Khulna	94	E4
Khurayş	101	B4
Khushab	94	B2
Khust	74	L1
Khuzdar	96	J4
Khvormūj	101	D2
Khvoy	98	L4
Khyber Pass	▣96	K3
Kibaya	110	F4
Kibombo	110	D4
Kibondo	110	E4
Kibre Mengist	110	F3
Kičevo	76	C3
Kichmengskiy Gorodok	78	J3
Kicking Horse Pass	▣34	H6
Kidal	106	F5
Kidderminster	64	K9
Kidira	108	B2
Kiel	60	F2
Kielce	58	K7
Kieler Bucht	⇒60	F2
Kiev = Kyyiv	⊟78	F4
Kiffa	106	C5
Kigali	▣110	E4
Kigoma	110	D4
Kihnu	⊟56	M7
Kıkıköy	76	L3
Kikinda	74	H4
Kikori	☑92	(2)F4
Kikwit	110	B5
Kilchu	88	E3
Kilifi	110	F4
Kilindoni	110	F4
Kilingi-Nõmme	56	N7
Kilis	98	G5
Kiliya	74	S4
Kilkenny	64	E9
Kilkis	76	E4
Killarney, Canada	40	D1
Killarney, Republic of Ireland ..	64	C9
Kilmarnock	64	H6
Kil'mez	78	K3
Kilosa	110	F5
Kilrush	64	C9
Kilttan	⊠94	B6
Kilwa	110	D5
Kilwa Masoko	110	F5
Kimberley	▣112	E3
Kimberley Plateau	▣116	E3
Kimch'aek	88	E3
Kimolos	⊟76	G8
Kimongo	108	G5
Kimry	78	G3
Kincardine	40	D2
Kinder	42	C3
Kindia	108	B2
Kindu	110	D4
Kineshma	78	H4
Kingaroy	116	K5
King City	38	B3
King George Islands	⊠34	R5
Kingisepp	56	Q7
King Island, Australia ..	⊟116	H7
King Island, Canada	⊠84	AA3
Kingman	44	D1
Kingri	96	J3
Kingscote	116	G7
Kingsland	42	E3
King's Lynn	64	N9
King Sound	⇒116	D3
Kings Peak	▲38	D2
Kingsport	42	E2
Kingston, Canada	40	E2
Kingston, Jamaica	⊟46	J5
Kingston, United States	40	F2
Kingston-upon-Hull	64	M8
Kingston upon Thames	62	B3
Kingstown	▣50	E1
Kingsville	42	B4
Kingville	46	E3
King William Island	⊟34	M3
King William's Town	▣112	D6
Kinik	76	K5
Kinka-san	⊟88	L4
Kinna	56	G8
Kinsale	64	D10
Kinshasa	▣110	B4
Kinsley	42	B2
Kinston	40	E3
Kintampo	108	D3
Kintyre	⊟64	G6
Kinyeti	▲110	E3
Kinzig	☑60	E6
Kipini	110	G4
Kipnuk	44	(1)E3
Kirchheim	70	E2
Kirchheimbolanden	62	L5
Kircudbright	64	H7
Kirenga	☑84	H5
Kirensk	84	H5
Kiribati	▲114	J6
Kirıkhan	98	G5
Kırıkkale	98	E4
Kirillov	78	G3
Kirinyaga	▲110	F4
Kirishi	78	F3
Kiritimati	⊞114	L5
Kirkağaç	76	K5
Kirk Bulāg Dāgh	▲96	E2
Kirkcaldy	64	J5
Kirkjubæjarklaustur	56	(1)E3
Kirkland Lake	40	D1
Kırklareli	76	K3
Kirkūk	98	L6
Kirkwall	64	K3
Kirov, Kyrgyzstan	82	N9
Kirov, Russia	78	F4
Kirov, Russia	78	J3
Kirovohrad	78	F5
Kiroyo-Chepetsk	78	K3
Kirs	78	K3
Kırsanov	78	H4
Kırşehir	98	F4
Kiruna	56	L3
Kiryū	88	K5
Kisangani	110	D3
Kisbér	74	E2
Kiselevsk	82	R7
Kishanganj	94	E3
Kishi	108	E3
Kishiwada	88	H6
Kishtwar	94	C2
Kisii	110	E4
Kiska Island	⊞44	(3)B1
Kiskőrös	74	G3
Kiskunfélegyháza	74	G3
Kiskunhalas	74	G3
Kiskunmajsa	74	G3
Kislovodsk	98	K2
Kismaayo	110	G4
Kissidougou	108	B3
Kisumu	110	E4
Kisvárda	74	K1
Kita	108	C2
Kitakami	88	L4
Kita-Kyūshū	⊞86	H4
Kita-Kyūshū	88	F7
Kitami	88	M2
Kitchener	40	D2
Kitgum	110	E3
Kitimat	34	F6
Kittilä	56	N3
Kitunda	110	E5
Kitwe	112	D2
Kitzingen	60	F7
Kiuruvesi	56	P5
Kivijärvi	56	N5
Kivik	58	D2
Kiya	☑84	D5
Kıyıköy	98	C3
Kizel	78	L3
Kizilalan	76	R8
Kızılırmak	☑98	F3
Kızılkaya	76	N7
Kizil'skoye	78	L4
Kızıltepe	98	J5
Kizlyar	98	M2
Kizlyarskiy Zaliv	⊟98	M1
Kladanj	74	F5
Kladno	58	D7
Klagenfurt	70	K4
Klaipėda	56	L9
Klamath	38	B2
Klamath	☑38	B2
Klamath Falls	38	B2
Klarälven	☑56	G6
Klatovy	60	J7
Klaus	70	K3
Klerksdorp	112	D5
Kleve	60	B5
Klin	78	G3
Klingenthal	60	H6
Klinovec	▲60	H6
Klintsy	78	F4
Ključ	70	M6
Klobuck	58	H7
Kłodzko	58	F7
Klosterneuburg	70	M2
Klosters	70	E4
Kluane	34	D4
Kluane Lake	☑44	(1)J3
Kluczbork	58	H7
Klyuchevskaya Sopka	▲84	U5
Klyuchi	84	U5
Knezha	74	M6
Knin	70	D5
Knittelfeld	70	K4
Knjaževac	74	K6
Knokke-Heist	62	F3
Knoxville	40	D3
Knysna	112	C6
Koba	92	(1)
Kōbe	88	
Kobe	92	(2)
København	▣56	
Koblenz	60	
Kobo	94	
Kobroör	⊞92	(2)
Kobryn	58	
Kobuk	44	(1)
Kobuk	☑44	(1)
Kočani	76	
Koçarli	76	
Kočevje	74	
Ko Chang	⊟90	
Kochechum	☑84	
Kochi	94	
Kōchi	88	
Kochkor	82	
Kochki	82	
Kochubey	98	
Kodiak	44	(1)
Kodiak Island	⊟44	(1)
Kodino	78	
Kodinsk	84	
Kodomari-misaki	⊟88	
Kodyma	74	
Köflach	70	
Kōfu	88	
Køge	74	
Køge Bugt	⊟58	
Kohat	94	
Kohima	94	
Koh-i-Qaisir	▲96	
Koh-i-Sangan	▲96	
Kohtla-Järve	56	
Koidu	108	
Koitere	⊟56	
Kokenau	92	(2)
Kokkola	56	
Kokomo	42	
Kokpekty	82	
Kokshetau	78	
Kokstad	112	
Kolaka	92	(2)
Kolar	94	
Kolari	56	
Kolašin	74	
Kolda	108	
Kolding	56	
Kole	110	
Kolhapur	94	
Kolin	58	
Kollam	94	
Köln	60	
Kolno	58	
Koło	58	
Kolobrzeg	58	
Kologriv	78	
Kolomna	78	
Kolomyya	74	
Kolonedale	92	(2)
Kolosovka	78	
Kolpashevo	82	
Kolpos Agiou Orous	⇒76	
Kolpos Kassandras	⇒76	
Kolpos Murampelou	⇒76	
Kolskijzaliv	⇒56	
Kolskiy Poluostrov	⊟78	
Kolumadulu Atoll	⊟94	
Koluton	78	
Kolva	☑78	
Kolwezi	112	
Kolyma	☑84	
Kolymskaya Nizmennost'	⊟84	
Kolymskaye	84	
Komandorskiye Ostrova ..	⊟84	
Komárno	74	
Komárom	74	
Komatsu	88	
Komi	▣78	
Komló	74	
Kom Ombo	104	
Komotini	76	
Komsa	82	
Komsomol'skiy	84	
Komsomol'sk-na-Amure	84	
Konārka	94	
Konda	☑78	
Kondagaon	94	
Kondinskoye	78	
Kondoa	110	
Kondopoga	78	
Kondrat'yeva	82	
Konduz	96	
Kong Frederik VI Kyst	⊟34	
Kongi	☑82	
Kongola	112	
Kongolo	110	
Kongsberg	56	
Kongur Shan	▲82	
Königsberg = Kaliningrad		58

146

Name	Page	Grid
Königswinter	60	C6
Königs-Wusterhausen	60	J4
Konin	58	H5
Konispol	76	C5
Konitsa	76	C4
Köniz	70	C4
Konjic	74	E6
Konosha	78	H2
Konotop	78	F4
Konstanz	70	E3
Konstinbrod	74	L7
Kontagora	108	F2
Kon Tum	90	D4
Konya	98	E5
Konz	60	B7
Kootenai	38	C1
Kootenay Lake	36	C2
Köpasker	56	(1)E1
Köpavogur	56	(1)C2
Koper	70	J5
Kopeysk	78	M3
Köping	56	J7
Koplik	74	G7
Koprivnica	74	D3
Korba, *India*	94	D4
Korba, *Tunisia*	72	E12
Korbach	60	D5
Korçë	76	C4
Korčula	74	D7
Korea Bay	88	B4
Korea Strait	88	E6
Korhogo	108	C3
Korinthiakos Kolpos	76	E6
Korinthos	76	E7
Köriyama	88	L5
Korkino	78	M4
Korkuteli	98	D5
Korla	82	R9
Korliki	84	C4
Körmend	74	D2
Kornat	74	C6
Koroba	92	(2)F4
Köroğlu Dağları	76	Q4
Köroğlu Tepesi	76	P4
Korogwe	110	F5
Koronowo	58	G4
Koror	114	D5
Korosten'	78	E4
Korsakov	84	Q7
Korsør	60	G1
Kortrijk	62	F4
Korumburra	116	J7
Koryakskiy Khrebet	84	V4
Koryazhma	82	H5
Kos	76	K8
Kos	76	K8
Kosa	78	L3
Ko Samui	90	C5
Kościerzyna	58	H3
Kosciusko	42	D3
Kosh Agach	82	R8
Koshoba	96	F1
Košice	58	L9
Koslan	78	J2
Košong	88	E4
Kosovo	76	C2
Kosovska Mitrovica	76	C2
Kosrae	114	H6
Kostajnica	70	M5
Kostenets	76	F2
Kosti	104	F5
Kostomuksha	56	R4
Kostroma	78	H3
Kostrzyn	58	D5
Kos'yu	78	L1
Koszalin	58	F3
Kőszeg	74	D2
Kota	94	C3
Kotaagung	92	(1)C4
Kotabaru	92	(1)F3
Kota Belud	92	(1)F1
Kota Bharu	92	(1)C1
Kotabumi	92	(1)C3
Kota Kinabalu	92	(1)F1
Kotamubagu	92	(2)B2
Kotapinang	92	(1)B2
Kotel'nich	78	J3
Kotel'nikovo	78	H5
Köthen	60	G5
Kotido	110	E3
Kotka	56	P6
Kotlas	78	J2
Kotlik	44	(1)E3
Kotor Varoš	74	E5
Kotov'sk	78	E5
Kottagudem	94	D5
Kotte	94	D7
Kotto	110	C2
Kotuy	84	G3
Kotzebue	44	(1)E2
Kotzebue Sound	44	(1)D2

Name	Page	Grid
Kouango	108	H3
Koudougou	108	D2
Koufey	108	G2
Koulamoutou	108	G5
Koum	108	G3
Koumra	108	H3
Koundâra	108	B2
Koupéla	106	C6
Kourou	50	G2
Koutiala	108	C2
Kouvola	78	E2
Kovdor	56	R3
Kovel'	78	D4
Kovin	74	H5
Kovrov	78	H3
Kowanyama	116	H3
Köyceğiz	76	L8
Koygorodok	78	K2
Koykuk	44	(1)E3
Koynas	78	J2
Koyukuk	44	(1)F2
Kozan	98	F5
Kozani	76	D4
Kozheynikovo	82	W3
Kozhikode	94	C6
Kozienice	58	L6
Kozloduy	74	L6
Kōzu-shima	88	K6
Kpalimé	108	E3
Kraai	112	D6
Krabi	90	B5
Kradeljevo	72	M5
Kragujevac	74	H5
Kraków	58	J7
Kraljeviča	70	K5
Kraljevo	74	H6
Kralovice	58	C8
Kramators'k	78	G5
Kramfors	56	J5
Kranj	74	B3
Krapina	72	K2
Krapinske Toplice	70	L4
Krasino	82	J3
Kráslava	56	P9
Kraśnik	58	M7
Krasnoarmeysk	78	N4
Krasnoborsk	78	J2
Krasnodar	78	G5
Krasnohrad	78	G5
Krasnokamensk	84	K6
Krasnosel'kup	84	C3
Krasnotur'insk	78	M3
Krasnoufimsk	78	L3
Krasnovishersk	78	L2
Krasnoyarsk	84	E5
Krasnoyarskoye Vodokhranilishche	82	S6
Krasnoznamensk	58	M3
Krasnystaw	58	N7
Krasnyy Chikoy	84	H6
Krasnyy Kut	78	J4
Krasnyy Yar	78	J5
Kratovo	76	E2
Kraynovka	98	M2
Krefeld	62	J3
Kremenchuk	78	F5
Kremmling	38	E2
Krems	70	L2
Kremsmünster	70	K2
Krestovka	78	K1
Krestyakh	84	K4
Kretinga	56	L2
Kribi	108	F4
Krichim	76	G2
Krishna	94	C5
Krishnagiri	94	C6
Kristiansand	56	E7
Kristianstad	56	H8
Kristiansund	56	D5
Kristinehamn	56	H7
Kristinestad	56	L5
Kriti	76	H10
Kriva Palanka	76	E2
Križevci	74	D3
Krk	70	K5
Krk	70	K5
Kroměříž	58	G8
Kronach	60	G6
Krŏng Kaôh Kŏng	90	C4
Kronotskiy Zaliv	84	U6
Kroonstadt	112	D3
Kroper	78	H3
Kropotkin	78	H5
Krosno	58	L8
Krško	70	L5
Krugē	76	C4
Krui	92	(1)C4
Krumbach	70	F2
Krung Thep	90	C4
Kruša	60	E2
Kruševac	74	J6
Krychaw	78	F4

Name	Page	Grid
Krym'	98	E1
Krymsk	98	H1
Krynica	58	L8
Krytiko Pelagos	76	G9
Kryve Ozero	74	T2
Kryvyy Rih	78	F5
Krzna	58	N5
Ksar el Boukhari	68	N9
Ksen'yevka	84	K6
Ksour Essaf	106	H1
Kuala Kerai	92	(1)C1
Kuala Lipis	92	(1)C2
Kuala Lumpur	92	(1)C2
Kuala Terengganu	92	(1)C1
Kuandian	88	C3
Kuantan	92	(1)C2
Kuçadasi	76	K7
Kučevo	74	J5
Kuching	92	(1)E2
Kucovë	76	B4
Kudat	92	(1)F1
Kudus	92	(1)E4
Kudymkar	78	K3
Kufstein	70	H3
Kugmallit Bay	34	E2
Kühbonän	101	G1
Kühdasht	98	M7
Küh-e Alijuq	101	D1
Küh-e Bâbâ	96	J3
Küh-e Bül	101	E1
Küh-e Dinär	101	D1
Küh-e Fürgun	101	G3
Küh-e Hazärän	101	G2
Küh-e Hormoz	101	F3
Küh-e Kalat	96	G3
Küh-e Kührän	101	H3
Küh-e Lâleh Zär	101	G2
Küh-e Masähün	101	F1
Küh-e Safidär	101	E2
Küh-e Sahand	98	M5
Kühestak	101	G3
Küh-e Taftän	96	H4
Kühhä-ye Bashäkerd	101	G3
Kühhä-ye Zägros	101	D1
Kuhmo	56	Q4
Kühpäyeh	101	G1
Kuito	112	B2
Kuji	88	L3
Kukës	74	H7
Kukhtuy	84	Q4
Kukinaga	88	F8
Kula	74	K6
Kulagino	78	K5
Kulandy	82	K8
Kuldiga	56	L8
Kulgera	116	F5
Kulmbach	60	G6
Kölob	96	J2
Kul'sary	78	K5
Kultsjön	56	H4
Kulu	98	E4
Kulunda	82	P7
Kulynigol	84	C4
Kuma	78	N3
Kumamoto	88	F7
Kumanovo	74	J7
Kumara, *New Zealand*	118	C6
Kumara, *Russia*	84	M6
Kumasi	108	D3
Kumba	108	F4
Kumbakonam	94	C6
Kumeny	78	K3
Kumertau	78	L4
Kumla	56	H7
Kumluca	76	N8
Kummerower See	60	H3
Kumo	108	G3
Kumta	94	B6
Kumukh	98	M2
Kunene	112	A3
Kungrad	82	K9
Kungu	110	B3
Kungur	78	L3
Kunhing	90	B2
Kunlun Shan	94	D1
Kunming	88	C6
Kunsan	88	D6
Kunszetmarton	58	K11
Künzelsau	60	E7
Kuolayarvi	56	Q3
Kuopio	78	E2
Kupang	116	B2
Kupino	82	P7
Kupreanof Point	44	(1)F4
Kup"yans'k	78	G5
Kuqa	82	Q9
Kür	98	M3
Kura	98	E2
Kuragino	84	E6
Kurashiki	88	G6
Kurasia	94	D4
Kurchum	82	Q8

Name	Page	Grid
Kürdämir	98	N3
Kurduvadi	94	C5
Kürdzhali	76	H3
Kure	88	G6
Kure Island	114	J3
Kuressaare	56	M7
Kureyka	84	D3
Kureyka	84	E3
Kurgal'dzhinskiy	82	N7
Kurgan	78	N3
Kurikka	56	M5
Kuril Islands = Kuril'skiye Ostrova	84	S7
Kuril'skiye Ostrova	84	S7
Kuril Trench	80	V5
Kuripapango	118	F4
Kurmuk	104	F5
Kurnool	94	C5
Kuroiso	88	K5
Kurow	118	C7
Kuršėnai	58	M1
Kursk	78	G4
Kuršumlija	74	J6
Kurşunlu	98	E3
Kuruman	112	C5
Kurume	88	F7
Kurumkan	84	J6
Kushikino	88	F8
Kushimoto	88	H7
Kushir	84	H6
Kushiro	88	N2
Kushmurun	78	M4
Kushva	78	K4
Kuskokwim Bay	44	(1)E4
Kuskokwim Mountains	44	(1)F3
Kussharo-ko	88	N2
Kustanay	78	M4
Kütahya	98	C4
K'ut'aisi	98	K2
Kutan	98	M1
Kutchan	88	L2
Kutina	74	D4
Kutno	58	J5
Kutu	108	H5
Kutum	104	D5
Kuujjua	34	J2
Kuujjuaq	34	T5
Kuujjuarapik	34	R5
Kuusamo	78	E1
Kuvango	112	B2
Kuybyshev	82	P6
Kuygan	82	N8
Kuytun	82	R9
Kuyumba	84	F4
Kuznetsk	78	J4
Kuzomen'	78	G1
Kvaløya, *Norway*	56	M1
Kvaløya, *Norway*	56	J2
Kvalynsk	82	H7
Kwale	110	F4
Kwangju	88	D6
Kwango	110	B5
Kwazulu Natal	112	E5
Kwekwe	112	D3
Kwidzyn	56	K10
Kwilu	108	H5
Kyakhta	84	H6
Kyancutta	116	G6
Kyaukse	94	G4
Kyeburn	118	C7
Kyenjetali	94	F5
Kyjov	70	N2
Kykkades	76	G7
Kyle of Lochalsh	64	G4
Kyll	62	J4
Kyllini	76	D7
Kymi	76	G6
Kyŏngju	88	G6
Kyonpyaw	88	H6
Kyparissia	76	D7
Kyperissiakos Kolpos	76	C7
Kyra Panagia	76	G5
Kyren	84	G6
Kyrgyzstan	82	N9
Kyrta	60	H4
Kyrta	82	P6
Kystatyam	84	L3
Kytalyktakh	84	N3
Kythira	76	E8
Kythira	76	F8
Kythnos	76	G7
Kythnos	76	F7
Kyüshü-sanchi	88	F7
Kyustendil	76	F2
Kyusyur	84	M2
Kyzyl	82	S7
Kzyl-Dzhar	78	N5

Kzyl-Orda 78 N6
Kzyltu 82 N7

L

Laascaanood 110 H2
Laatzen 60 E4
Laba 108 F2
La Banda 52 J4
La Bañeza 68 E2
La Baule 66 C6
Labbezenga 106 F5
Labe ☑58 E7
Labé 108 B2
Labin 70 K5
Labinsk 98 J1
Laboulaye 52 J5
Labrador ■34 U6
Labrador City 34 T6
Labrador Sea ■34 V4
Lábrea 50 E5
Labrieville 40 G1
Labuha 92 (2)C3
Labuhanbajo 92 (2)A4
Labytnangi 82 M4
Laç 74 G8
Lac à l'Eau Claire ☑34 R5
Lacanau 66 D8
La Carolina 68 G6
Lac Bienville ☑34 S5
Lac Brochet ☑34 L5
Laccadive Islands ▩94 B6
Lac d'Annecy ☑70 B5
Lac de Bizerte ☑72 D11
Lac Débo ☑106 E5
Lac de Kossou ☑108 C3
Lac de Lagdo ☑108 G3
Lac de Manantali ☑108 C2
Lac de Mbakaou ☑108 G3
Lac de Neuchâtel ☑70 B4
Lac de Retenue de la
  Lufira ☑110 D6
Lac de St-Croix ☑70 B7
Lac des Bois ☑34 G3
Lac de Sélingue ☑108 C2
Lac Do ☑106 E5
Lac du Bourget ☑70 A5
Lacedónia 72 K7
Lacepede Bay ▥116 G7
Lac Evans ☑34 R6
Lac Faguibine ☑106 E5
Lac Fitri ☑104 C5
La Charité-sur-Loire 66 J6
La Chaux-de-Fonds 70 B3
La Chorrera 50 C4
Lac Ichkeul ☑72 D11
La Ciotat 66 L10
Lac La Biche 34 J6
Lac La Martre ☑34 H4
Lac Léman =
  Lake Geneva ☑70 B4
Lac Mai-Ndombe ☑110 B4
Lac-Mégantic 40 F1
Lac Minto ☑34 R5
Lac Nzilo ☑110 D6
Lac Onangué ☑108 F5
Láconi 72 D9
Laconia 40 F2
Lac Payne ☑34 S5
La Crosse 40 B2
La Cruz 36 E7
Lac St-Jean ☑40 F1
Lac St. Joseph ☑34 N6
Lac Seul ☑34 N6
Lac Tumba ☑110 B4
Lacul Brateş ☑74 Q4
Lacul Razim ☑74 R5
Lacul Sinoie ☑74 R5
Lac Upemba ☑110 D5
La Dorada 50 C2
Ladozhskoye Ozero ☑78 F2
Ladysmith, South Africa 112 D5
Ladysmith, United States 40 B1
Ladyzhenka 78 N4
La Esmeralda 50 D3
Læsø ▩56 F8
Lafayette, Ind.,
  United States 40 C2
Lafayette, La.,
  United States 42 C3
Lafia 108 F3
Lafiagi 108 F3
La Flèche 66 E6
Lafnitz ☑70 M3
Laft 101 F3
Lagan ☑56 G8
Lagan' 78 J5
Lage 62 L3
Lågen ☑56 E6
Lage's 38 D2
Laghouat 106 F2

Lagkadas 76 F4
Lagoa dos Patos ☑52 L5
Lagoa Mirim ☑52 L5
Lago Argentino ☑52 G9
Lago de Cahora Bassa ☑112 E3
Lago del Coghinas ☑72 C8
Lago de Flumendosa ☑72 D9
Lago de Maracaibo ☑50 C2
Lago de Nicaragua ☑46 G6
Lago de Poopó ☑50 D7
Lago di Caine ☑70 D5
Lago di Como ☑70 E4
Lago di Garda ☑70 E5
Lago di Lecco ☑70 E5
Lago di Lugano ☑70 E5
Lago d'Iseo ☑70 E5
Lago di Verano ☑72 K7
Lago Maggiore ☑70 D5
Lago Omodeo ☑72 C8
Lago Rogaguado ☑50 D6
Lagos, Nigeria 108 E3
Lagos, Portugal 68 B7
Lago Titicaca ☑50 D7
Lago Trasimeno ☑72 G5
La Goulette 72 E12
La Grand-Combe 66 K9
La Grande 38 C1
La Grange 42 E3
La Gran Sabana ☑50 E6
Laguna 52 M4
Laguna de Caratasca ☑46 H5
Laguna Madre ▥42 B4
Laguna Mar Chiquita ☑48 E7
Lagunillas 50 E7
La Habana ■46 H4
Lahad Datu 90 F5
Lahat 92 (1)C3
La Haye-du-Puits 62 A5
Lähijän 96 F2
Lahn ☑62 L4
Lahnstein 62 K4
Laholmsbukten ☑58 B1
Lahore 94 B2
Lahri 70 C2
Lahti 56 N6
Laï 110 B2
Laiagam 92 (2)F4
Lai Chau 90 C2
L'Aigle 62 C4
Laihia 56 M5
Laingsburg 112 C6
Laiwu 86 F3
Laiyang 86 F3
Laiyuan 86 E3
Lajanurpekhi 98 K2
Lajes 52 L4
Lajosmizse 58 J10
La Junta 38 F3
Lake Abbe ☑110 G1
Lake Abitibi ☑40 E1
Lake Albert, Democratic
  Republic of Congo/
  Uganda ☑110 D3
Lake Albert, United States ☑38 B2
Lake Almanor ☑38 B2
Lake Amadeus ☑116 F4
Lake Andes 38 G2
Lake Argyle ☑116 E3
Lake Argyle Tourist
  Village 116 E3
Lake Athabasca ☑34 K5
Lake Austin ☑116 C5
Lake Balkhash = Ozero
  Balkhash ☑80 L5
Lake Bangweulu ☑112 E2
Lake Barlee ☑116 C5
Lake Benmore ☑118 C7
Lake Blanche ☑116 H5
Lake Buchanan ☑44 G2
Lake Callabonna ☑116 H5
Lake Carey ☑116 D5
Lake Carnegie ☑116 D5
Lake Chad ☑104 B5
Lake Charles 42 C3
Lake Chelan ☑38 B1
Lake Chilwa ☑112 F3
Lake City 42 E3
Lake Claire ☑34 J5
Lake Coleridge ☑118 C6
Lake Constance ☑70 E3
Lake Crowley ☑38 C3
Lake C. W. McConaughy ☑38 F2
Lake Diefenbaker ☑34 K6
Lake Disappointment ☑116 D4
Lake District ▩64 J7
Lake Dojran ☑76 E3
Lake Dora ☑116 D4
Lake Dundas ☑116 D5
Lake Edward ☑110 D4
Lake Elwall ☑38 D1
Lake Erie ☑40 D2
Lake Eyasi ☑110 E4
Lake Eyre ☑114 D8

Lake Eyre Basin ▩116 G5
Lake Eyre North ☑116 G5
Lake Eyre South ☑116 G5
Lake Francis Case ☑38 G2
Lake Frome ☑116 H6
Lake Gairdner ☑116 G6
Lake Geneva ☑70 B4
Lake Gordon ☑116 H8
Lake Grace 116 C6
Lake Harbour 34 T4
Lake Hauroko ☑118 A7
Lake Havasu ☑44 C2
Lake Havasu City 44 D2
Lake Hopkins ☑116 E4
Lake Hudson ☑42 B2
Lake Huron ☑40 D1
Lake Jackson 42 B4
Lake Kariba ☑112 D3
Lake Kemp ☑42 B2
Lake Kerkinitis ☑74 L8
Lake Kivu ☑110 D4
Lake Kyoga ☑110 E3
Lake Ladoga =
  Ladozhskoye Ozero ☑78 F2
Lakeland 42 E4
Lake Lefroy ☑116 D6
Lake Louis 34 H6
Lake Macdonald ☑116 E4
Lake Macleod ☑116 B4
Lake Manapouri ☑118 A7
Lake Manitoba ☑34 M6
Lake Manyara ☑110 E4
Lake Maurice ☑116 F5
Lake McDonald ☑38 D1
Lake McMillan ☑44 F2
Lake Mead ☑38 D3
Lake Melville ☑34 U6
Lake Michigan ☑40 C2
Lake Moore ☑116 C5
Lake Murray ☑92 (2)F4
Lake Mweru ☑110 D5
Lake Mweru Wantipa ☑110 E5
Lake Nash 116 G4
Lake Nasser ▥104 F3
Lake Natron ☑110 F4
Lake Neale ☑116 E4
Lake Nipigon ☑34 P6/7
Lake Nipissing ☑40 E1
Lake Nyasa ☑112 E2
Lake Oahe ☑38 F2
Lake of the Woods ☑40 B1
Lake Ohau ☑118 B7
Lake Ohrid ☑76 C4
Lake Okeechobee ☑42 E4
Lake Onega = Onezhskoye
  Ozero ☑54 H1
Lake Ontario ☑40 E2
Lake O' The Cherokees ☑40 B3
Lake O' The Pines ☑42 C3
Lake Paringa 118 B6
Lake Peipus ☑56 P7
Lake Placid 42 E4
Lakeport 38 B3
Lake Poteriteri ☑118 A8
Lake Powell ☑38 D3
Lake Prespa ☑76 D4
Lake Providence 42 C3
Lake Pskov ☑56 P7
Lake Pukaki ☑118 C7
Lake Rotorua ☑118 F4
Lake Rukwa ☑110 E5
Lake St. Lucia ▥112 E5
Lake Sakakawea ☑38 F1
Lake Scutari ☑74 G7
Lake Simcoe ☑40 E2
Lake Superior ☑40 C1
Lake Tahoe ☑38 C3
Lake Tanganyika ☑110 D5
Lake Taupo ☑118 F4
Lake Te Anau ☑118 A7
Lake Tekapo 118 C6
Lake Tekapo ☑118 C6
Lake Texoma ☑42 G2
Lake Torrens ☑116 G6
Lake Travis ☑44 G2
Lake Tschida ☑38 F1
Lake Turkana ☑110 F3
Lake Victoria ☑110 E4
Lakeview 38 B2
Lake Volta ☑108 D3
Lake Waikare ☑118 F3
Lake Waikaremoana ☑118 F4
Lake Wakatipu ☑118 B7
Lake Wanaka ☑118 B7
Lake White ☑116 E4
Lake Wills ☑116 E4
Lake Winnipeg ☑34 M6
Lake Winnipegosis ☑34 L6
Lakewood 38 E3
Lake Woods ☑116 F3
Lake Xau ☑112 C4

Lake Yamma Yamma ☑116 H8
Lakhdaria 68 P
Lakhimpur 94 D
Lakhpat 94 A4
Lakin 42 A
Lakki 94 B
Lakonikos Kolpos ▥76 E
Lakota 38 G
Lalín 68 B2
La Línea 68 E
Lalitpur 94 C
Lal-Lo 90 G
La Loche 34 K
La Louvière 62 G
La Maddalena 72 D
Lamar, Colo.,
  United States 44 F
Lamar, Mo.,
  United States 42 C
Lamard 101 F
La Marsa 72 E1
Lambaréné 108 G
Lambay Island ▩64 G
Lam Chi ☑90 C
Lamesa 44 F
Lamia 76 E
Lamone ☑70 G
Lampang 90 B
Lampasas 44 G
Lampedusa ▩106 H
Lamu 110 G
Lanai ▥44 (2)D
Lanai City 44 (2)E
Lancang 90 B
Lancaster,
  United Kingdom 64 K
Lancaster, Mo.,
  United States 40 B
Lancaster, N.H.,
  United States 40
Lancaster, Oh.,
  United States 40 D
Lancaster, Pa.,
  United States 40 E
Lancaster, S.C.,
  United States 42 E
Lancaster Sound ▥34 Q
Lanciano 72 J
Landau, Germany 62 L
Landau, Germany 70 H
Landeck 70 F
Lander 38 E
Landerneau 66 A
Landor 116 C
Land's End ▥64 F1
Landshut 70 H
Landskrona 58 B
Landstuhl 62 K
Land Wursten ☑60 D
Langarüd 98 N
Langdon 38 G
Langeland ▥60
Langen 62 L
Langenau 70 F
Langenhagen 60 F
Langeoog ▥60 C
Langfang 86 F
Langjökull ▩56 (1)C
Langkawi ▥90 B
Langkon 90 F
Langon 66 E
Langøya ▥56 H
Langreo 68 E
Langres 62 L
Langsa 90 B
Langtry 44 F
Langvatnet ☑56 G
Länkäran 98 N
Lannion 66 B
L'Anse 40 C
Lansing ☑40 C
Lanxi 86 H
Lanya 110 E
Lanzarote ▥106 C
Lanzhou 86 C
Laoag 90 G
Lao Cai 90 C
Laohekou 86 E
Laon 62 J
La Oroya 50 C
Laos ▣90 C
Laotougou 88 B
Lapa 52 M
La Palma ▩106 B
La Palma 46 C
La Paragua 50 E
La Paz, Argentina 50 E
La Paz, Bolivia 50 D
La Paz, Mexico 46 B
La Pedrera 50 D

Name	Page	Ref
La Perla	44	F3
La Pérouse Strait	86	L1
La Pesca	42	B5
La Pine	38	B2
Lapithos	100	A1
La Plant	38	F1
La Plata	52	K5
Lappajärvi	56	M5
Lappeenranta	56	Q6
Lappland =	56	M2
Laptev Sea = More Laptevykh	84	L1
Lapua	56	M5
Lapy	58	M5
La Quiaca	52	H3
L'Aquila	72	H6
Lär	101	F3
Larache	106	D1
Laramie	38	E2
Laramie Range	38	E2
Larantuka	92	(2)B4
Larat	92	(2)D4
Larba	68	P8
Laredo, Spain	68	G1
Laredo, United States	44	G3
Largo	42	E4
L'Ariana	72	E12
La Rioja	52	H4
Larisa	76	E5
Larkana	96	J4
Larne	100	A2
Larne	64	G7
La Rochelle	66	D7
La Roche-sur-Yon	66	D7
La Roda	68	H5
La Romana	46	L5
La Ronge	34	K5
Lar'yak	82	Q5
La Sarre	40	E1
Las Cabezas de San Juan	68	E7
Las Cruces	44	E2
La Serena	52	G4
La Seu d'Urgell	68	M2
La Seyne-sur-Mer	66	L10
Lashio	90	B2
Lashkar Gāh	96	H3
Łask	58	J6
Las Lomitas	52	J3
La Solana	68	G6
Las Palmas	106	B3
La Spézia	70	E6
Las Plumas	52	H7
Last Chance	38	F3
Lastoursville	108	G5
Lastovo	74	D7
Las Varas	36	E7
Las Varillas	52	J5
Las Vegas, Nev., United States	38	C3
Las Vegas, N.Mex., United States	44	E1
La Teste	66	D9
Latina	72	G7
Latisana	70	J5
La Toma	52	H5
La Tuque	40	F1
Latur	94	C5
Latvia	56	M8
Lauchhammer	60	J5
Lauenburg	60	F3
Lauf	60	G7
Lau Group	114	J7
Launceston, Australia	116	J8
Launceston, United Kingdom	64	H11
La Union	68	K7
Laupheim	70	E2
Laura	116	H3
Laurel	42	D3
Lauria	72	K8
Laurinburg	42	F3
Lausanne	70	B4
Laut, Indonesia	92	(1)F3
Laut, Malaysia	92	(1)D2
Lauter	62	K5
Lauterbach	60	E6
Lava	58	L3
Laval, Canada	40	F1
Laval, France	66	E5
La Vall de Uixo	68	K5
Lavant	70	K4
La Vega	46	K5
Laviana	68	E1
La Vila Joiosa	68	K6
Lavras	52	N3
Lavrentiya	84	Z3
Lavrio	76	G7
Lawdar	104	J5
Lawra	108	D2
Lawrence, New Zealand	118	B7
Lawrence, Kans., United States	40	A3
Lawrence, Mass., United States	40	F2
Lawrenceville	42	D2
Lawton	42	B3
Laya	78	L1
Laylä	104	J3
Laysan Island	114	J3
Layton	38	D2
Lazarev	84	Q6
Lázaro Cárdenas	46	D5
Lazdijai	58	N3
Lazo	84	P3
Leadville	38	E3
Leamington	40	D2
Leavenworth, Kans., United States	40	A3
Leavenworth, Wash., United States	38	B1
Lebach	62	J5
Lebanon	100	C3
Lebanon, Mo., United States	40	B3
Lebanon, N.H., United States	40	F2
Lebanon, Pa., United States	40	E2
Lebanon, Tenn., United States	40	C3
Lebel-sur-Quévillon	40	E1
Lębork	58	G3
Lebrija	68	D8
Lebu Victoria	52	G6
Lecce	72	N8
Lecco	70	E5
Lech	70	F3
Leck	60	D2
Le Creusot	66	K7
Łeczna	58	M6
Łęczyca	58	J5
Ledmozero	56	R4
Lee	64	D10
Leech Lake	40	B1
Leeds	64	L8
Leek	62	A1
Leer	62	K1
Leesburg	42	E4
Leeston	118	D6
Leesville	42	C3
Leeuwarden	62	H1
Leeward Islands	46	M5
Lefkada	76	C6
Lefkada	76	C6
Lefkimmi	76	C5
Lefkonikon	100	A1
Lefkosia	76	N9
Legaspi	90	G4
Legionowo	58	K5
Legnago	70	G5
Legnica	58	F6
Leh	94	C2
Le Havre	62	C5
Lehrte	60	F4
Leiah	94	B2
Leibnitz	70	L4
Leicester	64	A2
Leiden	62	G2
Leie	62	F4
Leigh Creek	116	G6
Leighton Buzzard	62	B3
Leine	60	E4
Leinster	116	D5
Leipzig	60	H5
Leiria	68	B5
Leitrim	64	D8
Leiyang	86	E5
Lek	62	G3
Lelystad	62	H2
Le Mans	66	F6
Le Mars	40	A2
Lemberg	60	D8
Lemesos	76	Q10
Lemgo	62	L2
Lemieux Islands	34	U4
Lemmer	62	H2
Lemmon	38	F1
Le Muret	66	E9
Lena	68	E1
Lena	84	L4
Lendinare	70	G5
Lengerich	62	K2
Lengshuijiang	86	E5
Lengshuitan	86	E5
Leninsk-Kuznetskiy	82	R7
Leninskoye	78	J3
Lenmalu	92	(2)D3
Lenne	62	K3
Lennestadt	62	L3
Lens	62	E4
Lensk	84	K4
Lenti	70	M4
Lentini	72	J11
Léo	108	D2
Leoben	70	L3
León, Mexico	46	D4
León, Nicaragua	46	G6
León, Spain	68	E2
Leonberg	70	E2
Leonforte	72	J11
Leonidi	76	E7
Leonora	116	D5
Le Perthus	66	H11
Lepsy	82	P8
Le Puy	66	J8
Léré	108	G3
Lérici	70	E6
Lerik	98	N4
Lerma	68	G2
Leros	76	J7
Lerwick	64	L1
Lešak	74	H6
Les Andelys	62	D5
Lesatima	110	F4
Lesbos = Lésvos	76	H5
Les Escaldes	66	G11
Les Escoumins	34	T7
Leshan	86	C5
Les Herbiers	66	D7
Leshukonskoye	78	J2
Leskovac	74	J7
Lesosibirsk	82	S6
Lesotho	112	D5
Lesozavodsk	88	G1
Les Sables-d'Olonne	66	D7
Les Sept Îles	66	B5
Lesser Antilles	46	L6
Lesser Slave Lake	34	J5
Lésvos	76	H5
Leszno	58	F6
Letaba	112	E4
Letchworth	62	B3
Letenye	70	M4
Lethbridge	38	D1
Lethem	50	F3
Leticia	50	D4
Letpadan	90	B3
Le Tréport	62	D4
Letterkenny	64	E7
Leutkirch	70	F3
Leuven	62	G4
Leuze	62	F4
Levadeia	76	E6
Lévanzo	72	G10
Levashi	98	M2
Levaya Khetta	78	P2
Leverkusen	62	J3
Levice	58	H9
Levico Terme	70	G4
Levin	118	E5
Lévis	40	F1
Levitha	76	J7
Levoča	58	K9
Levski	74	N6
Lewes	62	C4
Lewis	64	F3
Lewis and Clark Lake	38	G2
Lewis Range	34	J7
Lewiston, Id., United States	38	C1
Lewiston, Me., United States	40	F2
Lewistown, Mont., United States	38	E1
Lewistown, Pa., United States	40	E2
Lexington, Ky., United States	40	D3
Lexington, Nebr., United States	38	G2
Lexington, Va., United States	40	E3
Lexington Park	42	F2
Leyte	90	G4
Lezhë	74	G8
Lhari	94	F2
Lhasa	94	F3
Lhazä	94	E3
Lhokseumawe	90	B5
Lian Xian	90	E2
Lianyuan	90	E1
Lianyungang	86	F4
Liaocheng	86	F3
Liao He	88	B3
Liaoyang	88	B3
Liaoyuan	88	C2
Liard	34	F5
Liard River	34	F5
Libby	38	C1
Libenge	110	B3
Liberal	42	A2
Liberec	58	E7
Liberia	108	B3
Liberia	46	G6
Liberty	42	C1
Libjo	90	H4
Libourne	66	E9
Libreville	108	F4
Libya	104	C2
Libyan Desert	104	D2
Libyan Plateau	104	E1
Licata	72	H11
Lich	60	D6
Lichinga	112	F2
Lichtenfels	60	G6
Lida	56	N10
Lidköping	56	G7
Lido di Óstia	72	G7
Lidzbark Warmiński	58	K3
Liebenwalde	60	J4
Liechtenstein	70	E3
Liège	62	H4
Lieksa	56	R5
Lienz	70	H4
Liepāja	58	L1
Lier	62	G3
Liezen	70	K3
Lifford	64	E7
Lignières	66	H7
Ligueil	66	F6
Ligurian Sea	70	D7
Lihue	44	B2
Lijiang	90	C1
Likasi	110	D6
Lilienfeld	70	L2
Lille	62	F4
Lillebonne	62	C5
Lillehammer	56	F6
Lilleito	70	G3
Lilongwe	112	E2
Liloy	90	G5
Lima, Peru	50	B6
Lima, Mont., United States	38	D2
Lima, Oh., United States	40	D2
Limanowa	58	K8
Limassol = Lemesos	76	Q10
Limbaži	56	N8
Limburg	62	L4
Limeira	52	M3
Limerick	64	D9
Limingen	56	G4
Limni Kastorias	76	C4
Limni Kerkinitis	76	E3
Limni Koronia	76	F4
Limni Trichonida	76	D6
Limni Vegoritis	76	D4
Limni Volvi	76	F4
Limnos	76	H5
Limoges	66	G8
Limon	38	F3
Limón	46	H7
Limoux	66	H10
Limpopo	112	D4
Linares, Chile	52	G6
Linares, Mexico	44	G4
Linares, Spain	68	G6
Lincang	90	C2
Linchuan	86	F5
Lincoln, United Kingdom	62	B1
Lincoln, Ill., United States	40	C2
Lincoln, Me., United States	40	G1
Lincoln, Nebr., United States	38	G2
Lincoln, N.H., United States	40	F2
Lindenow Fjord	34	Y4
Lindesnes	56	D8
Lindi	110	D3
Lindi	110	F6
Lindos	76	L8
Line Islands	114	L5
Linfen	86	E3
Lingen	62	K2
Lingga	92	(1)C3
Lingshui	90	D3
Linguère	108	A1
Lingyuan	86	F2
Linhal	86	G5
Linhares	50	J7
Linhe	86	D2
Linjiang	88	D3
Linköping	56	H7
Linkou	88	F1
Linosa	72	G13
Lins	52	M3
Linton	38	F1
Linxia	86	C3
Lin Xian	86	E3
Linyi	86	F3
Linz	70	K2
Lipari	72	J10
Lipari	72	J10
Lipcani	74	P1

Lipetsk	78	G4	Locri	72	L10	Losheim	62	J5	Lucena, *Philippines*	90	G4
Lipin Bor	78	G2	Lodève	66	J10	Lošinj	70	K6	Lucena, *Spain*	68	F7
Lipno	58	J5	Lodeynoye	78	F2	Los Mochis	46	C3	Lučenec	58	J9
Lipova	74	J3	Lodge Grass	38	E1	Lospalos	92	(2)C4	Lucera	72	K7
Lippe	62	L3	Lodi, *Italy*	70	E5	Los Telares	52	J4	Lucero	44	E2
Lippstadt	62	L3	Lodi, *United States*	38	B3	Los Teques	50	D1	Lucira	112	A2
Lipsoi	76	J7	Lodja	110	C4	Lost Trail Pass	38	D1	Luckenwalde	60	J4
Liptovský-Mikuláš	58	J8	Lodwar	110	F3	Los'va	78	M2	Lucknow	94	D3
Lipu	90	E2	Łódź	58	J6	Los Vientos	52	H3	Luçon	66	D7
Liqeni i Fierzës	74	H7	Loei	90	C3	Lotta	56	O2	Lucusse	112	C2
Liqeni Komanit	74	G7	Lofoten	56	G3	Lotte	62	K2	Ludden	38	G1
Lira	110	E3	Logan, *Ia., United States*	40	A2	Louang Namtha	90	C2	Lüdenscheid	62	K3
Liri	72	H7	Logan, *N.Mex.,*			Louangphrabang	90	C3	Lüderitz	112	B5
Lisala	110	C3	*United States*	44	F1	Loubomo	108	G5	Ludhiana	94	C2
Lisboa	68	A6	Logan, *Ut., United States*	38	D2	Loudéac	66	C5	Ludington	40	C2
Lisbon = Lisboa	68	A6	Logansport	40	C2	Louga	108	A1	Ludlow	44	C2
Lisburn	64	G7	Logatec	70	K5	Loughborough	62	A2	Ludogori	74	P6
Liscannor Bay	64	C9	Logroño	68	H2	Lough Conn	64	C7	Luduş	74	M3
Lishi	86	E3	Lohiniva	56	N3	Lough Corrib	64	C8	Ludvika	56	H6
Lishui	86	F5	Lohr	60	E7	Lough Derg	64	D8	Ludwigsburg	70	E8
Lisieux	62	C5	Loikaw	90	B3	Lough Foyle	64	E6	Ludwigsfelde	60	J4
Liski	78	G4	Loir	66	F6	Lough Leane	64	C9	Ludwigshafen	62	L4
L'Isle-sur-la-Sorgue	66	L10	Loire	66	D6	Lough Mask	64	C8	Ludwigslust	60	G3
Lisse	62	G2	Loja, *Ecuador*	50	B4	Lough Neagh	64	F7	Ludza	56	P8
Lištica	72	M5	Loja, *Spain*	68	F7	Lough Ree	64	E8	Luebo	110	C5
Listowel	64	C9	Lokan tekojärvi	56	P3	Louhans	66	L7	Luena	112	B2
Listvyanka	84	H6	Lokeren	62	F3	Louisa	40	D3	Lufeng	90	F2
Litang	86	C5	Lokichar	110	F3	Louisiade Archipelago	116	K2	Lufira	110	D5
Litani	50	G3	Lokichokio	110	E3	Louisiana	42	C3	Lufkin	42	C3
Litava	58	F8	Lokoja	108	F3	Louis Trichardt	112	D4	Luga	56	Q7
Litchfield, *Ill.,*			Lokosovo	78	P2	Louisville, *Ga.,*			Luga	78	E3
United States	40	C3	Loks Land	34	U4	*United States*	42	E3	Lugano	70	D4
Litchfield, *Minn.,*			Lolland	60	G2	Louisville, *Ky.,*			Lugela	112	F3
United States	40	B1	Lollondo	110	F4	*United States*	42	D2	Lugenda	112	F2
Lithgow	116	K6	Lolo	38	D1	Louisville, *Miss.,*			Luggate	118	B7
Lithuania	56	L9	Lom	74	L6	*United States*	42	D3	Lugo	70	G6
Litke	84	Q6	Lomami	110	C4	Loukhi	56	S3	Lugoj	74	J4
Litomerice	60	K6	Lomas	50	C7	Loulé	68	C7	Lugovoy	82	N9
Litomyši	58	F8	Lomas de Zamora	52	K5	Louny	60	K5	Lugu	94	D2
Litovel	58	G8	Lombadina	116	D3	Loup	38	G2	Luhans'k	78	G5
Litovko	84	P7	Lomblen	92	(2)B4	Lourdes	66	E10	Luhuo	86	C4
Little Abaco	42	F4	Lombok	92	(1)F4	Louth, *Australia*	116	J6	Lui	90	C4
Little Andaman	94	F6	Lomé	108	E3	Louth, *United Kingdom*	62	C1	Luilaka	110	B4
Little Barrier Island	118	E3	Lomela	110	C4	Loutra Aidipsou	76	F6	Luino	70	D4
Little Current	40	D1	Lomela	110	C4	Louviers	62	D5	Luis Moya	44	F4
Little Desert	116	H7	Lommel	62	H3	Lovech	74	M6	Luiza	110	C5
Little Falls	40	B1	Lomonosovka	78	N4	Lovell	38	E2	Lukavac	74	F5
Littlefield	44	F2	Lompoc	44	B2	Lovelock	38	C2	Lukovit	74	M6
Little Inagua	46	K4	Łomża	58	M4	Lovosice	60	K6	Łuków	58	M6
Little Karoo	112	C6	London, *Canada*	40	D2	Lovran	70	K5	Lukulu	112	C2
Little Minch	64	E4	London, *United Kingdom*	62	B3	Lôvua	112	C2	Lukumburu	110	F5
Little Nicobar	94	F7	London, *United States*	42	E2	Lowa	110	D4	Lukuni	110	B5
Little Ouse	62	C2	Londonderry	64	E6	Lowell	40	F2	Luleå	56	M4
Little Rock	42	C3	Londrina	52	L3	Lower Hutt	118	E5	Luleburgaz	76	K3
Littleton	38	E3	Longarone	70	H4	Lower Lake	38	B2	Lulua	112	C2
Litvinov	60	J6	Long Bay	46	J2	Lower Lough Erne	64	E7	Lumala Kaquengue	112	C2
Liupanshui	86	C5	Long Beach	44	C2	Lower Post	34	F5	Lumberton	42	F3
Liuzhou	86	D6	Long Branch	40	F2	Lowestoft	62	D2	Lumbrales	68	D4
Live Oak	42	E3	Long Eaton	62	A2	Lowville	40	F2	Lumimba	112	E2
Liverpool	64	K8	Long Island, *Canada*	34	Q5	Loxstedt	60	D3	Lumsden	118	B7
Liverpool Bay	34	F2	Long Island,			Loyalty Islands	114	G8	Lund	58	C2
Livingston,			*United States*	40	F2	Loyno	78	K3	Lundazi	112	E2
United Kingdom	64	J6	Longlac	34	P7	Loznica	74	G5	Lundy	64	H10
Livingston, *United States*	38	D1	Long Lake	38	F1	L-Travemünde	60	F3	Lüneburg	60	F3
Livingstone	112	D3	Longmont	38	E2	Luama	110	D4	Lüneburger Heide	60	F3
Livingstonia	112	E2	Long Prairie	40	B1	Luampa	112	C3	Lunel	66	K10
Livno	74	E6	Long Range Mountains	34	V6	Lu'an	86	F4	Lünen	62	K3
Livny	78	G4	Longueuil	40	F1	Luanda	110	A5	Lunéville	70	B2
Livonia	40	D2	Longview, *Tex.,*			Luangwa	112	E2	Lungau	70	J3
Livorno	70	F7	*United States*	42	C3	Luangwa	112	E3	Luntai	82	Q9
Liwale	110	F5	Longview, *Wash.,*			Luanping	86	F2	Luohe	86	E4
Lizard Point	64	G12	*United States*	38	B1	Luanshya	112	D2	Luoyang	86	E4
Ljubljana	70	K4	Longwy	62	H5	Luarca	68	D1	Luozi	110	A5
Ljugarn	56	K8	Long Xuyên	90	D4	Luau	112	C2	Lupeni	74	L4
Ljungan	56	J5	Longyan	90	F1	Lubaczów	58	N7	Lürä Shīrīn	98	E3
Ljungby	56	G8	Löningen	62	K2	Luban	58	E6	Lure	70	B3
Ljusdal	56	J6	Lönsdalen	56	H3	Lubango	112	A2	Luremo	110	B5
Ljusnan	78	C2	Lons-le-Saunier	70	A4	Lubäns	56	P8	Lurio	112	F2
Llandovery	64	J9	Lookout Pass	38	C1	Lubao	110	D5	Lusaka	112	D3
Llandudno	64	J8	Loop Head	64	B9	Lubartów	58	M6	Lusambo	110	C5
Llanelli	64	H10	Lopez	90	G4	Lübbecke	62	L2	Lushnjë	74	G8
Llanes	68	F1	Lop Nur	82	S9	Lübben	60	J5	Lushui	86	B5
Llanos	50	C2	Lopphavet	56	L1	Lübbenau	60	J5	Lüshun	86	G3
Lleida	68	L3	Loptyuga	78	J2	Lubbock	44	F2	Lusk	38	F2
Lli	82	P9	Lora del Rio	68	E7	Lübeck	60	F3	Lutembo	112	C2
Lloret de Mar	68	N3	Lorain	40	D2	Lubefu	110	C4	Lutherstadt Wittenberg	60	H4
Llucmajor	68	N5	Loralai	94	A2	Lubero	110	D4	Luton	62	B3
Loano	70	D6	Lorca	68	J7	Lubilash	110	C5	Luts'k	78	E4
Lobatse	112	D5	Lordegân	101	D1	Lubin	58	F6	Lutto	78	O2
Lôbau	60	K5	Lord Howe Island	116	L6	Lublin	58	M6	Lützow-Holmbukta	120	(2)G3
Łobez	58	E4	Lordsburg	44	E2	Lubliniec	58	H7	Luverne	40	A2
Lobito	112	A2	Loreto	46	B3	Lubny	78	F4	Luvua	110	D5
Locarno	70	D4	Lorient	66	B6	Luboń	58	F5	Luwuk	92	(2)B3
Lochboisdale	64	E4	Lörrach	70	C3	Lubsko	60	D6	Luxembourg	62	J5
Lochinver	64	G3	Lorraine	116	G3	Lubudi	110	D5	Luxembourg	62	J5
Loch Linnhe	64	G5	Los Alamos	44	E1	Lubukklinggau	92	(1)C3	Luxeuil-les-Bains	70	B3
Loch Lomond	64	H5	Los Angeles, *Chile*	52	G6	Lubumbashi	110	D6	Luxor	100	F2
Lochmaddy	64	E4	Los Angeles,			Lubutu	110	D4	Luza	78	J2
Loch Ness	64	H4	*United States*	44	C2	Lucala	110	B5	Luza	78	J2
Lockhart	42	B4	Los Banos	38	B3	Lucca	70	F7	Luzern	70	D3
Lock Haven	40	E2	Los Blancos	52	J3	Luce Bay	64	H7	Luzhou	86	D5
Lockport	40	E2				Lucedale	42	D3			

Name	Page	Grid
uzilândia	50	J4
uznice	70	K1
uzon	90	G3
uzon Strait	90	G2
uzy	66	J7
viv	58	N8
yady	56	Q7
yapin	78	M2
ycksele	78	C2
ydenburg	112	E5
yme Bay	64	K11
ymington	62	A4
ynchburg	40	E3
ynn	40	F2
ynn Lake	34	L5
ynx Lake	34	K4
yon	66	K8
ys	62	E4
ys'va	78	L3
ysychans'k	78	G5
yttelton	118	D6

M

Name	Page	Grid
Maalosmadulu Atoll	94	B7
Ma'än	100	C6
Maardu	56	N7
Ma'arrat an Nu'mān	98	G6
Maas	62	J3
Maasin	90	G4
Maastricht	62	H4
Mabalane	112	E4
Mabanza-Ngungu	108	G6
Mabein	90	B2
Mablethorpe	62	C1
Macapá	50	G3
Macas	50	B4
Macassar Strait	114	F4
Macau	90	E2
Macau	90	E2
Macau	50	K5
Macaúba	50	G6
Macclesfield	64	K8
Macdonnell Ranges	116	F4
Macedonia	76	C3
Maceió	50	K5
Macerata	70	J7
Machakos	110	F4
Machala	50	B4
Macheng	86	F4
Machilipatnam	94	D5
Machiques	50	C1
Macia	112	E4
Măcin	74	R4
Mack	44	E1
Mackay	116	J4
Mackay Lake	34	J4
Mackenzie	34	G4
Mackenzie Bay	34	D3
Mackenzie Mountains	34	E3
Mackinaw City	40	D1
Macmillan	34	F4
Macmillan Pass	34	F4
Macomb	40	B2
Macomer	72	C8
Macon, *Ga., United States*	42	E3
Macon, *Mo., United States*	42	C2
Mâcon	66	K7
Macuje	50	C3
Mādabā	100	C5
Madagascar	112	H3
Madan	74	M8
Madaoua	108	F2
Madeira	106	B2
Madeira	50	E5
Maden	98	H4
Madera	44	E3
Madikeri	94	C6
Madison	40	C2
Madison, *Ind., United States*	40	C3
Madison, *Minn., United States*	40	A1
Madison, *S.D., United States*	38	G2
Madisonville	40	C3
Madiun	92	(1)E4
Mado Gashi	110	F3
Madoi	86	B4
Madona	56	P8
Madras = Chennai, *India*	94	D6
Madras, *United States*	38	B2
Madre de Dios	50	C6
Madrid, *Philippines*	90	H5
Madrid, *Spain*	68	G4
Madridejos	68	G5
Madura	92	(1)E4
Madurai	94	C6
Maebashi	88	K5
Mae Hong Son	90	B3
Mae Nam Mun	90	C3
Mae Sariang	90	B3
Maevatanana	112	H3
Mafeteng	112	D5
Maffighofen	70	J2
Mafia Island	110	G5
Mafra	52	M4
Mafraq	100	D4
Magadan	84	S5
Magadi	110	F4
Magdagachi	84	M6
Magdalena	50	C2
Magdalena, *Bolivia*	50	E6
Magdalena, *Mexico*	44	D2
Magdalena, *United States*	44	E2
Magdeburg	60	G4
Magdelaine Cays	116	K3
Magelang	92	(1)E4
Magenta	70	D5
Magerøya	56	N1
Maglaj	74	F5
Máglie	72	N8
Magnitogorsk	78	L4
Magnolia	42	C3
Mago	84	P6
Magog	40	F1
Magu	110	E4
Magwe	90	A2
Mahābād	98	L5
Mahagi	110	E3
Mahajamba	112	H3
Mahajanga	112	H3
Mahalapye	112	D4
Mahān	101	G1
Mahanadi	94	D4
Mahanoro	112	H3
Mahasamund	94	D4
Mahavavy	112	H3
Mahbubnagar	94	D5
Maḥḍah	101	G4
Mahé Island	112	(2)C1
Mahenge	110	F5
Mahesāna	94	B4
Mahia Peninsula	118	F4
Mahilyow	78	F4
Mahnomen	40	A1
Mahón	68	Q5
Mahuva	96	K5
Maicao	50	C1
Maidenhead	62	B3
Maidstone	62	C3
Maiduguri	108	G2
Mai Gudo	110	F2
Maimédy	60	B6
Main	60	E7
Mainburg	70	G2
Main-Donau-Kanal	60	G7
Maine	40	G1
Maïné Soroa	108	G2
Maingkwan	90	B1
Mainland, *Orkney Is., United Kingdom*	64	J2
Mainland, *Shetland Is., United Kingdom*	64	L1
Maintirano	112	G3
Mainz	60	D6
Maio	108	(1)B1
Majene	92	(2)A3
Majicana	52	H4
Majuro	114	H5
Makale	92	(2)A3
Makamba	110	D4
Makanza	110	B3
Makarora	118	B7
Makarov	84	Q7
Makarska	74	E6
Makar'yev	78	H3
Makat	78	K5
Makeni	108	B3
Makgadikgadi	112	C4
Makhachkala	98	M2
Makhorovka	82	M7
Makindu	110	F4
Makinsk	78	P4
Makiyivka	78	G5
Makkah	104	G3
Makó	74	H3
Makokou	108	G4
Makongolosi	110	E5
Makoralo	118	F4
Makoua	108	H4
Maków Mazowiecka	58	L5
Makran	96	G4
Makronisi	76	G7
Mākū	78	L4
Makumbako	110	E5
Makurazaki	88	F8
Makurdi	108	F3
Makūyeh	101	E2
Makuyuni	110	F4
Malabar Coast	94	B6
Malabo	108	F4
Malack	58	F9
Malacky	70	M2
Malad City	38	D2
Maladzyechna	78	E4
Málaga	68	F8
Malaimbandy	112	H4
Malaita	114	G6
Malakal	110	E2
Malakula	114	G7
Malamala	92	(2)B3
Malang	92	(1)E4
Malanje	110	B5
Malanville	108	E2
Malaryta	58	P6
Malatya	98	H4
Malaut	94	B2
Mālavi	98	M7
Malawi	112	E2
Malaya Baranikha	84	V3
Malaya Vishera	78	F3
Malaybalay	90	H5
Malâyer	96	E3
Malay Peninsula	90	C6
Malay Reef	116	J3
Malaysia	92	(1)C2
Malbork	58	J3
Malchin, *Germany*	60	H3
Malchin, *Mongolia*	82	S8
Malden Island	114	L6
Maldives	94	B8
Maldonado	52	L5
Malé	70	F4
Malé	94	B8
Male Atoll	94	B8
Malegaon	94	B4
Malé Karpaty	70	N2
Malesherbes	66	H5
Maleta	84	H6
Malheur	38	C2
Malheur Lake	38	C2
Mali	106	E5
Malindi	110	G4
Malin Head	64	E6
Malkara	76	J4
Malko Tŭrnovo	74	Q8
Mallaig	64	G4
Mallawi	104	F2
Mallorca	68	P5
Mallow	64	D9
Malmédy	62	J4
Malmesbury	112	B6
Malmö	58	C2
Malmyzh	78	K3
Malone	40	F2
Måløy	56	C6
Malozemel'skaya Tundra	78	K1
Mälselv	56	K2
Malta	72	J13
Malta	38	E1
Malta Channel	72	J12
Maltahöhe	112	B4
Malvern	40	B4
Malý Dunaj	70	N2
Malyy Uzen'	78	J4
Mama	84	J5
Mamadysh	78	K3
Mambasa	110	D3
Mamburao	90	G4
Mamelodi	112	D5
Mammoth Hot Springs	38	D2
Mamonovo	58	J3
Mamoré	50	D6
Mamou	108	B2
Mamoudzou	112	H2
Mamuju	92	(2)A3
Ma'mūl	96	G6
Mamuno	112	C4
Man	108	C3
Mana	44	(2)A1
Manacapuru	50	E4
Manacor	68	P5
Manado	92	(2)B2
Managua	46	G6
Manakara	112	H4
Manali	94	C2
Mananara	112	H4
Mananara Avaratra	112	H3
Mananjary	112	H4
Manantenina	112	H4
Manassas	40	E3
Manaus	50	E4
Manavgat	76	P8
Manbij	98	G5
Manchester, *United Kingdom*	64	K8
Manchester, *Ia., United States*	40	B2
Manchester, *Ky., United States*	40	D3
Manchester, *Tenn., United States*	40	C3
Manchester, *Vt., United States*	40	F2
Mand	96	H4
Mandabe	112	G4
Mandal	56	D7
Mandalay	90	B2
Mandalgovĭ	86	D1
Mandan	38	F1
Mandera	110	G3
Mandi	94	C2
Mandi Burewala	94	B2
Mandimba	112	F2
Manding	106	D6
Mandla	94	D4
Mandø	60	D1
Mandsaur	94	C4
Mandurah	116	C6
Mandúria	72	M8
Mandvi	94	A4
Mandya	94	C6
Manfredonia	72	K7
Manga	108	G2
Manga	50	J6
Mangaia	114	K8
Mangalia	74	R6
Mangalore	94	B6
Mangareva	114	N8
Mangatupopo	118	E4
Mangaweka	118	F4
Manggar	92	(1)D3
Mangit	96	H1
Mangnai	82	S10
Mango	108	E2
Mangoky	112	G4
Mangole	92	(2)C3
Mangonui	118	D2
Mangrove Cay	42	F5
Manhad	94	B5
Manhattan	42	B2
Manhuaçu	50	J8
Mania	112	H3
Maniamba	112	F2
Manicoré	50	E5
Manicouagan	34	T6
Manihiki	114	K7
Maniitsoq	34	W3
Manila	90	G4
Manisa	76	K6
Manistee	40	C2
Manistique	40	C1
Manitoba	34	M6
Manitou	38	G1
Manitoulin Island	40	D1
Manitouwadge	40	C1
Manitowoc	40	C2
Maniwaki	40	E1
Manizales	50	B2
Manja	112	G4
Manjimup	116	C6
Mankato	40	B2
Manley Hot Springs	34	A4
Manlleu	68	N3
Manna	92	(1)C3
Mannheim	62	L5
Manning, *Canada*	34	H5
Manning, *United States*	42	E3
Manokwari	92	(2)D3
Manono	110	D5
Manosque	66	L10
Manouane	40	F1
Manouane Lake	34	S6
Manp'o	88	D3
Manresa	114	J6
Manresa	68	M3
Mansa	112	D2
Mansel Island	34	Q4
Mansfield, *United Kingdom*	62	A1
Mansfield, *La., United States*	42	C3
Mansfield, *Oh., United States*	40	D2
Manta	50	A4
Manteo	42	F2
Mantes-la-Jolie	62	D5
Mántova	70	F5
Manturovo	78	H3
Manú	50	C6
Manuelzinho	50	G5
Manüjän	101	G3
Manukan	90	G5
Manukau	118	E3
Manukau Harbour	118	E3
Manyberries	38	D1
Manyinga	112	C2
Manyoni	110	E5
Manzanares	68	G5
Manzanillo	46	J4
Manzhouli	84	K7
Manzini	112	E5

Mao 104 C5
Maoming 90 E2
Mapam Yumco 94 D2
Mapi 92 (2)E4
Mapinhane 112 F4
Maple Creek 36 E2
Mapuera 50 E4
Maputo 112 E5
Maqueda 68 F4
Maquela do Zombo 110 B5
Maquinchao 52 H7
Maquoketa 40 B2
Maraba 50 H5
Maracaibo 50 C1
Maracay 50 D1
Marādah 104 C2
Maradi 108 F2
Marāgheh 98 M5
Maralal 110 F3
Marand 98 L4
Maranhão 50 H5
Marañón 50 B4
Mărăşeşti 74 Q4
Marathon, Canada 40 C1
Marathon, United States 44 F2
Marbella 68 F8
Marburg 62 L4
Marcal 70 N3
Marcali 70 N4
March 62 C2
Marche 62 H4
Marchena 68 E7
Mardan 94 B2
Mar del Plata 52 K6
Mardin 98 J5
Maré 114 G8
Mareeba 116 J3
Marettimo 72 F11
Marfa 44 F2
Margate 62 D3
Margherita di Savoia 72 L7
Marghita 74 K2
Margilan 96 K1
Marguerite Bay 120 (2)KK3
María Elena 52 H3
Marianas Trench 114 E4
Marianna 42 D3
Máriánská Lázně 60 H7
Mariazell 70 L3
Mar'ib 104 J4
Maribo 60 G2
Maribor 70 L4
Maridi 110 D2
Marie Byrd Land 120 (2)FF2
Marie Galante 46 M5
Mariehamn 56 K6
Marienberg 60 J6
Mariental 112 B4
Marietta 42 E2
Marietta, Oh.,
United States 40 D3
Marietta, Okla.,
United States 42 B3
Mariinsk 82 R6
Marijampolé 58 N3
Marília 52 M3
Marín 68 B2
Marinette 40 C1
Maringá 52 L3
Marino 72 G7
Marion, Ill.,
United States 40 C3
Marion, Ind.,
United States 40 C2
Marion, Oh.,
United States 40 D2
Maripa 50 D2
Mariscal Estigarribia 52 J3
Maritime Alps 70 C6
Marittimo 70 F7
Mariupol' 78 G5
Marīvān 98 M6
Mariy El 78 J3
Marjayoûn 100 C3
Marka 110 G3
Markam 86 B5
Markaryd 58 C1
Marked Tree 42 C2
Marken 62 H2
Markermeer 62 H2
Market Harborough 62 B2
Markham 40 E2
Marki 58 L5
Markit 82 P10
Markkleeberg 60 H5
Markovo 84 W4
Marktoberdorf 70 F3
Marktredwitz 60 H7
Marla 116 F5
Marle 62 F5
Marmande 66 F9
Marmara Adası 76 K4

Marmara Denizi 76 L4
Marmaris 76 L8
Marmolada 70 G4
Marne 62 F5
Maroansetra 112 H3
Marolambo 112 H4
Maroni 50 G3
Marotiri 114 M8
Maroua 108 G2
Marquesas Islands 114 M6
Marquette 40 C1
Marradi 70 G6
Marrakech 106 D2
Marra Plateau 104 D5
Marree 116 G5
Marrupa 112 F2
Marsa Alam 104 F2
Marsabit 110 F3
Marsala 72 G11
Marsberg 62 L3
Marsden 116 J6
Marseille 66 L10
Marseille-en-Beauvaisis 62 D5
Marshall, Ill.,
United States 42 D2
Marshall, Tex.,
United States 42 C3
Marshall Islands 114 G4
Marshalltown 40 B2
Marsh Harbour 42 F4
Marsh Island 42 C4
Martapura, Indonesia 92 (1)C3
Martapura, Indonesia 92 (1)E3
Martigny 70 C4
Martigues 66 L10
Martin, Slovakia 58 H8
Martin, United States 38 F2
Martina Franca 72 M8
Martinborough 118 E5
Martinique 46 M6
Martinsburg 40 E3
Martinsville, Ind.,
United States 40 C3
Martinsville, Va.,
United States 40 E3
Marton 118 E5
Martos 68 G7
Maruchak 96 H2
Mårvatn 56 E6
Mary 96 H2
Maryborough 116 K5
Maryland 40 E3
Marysville, Canada 40 G1
Marysville, Calif.,
United States 44 B1
Marysville, Kans.,
United States 42 B2
Maryville 40 B2
Masai Steppe 110 F4
Masaka 110 E4
Masalembu Besar 92 (1)E4
Masallı 98 N4
Masamba 92 (2)B3
Masan 88 E6
Masasi 110 F6
Masbate 90 G4
Masbate 90 G4
Mascara 106 F1
Maseru 112 D5
Mashhad 96 G2
Masi-Manimba 110 B4
Masindi 110 E3
Maşīrah 96 G5
Masjed Soleymān 96 E3
Maskanah 98 H5
Mason 42 B3
Mason Bay 118 A8
Mason City 40 B2
Massa 70 F6
Massachusetts 40 F2
Massachusetts Bay 40 G2
Massafra 72 M8
Massa Marittima 72 E5
Massawa 104 G4
Massena 40 F2
Masset 34 E6
Massif Central 66 H8
Massif de Guéra 104 C3
Massif de l'Aïr 106 G6
Massif des Écrins 70 B5
Massif du Chaillu 108 G5
Massif du Tsaratanana 112 H2
Massif Ennedi 104 D4
Massillon 40 D2
Massinga 112 F4
Masteksay 78 K5
Masterton 118 E5
Mastung 96 J4
Masty 56 N10
Masuda 88 F6
Masuguru 112 F2

Masvingo 112 E4
Maşyâf 100 D1
Matadi 110 A5
Matagami 40 E1
Matagorda Island 42 B4
Matakana Island 118 F3
Matakawau 118 E3
Matale 94 D7
Matam 108 B1
Matamoros, Mexico 44 F3
Matamoros, Mexico 44 G3
Matane 40 G1
Matanzas 36 K7
Matara 94 D7
Mataram 92 (1)F4
Mataranka 116 F3
Mataró 68 N3
Matawai 118 F3
Matawai 118 F4
Matehuala 44 F4
Matera 72 L8
Mátészalka 74 K2
Mateur 72 D11
Matheson 40 D1
Mathraki 76 B5
Mathura 94 C3
Mati 90 H5
Matlock 62 A1
Matmata 106 G2
Mato Grosso 50 F6
Mato Grosso 50 F6
Mato Grosso do Sul 50 F7
Matosinhos 68 B3
Matrah 101 H5
Matrel 70 H4
Matrûh 104 E1
Matsiatra 112 H4
Matsu 86 G5
Matsue 88 G6
Matsumae 88 L3
Matsumoto 88 J5
Matsusaka 88 J6
Matsuyama 88 G7
Mattawa 40 E1
Matterhorn 70 C5
Matthews Ridge 50 E2
Mattighofen 60 J8
Mattoon 40 C3
Maturín 50 E2
Maubeuge 62 F4
Maui 44 (2)F3
Maullín 52 G7
Maun 112 C3
Mauna Kea 44 (2)F4
Mauna Loa 44 (2)F4
Mauritania 106 C5
Mauritius 112 (1)B2
Mauron 66 C5
Mauthen 70 H4
Mavinga 112 C3
Mawlaik 90 A2
Max 38 F1
Maya 84 P5
Maya 92 (1)D3
Mayaguana 46 K4
Mayagüez 46 L5
Mayamba 110 B4
Maych'ew 104 G5
Maydh 110 H1
Mayenne 66 E5
Mayenne 66 E5
Mayer 44 D2
Maykamys 82 P8
Maykop 98 J1
Mayly-Say 96 K1
Maymecha 84 G3
Mayn 84 W4
Mayo 84 D4
Mayor Island 118 F3
Mayotte 112 H2
Mayrhofen 70 G3
Mayskiy 84 M6
Mayumba 108 G5
Mayya 84 N4
Mazagão 50 G4
Mazagran 66 K4
Mazama 38 B1
Mazamet 66 H10
Mazar 82 P10
Mazara del Vallo 72 G11
Mazár-e Sharīf 96 J2
Mazatlán 46 C4
Mažeikiai 58 M1
Mazocahui 44 D3
Mazomora 110 F5
Mazra 100 C5
Mazraat 78 E4
Mazzarino 72 J11
Mbabane 112 E5
Mbaïki 110 B3
Mbala 110 E5
Mbale 110 E3

Mbalmayo 108 G4
Mbamba Bay 112 E2
Mbandaka 110 B3
Mbanga 108 F4
M'banza Congo 110 A5
Mbarara 110 E4
Mbeya 110 E5
Mbomou 110 C3
Mbour 110 A3
Mbuji-Mayi 110 C3
Mbuyuni 110 F5
McAlester 42 B3
McBride 34 G6
McCamey 44 F3
McCammon 38 D3
McClintock 34 N5
McClintock Channel 34 L2
McComb 42 C3
McCook 38 F2
McDermitt 38 C2
McGehee 42 C3
McGrath 44 (1)F3
McKinlay 116 H4
McKinney 42 B3
McLaughlin 38 F1
McLennan 34 H4
McMinnville 40 C3
McPherson 42 B3
McRae 42 D3
Meadow Lake 34 K4
Meadville 40 D2
Meander River 34 H5
Meaux 62 E5
Mecca = Makkah 104 G5
Mechelen 62 G3
Mechernich 62 J4
Mecidiye 76 J4
Mecklenburger Bucht 60 G2
Mecula 112 F2
Meda 68 C3
Medak 94 C5
Medan 92 (1)B3
Médéa 68 N4
Medellín 50 B8
Medenine 106 H1
Medford 38 B2
Medgidia 74 R4
Mediaş 74 M3
Medicine Bow 38 E2
Medicine Hat 34 J2
Medicine Lodge 42 B2
Medina = Al Madīnah 104 G5
Medinaceli 68 H4
Medina de Campo 68 F4
Medina Sidonia 68 E8
Mediterranean Sea 54 L4
Mednogorsk 78 L1
Medvedica 78 H3
Medvezh'yegorsk 78 F2
Meeker 38 E2
Meerane 60 H4
Meerut 94 C3
Mega 92 (2)D3
Megalopoli 76 K8
Meganisi 76 C8
Megara 76 K8
Megisti 76 M8
Mehrān 98 M4
Mehriz 96 F3
Meiktila 90 A2
Meiningen 60 F4
Meißen 60 H4
Meizhou 90 F2
Mejez El Bab 72 D11
Mékambo 108 G4
Mek'elë 104 G6
Meknès 106 D2
Mekong 90 D2
Melaka 92 (1)C3
Melanesia 114 F4
Melbourne, Australia 116 H8
Melbourne, United States 42 E4
Melchor de Mencos 46 G4
Meldrum Bay 40 D1
Meleuz 78 L1
Mélfi 104 C0
Melfi 72 L8
Melfort 34 L1
Melide 68 B3
Melilla 68 H8
Melita 38 F1
Melitopol' 78 G5
Melk 70 L1
Melkosopochnik 82 N7
Mělník 60 K3
Melo 52 L4
Melton Mowbray 62 B2
Melun 62 E5
Melut 104 F5
Melvern Lake 42 B2
Melville 34 L1
Melville Island, Australia 116 F2

Name	Page	Grid
Melville Island, *Canada*	32	N2
Melville Peninsula	34	P3
Memberamo	92	(2)E3
Memboro	92	(2)A4
Memmert	62	J1
Memmingen	70	F3
Mempawah	92	(1)D2
Memphis, *Mo., United States*	40	B2
Memphis, *Tenn., United States*	40	C3
Mena	42	C3
Menai Strait	64	H8
Ménaka	106	F5
Mendawai	92	(1)E3
Mende	66	J9
Menden	62	K3
Mendī	110	F2
Mendoza	52	H5
Menemen	76	K6
Menen	62	F4
Menfi	72	G11
Menggala	92	(1)D3
Meniet	106	F4
Menkere	84	L3
Menominee	40	C1
Menomonee Falls	40	C2
Menongue	112	B2
Menorca	68	Q4
Mentok	92	(1)D3
Menyuan	86	C3
Menzel Bourguiba	72	D11
Menzel Bouzelfa	72	E12
Menzel Temime	72	E12
Menzies	116	D5
Meppel	62	J2
Meppen	62	K2
Meran Merano	70	G4
Merauke	92	(2)F4
Mercato Saraceno	70	H7
Merced	38	B3
Mercedes, *Argentina*	52	H5
Mercedes, *Argentina*	52	K4
Mercedes, *United States*	42	B4
Mercedes, *Uruguay*	52	K5
Mercury Islands	118	E3
Mergenevo	78	K5
Mergui	90	B4
Mergui Archipelago	90	B4
Mérida, *Mexico*	46	G4
Mérida, *Spain*	68	D6
Mérida, *Venezuela*	46	K7
Meridian	42	D3
Merinha Grande	68	B5
Meriruma	50	G3
Merke	82	N9
Merkys	56	N9
Merowe	104	F4
Merredin	116	C6
Merrill	40	C1
Merriman	38	F2
Merritt	34	G6
Merseburg	60	H5
Mers el Kébir	68	K9
Mersey	64	J8
Mersin = İcel	76	S8
Mērsrags	56	M8
Merthyr Tydfil	64	J10
Mérú	62	E5
Meru	110	F3
Merzifon	98	F3
Merzig	62	J5
Mesa	44	D2
Mesa de Yambi	50	C3
Mesagne	72	M8
Meschede	62	L3
Mesóaria Plain	100	A1
Mesolongi	76	D6
Mesopotamia	98	K6
Messaad	106	F2
Messina, *Italy*	72	K10
Messina, *South Africa*	112	D4
Messini	76	E7
Messiniakos Kolpos	76	D8
Mestre	70	H5
Meta	50	C2
Metairie	42	C4
Metaline Falls	38	C1
Metán	52	J4
Metangula	112	E2
Metema	104	G5
Meteor Depth	48	J9
Metković	74	E6
Metlika	70	L5
Metsovo	76	D5
Mettet	62	G4
Mettlach	62	J5
Metz	62	J5
Metzingen	70	F2
Meulaboh	90	B6
Meuse	62	G4
Mexia	42	B3
Mexicali	44	C2
Mexican Hat	44	E1
Mexico	40	B3
Mexico	46	D4
Meymaneh	96	H2
Mezdra	74	L6
Mezen'	78	H1
Mezenskaya Guba	78	H1
Mezhdurechensk	82	R7
Mezöberény	74	J3
Mezökövesd	74	H2
Mezötúr	74	H2
Mfuwe	112	E2
Miajadas	68	E5
Miami, *Fla., United States*	42	E4
Miami, *Okla., United States*	42	C2
Miandowáb	98	M5
Miandrivazo	112	H3
Miáneh	98	M5
Miangyang	86	E4
Mianning	86	C5
Mianwali	94	B2
Mianyang	86	C4
Miaodao Qundao	86	G3
Miao'ergou	82	Q8
Miass	78	M4
Miastko	58	G4
Michalovce	58	L9
Michigan	40	C1
Michipicoten Island	40	C1
Michurinsk	78	H4
Micronesia	114	F4
Mid-Atlantic Ridge	48	G1
Middelburg, *Netherlands*	62	F3
Middelburg, *South Africa*	112	D6
Middelfart	60	E1
Middelkerke	62	E3
Middle America Trench	32	L8
Middle Andaman	90	A4
Middlebury	40	F2
Middle Lake	38	C2
Middlesboro	40	D3
Middlesbrough	64	L7
Middletown, *N.Y., United States*	40	F2
Middletown, *Oh., United States*	40	D3
Midland, *Canada*	40	E2
Midland, *Mich., United States*	40	D2
Midland, *Tex., United States*	44	F2
Midway Islands	114	J3
Midwest City	42	B2
Midzor	74	K6
Miechów	58	K7
Mielan	66	F10
Mielec	58	L7
Miembwe	110	F5
Mien	58	D1
Miercurea-Ciuc	74	N3
Mieres	68	E1
Miesbach	70	G3
Mi'eso	110	G2
Miging	94	F3
Miguel Auza	44	F4
Mikhaylovka	78	H4
Mikhaylovskiy	82	P7
Mikino	84	U4
Mikkeli	56	P6
Mikulov	70	M2
Mikun'	78	K2
Mikuni-sammyaku	88	K5
Mikura-jima	88	K7
Mila	106	G1
Milaca	40	B1
Miladhunmadulu Atoll	94	B7
Milan = Milano, *Italy*	70	E5
Milan, *United States*	42	C2
Milano	70	E5
Milas	76	K7
Milazzo	72	K10
Miles	116	K5
Miles City	38	E1
Milford, *Fla., United States*	40	E3
Milford, *Ut., United States*	38	D3
Milford Haven	64	G10
Milford Sound	118	A7
Miliana	68	N8
Milicz	58	G6
Milk	34	G4
Mil'kovo	84	T6
Millau	66	J9
Millbank	38	G1
Milledgeville	42	E3
Miller	38	G2
Millerovo	78	H5
Millington	40	C3
Millinocket	40	G1
Miloro	110	E5
Milos	76	G8
Milton, *New Zealand*	118	B8
Milton, *United States*	42	D3
Milton Keynes	62	B2
Miluo	86	E5
Milwaukee	40	C2
Mily	82	L8
Mimizan-Plage	66	D9
Minab	101	G3
Mina Jebel Ali	101	F4
Minas	52	K5
Miná' Sa'üd	101	C2
Minas Gerais	50	H7
Minas Novas	50	J7
Minatitlán	46	F5
Minbu	90	A2
Minchinmávida	52	G7
Mincivan	98	M4
Mindanao	90	G5
Mindelheim	70	F2
Mindelo	108	(1)B1
Minden	62	L2
Mindoro	90	G4
Mindoro Strait	90	G4
Minehead	64	J10
Mineola	42	B3
Mineral'nyye Vody	98	K1
Minerva Reefs	114	J8
Minfeng	82	Q10
Minga	110	D6
Mingáçevir	98	M3
Mingáçevir Su Anbarı	98	M3
Mingulay	64	D5
Minicoy	94	B7
Minilya Roadhouse	116	B4
Minna	108	F3
Minneapolis	40	B2
Minnesota	40	A1
Minnesota	40	A2
Miño	68	C2
Minot	38	F1
Minsk	78	E4
Minturn	38	E3
Minusinsk	82	S7
Min Xian	86	C4
Min'yar	78	L3
Miquelon	40	E1
Miraflores	50	C3
Miramas	66	K10
Mirambeau	66	E8
Miranda	50	F8
Miranda de Ebro	68	H2
Miranda do Douro	68	D3
Mirandela	68	C3
Mirbāt	96	F6
Mīrjāveh	96	H4
Mirnyy	84	J4
Mirow	60	H3
Mirpur Khas	94	A3
Mirtoö Pelagos	76	F7
Mirzapur	94	D3
Miskolc	74	H1
Misoöl	92	(2)D3
Misrâtah	104	C1
Missinaibi	34	Q6
Missinipe	34	L5
Mission	38	F2
Mississippi	42	C3
Mississippi	42	D2
Mississippi River Delta	42	D4
Missoula	38	D1
Missouri	38	F1
Missouri	40	B3
Missouri City	42	B4
Mistassibi	34	S7
Mistelbach	70	M2
Mitchell	38	G2
Mithankot	96	K4
Mithaylov	78	G4
Mithymna	76	J5
Mito	88	L5
Mits'iwa	96	C6
Mittellandkanal	62	F2
Mittersill	70	H3
Mittweida	60	J6
Mitú	50	C3
Mitzic	108	G4
Miyake-jima	88	K6
Miyako	88	L4
Miyakonojō	88	F8
Miyazaki	88	F8
Miyoshi	88	G6
Mīzan Teferī	110	F2
Mizdah	106	H2
Mizen Head	64	B10
Mizhhir"ya	74	L1
Mizil	74	P4
Mizpe Ramon	100	B6
Mjölby	56	H7
Mjøsa	56	F6
Mkuze	112	E5
Mladá Boleslav	58	D7
Mladenovac	74	H5
Mława	58	K4
Mljet	74	E7
Mmabatho	112	D5
Moa	116	H2
Moanda	108	G5
Moapa	38	D3
Moba	110	D5
Mobaye	110	C3
Mobayi-Mbongo	110	C3
Moberly	40	B3
Mobile	42	D3
Moçambique	112	G3
Môc Châu	90	C2
Mochudi	112	D4
Mocímboa da Praia	112	G2
Mocuba	112	F3
Modane	70	B5
Módena	70	F6
Modesto	38	B3
Módica	72	J12
Mödling	70	M2
Modowi	92	(2)D3
Modriča	74	F5
Moenkopi	44	D1
Moers	62	J3
Moffat	64	J6
Moffat Peak	118	B7
Mogadishu = Muqdisho	110	H3
Mogilno	58	G5
Mogocha	84	K6
Mogochin	82	Q6
Mogok	90	B2
Mohács	74	F4
Mohammadia	68	L9
Mohe	84	L6
Mohembo	112	C3
Mohoro	110	F5
Mohyliv-Podil's'kyy	74	Q1
Moi	56	D7
Moincër	94	D2
Moinești	74	P3
Mo i Rana	56	H3
Moissac	66	G9
Mojave	44	C1
Mojave Desert	44	C1
Mokau	118	E4
Mokohinau Island	118	E2
Mokolo	108	G2
Mokoreta	118	B8
Mokp'o	88	D6
Mol	62	H3
Mola di Bari	72	M7
Molat	70	K6
Molde	56	D5
Moldova	74	P2
Moldova	74	R2
Moldova Nouă	74	J5
Molepolole	112	C4
Molfetta	72	L7
Molina de Aragón	68	J4
Molina de Segura	68	J6
Moline	40	B2
Möll	70	J4
Mollendo	50	C7
Molokai	44	(2)D2
Molopo	112	C5
Molsheim	70	C2
Molucca Sea	92	(2)C2
Moma	112	F3
Mombasa	110	G4
Momchilgrad	74	N8
Møn	60	H2
Monach Islands	64	E4
Monaco	70	C7
Monaco	70	C7
Monahans	44	F2
Mona Passage	46	L5
Monbetsu, *Japan*	88	M1
Monbetsu, *Japan*	88	M2
Moncalieri	70	C5
Monchegorsk	56	S3
Mönchengladbach	62	J3
Monclova	44	F3
Moncton	34	U7
Mondovi	70	C6
Mondragone	72	H7
Mondy	84	G6
Monfalcone	70	J5
Monforte	68	C5
Monforte de Lemos	68	C2
Monfredónia	72	K7
Monga	110	C3
Mongkung	90	B2
Mongo	104	C5
Mongolia	86	B2
Mongonu	108	G2
Mongora	94	B2
Mongu	112	C3
Mong Yai	90	B2
Mong Yu	90	B2

Name	Page	Grid
Monkoto	110	C4
Monmouth	40	B2
Mono	108	E3
Mono Lake	38	C3
Monopoli	72	M8
Monor	58	J10
Monowai	118	A7
Monreal del Campo	68	J4
Monreale	72	H10
Monroe, La., United States	42	C3
Monroe, Mich., United States	40	D2
Monroe, N.C., United States	42	E3
Monroe, Wash., United States	38	B1
Monroe City	42	C2
Monrovia	108	B3
Mons	62	F4
Monschau	62	J4
Monsélice	70	G5
Montabaur	62	K4
Montague Island	48	J9
Montalbán	68	K4
Montana	74	L6
Montana	38	E1
Montargis	66	H6
Montauban	66	G10
Montauk	40	F2
Mont aux Sources	112	D5
Montbard	66	K6
Montbéliard	70	B3
Montblanc	68	M3
Mont Blanc	70	B5
Montbrison	66	K8
Mont Cameroun	108	F4
Montceau-les-Mines	66	K7
Mont-de-Marsan	66	E10
Montdidier	62	E5
Monte Alegre	50	G4
Monte Azul	50	J7
Montebello	40	F1
Monte Bello Islands	116	B4
Montebelluna	70	H5
Monte Calvo	72	K6
Monte Cinto	72	C6
Montecristo	72	E6
Monte Etna	72	J11
Montefiascone	72	G6
Montego Bay	46	J5
Montélimar	66	K9
Monte Limbara	72	D8
Monte Lindo	52	K4
Montemorelos	42	B4
Monte Namuli	112	F3
Montenegro = Crna Gora	74	F7
Monte Perdino	68	L2
Monte Pollino	72	L9
Montepuez	112	F2
Montepulciano	72	F5
Monte Quemado	52	J4
Montereau-faut-Yonne	66	H5
Monterey	40	E3
Monterey Bay	38	B3
Montería	50	B2
Montero	50	E7
Monte Rosa	70	C6
Monterotondo	72	G6
Monterrey	44	F3
Monte Sant'Angelo	72	K7
Montes Claros	50	J7
Montesilvano Marina	72	J6
Montevarchi	70	G7
Montevideo, United States	40	A1
Montevideo, Uruguay	52	K5
Monte Viso	70	C6
Monte Vista	44	E1
Montgomery	42	D3
Monthey	70	B4
Monticello	38	E3
Montijo	68	D6
Montilla	68	F7
Mont Joli	40	G1
Mont-Laurier	40	E1
Montluçon	66	H7
Montmagny	40	F1
Montmedy	66	H5
Mont Mézenc	66	K9
Montone	70	G6
Montoro	68	F6
Mont Pelat	66	M9
Montpelier, Id., United States	38	D2
Montpelier, Vt., United States	40	F2
Montpellier	66	J10
Montréal	40	F1
Montreul	62	D4
Montreux	70	B4
Montrose, United Kingdom	64	K5
Montrose, United States	38	E3
Monts Bagzane	106	G5
Mont Serkout	106	G4
Montserrat	46	M5
Monts Nimba	108	C3
Monts Otish	34	S6
Mont Tahat	106	G4
Monywa	90	A2
Monza	70	E5
Monzón	68	L3
Moonie	116	K5
Moorcroft	38	F2
Moorhead	40	A1
Moosburg	70	G1
Moose Jaw	34	K6
Moose Lake	34	M6
Moosonee	34	Q6
Moosomin	34	L6
Mopti	106	E6
Moqor	96	J3
Môr	74	F2
Móra	56	H6
Móra	68	B6
Moradabad	94	C3
Morafenobe	112	G3
Morag	58	J4
Moramanga	112	H3
Moran	38	D2
Morane	114	N8
Moratuwa	94	D7
Morava	58	G8
Moravské Budějovice	70	L1
Morawhanna	50	F2
Moray Firth	64	J4
Morbach	62	K5
Morbi	94	B4
Mordoviya	78	H4
Moreau	38	F1
Morecambe	64	K7
Moree	116	J5
Morehead	40	D3
More Laptevykh	84	L1
Morelia	46	D5
Morella	68	K4
Moresby Island	44	(1)L5
Moreton Island	116	K5
Morez	66	M7
Morgan	116	G6
Morgan City	42	C4
Morgantown	40	D3
Morges	70	B4
Mori	88	L2
Morioka	88	L4
Morkoka	84	J4
Morlaix	62	B5
Mornington Island	116	G3
Morocco	102	C2
Morogoro	110	F5
Moro Gulf	90	G5
Morombe	112	G4
Mörön	84	G7
Morondava	112	G4
Morón de la Frontera	68	E7
Moroni	112	G2
Moron Us He	94	F2
Morotai	92	(2)C2
Moroto	110	E3
Morpeth	64	L6
Morris	38	G1
Morristown	42	E2
Mors	56	E8
Morshansk	78	H4
Mortain	62	B6
Morteros	52	J5
Morvern	64	H4
Morwell	116	J7
Mosbach	60	E7
Mosby	38	D1
Moscow = Moskva	78	G3
Mosel	62	K4
Moselle	62	G6
Moses Lake	38	C1
Mosgiel	118	C7
Moshi	110	F4
Mosjøen	56	G4
Moskenesøy	56	F3
Moskva	78	G3
Mosonmagyaróvár	70	N3
Mosquero	44	F1
Moss	56	F7
Mossburn	118	B7
Mosselbaai	112	C6
Mossoró	50	K5
Most	60	J6
Mostaganem	102	F1
Mostar	74	E6
Mostoles	68	G4
Møsvatn	56	F7
Mot'a	104	G5
Motala	56	H7
Motherwell	64	J6
Motihari	94	D3
Motilla del Palancar	68	J5
Motiti Island	118	F3
Motril	68	G8
Motru	74	K5
Motu One	114	L7
Motygino	82	S6
Mouchard	70	A4
Moudjéria	106	C5
Moudros	76	H5
Mouila	108	G5
Moulins	66	J7
Moulmein	90	B3
Moultrie	42	E3
Moundou	104	C6
Mount Adam	52	J9
Mount Adams	38	B1
Mountain Grove	40	B3
Mountain Home	40	B3
Mountain Nile = Bahr el Jebel	110	E2
Mount Alba	118	B7
Mount Aloysius	116	E5
Mount Anglem	118	A8
Mount Apo	90	H5
Mount Ararat	98	L4
Mount Arrowsmith	118	C6
Mount Aspiring	118	B7
Mount Assiniboine	34	H6
Mount Augustus	116	C4
Mount Baco	90	G3
Mount Baker	38	B1
Mount Bartle Frere	116	J3
Mount Bogong	116	J7
Mount Brewster	118	B7
Mount Bruce	116	C4
Mount Cameroun	102	D5
Mount Carmel	38	D3
Mount Columbia	34	H6
Mount Cook	118	C6
Mount Cook	118	C6
Mount Donald	118	A7
Mount Douglas	116	J4
Mount Egmont	118	E4
Mount Elbert	38	E3
Mount Elgon	110	E3
Mount Essendon	116	D4
Mount Evelyn	116	F2
Mount Everest	94	E3
Mount Fairweather	34	D5
Mount Gambier	116	H7
Mount Garnet	116	J3
Mount Hermon	100	C3
Mount Hood	38	B1
Mount Hutt	118	C6
Mount Huxley	118	B7
Mount Isa	116	G4
Mount Jackson	120	(2)MM2
Mount Karisimbi	110	D4
Mount Kendall	118	D5
Mount Kenya = Kirinyaga	110	F4
Mount Kilimanjaro	110	F4
Mount Kirkpatrick	120	(2)AA1
Mount Kosciuszko	116	J7
Mount Liebig	116	F4
Mount Lloyd George	34	G5
Mount Logan	34	C4
Mount Magnet	116	C5
Mount Maunganui	118	F3
Mount McKinley	44	(1)K3
Mount Meharry	116	C4
Mount Menzies	120	(2)L2
Mount Minto	120	(2)Y2
Mount Mulanje	112	F3
Mount Murchison	118	C6
Mount Nyiru	110	F3
Mount Olympus	38	B1
Mount Ord	116	E3
Mount Ossa	116	J8
Mount Owen	118	D5
Mount Paget	52	P9
Mount Pleasant, Ia., United States	40	B2
Mount Pleasant, Mich., United States	40	D2
Mount Pleasant, S.C., United States	42	F3
Mount Pleasant, Tex., United States	42	B3
Mount Pleasant, Ut., United States	38	D3
Mount Pulog	90	G3
Mount Rainier	38	B1
Mount Ratz	34	E5
Mount Richmond	118	D5
Mount Roberts	116	K5
Mount Robson	34	H6
Mount Roosevelt	34	F5
Mount Roraima	50	E2
Mount Ross	118	E5
Mount Shasta	38	B2
Mount Somers	118	C6
Mount Stanley	110	D3
Mount Tahat	102	D3
Mount Travers	118	D6
Mount Tuun	88	D3
Mount Usborne	52	K9
Mount Vernon, Al., United States	42	D3
Mount Vernon, Ill., United States	40	C5
Mount Vernon, Oh., United States	40	D2
Mount Vernon, Wash., United States	38	B1
Mount Victoria, Myanmar	90	A2
Mount Victoria, Papua New Guinea	114	E6
Mount Waddington	34	F6
Mount Washington	34	S8
Mount Whitney	38	C3
Mount Wilson	38	E3
Mount Woodroffe	116	F5
Mount Ziel	116	F4
Moura	88	C6
Mousa	64	(1)B2
Moussoro	104	C5
Moutamba	108	G5
Mouth of the Shannon	64	B9
Mouths of the Amazon	48	G3
Mouths of the Danube	74	S4
Mouths of the Ganges	94	E4
Mouths of the Indus	96	J5
Mouths of the Irrawaddy	90	A3
Mouths of the Krishna	94	D5
Mouths of the Mekong	90	D5
Mouths of the Niger	108	F4
Moûtiers	70	B5
Moutong	92	(2)B2
Moyale	110	F3
Moyen Atlas	106	D2
Moyenvic	62	J3
Moyeroo	82	U4
Moyynty	82	N8
Mozambique	112	E3
Mozambique Channel	112	F4
Mozdok	98	L2
Mozhga	78	K4
Mozirje	70	K4
Mpanda	110	E5
Mpika	112	E2
Mporokoso	110	E5
Mpumalanga	112	D5
Mragowo	58	L4
Mrkonjić-Grad	70	N6
M'Sila	106	F1
Mtsensk	78	G4
Mtwara	110	G6
Muang Khammouan	90	C3
Muang Không	90	D3
Muang Khôngxédôn	90	D3
Muang Khoua	90	C2
Muang Pakxan	90	C3
Muang Phin	90	D3
Muang Sing	90	C2
Muang Xai	90	C2
Muar	92	(1)C2
Muarabungo	92	(1)C3
Muarawahau	92	(1)F2
Mubarek	82	M10
Mubende	110	E3
Mubrani	92	(2)D3
Muck	64	G4
Muckadilla	116	J5
Muconda	110	C6
Mucur	76	S5
Mudanjiang	88	C4
Mudanya	76	L4
Muddy Gap	38	E2
Mudurnu	76	P4
Mufulira	112	D2
Mughshin	96	F6
Muğla	76	L7
Mugodzhary	78	L5
Mühldorf	70	H2
Mühlhausen	60	F5
Muhos	56	N4
Muhu	56	M7
Muhulu	110	D4
Mukacheve	58	M9
Mukah	92	J2
Mukdahan	90	C2
Mukuku	112	C2
Mulanje	94	B8
Mulaku Atoll	94	B8
Mulde	60	H2
Muleshoe	44	F2
Mulgrave Island	116	H2
Mulhacén	68	G7
Mülheim	62	C3
Mulhouse	70	C3
Muling	88	C4
Mull	64	G5

Mullaittivu 94 D7
Mullewa 116 C5
Müllheim 70 C3
Mulingar 64 E8
Mulobezi 112 D3
Multan 96 K3
Mumbai 94 B5
Mumbwa 112 D2
Muna .... ⊠ 92 (2)B4
Münchberg 60 G6
München 70 G2
Münden 60 E5
Mundo Novo 50 J6
Mungbere 110 D3
Munger 94 E3
Munich = München 70 G2
Münster 62 K3
Munster, France 70 C2
Munster, Germany 60 F4
Munte .... 92 (2)A2
Muojärvi .... ☑ 56 Q4
Muonio 56 M3
Muqdisho .... ■ 110 H3
Mur .... ☑ 70 L4
Muradiye 98 K4
Murang'a 110 F4
Murashi 78 J3
Murat .... ☑ 98 K4
Muratli 76 K3
Murchison 118 D5
Murcia 68 J7
Murdo 38 F2
Mureş .... ☑ 74 J3
Muret 66 G10
Murfreesboro, N.C.,
      United States ... 42 F2
Murfreesboro, Tenn.,
      United States ... 42 D2
Murghob 96 K2
Muriaé 50 J8
Müritz .... ☑ 60 H3
Muriwai 118 F4
Murmansk 56 S2
Murnau 70 G3
Murom 78 H3
Muroran 88 L2
Muros 68 A2
Muroto 88 H7
Murphy 42 E2
Murray .... ☑116 H6
Murray 40 C3
Murray Bridge 116 G7
Murray River Basin ... ◉ 116 H6
Murska Sobota 70 M4
Murter .... ☑ 70 L7
Murtosa 68 B4
Murud 94 B5
Murupara 118 F4
Mururoa .... ⊠ 114 M8
Murwara 94 D4
Murzüg 106 H3
Mürzzuschlag 70 L3
Muş 98 J4
Müsa .... ☑ 58 N1
Musala .... ☑ 76 F2
Musandam Peninsula ... ◉ 101 G3
Musay'id 101 D4
Muscat = Masqaţ ...... ■ 101 H5
Musgrave Ranges ...... ▲ 116 E5
Mushin 108 E3
Muskegon 40 C2
Muskogee 42 B2
Musoma 110 E4
Mustafakemalpaşa 76 L4
Mut, Egypt 104 E2
Mut, Turkey 76 R8
Mutare 112 E3
Mutarnee 116 J3
Mutnyy Materik 78 L1
Mutoray 82 U5
Mutsamudu 112 G2
Mutsu 88 L3
Mutsu-wan .... ⊠ 88 L3
Muttaburra 116 H4
Muyezerskiy 56 R5
Muyinga 110 E4
Muynak 82 K9
Muzaffarnagar 94 C3
Muzaffarpur 94 E3
Muzillac 66 C6
Múzquiz 44 F3
Muztagata .... ▲ 82 N10
Mwali .... ☑112 G2
Mwanza 110 E4
Mweka 110 C4
Mwenda 110 D6
Mwene-Ditu 110 C5
Mwenezi 112 E4
Mwenezi .... ☑112 E4
Mwinilunga 112 C2
Myanmar .... ▲ 90 B2
Myingyan 90 B2

Myitkyina 90 B1
Myjava 70 N2
Myjava .... ☑ 70 N2
Mykolayiv 58 N8
Mykonos .... ⊠ 76 H7
Mymensingh 94 F4
Mynbulak 82 L9
Myndagayy 84 N4
Myōjin .... ⊠ 86 K4
Myonggan 88 E3
Myrdalsjökull .... ◉ 56 (1)D3
Myrina 76 H5
Myrtle Beach 42 F3
Mys Alevina .... ⊠ 84 S5
Mys Aniva .... ⊠ 86 L1
Mys Buorkhaya .... ⊠ 84 N2
Mys Dezhneva .... ⊠ 84 Z3
Mys Elizavety .... ⊠ 84 Q6
Mys Enkan .... ⊠ 84 P5
Mys Govena .... ⊠ 84 V5
Mys Kanin Nos .... ⊠ 78 H1
Mys Kekurskij .... ⊠ 56 S2
Mys Kril'on .... ⊠ 86 L1
Myślenice 58 J8
Myślibórz 58 D5
Mys Lopatka, Russia .. ⊠ 84 T6
Mys Lopatka, Russia .. ⊠ 84 S2
Mys Navarin .... ⊠ 84 X4
Mys Olyutorskiy ...... ⊠ 84 W5
Mysore 94 C6
Mys Peschanyy .... ⊠ 82 J9
Mys Povorotnyy .... ⊠ 88 G2
Mys Prubiynyy .... ⊠ 78 F5
Mys Shelagskiy .... ⊠ 84 V2
Mys Sivuchiy .... ⊠ 84 U5
Mys Terpeniya .... ⊠ 84 Q7
Mys Tolstoy .... ⊠ 84 T5
Mys Yuzhnyy .... ⊠ 84 T5
Mys Zhelaniya .... ⊠ 82 M2
Myszksw 58 J7
My Tho 90 D4
Mytilini 76 J5
Mývatn .... ☑ 56 (1)E2
Mže .... ☑ 60 H7
Mzimba 112 E2
Mzuzu 112 E2

N

Naalehu .... 44 (2)F4
Naas 64 F8
Nabas 90 G4
Naberezhnyye Chelny .. 78 K3
Nabeul 72 E12
Nabïd 101 G2
Nabire .... 92 (2)E3
Nablus 100 C4
Nacala 112 G2
Náchod 58 F7
Nacogdoches 42 C3
Nadiad 94 B4
Nador 106 E2
Nadvirna 74 M1
Nadym 78 P1
Nadym .... ☑ 78 P2
Næstved 60 G1
Nafpaktos 76 D6
Nafplio 76 E7
Nagano 88 K5
Nagaoka 88 K5
Nagaon 94 F3
Nagarzê 94 F3
Nagasaki 88 E7
Nagaur 94 B3
Nagercoil 94 C7
Nago 86 H5
Nagold 60 D8
Nagorsk 78 K3
Nagoya 88 J6
Nagpur 94 C4
Naggu 94 F2
Nagyatád 70 N4
Nagykálló 74 J2
Nagykanizsa 70 N4
Nagykáta 58 J10
Nagykörös 74 G2
Naha 86 H5
Nahanni .... ☑ 34 G4
Nahanni Butte 34 G4
Nahr en Nile = Nile .. ☑104 F2
Naiman Qi 86 G2
Nain 34 U5
Nairn 64 J4
Nairobi .... ■110 F4
Naivasha 110 F4
Naizishan 88 D2
Najafābād 96 F3
Nájera 68 H2
Najibabad 94 C3
Najin 88 F2
Najrān 104 H4

Nakamura 88 G7
Nakatsu 88 F7
Nakhl 100 A7
Nakhodka, Russia 82 P4
Nakhodka, Russia 88 G2
Nakhon Ratchasima 90 C3
Nakhon Sawan 90 B3
Nakhon Si Thammarat .. 90 B5
Nakina 34 P6
Naknek .... 44 (1)F4
Nakonde 110 E5
Nakskov 60 G2
Nakten .... ☑ 56 H5
Nakuru 110 F4
Nal'chik .... ☑ 98 K2
Nalihan 76 P4
Nälüt 106 H2
Namagan 82 N9
Namakzar-e Shadad .... ☑101 G1
Namanga 110 F4
Namapa 112 F2
Namasagali 110 E3
Nam Can 90 C5
Nam Co .... ☑ 94 F2
Namdalen .... ☑ 56 G4
Nam Dinh 90 D2
Namib Desert .... ◉112 A4
Namibe 112 A3
Namibia .... ▲112 B4
Namlea .... 92 (2)C3
Namo .... 92 (2)A3
Nampa 38 C2
Nam Ping .... ☑ 90 B3
Namp'o 88 C4
Nampula 112 F3
Namsos 56 F4
Namtsy 84 M4
Namur 62 G4
Namwala 112 D3
Namwŏn 88 D6
Nan 90 C3
Nanaimo 38 B1
Nanao 88 J5
Nanchang 86 F5
Nanchong 86 D4
Nancy 70 B2
Nanda Devi .... ▲ 94 C2
Nānded 94 C5
Nandurbar 94 B4
Nangalala 116 G2
Nangapinoh .... 92 (1)E3
Nangatayap .... 92 (1)E3
Nangis 66 J5
Nangong 86 F3
Nang Xian 94 F3
Nanjing 86 F4
Nankoku 88 G7
Nannine 116 C5
Nanning 90 D2
Nanortalik 34 X4
Nanpan .... ☑ 90 D2
Nanping 86 F5
Nansei-shotō .... ⊠ 86 H5
Nantes 66 D6
Nanton 36 D1
Nantong 86 G4
Nanumea .... ⊠114 H6
Nanuque 50 J7
Nanyang 86 E4
Napa 38 B3
Napalkovo 82 N3
Napamute .... 44 (1)F3
Napas 84 C4
Napasoq 34 W3
Napier 118 F4
Naples = Napoli 72 J8
Naples 42 E4
Napo .... ☑ 50 C4
Napoli 72 J8
Naqb Ashtar 100 C6
Nara, Japan 88 H6
Nara, Mali 106 D5
Narathiwat 90 C5
Narbonne 66 H10
Nardò 72 N8
Nares Strait .... ▸ 32 J2
Narev .... ☑ 58 N5
Narew .... ☑ 58 L5
Narmada .... ☑ 94 C4
Narnaul 94 C3
Narni 72 G6
Narok 110 F4
Närpes 56 L5
Narrabri 116 J6
Narrandera 116 J6
Narsimhapur 94 C4
Nart 86 F2
Narva .... ☑ 56 P7
Narva 56 Q7
Narva Bay .... ☑ 56 P7
Narvik 56 J2
Nar'yan Mar 78 K1

Naryn 84 F6
Näsåud 74 M2
Nashua 40 F2
Nashville .... ◉ 42 D2
Našice 74 F4
Nasik 94 B4
Nasir 110 E2
Nassarawa 108 F3
Nassau .... ■ 42 F4
Nässjö 56 H8
Nastapoka Islands .... ⊠ 34 R5
Nasugbu 90 G4
Naswá 101 G5
Nata 112 D4
Natal .... ☑ 50 K5
Natara 84 L3
Natashquan 34 U6
Natchez 42 C3
Natchitoches 42 C3
National Park 118 E4
Natitingou 108 E2
Natuna Besar .... ⊠ 92 (1)D2
Naujoji Akmenė 58 M1
Naumburg 60 G5
Na'ūr 100 C5
Nauru .... ▲114 G6
Nauta 50 C4
Nautonwa 94 D3
Navahermosa 68 F5
Navahrudak 56 N10
Navajo Reservoir ..... ☑ 38 E3
Navalmoral de la Mata 68 E5
Navalvillar de Pela .. 68 E5
Navapolatsk 78 E3
Navlya 78 F4
Navoi 82 M9
Navojoa 36 E6
Navrongo 108 D2
Nawabshah 94 B4
Nāwah 96 J3
Naxçıvan 98 L4
Naxos 76 H7
Naxos .... ⊠ 76 H7
Nayakhan 84 T4
Näy Band, Iran 96 G3
Näy Band, Iran 101 E3
Nayoro 88 M1
Nazaré 68 A5
Nazareth 100 C4
Nazarovo 82 S6
Nazca 50 C6
Nazca Ridge .... ◉ 52 E3
Naze 86 H5
Nazilli 76 L7
Nazino 82 P6
Nazran' .... ◉ 98 L2
Nazrēt 110 F2
Nazwá 96 G5
Nazyvayevsk 78 P3
Ndélé 110 C2
Ndjamena .... ■104 B5
Ndjolé 108 G5
Ndola 112 D2
Neale Junction 116 E5
Neapoli 76 F8
Nea Zichni 76 F3
Nebbi 110 E3
Nebitdag 96 F2
Nebo 116 J4
Nebraska .... ▲ 38 G2
Neckar .... ☑ 60 D7
Neckar .... ☑ 60 D8
Neckarsulm 60 E7
Necker Island .... ⊠114 K3
Necochea 52 K6
Nédély 104 C4
Needles 44 D2
Nefedovo 78 P3
Nefta 106 G2
Neftçala 98 N4
Neftekamsk 78 K3
Neftekumsk 98 L1
Nefteyugansk 78 P2
Nefza 72 D12
Negage 110 B5
Negār 101 G2
Negēlē 110 F2
Negele 110 F2
Negev .... ◉100 B6
Negomane 112 F2
Negombo 94 C7
Negotin 74 K5
Negotino 76 E3
Négrine 106 G2
Negro, Argentina ..... ☑ 52 J7
Negro, Brazil .... ☑ 50 E4
Negro .... ☑ 50 G5
Negru Vodă 74 R6
Nehbandān 96 G3
Nehe 84 M7
Nehoiu 74 P4

INDEX

Neijiang	86	C5	New Britain	▣114	F6	Nieuw Nickerie	50	F2	Norden	60	C
Nei Monggol	▣86	E2	New Brunswick	▣34	T7	Nieuwpoort	62	E3	Nordenham	60	D
Neiva	50	B3	Newburgh	40	F2	Niğde	76	S7	Norderney	▣60	C
Neixiang	86	E4	Newbury	62	A3	Niger	Ⓐ106	G5	Norderstedt	60	F
Nejanilini Lake	◪34	M5	New Bussa	108	E3	Niger	◪108	E2	Nordfriesische Inseln	▣60	D
Nek'emtē	110	F2	Newcastle, Australia	116	K6	Nigeria	Ⓐ108	F2	Nordhausen	60	F
Nelidovo	78	F3	Newcastle, United States	38	F2	Nigoring Hu	◪86	B3	Nordhorn	62	K
Neligh	38	G2	Newcastle-under-Lyme	64	K8	Niigata	88	K5	Nordkapp	▣56	N
Nellore	94	C6	Newcastle-upon-Tyne	64	L6	Niihau	▣44	(2)A2	Nordkinn	▣56	P
Nel'ma	84	P7	Newcastle Waters	116	F3	Nii-jima	▣88	K6	Nordkinnhalvøya	▣56	P
Nelson	◪34	N5	New Delhi	▣94	C3	Nijar	68	H8	Nordkvaløya	▣56	J
Nelson, Canada	38	C1	New England	38	F1	Nijmegen	62	H3	Nordli	56	G
Nelson, New Zealand	118	D5	Newe Zohars	100	C5	Nikolayevsk-na-Amure	84	Q6	Nördlingen	60	F
Nelspruit	▣112	E5	Newfoundland	▣34	V5	Nikol'sk	78	J3	Nord-Ostsee-Kanal	◪60	E
Nēma	106	D5	Newfoundland	▣34	V7	Nikopol'	78	F5	Nordstrand	▣60	D
Nēman	◪56	N10	New Georgia Island	▣114	F6	Nik Pey	98	N5	Nordvik	82	W
Neman	58	M2	New Glasgow	34	U7	Nikšić	74	F7	Nore	◪64	E
Nemours	66	H5	New Guinea	▣80	S10	Nilande Atoll	▣94	B8	Norfolk, Nebr.,		
Nemperola	92	(2)B5	New Hampshire	Ⓐ40	F2	Nile	◪104	F3	United States	38	G
Nemunas	◪58	P3	New Hampton	40	B2	Niles	40	C2	Norfolk, Va.,		
Nemuro	88	N2	New Hanover	▣114	F6	Nimach	94	B4	United States	40	E
Nen	◪84	L7	Newhaven	62	C4	Nîmes	66	K10	Norfolk Island	▣114	G
Nenagh	64	D9	New Haven	40	F2	Nimule	110	E3	Noril'sk	82	K
Nenana	44	(1)H3	New Iberia	42	C3	Nin	70	L6	Norman	42	B
Nene	◪62	B2	New Ireland	▣114	F6	Nine Degree Channel	▣94	B7	Normanton	116	H
Nenjiang	84	M7	New Jersey	Ⓐ40	F2	9 de Julio	52	J6	Norman Wells	34	F
Neosho	40	B3	New Liskeard	40	E1	Ning'an	88	E1	Nørre Åby	60	E
Nepa	84	H5	New London	40	F2	Ningbo	86	G5	Nørre Alslev	60	G
Nepal	Ⓐ94	D3	Newman	116	C4	Ningde	86	F5	Norristown	40	E
Nepalganj	94	D3	Newmarket	62	C2	Ninghai	86	G5	Norrköping	56	K
Nepean	40	E1	New Meadows	38	C2	Ninh Hoa	90	D4	Norrtälje	56	K
Nepomuk	60	J7	New Mexico	Ⓐ44	E2	Ninohoe	88	L3	Norseman	116	D
Ner	◪58	H5	Newnan	42	E3	Niobrara	◪38	F2	Norsk	84	N
Nera	◪72	G6	New Orleans	42	D4	Niobrara	38	G2	Northallerton	64	L
Neratovice	60	K6	New Plymouth	118	E4	Nioro	106	D5	Northam	116	C
Neris	◪58	P2	Newport, Eng.,			Nioro du Sahel	108	C1	Northampton	62	B
Nerja	68	G8	United Kingdom	62	A4	Niort	66	E7	North Andaman	▣90	A
Neryungri	84	L5	Newport, Wales,			Nipigon	40	C1	North Battleford	34	K
Nesebŭr	74	Q7	United Kingdom	64	K10	Niquelândia	50	H6	North Bay	40	E
Ness City	42	B2	Newport, Ark.,			Nirmal	94	C5	North Cape	▣118	C
Netanya	100	B4	United States	42	C2	Niš	74	J6	North Carolina	Ⓐ42	F
Netherlands	Ⓐ62	H2	Newport, Oreg.,			Nisa	68	C5	North Channel	◪64	G
Netherlands Antilles	▣46	L6	United States	38	B2	Niscemi	72	J11	North Charleston	42	F
Nettilling Lake	◪34	S3	Newport, R.I.,			Nishinoomote	88	F8	North Dakota	Ⓐ38	F
Neubrandenburg	60	J3	United States	40	F2	Nisyros	▣76	N8	Northeast Providence		
Neuburg	60	G8	Newport, Vt.,			Niterói	52	N3	Channel	▣42	F
Neuchâtel	70	B3	United States	40	F2	Nitra	58	H9	Northeim	60	F
Neuenhagen	60	J4	Newport, Wash.,			Nitra	◪58	H9	Northern Cape	Ⓐ112	C
Neufchâteau, Belgium	62	H5	United States	38	C1	Nitsa	◪78	M3	Northern Ireland	Ⓐ64	E
Neufchâteau, France	66	L5	New Providence	▣42	F5	Niue	▣114	K7	Northern Mariana		
Neufchâtel-en-Bray	62	D5	Newquay	64	G11	Nivelles	62	G4	Islands	▣114	E
Neuhof	60	E6	Newry	64	F7	Nizamabad	94	C5	Northern Province	Ⓐ112	E
Neumarkt	60	G7	New Siberia Islands =			Nizhnekamsk	78	K3	Northern Territory	Ⓐ116	F
Neumünster	60	F2	Novosibirskiye			Nizhnekamskoye			North Foreland	▣62	D
Neunkirchen, Austria	70	M3	Ostrova	▣84	P1	Vodokhranilishche	▣78	K3	North Horr	110	F
Neunkirchen, Germany	60	C7	New Smyrna Beach	42	E4	Nizhneudinsk	84	F5	North Iberia	46	F
Neuquén	52	H6	New South Wales	▣116	H6	Nizhnevartovsk	78	Q2	North Island	▣118	D
Neuruppin	60	H4	Newton, Ia.,			Nizhneyansk	84	P2	North Korea	Ⓐ88	C
Neusiedler	◪58	F10	United States	40	B2	Nizhniy Lomov	78	H4	North Little Rock	42	C
Neusiedler See	◪70	M3	Newton, Kans.,			Nizhniy Novgorod	78	H3	North Platte	◪36	F
Neuss	62	J3	United States	42	B2	Nizhniy Tagil	78	M3	North Platte	38	F
Neustadt, Germany	62	L5	Newtownards	64	G7	Nizhnyaya Tunguska	◪84	H4	North Ronaldsay	▣64	K
Neustadt, Germany	60	F2	New Ulm	40	B2	Nizhyn	78	F4	North Sea	▣64	N
Neustadt, Germany	60	F7	New York	Ⓐ40	F2	Nizip	98	G5	North Stradbroke Island	▣116	K
Neustadt, Germany	60	G6	New York	40	F2	Nizza Monferrato	70	D6	North Taranaki Bight	▣118	D
Neustadt, Germany	60	G8	New Zealand	Ⓐ118	B5	Njazidja	▣112	G2	North Uist	▣64	E
Neustadt, Germany	60	H7	Neya	78	H3	Njombe	110	E5	Northumberland Strait	▣34	U
Neustrelitz	60	J3	Neyrīz	101	F2	Njombe	◪110	E5	North Vancouver	38	B
Neu-Ulm	60	F8	Neyshābūr	96	G2	Nkambe	108	G3	North West	Ⓐ112	C
Neuwerk	▣60	D3	Ngabang	92	(1)D2	Nkhotakota	112	E2	North West Basin	▣116	C
Neuwied	62	K4	Ngalu	92	(2)B5	Nkongsamba	108	F4	North West Cape	▣116	B
Nevada	Ⓐ38	C3	Ngaoundéré	108	G3	Noatak	◪44	(1)F2	North West Christmas		
Nevada	40	B3	Ngara	110	E4	Nobeoka	88	F7	Island Ridge	▣114	J
Nevado Auzangate	Ⓐ50	C6	Ngawihi	118	E5	Noci	72	M8	North West Highlands	▣64	G
Nevado de Colima	Ⓐ46	D5	Ngo	108	H5	Nogales, Mexico	44	D2	Northwest Territories	Ⓐ34	G
Nevado de Cumbal	Ⓐ50	B3	Ngoura	104	C5	Nogales, United States	44	D2	Norton	42	B
Nevado de Huascaran	Ⓐ50	B5	Ngozi	110	D4	Nogat	◪58	J3	Norton Sound	▣44	(1)E
Nevado de Illampu	Ⓐ50	D7	Nguigmi	108	G2	Nogent-le-Rotrou	66	F5	Norway	Ⓐ56	F
Nevado Sajama	Ⓐ50	D7	Nguru	108	G2	Noginsk	78	G3	Norwegian Sea	▣56	B
Nevados de Cachi	Ⓐ52	H4	Nha Trang	90	D4	Noginskiy	82	S5	Norwich, United Kingdom	62	D
Never	84	L6	Nhulunbuy	116	G2	Nogliki	84	Q6	Norwich, United States	40	F
Nevers	66	J7	Niafounké	106	E5	Nohēji	88	L3	Nos	78	H
Nevesinje	74	F6	Niagara Falls	40	E2	Noia	68	B2	Nos Emine	▣74	Q
Nevėžis	◪56	M9	Niamey	▣108	E2	Noire	◪90	C2	Nosevaya	78	K
Nevinnomyssk	98	J1	Niangara	110	D3	Nojima-zaki	▣88	K6	Noshiro	88	K
Nevşehir	76	S6	Nia-Nia	110	D3	Nok Kundi	96	H4	Nos Kaliakra	▣74	R
Newala	110	F6	Nias	▣92	(1)B2	Nola, Central African			Noşratābād	96	G
New Albany, Ind.,			Nicaragua	Ⓐ46	G6	Republic	110	B3	Nosy Barren	▣112	G
United States	40	C3	Nicastro	72	L10	Nola, Italy	72	J8	Nosy Bé	▣112	H
New Albany, Miss.,			Nice	70	C7	Nolinsk	78	J3	Nosy Boraha	▣112	J
United States	42	D3	Nicholls Town	42	F4	Noma-misaki	▣88	F8	Nosy Mitsio	▣112	H
New Amsterdam	50	F2	Nicobar Islands	▣90	A5	Nome	44	(1)D3	Nosy Radama	▣112	H
Newark, N.J.,			Nicosia = Lefkosia	▣76	R9	Nomoi Islands	▣114	F5	Nosy-Varika	112	H
United States	40	F2	Nida	◪58	K7	Nomo-saki	▣88	E7	Notec	◪58	G
Newark, Oh.,			Nidym	84	F4	Nong'an	88	C1	Notia Pindos	▣76	J
United States	40	D3	Nidzica	58	K4	Nong Khai	90	C3	Notios Evvoïkos Kolpos	▣76	F
Newark-on-Trent	62	B1	Niebüll	60	D2	Noord-Beveland	▣62	F3	Notre Dame Bay	▣34	V
New Bedford	40	F2	Niedere Tauern	▣70	J3	Noord-Oost-Polder	▣62	H2	Notsé	108	E
Newberg	38	B1	Niefang	108	G4	Noordwijk aan Zee	62	G2	Nottingham	62	A
New Bern	42	F2	Nienburg	60	E4	Norak	96	J2	Nottingham Island	▣34	R
Newberry	42	E3	Niesky	60	K5	Noranda	40	E1	Nouâdhibou	106	B
New Braunfels	42	B4	Nieuw Amsterdam	50	F2	Nordaustlandet	▣120	(1)L1	Nouakchott	▣106	B

Name	Page	Grid
ouméa	⊡14	G8
ouvelle Calédonie	⊠114	G8
ova Gorica	70	J5
ova Gradiška	74	E4
ova Iguaçu	52	N3
ova Mambone	112	F4
ova Pazova	74	H5
ovara	70	D5
ova Scotia	▣34	T8
ovaya Igirma	84	G5
ovaya Karymkary	78	N2
ovaya Kasanka	78	J5
ovaya Lyalya	78	M3
ovaya Zemlya	▣82	J3
ova Zagora	74	P7
ovelda	68	K6
ové Mĕsto	58	F8
ové Mesto	58	G9
ové Zámky	58	H10
ovgorod	78	F3
ovi Bečej	74	H4
ovi Iskŭr	74	L7
ovi Ligure	70	D6
ovi Marof	70	M4
ovi Pazar, *Bulgaria*	74	Q6
ovi Pazar, *Yugoslavia*	74	H6
ovi Sad	74	G4
ovi Vinodolski	70	K5
ovoaleksandrovsk	78	H5
ovoalekseyevka	78	L4
ovoanninsky	78	H4
ovocheboksarsk	78	J3
ovocherkassk	78	H5
ovodvinsk	78	H2
ovo Hamburgo	52	L4
ovohrad-Volyns'kyy	78	E4
ovokazalinsk	78	M5
ovokutznetsk	82	R7
ovokuybyshevsk	78	J4
ovo Mesto	70	L5
ovomikhaylovskiy	98	H1
ovomoskovsk	78	G4
ovonazimovo	84	E5
ovorossiysk	98	G1
ovorybnoye	84	H2
ovoselivka	74	S2
ovosergiyevka	78	K4
ovosibirsk	82	Q6
ovosibirskiye Ostrova	▣84	P1
ovosil'	78	G4
ovotroitsk	78	L4
ovouzensk	78	J4
ovozybkov	78	F4
ový Bor	60	K6
ový Jičín	58	H8
ovyy Port	82	N4
ovyy Uoyan	84	J5
ovyy Urengoy	82	P4
ovyy Uzen'	82	J9
owa Ruda	58	F7
owata	42	B2
owogard	58	E4
owo Warpno	60	K3
owra	116	K6
ow Shahr	96	F2
owy Dwór Mazowiecki	58	K5
owy Sącz	58	K8
owy Targ	58	K8
owy Tomyśl	58	F5
oyabr'sk	82	P5
oyon	62	E5
sombo	112	D2
tem	☑108	D2
twetwe Pan	☑112	C4
u	☑94	G2
uasjärvi	☑56	Q4
ubian Desert	⊠104	F3
udo Coropuna	▲50	C7
ueltin Lake	☑34	M4
ueva Rosita	44	F3
ueva San Salvador	46	G6
uevo Casas Grandes	44	E2
uevo Laredo	44	G3
ugget Point	⊟118	B8
uhaka	118	F4
uku'alofa	■114	J8
uku Hiva	⊠114	M6
ukumanu Islands	⊠114	H6
ukunonu	⊠114	J6
ukus	82	K9
ullarbor Plain	▣116	E6
uman	108	G3
umazu	88	K6
umbulwar	116	G2
umfor	⊠92	(2)E3
umto	78	P2
unarsuit	⊟34	X4
unavut	▣34	M3
uneaton	62	A2
univak Island	▣44	(1)D3
unligram	84	Y3
Nüoro	72	D8
Nuqui	50	B2
Nura	☑78	P4
Nurābād	101	D1
Nurata	96	J1
Nurmes	56	Q5
Nürnberg	60	G7
Nürtingen	70	E2
Nurzec	☑58	M5
Nushki	96	J4
Nutak	34	U5
Nuuk	⊡34	W4
Nuussuaq	⊠34	W2
Nyagan'	78	N2
Nyahururu	110	F3
Nyala	104	D5
Nyalam	94	E3
Nyamlell	110	D2
Nyamtumbo	110	F6
Nyandoma	78	H2
Nyantakara	110	E4
Nyborg	60	F1
Nybro	56	H8
Nyda	82	N4
Nyima	94	E2
Nyingchi	94	F3
Nyírbátor	74	K2
Nyiregyháza	58	L10
Nykarleby	56	M5
Nyköbing	60	G2
Nyköping	56	J7
Nylstroom	112	D4
Nymburk	58	E7
Nynäshamn	56	J7
Nyngan	116	J6
Nyon	70	B4
Nysa	☑58	D6
Nysa	58	G7
Nyukhcha	78	J2
Nyunzu	110	D5
Nyurba	84	K4
Nyuya	84	K4
Nzega	110	E4
Nzérékoré	108	C3
N'zeto	110	A5
Nzwami	⊠112	G2

O

Name	Page	Grid
Oaho	⊠44	(2)D2
Oahu	⊠114	L3
Oakdale	42	C3
Oakham	62	B2
Oak Lake	☑38	F1
Oakland	38	B3
Oak Lawn	40	C2
Oakley	42	A2
Oak Ridge	40	D3
Oamaru	118	C7
Oaxaca	46	E5
Ob'	☑78	N2
Obama	88	H6
Oban	64	G5
O Barco	68	D2
Oberdrauburg	70	H4
Oberhausen	62	J3
Oberkirch	60	D8
Oberlin	42	A2
Oberndorf	70	H3
Oberstdorf	70	F3
Oberursel	60	D6
Obervellach	70	M3
Oberwart	58	C11
Obi	⊠92	(2)C3
Obidos	50	F4
Obigarm	96	M2
Obihiro	88	M2
Obluch'ye	84	N7
Obninsk	78	G3
Obo, *Central African Republic*	110	D2
Obo, *China*	86	C3
Oborniki	58	F5
Obouya	108	H5
Oboyan'	78	G4
Obskaya Guba	▣82	N4
Obuasi	108	D3
Ob'yachevo	78	J2
Ocala	42	E4
Ocaña, *Colombia*	50	C2
Ocaña, *Spain*	68	G5
Ocean City	80	E3
Ocean Falls	34	F6
Oceanside	44	C2
Och'amch'ire	98	J2
Ochsenfurt	60	E7
Oconto	40	C2
Oda	108	D3
Ōda	88	G6
Ōdate	88	L3
Odda	56	D6
Odemira	68	B7
Ödemiş	76	L6
Odense	60	F1
Oder = Odra	☑58	F6
Oderzo	70	H5
Odesa	78	F5
Odessa = Odesa, *Ukraine*	78	F5
Odessa, *United States*	44	F2
Odienné	108	C3
Odorheiu Secuiesc	74	N3
Odra	☑58	F6
Odžaci	74	G4
Oeiras	50	J5
Oelrichs	38	F2
Oelsnitz	60	H6
Oeno	⊠114	N8
Oestev	52	H7
Ofaqim	100	B5
Offenbach	60	D6
Offenburg	70	C2
Ōgaki	88	J6
Ogasawara-shotō	⊠80	T7
Ogbomosho	108	E3
Ogden	38	D2
Ogdensburg	34	R8
Ogilvie Mountains	▲34	C4
Oglio	☑70	E5
Ogosta	☑74	L6
Ogre	56	N8
Ogre	☑56	N8
O Grove	68	B2
Ogulin	70	L5
Ohai	118	A7
Ohio	☑40	C3
Ohio	▣40	D2
Ohre	☑60	J6
Ohrid	76	C3
Ohura	118	E4
Oiapoque	50	G3
Oil City	40	E2
Oise	☑62	E5
Oita	88	F7
Ojinaga	44	F3
Ojos del Salado	▲52	H4
Oka	☑84	G6
Okaba	92	(2)E4
Okahandja	112	B4
Okanagan Lake	☑36	C2
Okano	☑108	G4
Okanogan	☑38	C1
Okara	94	B2
Okarem	96	F2
Okato	118	D4
Okavango Delta	⊠112	C3
Okaya	88	K5
Okayama	88	G6
Okene	108	F3
Oker	☑60	F4
Okha, *India*	96	J5
Okha, *Russia*	84	Q6
Okhansk	78	L3
Okhotsk	84	Q5
Okhtyrka	78	F4
Okinawa	86	H5
Okinawa	☑86	H5
Oki-shotō	⊠88	G5
Okitipupa	108	E3
Oklahoma	▣42	B2
Oklahoma City	▣42	B2
Okoppe	88	M1
Okoyo	108	H5
Okranger	56	E5
Øksino	78	K1
Oktinden	▲56	H4
Oktyabr'sk	78	L5
Oktyabr'skiy	78	K4
Okurchan	84	S5
Okushiri-tō	☑88	K2
Olancha	38	C3
Øland	☑56	J8
Olanga	☑56	Q3
Olathe	42	C2
Olava	☑60	J7
Olavarría	52	J6
Oława	58	G7
Ólbia	72	D8
Olching	70	G2
Old Crow	44	(1)K2
Oldenburg, *Germany*	60	D3
Oldenburg, *Germany*	60	F2
Oldenzaal	62	J2
Oldham	64	L8
Old Head of Kinsale	⊟64	D10
Olean	40	E2
Olekma	☑84	L5
Olekminsk	84	L4
Oleksandriya	78	F5
Olenegorsk	56	S2
Olenek	84	J3
Olenëk	☑84	L2
Olenëkskiy Zaliv	⊟84	L2
Olhão	68	C7
Olib	⊠70	K6
Olinda	50	L5
Oliva	68	K6
Olivet	38	G2
Olivia	40	B2
Olmos	50	B5
Olney	42	B3
Olochi	84	K6
Olonets	78	F2
Olongapo	90	G4
Oloron-Ste-Marie	66	L10
Olot	68	N2
Olovyannaya	84	K6
Olpe	62	K3
Olsztyn	58	K4
Olt	☑74	M4
Olten	70	C3
Oltenița	74	P5
Oltu	98	K3
Oluan-pi	⊟90	G2
Olvera	68	E8
Olympia	⊡38	B1
Olympos	▲76	E4
Olympus	▲76	Q10
Olyutorskiy	84	W4
Olyutorskiy Zaliv	⊟84	V4
Om'	☑82	N6
Oma	94	D2
Omae-saki	⊟88	K6
Omagh	64	E7
Omaha	38	G2
Omak	38	C1
Omakau	118	B7
Oman	▣96	F5
Omapere	118	D2
Omarama	118	B7
Omaruru	112	B4
Omba	94	E2
Ombrone	☑72	F6
Omdurman = Umm Durman	104	F4
Omegna	70	D5
Omeo	116	J7
Om Hajer	104	G5
Omīdeyeh	101	C1
Omis	70	M7
Ommen	62	J2
Omolon	☑84	T3
Omoloy	☑84	N3
Omo Wenz	☑110	F2
Omsk	82	N6
Omsukchan	84	S4
Ōmū	88	M1
Omulew	☑58	L4
Omuta	88	F7
Onautha	68	K5
Ondangwa	112	B3
Ondjiva	112	B3
Ondo	108	E3
Ondörhaan	86	E1
One and a Half Degree Channel	⊟94	B8
Onega	78	G2
O'Neill	38	G2
Oneonta	40	F2
Onești	74	P3
Onezhskoye Ozero	⊟78	F2
Ongjin	88	C5
Ongole	94	D5
Onguday	82	R7
Oni	98	K2
Onilahy	☑112	G4
Onitsha	108	F3
Ono	88	J6
Onon	84	J7
Onon	☑84	J7
Onslow Bay	⊟46	J2
Onsong	88	E2
Ontario	▣34	N6
Ontinyent	68	K6
Ontonagon	40	C1
Onyx	44	C1
Oodnadatta	116	G5
Oologah Lake	☑42	B2
Oostburg	62	H2
Oostelijk-Flevoland	⊠62	H2
Oostende	62	E3
Oosterhout	62	G3
Oosterschelde	☑62	F3
Ootsa Lake	☑34	F6
Opala	110	C4
Oparino	78	J3
Opava	58	G8
Opelika	42	D3
Opelousas	42	C3
Opheim	38	E1
Opochka	78	E3
Opoczno	58	K6
Opole	58	G7
Opornyy	82	J8
Opotiki	118	F4
Opp	42	D3
Opunake	118	D4

Name	Page	Ref
Opuwo	112	A3
Oradea	74	J2
Orahovac	74	H7
Orai	94	C3
Oran	68	K9
Orán	52	J3
Orange	✓112	C5
Orange, *Australia*	116	J6
Orange, *France*	66	K9
Orange, *United States*	42	C3
Orangeburg	42	E3
Orangeville	40	D2
Orango	▦108	A2
Oranienburg	60	J4
Orapa	112	D4
Orăştie	74	L4
Oraviţa	74	J4
Orbetello	72	F6
Orco	✓70	C5
Ordes	68	B1
Ordes Santa Comba	68	B1
Ordu	98	G3
Ordway	38	F3
Öreälven	✓56	K4
Örebro	56	H7
Oregon	▣38	B2
Oregon	40	A3
Orekhovo-Zuyevo	78	G3
Orel	78	G4
Orem	38	D2
Orenburg	78	L4
Orestiada	76	J3
Orford Ness	✓62	D2
Orhei	74	R2
Orihuela	68	K6
Orillia	40	E2
Orinoco	✓50	D2
Orinoco Delta = Delta del Orinoco	✓50	E2
Orissaare	56	M7
Oristano	72	C9
Orivesi	✓56	Q5
Orkla	✓56	F5
Orkney Islands	▦64	K3
Orlando	42	E4
Orléans	66	G6
Orlik	84	F6
Orly	62	E6
Ormara	96	H4
Ormoc	90	G4
Ormos Almyrou	✓76	G9
Ormos Mesara	✓76	G9
Ornans	66	M6
Örnö	✓56	K7
Örnsköldsvik	56	K5
Orocué	50	C3
Orofino	38	C1
Oromocto	40	G1
Orona	▦114	J6
Oronoque	50	F3
Oroqen Zizhiqi	84	L6
Orosei	72	D8
Oroszháza	74	H3
Oroszlany	58	H10
Orotukan	84	S4
Oroville	38	B3
Orroroo	116	G6
Orsay	66	H5
Orsha	78	F4
Orsk	78	L4
Orşova	74	K5
Ørsta	56	D5
Ortaklar	76	K7
Orthez	66	E10
Ortigueira	68	C1
Ortisei	70	G4
Ortles	▣70	E4
Ortona	72	J6
Ortonville	40	A1
Orümíyeh	98	L5
Oruro	50	D7
Orvieto	72	G6
Orville	66	L6
Ōsaka	88	H6
Osám	✓74	M6
Osceola	40	B2
Oschatz	60	J5
Oschersleben	60	G4
Osh	82	N9
Oshamambe	88	L2
Oshawa	40	E2
Oshkosh, *Nebr., United States*	38	F2
Oshkosh, *Wis., United States*	40	C2
Oshogbo	108	E3
Osijek	74	F4
Osimo	70	J7
Oskaloosa	40	B2
Oskarshamn	56	J8
Oslo	▣56	F7
Oslofjorden	◪56	F7
Osmancık	98	F3
Osmaniye	98	G5
Osnabrück	62	L2
Osor	70	K6
Osorno	52	G7
Osprey Reef	▦116	J2
Oss	62	H3
Osseo	40	B2
Ossora	84	U5
Ostashkov	78	F3
Oste	✓60	E3
Osterburg	60	G4
Østerdalen	▦56	F6
Osterholz-Scharmbeck	60	D3
Osterode	60	F5
Östersund	56	H5
Ostfriesische Inseln	◪60	C3
Ostiglia	70	G5
Ostrava	58	H8
Ostróda	58	K4
Ostrołęka	58	L4
Ostrov, *Czech Republic*	60	H6
Ostrov, *Russia*	78	E3
Ostrova Medvezh'i	▦84	T2
Ostrova Atlasova	▦84	S6
Ostrova Vrangelya	▦32	V4
Ostrov Ayon	▦84	V2
Ostrov Belyy	▦82	N3
Ostrov Beringa	▦84	V6
Ostrov Bol'shevik	▦82	V2
Ostrov Bol'shoy Begichev	▦84	J2
Ostrov Bol'shoy Lyakhovskiy	▦84	Q2
Ostrov Bol'shoy Shantar	▦84	P6
Ostrov Chechen'	▦98	M2
Ostrov Iturup	▦88	P1
Ostrov Kil'din	▦56	T2
Ostrov Kolguyev	▦82	H4
Ostrov Komsomolets	▦82	T1
Ostrov Kotel'nyy	▦84	P1
Ostrov Kunashir	▦88	P1
Ostrov Mednyy	▦84	V6
Ostrov Mezhdusharskiy	▦82	H3
Ostrov Novaya Sibir'	▦84	S2
Ostrov Ogurchinskiy	▦96	F2
Ostrov Oktyabr'skoy	▦82	S2
Ostrov Onekotan	▦84	S7
Ostrov Paramushir	▦84	T6
Ostrov Rasshua	▦84	S7
Ostrov Shiashkotan	▦84	S7
Ostrov Shumshu	▦84	T6
Ostrov Simushir	▦84	S7
Ostrov Urup	▦84	S7
Ostrov Ushakova	▦82	Q1
Ostrov Vaygach	▦82	K3
Ostrov Vise	▦82	P1
Ostrov Vosrozhdeniya	▦82	K9
Ostrov Vrangelya	▦84	W2
Ostrowiec Świętokrzyski	58	L7
Ostrów Mazowiecka	58	L5
Ostrów Wielkopolski	58	G6
Ostuni	72	M8
Osum	✓76	C4
Osumi-shotō	▦88	F8
Osuna	68	E7
Oswego	40	E2
Oświęcim	58	J7
Otago Peninsula	▣118	C7
Otaki	118	E5
Otaru	88	L2
Oţelu Roşu	74	K4
Othonoi	▦76	B5
Oti	✓108	E2
Otjiwarongo	112	B4
Otočac	70	L6
Otog Qi	86	D3
Otoineppu	88	M1
Otorohanga	118	E4
Ótranto	72	N8
Otrøy	▦56	D5
Ōtsu	88	H6
Otta	56	E6
Ottawa	▣40	E1
Ottawa, *Canada*	✓40	E1
Ottawa, *Ill., United States*	40	C2
Ottawa, *Kans., United States*	42	B2
Ottawa Islands	▦34	Q5
Otterøy	▦56	F8
Ottobrunn	70	G2
Ottumwa	40	B2
Otukpo	108	F3
Ouachita Mountains	▦42	C4
Ouadâne	106	C4
Ouadda	110	C2
Ouagadougou	▣108	D2
Oualâta	106	D5
Ouarâne	106	D5
Ouarzazate	106	D2
Oudenbosch	62	F4
Oudenbosch	62	G3
Oudtshoorn	112	C6
Oued Medjerda	✓72	D12
Oued Meliane	✓72	D12
Oued Tiélat	68	K9
Oued Zem	106	D2
Ouésso	108	H4
Ouezzane	106	D2
Oujda	106	E2
Oulainen	56	N4
Oulu	56	N4
Oulujärvi	▦56	P4
Oulujoki	✓56	P4
Oulx	70	B5
Oum-Chalouba	104	D4
Oum-Hadjer	104	C5
Ounarjoki	▦56	N3
Our	✓62	J4
Ouray	38	E3
Ourense	68	C2
Ouricuri	50	J5
Ourthe	✓62	H4
Oustreham	62	B5
Outer Hebrides	▦64	D4
Outjo	112	B4
Outokumpu	56	Q5
Out Skerries	▦64	M1
Ouyen	116	H7
Ovacık	76	R8
Ovada	70	D6
Ovalle	52	G5
Ovareli	98	L3
Overflakkee	▦62	G3
Overlander Roadhouse	116	B5
Overland Park	42	C2
Overton	38	D3
Övertorneå	56	M3
Ovidiopol'	74	T3
Oviedo	68	E1
Owaka	118	B8
Owando	108	H5
Owase	88	J6
Owatonna	40	B2
Owensboro	40	C3
Owens Lake	▣38	C3
Owen Sound	40	D2
Owerri	108	F3
Owo	108	F3
Owosso	40	D2
Owyhee	38	C2
Owyhee	✓38	C2
Oxford, *New Zealand*	118	D6
Oxford, *United Kingdom*	62	A3
Oxnard	44	C2
Oyama	88	K5
Oyapock	✓50	G3
Oyem	108	G4
Oyen	36	D1
Oyonnax	70	A4
Özd	58	K9
Ozernovskiy	84	T6
Ozero Alakol'	▦82	Q8
Ozero Aralsor	▦82	J5
Ozero Aydarkul'	▦82	M9
Ozero Balkhash	▦82	N8
Ozero Baykal	▦84	H6
Ozero Beloye	▦78	G2
Ozero Chany	▦82	P7
Ozero Chernoye	▦78	N3
Ozero Il'men'	▦78	F3
Ozero Imandra	▦56	R2
Ozero Inder	▦82	J8
Ozero Janis'järvi	▦56	R5
Ozero Kamennoje	▦56	R4
Ozero Kanozero	▦56	T3
Ozero Karaginskiy	▦84	U3
Ozero Khanka	▦88	G1
Ozero Kolvitskoye	▦56	S3
Ozero Kovdozero	▦56	S3
Ozero Kulundinskoye	▦82	P7
Ozero Kushmurun	▦78	N4
Ozero Lama	▦84	D2
Ozero Leksozero	▦56	R5
Ozero Lovozero	▦56	T2
Ozero Morzhovets	▦56	H1
Ozero Njuk	▦56	R4
Ozero Ozhogino	▦84	R3
Ozero Pirenga	▦56	R3
Ozero Pyaozero	▦56	R3
Ozero Saltaim	▦78	P3
Ozero Sarpa	▦78	J5
Ozero Segozeroskoye	▦78	F8
Ozero Seletyteniz	▦82	N7
Ozero Sredneye Kuyto	▦56	R4
Ozero Teletskoye	▦82	R7
Ozero Tengiz	▦78	N4
Ozero Topozero	▦56	R3
Ozero Umbozero	▦56	T3
Ozero Vygozero	▦78	G2
Ozero Yalpug	▦74	R4
Ozero Zaysan	▦82	Q8
Ozero Zhaltyr	▦78	K5
Ozero Zhamanakkol'	▦78	M5
Ozersk	58	M
Ozhogina	✓84	R
Ozhogino	84	R
Ozieri	72	C
Ozinki	78	J
Ozona	44	F
Ozurget'i	98	J

P

Name	Page	Ref
Paamiut	34	X
Paar	✓60	G
Paarl	112	B
Pabbay	▦64	E
Pabianice	58	J
Pabna	94	E
Pacasmayo	50	B
Pachino	72	K1
Pachuca	46	E
Pacific Ocean	▣114	M
Pacitan	92	(1)E
Packwood	38	B
Padalere	92	(2)B
Padang	92	(1)C
Padangpanjang	92	(1)B
Padangsidempuan	92	(1)B
Paderborn	60	D
Pádova	70	G
Padre Island	▦44	B
Padrón	68	B
Paducah, *Ky., United States*	40	C
Paducah, *Tex., United States*	44	F
Padum	94	C
Paekdu San	▣88	D
Paeroa	118	E
Pafos	76	Q1
Pag	▦70	K
Pag	70	L
Pagadian	90	G
Pagai Selatan	▦92	(1)B
Pagai Utara	▦92	(1)B
Pagalu = Annobón	▦108	F
Pagan	▦114	G
Pagatan	92	(1)F
Page, *Ariz., United States*	42	C
Page, *Okla., United States*	42	C
Pagosa Springs	38	E
Pagri	94	E
Pahiatua	118	E
Paia	44	(2)E
Paide	56	N
Päijänne	▦56	N
Painan	92	(1)C
Painesville	40	D
Paisley	64	H
Paita	50	A
Pakaraima Mountains	▦50	E
Pakch'ŏn	88	C
Paki	108	F
Pakistan	▣96	J
Pakokku	94	A
Pakotai	118	D
Pakrac	70	E
Paks	74	F
Pakxé	90	D
Pala	104	B
Palafrugell	68	P
Palagónia	72	J1
Palagruža	▦72	L
Palamós	68	P
Palana	84	U
Palanga	56	L
Palangkaraya	92	(1)E
Palanpur	94	B
Palantak	96	H
Palatka, *Russia*	84	S
Palatka, *United States*	42	E
Palau	72	D
Palau	▣114	D
Palawan	▣90	F
Palazzolo Arceide	72	J1
Palembang	92	(1)C
Palencia	68	F
Paleokastritsa	76	H10
Palermo	72	H
Palestine	42	B
Palestrina	72	G
Paletwa	90	A
Palghat	94	C
Pali	94	B
Palikir	▣114	F
Palimbang	90	G
Palk Strait	◪94	C
Palma	68	P
Palma del Rio	68	E
Palma di Montechiaro	72	H1
Palmanova	70	J

Name	Page	Ref
almares	50	K5
aimarola	72	G8
almas	50	H6
almas	52	L4
alm Bay	42	E4
almdale	44	C2
almerston	118	C7
almerston Island	114	K7
almerston North	118	E5
alm Harbor	42	E4
almi	72	K10
almira	50	B3
almyra Island	114	K5
alojärvi	56	M2
alopo	92	(2)B3
alu, Indonesia	92	(2)A3
alu, Turkey	98	J4
aluostrov Taymyr	82	R3
alyavaam	84	W3
ama	108	E2
amhagen	70	M3
amiers	66	G10
amlico Sound	42	F2
ampa	44	F1
ampas	52	J6
amplona, Colombia	46	K7
amplona, Spain	68	J2
ana	40	C3
anagyurishte	74	M7
anaji	94	B5
anama	46	H7
anamá	50	B2
anama Canal = Canal de Panamá	46	J7
anama City	42	D3
anara	70	G6
anaria	72	K10
anarik	92	(1)D2
anay	90	G4
ančevo	74	H5
anciu	74	Q4
andharpur	94	C5
anevėžys	58	P2
angin	94	F3
angkajene	92	(2)A3
angkalpinang	92	(1)D3
angnirtung	34	T3
anguitch	38	D3
angutaran Group	90	G5
anhandle	44	F1
anipat	74	C3
anjāb	96	J3
anjgur	96	H4
ankshin	108	F3
antanal	50	F7
antar	92	(2)B4
antelleria	106	H1
áola	72	L9
aoua	110	B2
ápa	74	E2
apa	44	(2)F4
apakura	118	E3
apantla	46	E4
aparoa	118	E3
apa Stour	64	L1
apa Westray	64	K2
apenburg	60	C3
apey	56	(1)F2
apua New Guinea	114	A
apun	90	B3
ará	50	G5
ara	50	H4
arabel'	82	Q6
aracatu	50	H7
aracel Islands	90	E3
aracin	74	J6
ará de Minas	50	J2
aragould	42	C2
aragua, Bolivia	50	E6
aragua, Venezuela	50	E2
araguay	48	F6
araguay	52	J3
araíba	50	K5
arakou	108	E3
aralimni	100	A1
aramaribo	50	F2
araná	50	H6
araná	50	H6
araná	52	J5
araná	52	K4
araná	52	L3
aranaguá	52	M4
aranaíba	50	G7
aranaíba	50	G7
aranavaí	52	L3
aranestio	76	G3
araparaumu	118	E5
aray-le Monial	66	K7
arbhani	94	C5
archim	60	G3
ardo	50	J7
ardubice	58	E7
Pareh	98	L4
Parepare	92	(2)A3
Parga	76	C5
Parigi	92	(2)B3
Parika	50	F2
Parintins	50	F4
Paris, France	66	H5
Paris, Tenn., United States	42	D2
Paris, Tex., United States	42	B3
Parkersburg	40	D3
Park Rapids	40	A1
Parla	68	G4
Parma	70	F6
Parma, Italy	70	F6
Parma, United States	40	D2
Parnaíba	50	J4
Parnassus	118	D6
Pärnu	56	N7
Pärnu	56	N7
Paros	76	H7
Paros	76	H7
Parry Bay	34	Q3
Parry Islands	34	L1
Parry Sound	40	D2
Parsons	42	B2
Parthenay	66	E7
Partinico	72	H10
Partizansk	88	G2
Paru	50	G4
Parvatipuram	94	D5
Paryang	94	D2
Pasadena, Calif., United States	44	C2
Pasadena, Tex., United States	42	B4
Paşalimani Adası	76	K4
Pasawng	90	B3
Paşcani	74	P2
Pasco	38	C1
Pasewalk	60	K3
Pasig	90	G4
Pasinler	98	J3
Pasłęk	58	J3
Paslek	58	J3
Pasleka	56	L9
Pašman	70	L7
Pasni	96	H4
Paso de Hachado	52	G6
Paso de Indios	52	H7
Paso de la Cumbre	52	H5
Paso de San Francisco	52	H4
Paso Río Mayo	52	G8
Paso Robles	44	B1
Passau	60	J8
Passo Fundo	52	L4
Passos	50	H8
Pastavy	56	P9
Pasto	50	B3
Pastos Bons	50	J5
Pásztó	74	G2
Patagonia	52	G8
Patan, India	94	B4
Patan, Nepal	94	E3
Patea	118	E4
Pate Island	110	G4
Paterna	68	K5
Paterno	72	J11
Paterson	40	F2
Pathankot	94	C2
Pathein	90	A3
Pathfinder Reservoir	38	E2
Patia	50	B3
Patiala	94	C2
Patmos	76	J7
Patna	94	E3
Patnos	98	K4
Patos de Minas	50	H7
Patra	76	D6
Patraikis Kolpos	76	D6
Patreksfjörður	56	(1)B2
Pattani	90	C5
Pattaya	90	C4
Patti	72	J10
Paturau River	118	D5
Pau	68	K1
Pauini	50	D5
Pauini	50	D5
Paulatuk	44	(1)N2
Paulo Afonso	50	K5
Paul's Valley	42	B3
Päveh	98	M6
Pavia	70	E5
Pävilosta	56	L8
Pavlikeni	74	N6
Pavlodar	82	P7
Pavlohrad	78	G5
Pavlovsk	78	H4
Pavlovskaya	78	G5
Pavullo nel Frignano	70	F6
Paxoi	76	C5
Paxson	44	(1)H3
Payerne	70	B4
Payette	38	C2
Payne's Find	116	C5
Paysandu	52	K5
Payson	44	D2
Payturma	82	S3
Pazar	98	J3
Pazardzhik	74	M7
Pazin	70	J5
Peace	34	H5
Peace River	34	H5
Peach Springs	44	D1
Pearsall	42	B4
Pebane	112	F3
Pebas	50	C5
Peć	74	H7
Pecan Island	42	C4
Pechora	78	K1
Pechora	78	L1
Pechorskoye More	82	J4
Pechory	56	P8
Pecos	44	F2
Pecos	44	F2
Pécs	74	F3
Pedja	56	P7
Pedra Azul	50	J7
Pedra Lume	108	(1)B1
Pedreiras	50	J4
Pedro Afonso	50	H5
Pedro Juan Caballero	52	K3
Pedro Luro	52	J6
Peel Sound	34	M2
Peene	60	J3
Peenemünde	60	J2
Pegasus Bay	118	D6
Pegnitz	60	G7
Pegu	90	B3
Pegunungan Barisan	92	(1)B2
Pegunungan Iban	92	(1)F2
Pegunungan Maoke	92	(2)E3
Pegunungan Meratus	92	(1)F3
Pegunungan Schwaner	92	(1)E3
Pegunungan Van Rees	92	(2)E3
Pehuajó	52	J6
Peine	60	F4
Peißenberg	70	G3
Peixe	50	H6
Pekalongan	92	(1)D4
Pekanbaru	92	(1)C2
Peking = Beijing	86	F3
Peleduy	84	J5
Peleng	92	(2)B3
Pello	56	N3
Pellworm	60	D2
Pelly Bay	34	P3
Peloponnisos	76	D7
Pelotas	52	L5
Pelym	78	M2
Pemangkat	92	(1)D2
Pematangsiantar	92	(1)B2
Pemba	112	G2
Pemba Island	110	F5
Pembina	38	G1
Pembine	40	C1
Pembroke, Canada	40	E1
Pembroke, United Kingdom	64	H10
Pembroke, United States	42	E3
Peñafiel	68	F3
Peñaranda de Bracamonte	68	E4
Peñarroya-Pueblonuevo	68	E6
Pendleton	38	C1
Pendolo	92	(1)G3
Pend Oreille Lake	38	C1
Pfunds	70	F4
Peniche	68	A5
Península de Azuero	46	H7
Península de Guajira	46	K6
Península Valdés	52	J7
Péninsule de Gaspé	34	T7
Péninsule d'Ungava	34	R4
Penmarch	66	A6
Penne	72	H6
Pennines	64	K7
Pennsylvania	40	E2
Penrith	64	K7
Pensacola	46	G2
Penticton	38	C1
Penza	78	J4
Penzance	64	G11
Penzhina	84	U3
Penzhinskaya Guba	84	U4
Penzhinskiy Khrebet	84	V4
Peoria, Ariz., United States	44	D2
Peoria, Ill., United States	40	C2
Percival Lakes	116	D3
Peregrebnoye	78	N2
Pereira	50	B3
Pergamino	52	J5
Périgueux	66	F8
Peristera	76	G5
Perito Moreno	52	G8
Perleberg	60	G3
Perm'	78	L3
Përmet	76	C4
Pernambuco	50	K5
Pernik	74	L7
Péronne	62	E5
Perpignan	66	H11
Perrine	42	E4
Perry, Fla., United States	42	E3
Perry, Ga., United States	42	E3
Persepolis	101	E2
Persian Gulf	101	C2
Perth, Australia	116	C6
Perth, United Kingdom	64	J5
Pertuis Breton	66	D7
Peru	40	C2
Peru	50	C6
Peru-Chile Trench	48	D5
Perúgia	72	G5
Pervomays'k	78	F5
Pervoural'sk	78	L3
Pésaro	70	H7
Pescara	72	J6
Pescia	70	F7
Peshawar	94	B2
Peshkopi	76	C3
Peshtera	76	G2
Peski Karakumy	96	G2
Peski Kzylkum	82	L9
Peski Priaral'skiye Karakumy	82	L8
Pesnica	70	L4
Pessac	66	E9
Petah Tiqwa	100	B4
Petalioi	76	G7
Petaluma	38	B3
Pétange	62	H5
Petare	46	L6
Petauke	112	E2
Peterborough, Canada	40	E2
Peterborough, United Kingdom	64	M9
Peterhead	64	L4
Peter I Øy	120	(2)JJ3
Petersburg	40	E3
Petersfield	62	B3
Petershagen	60	D4
Petilia	72	L9
Petit Mécatina	34	U6
Petre Bay	118	(1)B1
Petrich	76	F3
Petrila	74	L4
Petrinja	70	M5
Petrolina	50	J5
Petropavlovka	84	H6
Petropavlovsk	78	N4
Petropavlovsk-Kamchatskiy	84	T6
Petrópolis	52	N3
Petroşani	74	L4
Petrovac	74	J5
Petrovsk-Zabaykal'skiy	84	H6
Petrozavodsk	78	F2
Petrun	78	M1
Petukhovo	78	N3
Pevek	84	W3
Pezinok	58	G9
Pfaffenhofen	60	G8
Pfarrkirchen	60	H8
Pflach	70	F3
Pforzheim	60	D8
Pfunds	70	F4
Pfungstadt	60	D7
Phalaborwa	112	E4
Phalodi	94	B3
Phan Rang	90	D4
Phan Thiêt	90	D4
Phatthalung	90	C5
Phet Buri	90	C4
Phichit	90	C3
Philadelphia, Miss., United States	42	D3
Philadelphia, Pa., United States	42	F2
Philippeville	62	G4
Philippines	90	G5
Philippine Trench	80	R8
Philips	34	K7
Phillipsburg	38	G3
Phitsanulok	90	C3
Phnom Penh	90	C4
Phoenix	44	D2
Phoenix Islands	114	J6
Phôngsali	90	C2
Phuket	90	B5
Piacenza	70	E5
Pádena	70	F5
Pianosa	72	E6

Name	Page	Grid
'ort-Vila	■114	G7
'ort Warrender	116	E2
'osadas	52	K4
'oschiavo	70	F4
'oshekhon'ye	78	G3
'oso	92	(2)B3
osŏng	88	D6
osse	50	H6
öβneck	60	G6
ost	44	F2
ostmasburg	112	C5
ostojna	70	K5
osušje	74	E6
otapovo	82	R4
oteau	42	C2
otenza	72	K8
'ot'i	98	J2
otiskum	108	G2
otlatch	38	C1
otosi	50	D7
otsdam, Germany	60	J4
otsdam, United States	40	F2
ottuvil	94	D7
oughkeepsie	40	F2
ourerere	118	F5
outo	118	E3
óvoa de Varzim	68	B3
ovorino	78	H4
owder	☑38	E1
owder River	38	E2
owell River	34	G7
oyang Hu	☑86	F5
ožarevac	74	J5
oza Rica	46	E4
ožega	74	H6
oznań	58	F5
ozoblanco	68	F6
rabumulih	92	(1)C3
rachatice	58	D8
rachuap Khiri Khan	90	B4
rado	50	K7
rastø	60	H1
rague = Praha	■58	D7
raha	■58	D7
raia	■108	(1)B2
rainha	50	G4
rairie du Chien	40	B2
rapat	92	(1)B2
raslin Island	🖫112	(2)B1
ratas = Dongsha Qundao	🖫90	F2
rato	70	G7
ratt	38	G3
rattville	42	D3
raya	92	(1)F4
reetz	60	F2
reilj	56	P8
remnitz	60	H4
remuda	🖫70	K6
rentice	40	B1
renzlau	58	C4
reobrazhenka	84	H4
reparis Island	🖫90	A4
reparis North Channel	🖪90	A3
reparis South Channel	🖪90	A4
ŕerov	58	G8
resa de la Boquilla	☑44	E3
resa de las Adjuntas	☑44	G4
resa Obregón	☑44	E3
rescott	38	D4
reševo	74	J7
resho	38	G2
residencia Roque Sáenz Peña	52	J4
residente Prudente	52	L3
residio	44	F3
reslav	74	P6
resnogorkovka	78	N4
rešov	58	L9
resque Isle	40	G1
reštice	60	J7
reston, United Kingdom	64	K8
reston, Minn., United States	40	B2
reston, Mo., United States	40	B3
retoria	■112	D5
reveza	76	C6
riargunsk	84	K6
ribilof Islands	🖫44	(1)D4
riboj	74	G6
ŕibram	58	D8
rice	38	D3
richard	42	D3
riego de Córdoba	68	F7
riekule	76	L8
rienai	58	N3
rieska	112	C5
riest Lake	☑38	C1
rievidza	58	H9
rijedor	74	D5

Name	Page	Grid
Prijepolje	74	G6
Prikaspiyskaya Nizmennost'	🖫78	K5
Prilep	76	D3
Primorsk	56	Q6
Primorsko Akhtarsk	78	G5
Prince Albert	34	K6
Prince Albert Peninsula	🖪34	H2
Prince Albert Sound	🖪34	H2
Prince Charles Island	🖪34	R3
Prince Edward Island	🖫102	G10
Prince Edward Island	🖪34	U7
Prince George	34	G6
Prince of Wales Island, Australia	🖫116	H2
Prince of Wales Island, Canada	🖪34	L2
Prince of Wales Island, United States	🖪34	E5
Prince of Wales Strait	🖪34	H2
Prince Patrick Island	🖪32	Q2
Prince Regent Inlet	🖪34	N2
Prince Rupert	34	E6
Princess Charlotte Bay	🖪116	H2
Princeton, Canada	38	B1
Princeton, Ill., United States	40	C2
Princeton, Ky., United States	40	C3
Princeton, Mo., United States	40	B2
Prince William Sound	🖪34	B4
Príncipe	🖫108	F4
Prineville	38	B2
Priozersk	56	R6
Priština	74	J7
Pritzwalk	60	H3
Privas	66	K9
Privolzhskaya Vozvyshennost'	🖫78	H4
Prizren	74	H7
Probolinggo	92	(1)E4
Proddatur	94	C6
Progreso	46	G4
Prokhladnyy	98	L2
Prokop'yevsk	82	R7
Prokuplje	74	J6
Proletarsk	78	H5
Proliv Longa	🖪84	X2
Proliv Vil'kitskogo	🖪82	U2
Prophet	☑34	G5
Propriano	72	C7
Prorer Wiek	🖪60	J2
Proserpine	116	J4
Prosna	☑58	G6
Prosperidad	90	H5
Prostojov	58	G8
Proti	🖫76	D7
Provadiya	74	Q6
Prøven = Kangersuatsiaq	34	W2
Providence	☑40	F2
Providence Island	🖫112	(2)B2
Provideniya	84	Z4
Provincetown	40	F2
Provins	66	J5
Provo	38	D2
Provost	34	J6
Prudhoe Bay	44	(1)H1
Prudnik	58	G7
Prüm	62	J4
Pruszków	58	K5
Prut	☑74	R4
Pružany	58	P5
Prvić	🖫70	K6
Pryluky	78	F4
Prypyats'	☑54	G2
Przasnysz	58	K4
Przemyśl	58	M8
Przeworsk	58	M7
Psara	🖫76	H6
Psebay	98	J1
Pskov	78	E3
Ptolemaída	76	D4
Ptuj	70	L4
Pucallpa	50	C5
Pucheng	86	F5
Puch'ŏn	88	D5
Púchov	58	H8
Pucioasa	74	N4
Puck	58	H3
Pudasjärvi	56	P4
Pudozh	78	G2
Puebla	46	E5
Pueblo	38	F3
Puelches	52	H6
Puelén	52	H6
Puente-Genil	68	F7
Puerto Acosta	50	D7
Puerto Aisén	52	G8
Puerto Alegre	50	E6
Puerto Angel	46	E5
Puerto Ayacucho	46	L7

Name	Page	Grid
Puerto Barrios	46	G5
Puerto Berrío	50	C2
Puerto Cabezas	46	H6
Puerto Carreño	46	L7
Puerto del Rosario	106	C3
Puerto de Navacerrada	🖫68	G4
Puerto Guarini	50	F8
Puerto Heath	50	D6
Puerto Inírida	50	D3
Puerto Leguizamo	50	C4
Puerto Libertad	44	D3
Puerto Limón	50	B3
Puertollano	68	F6
Puerto Maldonado	50	D6
Puerto Montt	52	G7
Puerto Nuevo	46	K7
Puerto Peñasco	44	D2
Puerto Princesa	90	F5
Puerto Real	68	D8
Puerto Rico	🖫46	L5
Puerto Rico	50	D6
Puerto Rico Trench	🖫48	E1
Puerto Santa Cruz	52	H9
Puerto Suárez	50	F7
Pukapuka	🖫114	N7
Pukatawagen	34	L5
Pukch'ŏng	88	E3
Pukě	74	G7
Pula	70	J6
Puławy	58	M6
Pullman	38	C1
Pułtusk	56	L10
Pulu	82	Q10
Pülümür	98	H4
Puncak Jaya	🖪92	(2)E3
Puncak Mandala	🖪92	(2)F3
Pune	94	B5
Punia	110	D4
Puno	50	C7
Punta Albina	🗁112	A3
Punta Alice	🗁72	M9
Punta Angamos	🗁52	G3
Punta Arena	🗁38	B3
Punta Arenas	52	G9
Punta Ballena	🗁52	G3
Punta Dungeness	🗁52	H9
Punta Eugenia	🗁46	A3
Punta Galera	🗁52	G6
Punta Gallinas	🗁46	K6
Punta Gorda	42	E4
Punta La Marmora	🖪72	D8
Punta Lavapié	🗁52	G6
Punta Lengua de Vaca	🗁52	G5
Punta Mala	🗁50	B2
Punta Mariato	🗁46	H7
Punta Medanosa	🗁52	H8
Punta Negra	🗁50	A5
Punta Norte, Argentina	🗁52	J7
Punta Norte, Argentina	🗁52	K6
Punta Pariñas	🗁50	A5
Punta Rasa	🗁52	J7
Puntarenas	46	H6
Punta San Gabriel	🗁44	D3
Punta San Telmo	🗁46	D5
Punta Sarga	🗁106	B4
Puponga	118	D5
Puri	94	E5
Purmerend	62	G2
Purpe	☑84	B4
Purukcahu	92	(1)E3
Purus	☑50	E5
Puruvesi	🖪56	Q6
Pusan	88	E6
Püshkin	78	F3
Püspökladany	58	L10
Putao	90	B1
Putaruru	118	E3
Putian	86	F5
Putna	☑74	P4
Puttalami	94	C7
Putten	🖪62	G3
Puttgarden	60	G2
Putumayo	☑50	C4
Puuwai	44	(2)A2
Puy de Dôme	🖪66	H8
Puy de Sancy	🖪66	H8
Puysegur Point	🗁118	A8
Pweto	110	D5
Pwllheli	64	H9
Pyapon	78	G2
Pyatigorsk	98	K1
Pyhäjärvi	🖪56	M6
Pylos	76	D8
Pyöktong	88	C3
P'yŏnggang	88	D4
P'yŏngyang	■88	C4
Pyramid Island	🖫118	(1)B2
Pyramid Lake	🖪38	C2/3
Pyrenees	🖪66	E11

Name	Page	Grid
Pyrgos	76	D7
Pyrzyce	58	D4
Pyshchug	78	J3
Pytalovo	56	P8

Q

Name	Page	Grid
Qadīmah	96	C5
Qādub	96	F7
Qagan Nur	☑86	F2
Qal'aikhum	96	K2
Qalamat Nadqān	101	D5
Qalāt	96	J3
Qal'at Bīshah	96	D5
Qal'eh-ye Now	96	H3
Qamdo	86	B4
Qaminis	104	C1
Qaraaoun	98	F7
Qardho	110	H2
Qartaba	100	C2
Qasr Farafra	104	E2
Qaţanā	100	D3
Qatar	▲101	D4
Qatrāna	100	D5
Qattāra Depression	🖫104	E2
Qāyen	96	G3
Qazangöldag	▲98	M4
Qazax	98	L3
Qazimämmäd	98	N3
Qazvīn	96	E2
Qena	104	F2
Qeqertarsuatsiaat	34	W4
Qeqertarsuatsiaq	🖫34	V3
Qeqertarsuup Tunua	🖪34	V3
Qeshm	🖫101	F3
Qeshm	101	G3
Qeys	🖫101	E3
Qezel Owzan	☑98	N5
Qezi'ot	100	B6

Name	Page	Grid
Qianshanlaoba	82	Q8
Qiaowan	86	B2
Qidukou	94	G2
Qiemo	82	R10
Qijiang	86	D5
Qijiaojing	82	S9
Qila Saifullah	96	J3
Qilian	86	C3
Qilian Shan	🖪86	B3
Qingdao	86	G3
Qinghai Hu	☑86	B3
Qinghai Nanshan	🖪86	B3
Qingjiang	86	F4
Qingshuihe	86	E3
Qingyang	86	D3
Qingyuan, China	86	E6
Qingyuan, China	86	G2
Qinhuangdao	86	F3
Qinzhou	90	D2
Qionghai	90	D3
Qiqian	84	L6
Qiqihar	84	L7
Qīr	101	E2
Qira	82	Q10
Qiryat Motzkin	100	C4
Qiryat Shemona	100	C3
Qishn	96	F6
Qolleh-ye Damāvand	▲96	F2
Qom	96	F3
Qomishèh	96	F3
Qornet es Saouda	▲100	D2
Qorveh	98	M6
Qotūr	98	L4
Quang Ngai	90	D3
Quangolodougou	108	C3
Quang Tri	90	D2
Quanzhou	90	F2
Quaqtaq	34	T4
Quarto Sant'Elena	72	D9
Quba	98	N3
Quchan	96	G2
Québec	🖾40	F1
Quedlinburg	60	G5
Queen Charlotte	34	E6
Queen Charlotte Islands	🖫34	E6
Queen Charlotte Sound	🖪34	E6
Queen Charlotte Strait	🖪34	F6
Queen Elizabeth Islands	🖫32	M2
Queen Maud Gulf	🖪34	L3
Queensland	■116	J8
Queenstown, Australia	116	J8
Queenstown, New Zealand	118	B7
Queenstown, South Africa	112	D6
Queets	38	B1
Quelimane	112	F3
Quemado	44	E2
Querétaro	46	D4
Quesnel	34	G6
Quetta	96	J3

Quezaltenango ... 46 F6
Quezon ... 90 F5
Quezon City ... 90 G4
Qufu ... 86 F3
Quibala ... 112 A2
Quibdó ... 46 J7
Quijotoa ... 44 D2
Quilmes ... 52 K5
Quilpie ... 116 H5
Quimbele ... 110 B5
Quimili ... 52 J4
Quimper ... 66 A5
Quimperlé ... 66 B6
Quincy ... 40 B3
Qui Nhon ... 90 D4
Quionga ... 110 G6
Quirindi ... 116 K6
Quito ... ■ 50 B4
Qujing ... 90 C1
Qumar He ... ☒ 94 F1
Qumaryan ... 94 F1
Qurayyāt ... 96 G5
Qurghonteppa ... 34 J2
Qurlurtuuq ... 34 H3
Qus ... 104 F2
Quseir ... 104 F2
Quzhou ... 86 F5

R

Raab ... ☒ 70 L3
Raahe ... 56 N4
Raalte ... 62 J2
Raasay ... ☒ 64 G4
Raas Caseyr ... ▷110 J1
Raas Xaafuun ... ▷110 J1
Rab ... 70 K6
Rab ... ☒ 70 K6
Rába ... ☒ 74 E2
Raba ... 92 (2)A4
Rabak ... 104 F5
Rabat ... 72 J13
Rabat ... ■106 D2
Rabca ... ☒ 70 N3
Rābigh ... 96 C5
Rabka ... 58 K8
Rach Gia ... 90 D5
Racine ... 40 C2
Ráckeve ... 74 F2
Rădăuți ... 74 N2
Radbuza ... ☒ 60 H7
Radeberg ... 60 J5
Radebeul ... 60 J5
Radhanpur ... 94 B4
Radnevo ... 74 N7
Radom ... 58 L6
Radomir ... 74 K7
Radomsko ... 58 J6
Radoviš ... 76 E3
Radstadt ... 58 C10
Raduzniy ... 82 P5
Radviliškis ... 58 N2
Rae-Edzo ... 34 H4
Raethi ... 118 E4
Raevavae ... ☒114 M8
Rafaela ... 52 J4
Rafah ... 100 B5
Rafaï ... 110 C3
Rafțā ... 96 D4
Rafsanjān ... 101 G1
Raglan ... 118 E3
Ragusa ... 72 J12
Raha ... 92 (2)B3
Rahad el Berdi ... 104 D5
Rahimyar Khan ... 96 K4
Raichur ... 94 C5
Raiganj ... 94 E3
Raigarh ... 94 D4
Rainach ... ☒ 70 L4
Rainbow Lake ... 34 H5
Rainier ... 38 B1
Rainy Lake ... ☒ 40 B1
Rainy River ... 40 B1
Raipur ... 94 D4
Rai Valley ... 118 D5
Rajahmundry ... 94 D5
Raja-Jooseppi ... 56 Q2
Rajapalaiyam ... 94 C7
Rajgarh ... 94 C3
Rajkot ... 96 K5
Raj Nangaon ... 94 D4
Rajshahi ... 94 E4
Rakhiv ... 74 M1
Rakovica ... 70 L6
Rakovnik ... 58 C7
Rakovski ... 74 M7
Rakvere ... 56 P7
Raleigh ... ◙ 42 F2
Ralik Chain ... ☒114 G5
Ram ... 100 C7
Rama ... 46 H6

Ramallah ... 100 C5
Rambouillet ... 66 G5
Rameswaram ... 94 C7
Rämhormoz ... 101 C1
Ramla ... 100 B5
Ramlat Rabyānah ... ◙104 C3
Râmnicu Sărat ... 74 Q4
Râmnicu Vâlcea ... 74 M4
Rampur, India ... 94 C2
Rampur, India ... 94 C3
Ramree Island ... ☒ 90 A3
Ramsgate ... 64 P10
Ramtha ... 100 D4
Ranau ... 92 (1)F1
Rancagua ... 52 G5
Ranchi ... 94 E4
Randazzo ... 72 J11
Randers ... 78 F4
Randijaure ... ☒ 56 K3
Randolph ... 38 G2
Rânes ... 62 B6
Rangamati ... 94 F4
Rangiora ... 118 D6
Rangoon = Yangon ... ■ 90 B3
Rankin ... 44 F2
Rankin Inlet ... 34 N4
Ranong ... 90 B5
Ransiki ... 92 (2)D3
Rānya ... 98 L5
Rapa ... ☒114 M8
Rapalla ... 72 D4
Rapallo ... 70 E6
Rapar ... 96 K5
Raperswil ... 70 D3
Rapid City ... 38 F2
Rapid River ... 40 C1
Rapla ... 56 N7
Rapur ... 96 J5
Raroia ... ☒114 N7
Rarotonga ... ☒114 K8
Râs Abu Shagara ... ▷104 G3
Ra's al Ḥadd ... ▷ 96 G5
Ra's al Ḥazrah ... ▷101 D4
Ra's al Hilāl ... ▷104 D1
Ra's al Khajī ... 101 C2
Ra's al Khaymah ... 101 F4
Ra's al Kūh ... ▷101 G4
Ra's al Muraysah ... ▷104 E1
Ra's al 'Udayd ... 101 D4
Ra's az Zawr ... ▷101 C3
Rās Banâs ... ▷104 G3
Ras Beddouza ... ▷106 C1
Ras Bir ... ▷104 H5
Ras Dashen Terara ... ▲104 G5
Ra's-e Barkan ... ▷101 C2
Raseiniai ... 56 M9
Ra's el Nafas ... ▲100 B7
Ra's Fartak ... ▷ 96 F6
Râs Ghârib ... 104 F2
Rasht ... 98 N5
Râsk ... 96 H4
Raška ... 74 H6
Ras Kasar ... ▷104 G4
Ra's Madrakah ... ▷ 96 G6
Râs Nouâdhibou ... ▷106 B4
Rason Lake ... ☒116 D5
Rass Jebel ... 72 E11
Rass Mostefa ... ▷ 72 F12
Rassokha ... ☒ 84 H2
Rast ... 74 L6
Ras Tannūrah ... 101 D3
Rastatt ... 62 L6
Rastede ... 60 D3
Ratak Chain ... ☒114 H4
Ratangarh ... 96 K4
Rat Buri ... 90 B4
Rath ... 94 C3
Rathenow ... 60 H4
Rathlin Island ... ☒ 64 F6
Ratlam ... 94 C4
Ratnagiri ... 96 K6
Raton ... 38 F3
Ratta ... 84 C4
Ratten ... ☒ 70 D4
Ratzeburg ... 60 F3
Raudhatain ... 101 B1
Raukumara Range ... ▲118 F4
Rauma ... 56 L6
Rausu ... 88 N1
Ravalli ... ☒ 74 R2
Ravānsar ... 98 M6
Rāvar ... 101 G1
Ravenna ... 70 H6
Ravensburg ... 70 E3
Ravensthorpe ... 116 D6
Ravnina ... 96 H2
Râwah ... 98 J6
Rawaki ... ☒114 J6
Rawalpindi ... 96 K3
Rawa Mazowiecka ... 58 K6
Rawāndiz ... 98 L5

Rawicz ... 58 F6
Rawlinna ... 116 E6
Rawlins ... 38 E2
Rawson ... 52 J7
Rawu ... 94 G3
Raychikhinsk ... 84 M7
Raymond ... 38 B1
Raymondville ... 44 G3
Rayong ... 90 C4
Razdol'noye ... 88 F2
Razgrad ... 74 P6
Razlog ... 74 L8
Reading, United Kingdom ... 64 M10
Reading, United States ... 40 E2
Realicó ... 52 J6
Rebbeneseya ... ☒ 56 J1
Rebun-tō ... ☒ 86 L1
Recife ... ◙ 50 L5
Recklinghausen ... 62 K3
Recknitz ... ☒ 60 H3
Reconquista ... 52 K4
Recreo ... 52 H4
Red, Canada/
  United States ... ☒ 38 G1
Red, United States ... ☒ 42 B3
Reda ... 58 H3
Red Bluff ... 44 B1
Red Cloud ... 42 B1
Red Deer ... 34 J6
Redding ... 38 B2
Redditch ... 62 A2
Redfield ... 38 G2
Red Lake ... 34 N6
Red Lakes ... ☒ 36 H2
Red Lodge ... 38 E1
Red Oak ... 40 A2
Redon ... 66 C6
Redondela ... 68 B2
Red River = Song Hông ... ☒ 90 C2
Red Sea ... ◫104 G3
Redwater ... 34 J6
Red Wing ... 40 B2
Redwood City ... 38 B3
Redwood Falls ... 40 A2
Reed City ... 40 C2
Reedsport ... 38 B2
Reefton ... 118 C6
Rega ... ☒ 58 E4
Regen ... ☒ 60 H7
Regen ... 60 J8
Regensburg ... 60 H7
Regenstauf ... 60 H7
Reggane ... 106 F3
Réggio di Calabria ... 72 K10
Réggio nell'Emília ... 70 F6
Reghin ... 74 M3
Regina ... ◫ 36 F1
Rehau ... 60 H6
Rehoboth ... 112 B4
Rehovot ... 100 B5
Reichenbach ... 60 H6
Reigate ... 64 M10
Reims ... 62 G5
Reinach Bad ... 70 C3
Reindeer Lake ... ☒ 34 L5
Reinosa ... 68 F1
Reisi ... 72 J11
Relizane ... 106 F1
Remada ... 106 H2
Remagen ... 62 K4
Rembang ... 92 (1)E4
Remeshk ... 101 H3
Remiremont ... 66 M6
Remscheid ... 62 K3
Rena ... 56 F6
Rendína ... 76 F4
Rendsburg ... 60 E2
Rengat ... 92 (1)C3
Reni ... 74 R4
Renmark ... 116 H6
Rennes ... 66 D5
Reno ... ☒ 70 G6
Reno ... 38 C3
Rentería ... 68 J1
Renton ... 38 B1
Renukut ... 94 D4
Reo ... 92 (2)B4
Replot ... ☒ 56 L5
Reprêsa de Balbina ... ☒ 50 F4
Represa de Samuel ... ☒ 50 E5
Represa de Sao Simao ... ☒ 50 G4
Represa Ilha Solteira ... ☒ 50 G4
Represa Tucuruí ... ☒ 50 H4
Republic of Ireland ... ▲ 64 D8
Repulse Bay ... ◫116 C4
Reşadiye ... 98 G3
Resen ... 74 J8
Réservoir Cabonga ... ☒ 40 E1

Réservoir Caniapiscau ... ☒ 34 T
Réservoir de La Grande 2 ... ☒ 34 P
Réservoir de La Grande 3 ... ☒ 34 P
Réservoir de La Grande 4 ... ☒ 34 S
Réservoir Gouin ... ☒ 40 E
Réservoir Manicouagan ... ☒ 34
Réservoir Opinaca ... ☒ 34 P
Réservoir Pipmuacan ... ☒ 40
Reshteh-ye Kūhhā-ye
  Alborz ... ■ 96
Resistencia ... 52 H
Reşița ... 74
Resolute ... 34 N
Resolution Island,
  Canada ... ☒ 34 U
Resolution Island,
  New Zealand ... ☒118
Resovo ... 76 H
Rethel ... 62 G
Rethymno ... 76 C
Réunion ... ☒112 (1)E
Reus ... 68 M
Reutlingen ... 60
Revda ... 78
Revillagigedo Island ... ☒ 44 (1)L
Revin ... 62
Revivim ... 100 B
Revúca ... 58
Rewa ... 94 D
Rexburg ... 38
Reykjanes ... ☒ 56 (1)B
Reykjavík ... ■ 56 (1)C
Reynosa ... 42
Rezat ... ☒ 60
Rezé ... 66
Rēzekne ... 56
Rezina ... 74 R
Rezovo ... 74
Rheda-Wiedenbrück ... 60
Rhein = Rhine ... ☒ 70
Rheinbach ... 62 K
Rheine ... 62
Rheinfelden ... 70 C
Rhin = Rhine ... ☒ 70
Rhine ... ☒ 70 C
Rhinelander ... 40 C
Rho ... 70
Rhode Island ... ◙ 40 F
Rhodes = Ródos ... ☒ 76 D
Rhondda ... 64 J
Rhône ... ☒ 66 K
Rhyl ... 64
Ribadeo ... 68 C
Ribas do Rio Pardo ... 52
Ribe ... 66
Ribeauville ... 66
Ribeirão Prêto ... 52 N
Ribeira = Santa Eugenia ... 68
Ribera ... 72 H
Riberalta ... 52
Ribnica ... 72
Ribnița ... 74
Ribnitz-Damgarten ... 60
Ričany ... 60
Riccione ... 70
Richardson Mountains ... ▲ 44 (1)H
Richfield ... 38 D
Richland ... 38
Richlands ... 40 D
Richmond, Australia ... 116
Richmond, New Zealand ... 118
Richmond, Ky.,
  United States ... 40
Richmond, Va.,
  United States ... ◙ 40
Ridgecrest ... 44
Ridgway ... 40
Ried ... 70
Riesa ... 60
Rieti ... 72
Rifle ... 38
Rīga ... ■ 56
Riggins ... 34
Rigolet ... 34
Rijeka ... 72
Riley ... 38
Rimava ... ☒ 58
Rimavská Sobota ... 58
Rímini ... 70
Rimouski ... 40
Rineia ... ☒ 76
Ringe ... 60
Ringkøbing ... 56
Ringkøbing Fjord ... ☒ 56
Ringsted ... 56
Ringvassøya ... ☒ 56
Rinteln ... 60
Rio Branco ... ◙ 50
Rio Colorado ... 52
Rio Cuarto ... 52
Rio de Janeiro ... ◙ 52
Rio de Janeiro ... ◙ 52

	Page	Grid
Río de la Plata	52	K6
Río Gallegos	52	H9
Río Grande	44	E2
Río Grande, Argentina	52	H9
Río Grande, Mexico	44	F4
Rio Grande	52	L5
Rio Grande City	42	B4
Rio Grande do Norte	50	K5
Rio Grande do Sul	52	L4
Ríohacha	46	K6
Río Largartos	46	G4
Riom	66	J8
Río Mulatos	50	D7
Rionero	72	K8
Rionero in Vulture	74	C9
Rio Tigre	50	B4
Rio Verde	50	G7
Rio Verde de Mato Grosso	50	G7
Ripley, Oh., United States	40	D3
Ripley, Tenn., United States	40	C3
Ripley, W.Va., United States	40	D3
Ripoll	68	N2
Ripon	64	L7
Rishiri-tō	84	Q7
Rishon le Ẕiyyon	100	B5
Ritchie's Archipelago	90	A4
Ritzville	38	C1
Rivadavia	52	G4
Riva del Garda	70	F5
Rivarolo	70	C5
Rivas	46	G6
Rivera, Argentina	52	J6
Rivera, Uruguay	52	K5
Riversdale	112	C6
Riversdale Beach	118	E5
Riverton, Canada	34	M6
Riverton, New Zealand	118	A8
Rivesaltes	66	H11
Rivière-du-Loup	40	G1
Rivne	78	E4
Rivoli	70	C5
Riwoqê	94	G2
Riyadh = Ar Riyāḍ	101	H4
Rize	98	J3
Rizhao	86	F3
Roanne	66	K7
Roanoke	40	D3
Roanoke Rapids	42	F2
Robe	116	G7
Robertsfors	56	L4
Robertval	40	F1
Roboré	50	F7
Robstown	42	B4
Roccastrada	72	F6
Rochefort, Belgium	62	H4
Rochefort, France	66	E8
Rochelle	40	C2
Rocher River	34	J4
Rochester, United Kingdom	62	C3
Rochester, Minn., United States	40	B2
Rochester, N.H., United States	40	F2
Rochester, N.Y., United States	40	E2
Rockall	54	C2
Rockefeller Plateau	120	(2)EE2
Rockford	40	C2
Rockhampton	116	K4
Rock Hill	40	D4
Rock Island	40	B2
Rocklake	38	G1
Rockport	38	B1
Rock Rapids	40	A2
Rock Springs	38	E2
Rocksprings	44	F3
Rocky Mount	40	E3
Rocky Mountains	34	F5
Rødby Havn	60	G2
Roddickton	34	V6
Rodez	66	H9
Rodi Gargánico	72	K7
Roding	60	H7
Rodney	40	D2
Rodopi Planina	74	M7
Rodos	76	L8
Rodos	76	L8
Roebourne	116	C4
Roermond	62	J3
Roeselare	62	F4
Roes Welcome Sound	34	P4
Rogers City	40	D1
Rogerson	38	D2
Rogliano	72	D6
Rogue	38	B2
Rohrbach	70	K2
Rohtak	94	C3
Roi Et	90	C3
Roja	56	M8
Rokiškis	56	N9
Rokycany	58	C8
Rolla	40	B3
Rolleston	118	D6
Rolvsøya	56	M1
Roma	92	(2)C4
Roma, Australia	116	J5
Roma, Italy	72	G7
Roman	74	P3
Romania	74	L4
Romans-sur-Isère	66	L8
Rombas	62	J5
Rome = Roma	72	G7
Rome, Ga., United States	42	D3
Rome, N.Y., United States	40	E2
Romney	40	E3
Romny	78	F4
Rømø	60	D1
Romorantin-Lanthenay	66	G6
Rona	64	G2
Ronan	36	D2
Roncesvalles	68	J2
Ronda	68	E8
Rondônia	50	E6
Rondônia	50	E6
Rondonópolis	50	G7
Rondu	96	L2
Rongcheng	86	G3
Rønne	58	D2
Ronneby	56	H8
Ronne Entrance	120	(2)JJ3
Ronne Ice Shelf	120	(2)MM2
Ronse	62	F4
Roosendaal	62	G3
Roper Bar	116	F2
Roraima	50	E3
Røros	56	F5
Rosário	50	J4
Rosario, Argentina	52	J5
Rosario, Mexico	36	D6
Rosario, Mexico	36	E7
Rosario, Paraguay	52	K3
Rosário Oeste	50	F6
Rosarito	36	C6
Rosarno	72	K10
Roscommon	64	D8
Roseau	46	M5
Roseburg	38	B2
Roseires Reservoir	104	F5
Rose Island	114	K7
Rosenburg	44	G3
Rosenheim	70	H3
Roses	68	P2
Rosetown	34	K6
Rosica	74	N6
Rosignano Solvay	70	F7
Roşiori de Vede	74	N5
Roskilde	56	G9
Roslavl'	78	F4
Rossano	72	L9
Ross Ice Shelf	120	(2)Z1
Ross Lake	38	B1
Roßlau	60	H5
Rosso	106	B5
Rossosh'	78	G4
Ross River	34	E4
Ross Sea	120	(2)AA2
Røssvatnet	56	G4
Røst	56	G3
Roståq	101	E3
Rosthern	34	K6
Rostock	60	H2
Rostov	78	G3
Rostov-na-Donu	78	G5
Rostrenen	66	B5
Roswell	44	F2
Rota	114	E4
Rotarua	118	F4
Rote	92	(2)B5
Rotenburg, Germany	60	E3
Rotenburg, Germany	60	E5
Roth	60	G7
Rothenburg	60	F7
Roto	116	J6
Rott	70	H2
Rottnen	58	E1
Rottumeroog	62	J1
Rottumerplaat	62	J1
Rottweil	70	D2
Rotuma	114	H7
Roubaix	62	F4
Rouen	66	D5
Rouiba	68	P8
Round Mountain	116	K6
Round Rock	42	B3
Roundup	38	E1
Rousay	64	J2
Rouyn	40	E1
Rovaniemi	56	N3
Rovereto	70	G5
Rovigo	70	G5
Rovinj	70	J5
Rovuma	110	F6
Rowley Island	34	R3
Rowley Shoals	116	C3
Roxas	90	G4
Roxburgh	118	B7
Royal Leamington Spa	62	A2
Royal Tunbridge Wells	62	C3
Royan	66	D8
Roye	62	E5
Royston	62	C2
Rozdil'na	74	T3
Rožňava	58	K9
Rrëshen	76	B3
Rtishchevo	78	H4
Ruacana	112	A3
Ruahine Range	118	E5
Ruapehu	118	E4
Ruapuke Island	118	B8
Ruarkela	94	D4
Ruatahuna	118	F4
Ruatoria	118	G3
Ruawai	118	D3
Rub' al Khālī	96	E6
Rubi	110	C3
Rubtsovsk	82	Q7
Ruby	44	(1)F3
Rudan	101	G3
Ruda Śląska	58	H7
Rudbar	96	H3
Rüdersdorf	60	J4
Rudkøbing	60	F2
Rudnaya Pristan'	88	H2
Rudnyy	78	M4
Rudolstadt	60	G6
Rüdsar	98	P5
Rue	62	D4
Ruffec	66	F7
Rufiji	110	F5
Rugby, United Kingdom	62	A2
Rugby, United States	36	G2
Rügen	58	C3
Ruhnu	56	M8
Ruhr	62	L3
Rum	64	F5
Ruma	74	G4
Rumäh	101	B4
Rumaylah	101	B1
Rumbek	110	D2
Rum Cay	46	K4
Rumigny	62	G5
Rumoi	88	L2
Runanaga	118	C6
Rundu	112	B3
Ruoqiang	82	R10
Ruo Shui	86	C2
Rupa	70	K5
Rupat	92	(1)C2
Rupert	34	R6
Rupert	38	D2
Rururu	114	L8
Ruse	74	N6
Rushon	94	G3
Rushville, Ill., United States	40	B2
Rushville, Ind., United States	40	C3
Rushville, Nebr., United States	38	F2
Russell	38	G3
Russellville, Ark., United States	42	C2
Russellville, Ky., United States	40	D2
Rüsselsheim	60	D7
Russia	56	L9
Russia	80	M3
Rust'avi	98	L3
Ruston	42	C3
Rutana	110	D4
Rute	68	F7
Ruteng	92	(2)B4
Rutland	40	F2
Rutog	94	C2
Ruvo di Puglia	72	L7
Ruvuma	110	F6
Ruzayevka	78	H4
Ružomberok	58	J8
Rwanda	110	D4
R-Warnemünde	60	H2
Ryazan'	78	G4
Ryazhsk	78	H4
Rybinsk	78	G3
Rybinskoye Vodokhranilishche	78	G3
Rybnik	58	H7
Rychnov	58	F7
Ryde	62	A4
Rye Patch Reservoir	38	C2
Ryki	58	L6
Ryl'sk	78	F4
Ryn-Peski	78	J5
Ryōtsu	88	K4
Rypin	58	J4
Ryukyu Islands = Nansei-shotō	86	H5
Rzeszów	58	M7
Rzhev	78	F3

S

	Page	Grid
Sa'ādatābād, Iran	101	E1
Sa'ādatābād, Iran	101	F2
Saale	60	G6
Saalfeld	60	G6
Saalfelden	70	H3
Saanen	72	B2
Saar	62	J5
Saarbrücken	62	J5
Saarburg	62	J5
Saaremaa	56	L7
Saarlouis	62	J5
Saatli	98	N4
Saatly	96	E2
Saba	46	M5
Sab' Ābār	100	E3
Šabac	74	G5
Sabadell	68	N3
Sabah	92	(1)F1
Sabang	90	B5
Sabhā	106	H3
Sabiñánigo	68	K2
Sabinas	44	F3
Sabinas Hidalgo	44	F3
Sabine	42	B3
Sabine Lake	42	C3
Sabinov	58	L8
Sabkhet el Bardawīl	100	A5
Sable Island	34	V8
Sablé-sur-Sarthe	66	E6
Sabôr	68	D3
Sabun	82	Q5
Sabzevär	96	G2
Săcele	74	N4
Sachanga	112	B2
Sachs Harbour	34	G2
Säckingen	70	C3
Sacramento	38	B3
Sacramento	38	B3
Şad'ah	96	D6
Sadiqabad	96	K4
Sadiya	94	G3
Sado	68	B6
Sadoga-shima	88	K4
Sadon	98	K2
Sado-shima	86	K3
Sä Dragonera	68	N5
Säffle	56	G7
Safford	44	E2
Safi, Jordan	100	C5
Safi, Morocco	106	D2
Safonovo, Russia	78	F3
Safonovo, Russia	78	J1
Safranbolu	76	Q3
Saga, China	94	E3
Saga, Japan	88	F7
Sagami-nada	88	K6
Sagar	94	C4
Sagastyr	82	Z3
Sage	38	D2
Saginaw	40	D2
Sagiz	78	K5
Sagiz	78	K5
Saguache	38	E3
Sagua la Grande	46	H4
Sagunt	68	K5
Sahāb	100	D5
Sahagún	68	E2
Sahara	102	C3
Saharah el Gharbïya	104	E2
Saharanpur	94	C3
Saharsa	94	E3
Şahbuz	98	L4
Sahel	102	C4
Sahiwal	94	K3
Sahuaripa	44	E3
Sähy	74	F1
Saïda, Algeria	106	C2
Saïda, Lebanon	100	C3
Sa'idābād	101	F2
Saidpur	94	E3
Saigo	88	G5
Saigon = Hồ Chi Minh	90	D4
Saiha	94	F4
Saihan Toroi	86	C2
Saiki	88	F7
Saimaa	56	P6
Saimbeyli	98	G4
Sä'in	101	F1
Saindak	96	H4
St. Albans	62	B3

163

Santa Ana, *United States* ..		44	C2
Santa Bárbara		36	E6
Santa Barbara		44	C2
Santa Barbara Island	◫ 44	44	C2
Santa Catalina		52	H4
Santa Catalina Island	◫ 44	44	C2
Santa Catarina	◪ 52	52	L4
Santa Clara, *Columbia*		50	D4
Santa Clara, *Cuba*		36	K7
Santa Clarita		44	C2
Santa Comba Dão		68	B4
Santa Cruz	◪ 52	52	G9
Santa Cruz, *Bolivia*		50	E7
Santa Cruz, *United States*		44	B1
Santa Cruz de Tenerife		106	B3
Santa Cruz Island	◫ 44	44	B2
Santa Cruz Islands	◫114	114	G7
Santa Eugenia		68	A2
Santa Fe	◨ 38	38	E3
Santa Fé		52	J5
Sant'Agata di Militello		72	J10
Santa Isabel	◫114	114	F6
Santa Isabel		52	H6
Santa la Grande		36	K7
Santa Margarita	◪ 36	36	D7
Santa Maria	◫106	106	(1)B2
Santa Maria, *Brazil*		52	L4
Santa Maria, *United States* .		44	B2
Santa Maria das Barreiras .		50	H5
Santa Marta		46	K6
Santana do Livramento		52	K5
Santander		68	G1
Sant'Antioco	◪ 72	72	C9
Santa Pola		68	K6
Santarém, *Brazil*		50	G4
Santarém, *Spain*		68	B5
Santa Rosa, *Argentina*		52	J6
Santa Rosa, *Acre, Brazil* ..		50	C5
Santa Rosa, *R.G.S., Brazil* .		52	L4
Santa Rosa, *Calif.,* *United States*		38	B3
Santa Rosa, *N.Mex.,* *United States*		44	F2
Santa Rosa Island	◫ 44	44	B2
Santa Vitória do Palmar ..		52	L5
Sant Boi		68	N3
Sant Carlos de la Ràpita ..		68	L4
Sant Celoni		68	N3
Sant Feliu de Guixols		68	P3
Santiago	◪ 52	52	G5
Santiago, *Brazil*		52	L4
Santiago, *Dominican Republic* ..		46	K5
Santiago, *Philippines*		90	G3
Santiago, *Spain*		68	B2
Santiago de Cuba		46	J5
Santiago del Estero		52	J4
Santo André		52	M3
Santo Antão	◫108	108	(1)A1
Santo Antônio de Jesus ..		50	K6
Santo Antônio do Içá		50	D4
Santo Domingo	■ 46	46	L5
Santo Domingo de los Colorados		50	B4
Santoña		68	G1
Santos		52	M3
San Vicente		90	G3
San Vincenzo		72	E5
Sanya		90	D3
Sao Bernardo do Campo ..		50	E4
São Borja		52	K4
São Carlos		52	M3
São Félix, *M.G., Brazil* ..		50	G6
São Félix, *Pará, Brazil* ...		50	G5
São Filipe		108	(1)B2
São Francisco	◪ 50	50	J6
São João de Madeira		68	B4
São Jorge	◫106	106	(1)B2
São José do Rio Prêto		52	L3
São Luís	◨ 50	50	J4
São Miguel	◫106	106	(1)B2
Saône	◪ 66	66	K7
São Nicolau	◫108	108	(1)B1
São Paulo	◪ 52	52	L3
São Paulo	◨ 52	52	M3
São Paulo de Olivença ...		50	D4
São Raimundo Nonato		50	J5
São Tiago	◫108	108	(1)B1
São Tomé	◫108	108	F4
São Tomé	◫108	108	F4
São Tomé and Príncipe ...	▣108	108	F4
São Vicente	◫108	108	(1)A1
São Vicente		52	M3
Saparua		92	(2)C3
Sapele		108	F3
Sapes		76	H4
Sapientza	◫ 76	76	D8
Sa Pobla		68	P5
Sapporo		88	L2
Sapri		72	K8
Sapudi	◫ 92	92	(1)E4
Sapulpa		42	B2

Saqqez		98	M5
Saráb		98	M5
Sara Buri		90	C4
Sarajevo	■ 74	74	F6
Sarakhs		96	H2
Saraktash		78	L4
Saramati	◢ 94	94	G3
Saran		82	N8
Saranac Lake		40	F2
Sarandë		76	C5
Sarangani Islands	◫ 92	92	(2)C1
Saranpul		78	M2
Saransk	◫ 78	78	J4
Sarapul		78	K3
Sarapul'skoye		84	P7
Sarasota		42	E4
Sarata		74	S3
Saratoga		38	E2
Saratoga Springs		40	F2
Saratov		78	J4
Saravan		96	H4
Sarawak	▩ 92	92	(1)E2
Saray		76	K3
Sarayköy		76	L7
Sarayönü		76	Q6
Sarbāz		96	H4
Sarbîsheh		96	G3
Sárbogárd		74	F3
Sar Dasht		98	L5
Sardegna	◫ 72	72	E8
Sardinia = Sardegna	◫ 72	72	E8
Sardis Lake	◪ 42	42	B3
Sar-e Pol		96	J2
Sargodha		96	K3
Sarh		108	H3
Sārī		96	F2
Saria	◫ 76	76	K9
Sarıkamış		98	K3
Sarıkaya		76	K4
Sarikei		92	(1)E2
Sarina		116	J4
Sariñena		68	K3
Sarīr Tibesti	◉104	104	C3
Sariwŏn		88	C4
Sark	◫ 66	66	C4
Sarkad		74	J3
Sarkand		82	P8
Sarıkaraağaç		76	P6
Şarkişla		98	G4
Şarköy		76	K4
Şarmi		92	(2)E3
Särna		56	G6
Sarnia		40	D2
Sarny		78	E4
Sarolangun		92	(1)C3
Saronno		70	E5
Saros Körfezi	◫ 76	76	J4
Sárospatak		58	L9
Sarre	◪ 66	66	M5
Sarrebourg		66	N5
Sarreguemines		66	N4
Sarria		68	C2
Sartène		72	C7
Sartyn'ya		78	M2
Saruhanli		76	K6
Sārur		98	L4
Sárvár		70	M3
Sarvestān		101	E2
Sarviz	◪ 74	74	F2
Sarykamyshkoye Ozero ..	◪ 82	82	K9
Saryozek		82	P9
Saryshagan		82	N8
Sarysu	◪ 82	82	M8
Sary-Tash		96	K2
Sarzana		70	E6
Sasaram		94	D4
Sasebo		88	E7
Saskatchewan	◩ 34	34	K6
Saskatchewan	◪ 34	34	L6
Saskatoon		34	K6
Saskylakh		82	W3
Sassandra		108	C4
Sassari		72	C8
Sassnitz		60	J2
Sassuolo		70	F6
Satadougou		108	B2
Satara		94	B5
Satna		94	D4
Sátoraljaújhely		58	L9
Satti		94	C2
Sättna		52	J5
Satu Mare		58	J3
Satun		92	(1)B1
Sauce		52	K5
Saudi Arabia	▲ 96	96	C4
Sauk Center		40	B1
Saulgau		70	E2
Saulieu		66	K6
Sault Ste. Marie, *Canada*		40	D1
Sault Ste. Marie, *United States*		40	D1

Saumlakki		92	(2)D4
Saumur		66	E6
Saunders Island	◫ 48	48	J9
Saurimo		110	C5
Sauðarkrókur		56	(1)D2
Sava	◪ 70	70	L5
Savaii	◫114	114	J7
Savalou		108	E3
Savannah	◪ 32	32	K6
Savannah, *United States*		42	E3
Savannah, *Tenn., United States*		42	D2
Savannakhet		90	C3
Savaştepe		76	K5
Savè		108	E3
Save	◪112	112	E4
Sāveh		96	F2
Saverne		60	C8
Savigliano		70	C6
Savona		70	D6
Savonlinna		56	Q6
Savu	◫ 92	92	(2)B5
Sawahlunto		92	(1)C3
Sawai Madhopur		94	C3
Sawqirah		96	G6
Sawu Sea	◪ 92	92	(2)B4
Sayanogorsk		82	S7
Sayansk		84	G6
Sayhūt		96	F6
Sāylac		104	H5
Saynshand		86	E2
Sayram Hu	◪ 82	82	Q9
Say'ün		96	E6
Say-Utes		82	J9
Sazan	◪ 76	76	B4
Sazin		96	K2
Scafell Pike	◢ 64	64	J7
Scalea		72	K9
Scarborough		64	M7
Scarp	◫ 64	64	E3
Schaalsee	◪ 60	60	F3
Schaffhausen		70	D3
Schagen		62	G2
Scharbeutz		60	F2
Schärding		70	J2
Scharhörn	◫ 60	60	D3
Scheeßel		60	E3
Schefferville		34	T6
Scheibbs		70	L3
Schelde	◪ 62	62	F3
Schenectady		40	F2
Scheveningen		62	G2
Schiedam		62	G3
Schiermonnikkoog	◪ 62	62	H1
Schio		70	G5
Schiza	◫ 76	76	D8
Schkeuditz		60	H5
Schlei	◪ 60	60	E2
Schleiden		62	J4
Schleswig		60	E2
Schlieben		60	J5
Schlüchtern		60	E6
Schneeberg	◢ 60	60	G6
Schneeberg		60	H6
Schönebeck		60	G4
Schongau		70	F3
Schöningen		60	F4
Schouwen	◫ 62	62	F3
Schramberg		70	D2
Schreiber		40	C1
Schrems		70	L2
Schull		64	C10
Schwabach		60	G7
Schwäbische Alb	◫ 70	70	E2
Schwäbisch-Gmünd		70	E2
Schwäbisch-Hall		60	E7
Schwalmstadt		60	E6
Schwandorf		60	H7
Schwarzenbek		60	F3
Schwarzenberg		60	H6
Schwarzwald	◪ 70	70	D3
Schwaz		70	G3
Schwechat		58	F9
Schwedt		58	D4
Schweich		62	J5
Schweinfurt		60	F6
Schwenningen		70	D2
Schwerin		60	G3
Schweriner See	◪ 60	60	G3
Schwetzingen		60	D7
Schwyz		70	D3
Sciacca		72	H11
Scicli		72	J12
Scobey		38	E1
Scotia Ridge	◪ 52	52	K9
Scotia Sea	◪120	120	(2)A4
Scotland	◨ 64	64	H5
Scott City		38	F3
Scott Inlet	◪ 34	34	T2
Scott Island	◫120	120	(2)Z3
Scott Reef	◫116	116	D2

Scottsbluff		38	F2
Scottsboro		40	C4
Scotty's Junction		44	C1
Scranton		40	E2
Scunthorpe		64	M8
Seal	◪ 34	34	M5
Sea of Azov	◪ 78	78	G5
Sea of Galilee	◪100	100	C4
Sea of Japan	◪ 88	88	G3
Sea of Marmara = Marmara Denizi	◪ 76	76	L4
Sea of Okhotsk	◪ 84	84	Q5
Sea of the Hebrides	◪ 64	64	E4
Searchlight		44	D1
Searcy		40	B3
Seaside		38	B1
Seattle		38	B1
Sebeş		74	L4
Sebkha Azzel Matti	◪106	106	F3
Sebkha de Timimoun	◪106	106	E3
Sebkha de Tindouf	◪106	106	D3
Sebkha Mekerrhane	◪106	106	F3
Sebkha Oum el Drouss Telli	◪106	106	C4
Sebkhet de Chemchâm ...	◪106	106	C4
Sebnitz		60	K6
Sebring		42	E4
Secchia	◪ 70	70	F6
Sechura		50	A5
Secretary Island	◫118	118	A7
Secunderabad		94	C5
Sécure	◪ 50	50	D7
Sedalia		40	B3
Sedan		62	G5
Sedano		68	G2
Seddonville		118	C5
Sede Boqer		100	B6
Sedeh		96	G3
Sederot		100	B5
Sédico		70	H4
Sedom		100	C5
Seeheim		112	B5
Seelow		60	K4
Seesen		60	F5
Seevetal		60	E3
Séez		70	B5
Seferihisar		76	J6
Segamat		92	(1)C2
Segezha		78	F2
Seghnān		96	K2
Ségou		108	C2
Segovia		68	F4
Segré		66	E6
Séguédine		106	H4
Seguin		42	B4
Segura	◪ 68	68	H6
Sehithwa		112	C4
Sehnde		60	E4
Seiland	◫ 56	56	M1
Seiling		42	B2
Seinäjoki		56	M5
Selkirk		36	B1
Selaru	◫ 92	92	(1)E4
Selassi		92	(2)D3
Selat Bangka	◪ 92	92	(1)D3
Selat Berhala	◪ 92	92	(1)C3
Selat Dampir	◪ 92	92	(2)D3
Selat Karimata	◪ 92	92	(1)D3
Selat Makassar	◪ 92	92	(1)F3
Selat Mentawai	◪ 92	92	(1)B3
Selat Sunda	◪ 92	92	(1)D4
Selawik		44	(1)F2
Selb		60	H6
Selby		38	G1
Selçuk		76	K7
Selebi-Phikwe		112	D4
Sélestat		70	C2
Selfoss		56	(1)C3
Seligman		44	D1
Seljord		56	E7
Selkirk		36	B1
Selkirk Mountains	◪ 36	36	C1
Sells		44	D2
Selm		62	K3
Selmer		40	C3
Selpele		92	(2)D3
Selvas	◪ 50	50	C5
Selwyn Lake	◪ 34	34	L5
Selwyn Mountains	◪ 44	44	(1)L3
Semanit	◪ 76	76	B4
Semarang		92	(1)E4
Sematan		92	(1)D2
Sembé		108	G4
Seminoe Reservoir	◪ 38	38	E2
Seminole, *Okla., United States*		38	G3
Seminole, *Tex., United States*		44	F2
Semiozernoye		82	L7
Semipalatinsk		82	Q7
Semiyarka		82	P7
Semois	◪ 62	62	H5

165

Semporna	92	(1)F2
Sena Madureira	50	D5
Senanga	112	C3
Senatobia	42	D3
Sendai	88	L4
Senec	70	N2
Seneca	42	E3
Senegal	▲108	A2
Sénégal	✓108	B1
Senftenberg	60	J5
Senhor do Bonfim	50	J6
Senica	58	G9
Senigallia	70	J7
Senj	70	K6
Senja	⊞ 56	J2
Senlis	62	E5
Sennar	96	B7
Senneterre	40	E1
Sens	66	J5
Senta	74	H4
Seoni	94	C4
Seoul = Sŏul	■ 88	D5
Separation Point	➤118	D5
Sept-Îles	34	T6
Seraing	62	H4
Serakhs	96	H2
Seram	✓ 92	(2)D3
Seram Sea	⊞ 92	(2)C3
Serang	✓ 92	(1)D4
Serbia = Srbija	✓ 74	H6
Serdobsk	78	H4
Serebryansk	82	Q8
Sered'	74	E1
Şereflikoçhisar	76	R6
Seregno	70	E5
Serein	✓ 66	J6
Seremban	92	(1)C2
Serenje	112	E2
Sergelen	86	E1
Sergeyevka	78	N4
Sergipe	▣ 50	K6
Sergiyev Posad	78	G3
Seria	92	(1)E2
Serifos	⊞ 76	G7
Serik	76	P8
Seringapatam Reef	⊞116	D2
Sermata	⊞ 92	(2)C4
Seronga	112	C3
Serov	78	M3
Serowe	112	D4
Serpa	68	C7
Serpukhov	78	G4
Serra Acari	⊠ 50	F3
Serra Curupira	⊠ 50	E3
Serra da Chela	⊠112	A3
Serra da Espinhaço	⊠ 50	J7
Serra da Ibiapaba	⊠ 50	J4
Serra da Mantiqueira	⊠ 52	M3
Serra de Maracaju	⊠ 52	K3
Serra do Cachimbo	⊠ 50	F5
Serra do Caiapó	⊠ 50	G7
Serra do Roncador	⊠ 50	G6
Serra dos Carajás	⊠ 50	G5
Serra dos Dois Irmãos	⊠ 50	J5
Serra dos Parecis	⊠ 50	E6
Serra do Tiracambu	⊠ 50	H4
Serra Estrondo	⊠ 50	H5
Serra Formosa	⊠ 50	F6
Serra Geral de Goiás	⊠ 50	H6
Serra Geral do Paraná	⊠ 50	H7
Serra Lombarda	⊠ 50	G3
Serra Pacaraima	⊠ 50	E3
Serra Parima	⊠ 50	E3
Serra Tumucumaque	⊠ 50	F3
Serre da Estrela	⊠ 68	C4
Serres, France	66	L9
Serres, Greece	76	F3
Serrinha	50	K6
Sertã	68	B5
Serui	92	(2)E3
Servia	76	D4
Sêrxü	86	B4
Sese Islands	⊞110	E4
Sesfontein	112	A3
Sesheke	112	C3
Sessa Aurunca	72	H7
Sestri Levante	70	E6
Sestroretsk	56	Q6
Sestrunj	⊞ 70	K6
Sesvete	70	M5
Setana	88	K2
Sète	66	J10
Sete Lagoas	50	J7
Setesdal	⊠ 56	D7
Sétif	106	D2
Settat	106	D2
Setúbal	68	B6
Sŏul	■114	C2
Seurre	66	L7
Sevana Lich	✓ 84	L3
Sevastopol'	98	E1
Seven Lakes	44	E1

Sevenoaks	62	C3
Severn, Canada	✓ 34	P5
Severn, United Kingdom	✓ 64	K10
Severnaya Dvina	✓ 78	H2
Severnaya Osetiya	▣ 98	L2
Severnaya Zemlya	⊞ 82	U1
Severn Estuary	➤ 64	J10
Severnoye	78	K4
Severnyy	82	L4
Severobaykal'sk	84	H5
Severodvinsk	78	G2
Severomorsk	56	S2
Severoural'sk	78	M2
Severo-Yeniseyskiy	82	S5
Sevier Lake	☑ 38	D3
Sevilla	68	E7
Sevlievo	74	N7
Seward Peninsula	▣◉ 44	(1)E2
Seyakha	82	N3
Seychelles	▲112	(2)B2
Seychelles Islands	⊞102	J6
Seydişehir	76	P7
Seydisfjördur	56	(1)G2
Seyhan	✓ 98	F5
Seymchan	84	S4
Seymour, Australia	116	J7
Seymour, Ind., United States	42	D2
Seymour, Tex., United States	42	B3
Sézanne	66	J5
Sezze	72	H7
Sfakia	76	G9
Sfântu Gheorghe	74	N4
Sfax	106	H2
's-Gravenhage	62	G2
Sha'am	101	G3
Shabunda	110	D4
Shabwah	96	E6
Shache	82	P10
Shädegän	101	C1
Shadehill Reservoir	☑ 38	F1
Shagamu	108	E3
Shagonar	82	S7
Shag Rocks	⊞ 52	N9
Shahbā'	100	D4
Shahdāb	101	G1
Shahdol	94	D4
Shah Fuladi	▲ 96	J3
Shahjahanpur	94	C3
Shahrak	96	H3
Shahr-e Bābāk	101	F1
Shahrtuz	96	J2
Shakhrisabz	96	J2
Shakhtērsk	84	Q7
Shakhty	78	H5
Shakhun'ya	78	J3
Shaki	108	E3
Shakotan-misaki	➤ 88	L2
Shama	✓110	E6
Shamattawa	34	N5
Shamrock	44	F1
Shand	96	H3
Shandong Bandao	◉ 86	G3
Shangani	✓112	D3
Shangdu	86	E2
Shanghai	86	G4
Shangqui	86	F4
Shangrao	86	F5
Shangshi	86	H1
Shangzhou	86	D4
Shantarskiye Ostrova	⊞ 84	P5
Shantou	86	F6
Shanwei	90	F2
Shanyin	86	E3
Shaoguan	86	E6
Shaoxing	86	G5
Shaoyang	86	E5
Shapkina	✓ 78	K1
Shaqrā'	101	A4
Sharga	82	T8
Sharjah = Ash Shāriqah	101	G4
Shark Bay	➤114	B8
Shark Reef	⊞116	J2
Sharm el Sheikh	104	F2
Sharūrah	96	E6
Shashe	✓112	D4
Shashi	✓ 38	B2
Shasta Lake	☑ 38	B2
Shatsk	78	H4
Shatubak	58	N6
Shawano	40	C6
Shcherbakove	84	U3
Shchigry	78	G4
Shchuch'ye	82	L6
Shchuchyn	56	N10
Sheberghān	96	J2
Sheboygan	40	C2
Sheffield, New Zealand	118	D6
Sheffield, United Kingdom	64	L8

Sheffield, Al., United States	40	C4
Sheffield, Tex., United States	44	F2
Shegmas	78	J2
Shelburne	34	T8
Shelby	38	D1
Shelbyville	40	C3
Shelikof Strait	➤ 44	(1)F4
Shenandoah	40	A2
Shendam	108	F3
Shendi	104	F4
Shenkursk	78	H2
Shenyang	88	B3
Shenzhen	86	E6
Shepetivka	78	E4
Shepparton	116	J7
Sherbro Island	⊞108	B3
Sherbrooke	40	F1
Sheridan	38	E2
Sherkaly	78	N2
Sherlovaya Gora	84	K6
Sherman	42	B3
's-Hertogenbosch	62	H3
Shetland Islands	⊞ 64	M1
Shetpe	82	J9
Sheyenne	✓ 38	G1
Sheykh Sho'eyb	⊞101	E3
Shiant Islands	⊞ 64	F4
Shibata	88	K5
Shibetsu, Japan	88	M1
Shibetsu, Japan	88	N2
Shibotsu-jima	⊞ 88	P2
Shiderty	✓ 82	N7
Shihezi	82	R9
Shijiazhuang	86	E3
Shikarpur	96	J4
Shikoku	⊞ 88	G7
Shikoku-sanchi	◉ 88	G7
Shikotan-tō	⊞ 88	P2
Shikotsu-ko	✓ 88	L2
Shiliguri	94	E3
Shilka	84	K6
Shilka	✓ 84	K6
Shillong	94	F3
Shilovo	78	H4
Shimabara	88	F7
Shimla	94	C2
Shimoda	88	K6
Shimoga	94	C6
Shimo-Koshiki-jima	⊞ 88	E8
Shimoni	110	F4
Shimonoseki	88	F7
Shinäs	101	G4
Shindan	96	H3
Shingū	88	H7
Shinjō	88	L4
Shinyanga	110	E4
Shiono-misaki	➤ 88	H7
Shiprock	38	E3
Shiquan	86	D4
Shirakawa	88	L5
Shīrāz	101	E2
Shire	✓112	E3
Shiretoko-misaki	➤ 88	N1
Shiriya-zaki	➤ 88	L3
Shir Kūh	▲ 96	F3
Shivpuri	94	C3
Shiyan	86	E4
Shizuishan	86	D3
Shizuoka	88	K6
Shkodër	74	G7
Shomishko	82	K8
Shorap	96	J4
Shoreham	62	B4
Shoshone, Calif., United States	38	C3
Shoshone, Id., United States	38	D2
Shoshoni	38	E2
Shostka	78	F4
Show Low	44	E2
Shoyna	78	H1
Shreveport	42	C3
Shrewsbury	64	K9
Shuangliao	88	B2
Shuangyashan	84	N7
Shubarkuduk	82	K8
Shulan	88	D1
Shumagin Islands	⊞ 44	(1)E5
Shumen	74	P6
Shumikha	78	M3
Shuqrah	96	E7
Shurchi	96	J2
Shūr Gaz	101	H2
Shurinda	84	J5
Shuryshkary	78	N1
Shuya	78	H3
Shuyang	86	F4
Shwebo	90	B2
Shymkent	82	M9
Sialkot	96	K3

Siatista	76	D4
Šiauliai	58	N2
Sibay	78	L4
Šibenik	74	C6
Siberia = Sibir	⊞ 80	N3
Siberut	⊞ 92	(1)B3
Sibi	96	J4
Sibigo	92	(1)B2
Sibir	⊞ 80	N3
Sibiu	74	M4
Sibolga	92	(1)B2
Sibu	92	(1)E2
Sibuco	90	G5
Sibut	110	B2
Sicilia	⊞ 72	G11
Sicilian Channel	➤ 72	F11
Sicily = Sicilia	⊞ 72	G11
Šid	74	G4
Siddipet	94	C5
Siderno	72	L10
Sidi Barrani	104	E1
Sidi Bel Abbès	106	E1
Sidi Kacem	106	D2
Sidirokastro	76	F3
Sidney	38	F2
Sidoan	92	(2)B2
Sidorovsk	82	Q4
Sieburg	62	K4
Siedlce	58	M5
Sieg	✓ 62	K4
Siegen	62	L4
Siemiatycze	58	M5
Siĕmréab	90	C4
Siena	70	G7
Sierpc	58	J5
Sierra Blanca	44	E2
Sierra Colorada	52	H7
Sierra de Calalasteo	⊠ 52	H4
Sierra de Córdoba	⊠ 52	H5
Sierra de Gata	⊠ 68	D3
Sierra de Gúdar	⊠ 68	K4
Sierra del Nevado	⊠ 52	H6
Sierra de Perijá	⊠ 46	K7
Sierra Grande	52	H7
Sierra Leone	▲108	B3
Sierra Madre	⊠ 46	F5
Sierra Madre del Sur	⊠ 46	E5
Sierra Madre Occidental	⊠ 36	E6
Sierra Madre Oriental	⊠ 44	F3
Sierra Morena	⊠ 68	E6
Sierra Nevada, Spain	⊠ 68	G7
Sierra Nevada, United States	⊠ 44	B1
Sierra Vizcaino	⊠ 36	D6
Sierre	70	C4
Sifnos	⊞ 76	G7
Sig	68	K9
Sigean	66	H10
Sighetu Marmaţiei	74	L2
Sighişoara	74	M3
Siglufjördur	56	(1)D1
Sigmaringen	70	E2
Siguiri	108	C2
Sihanoukville	90	C4
Siilinjärvi	56	P5
Siirt	98	J5
Sikar	94	C3
Sikasso	108	C2
Sikea	76	F4
Sikeston	40	C3
Sikhote Alin	⊠ 88	H1
Sikinos	⊞ 76	G8
Siklós	74	F4
Siktyakh	84	L3
Sil	✓ 68	C2
Šilalé	58	M2
Silandro	70	F4
Silba	⊞ 70	K6
Silchar	94	F4
Šile	76	M3
Silhouette Island	⊞112	(2)B1
Siliana	72	D12
Silifke	98	E5
Siling Co	☑ 94	Q5
Silistra	74	Q5
Silivri	76	L3
Siljan	⊞ 56	H6
Sillamäe	56	P7
Silsbee	42	C3
Siluas	92	(1)D2
Šilutė	58	L2
Silvan	98	J4
Silver Bay	40	B1
Silver City	44	E2
Silver Lake	38	B2
Silver Plains	116	H2
Simanggang	92	(1)E2
Simao	86	C6
Simav	98	C4
Simcoe	40	F2
Simeonovgrad	74	N7

Simeria	**58**	N12	Skien	**56**	E7	Sohâg	**104**	F2	Soubré	**108**	C3
Simeuluë	▣ **92**	(1)A2	Skikda	**106**	G1	Soignies	**62**	G4	Soufli	**76**	J3
Simferopol'	**98**	F1	Skipton	**64**	L8	Soissons	**62**	F5	Souilly	**62**	H5
Şimleu Silvaniei	**74**	K2	Skjern	**56**	E9	Sokch'o	**88**	E4	Souk Ahras	**72**	B12
Simmerath	**62**	J4	Škofja Loka	**70**	K4	Söke	**76**	K7	Sŏul	◼ **88**	D5
Simojärvi	✓ **56**	P3	Skopelos	▣ **76**	F5	Sokhumi	**98**	J2	Soulac-sur-Mer	**66**	D8
Simpang	**92**	(1)C3	Skopje	◼ **74**	J7	Sokode	**108**	E3	Soumussalmi	**56**	Q4
Simpson Desert	◼ **116**	G4	Skövde	**56**	G7	Sokol	**78**	H3	Soûr	**100**	C3
Sinabang	**92**	(1)B2	Skovorodino	**84**	L6	Sokółka	**56**	M10	Soure	**68**	B5
Sinai	◼ **104**	F2	Skowhegan	**40**	G2	Sokolo	**108**	C2	Sour el Ghozlane	**68**	P8
Sinaia	**74**	N4	Skuodas	**56**	L8	Sokolov	**60**	H6	Souris	✓ **36**	F2
Şinak	**98**	K5	Skye	◄ **64**	F4	Sokołów Podlaski	**58**	M5	Souris	**36**	G2
Sinalunga	**72**	F5	Skyros	**76**	G6	Sokoto	**108**	F2	Sousa	**50**	K5
Sinanju	**88**	C4	Skyros	▣ **76**	G6	Sokoto	◼ **108**	F2	Sousse	**106**	H1
Sincelejo	**50**	B2	Slagelse	**60**	G1	Sokyryany	**74**	Q1	South Africa	Ⓐ **112**	C6
Sinclair's Bay	◄ **64**	J3	Slaney	✓ **64**	F9	Solander Island	▣ **118**	A8	Southampton, *Canada*	**40**	D2
Sindangbarang	**92**	(1)D4	Slano	**74**	E7	Solapur	**94**	C5	Southampton,		
Sindelfingen	**60**	E8	Slantsy	**56**	Q7	Sölden	**70**	F4	*United Kingdom*	**62**	A4
Sines	**68**	B7	Slaný	**60**	K6	Solenzara	**72**	D7	Southampton Island	▣ **34**	Q4
Singa	**104**	F5	Slatina	**74**	M5	Solikamsk	**78**	L3	South Andaman	▣ **94**	F6
Singapore	Ⓐ **92**	(1)C2	Slave	✓ **32**	N3	Sol'-Iletsk	**78**	L4	South Atlantic Ocean	◄ **52**	P6
Singapore	◼ **92**	(1)C2	Slave Lake	**34**	J5	Soliman	**72**	E12	South Australia	◼ **116**	F5
Singaraja	**92**	(1)E4	Slavonska Požega	**74**	E4	Solingen	**62**	K3	South Baymouth	**40**	D1
Singen	**70**	D3	Slavonski Brod	**74**	F4	Sollefteå	**56**	J5	South Bend	**40**	C2
Singerei	**74**	R2	Slavyanka	**88**	F2	Soller	**68**	N5	South Boston	**40**	E3
Singida	**110**	E4	Slavyansk-na-Kubani	**98**	H1	Solna	**56**	J7	South Carolina	◼ **42**	E3
Singkawang	**92**	(1)D2	Sławno	**58**	F3	Solomon Islands	Ⓐ **114**	F6	South Charleston	**42**	E2
Singkep	▣ **92**	(1)C3	Sleaford	**62**	B1	Solothurn	**70**	C3	South China Sea	✓ **90**	E4
Singkilbaru	**92**	(1)B2	Sleeper Islands	▣ **34**	Q5	Solov'yevsk	**84**	K6	South Dakota	◼ **38**	F2
Singleton	**116**	K6	Slidell	**42**	D3	Šolta	▣ **74**	D6	South Downs	◄ **62**	B4
Siniscóla	**72**	D8	Sligo	**64**	D7	Soltau	**60**	E4	South East Cape	✓ **116**	J8
Sinj	**74**	D6	Sligo Bay	◄ **64**	D7	Sol'tsy	**78**	F3	South East Point	▣ **116**	J7
Sinjär	**98**	J5	Sliven	**74**	P7	Solway Firth	◄ **64**	J7	Southend-on-Sea	**62**	C3
Sinkat	**104**	G4	Slobozia, *Moldova*	**74**	S3	Solwezi	**112**	D2	Southern Alps	◄ **118**	B6
Sinni	✓ **72**	L8	Slobozia, *Romania*	**74**	Q5	Soma	**76**	K5	Southern Cross	**116**	C6
Sinop	**98**	F2	Slonim	**56**	N10	Sōma	**88**	L5	Southern Indian Lake	✓ **34**	M5
Sinsheim	**60**	D7	Slough	**62**	B3	Somalia	Ⓐ **110**	H2	South Georgia	▣ **52**	P9
Sinton	**42**	B4	Slovakia	Ⓐ **58**	H9	Sombor	**74**	G4	South Harris	◄ **64**	F4
Sinūiju	**88**	C3	Slovenia	Ⓐ **70**	K4	Sombrerete	**44**	F4	South Haven	**40**	C2
Sinyaya	✓ **84**	L4	Slovenj Gradec	**70**	L4	Somerset, *Australia*	**116**	H2	South Hill	**40**	E3
Sió	✓ **74**	F3	Slovenska Bistrica	**70**	L4	Somerset, *Ky.,*			South Island	**118**	B6
Siófok	**74**	F3	Slov''yans'k	**78**	G5	*United States*	**40**	C3	South Korea	Ⓐ **88**	D5
Sion	**70**	C4	Słubice	**58**	D5	Somerset, *Pa.,*			South Lake Tahoe	**38**	B3
Sioux City	**40**	A2	Slunj	**70**	L5	*United States*	**40**	E2	South Orkney Islands	▣ **120**	(2)A3
Sioux Falls	**40**	A2	Słupca	**58**	G5	Somerset Island	▣ **34**	M4	South Pacific Ocean	✓ **52**	P6
Sioux Lookout	**36**	H2	Słupsk	**58**	G3	Someş	✓ **74**	K2	South Platte	✓ **38**	F2
Siping	**88**	C2	Slutsk	**78**	E4	Somme	✓ **62**	E4	Southport	**64**	J8
Sipiwesk	**34**	M5	Slyudyanka	**84**	G6	Sommen	✓ **56**	H8	South Ronaldsay	▣ **64**	K3
Sipura	▣ **92**	(1)B3	Smålandsfarvandet	◄ **60**	G1	Sömmerda	**60**	G5	South Sandwich Islands	▣ **120**	(2)C4
Sira	✓ **56**	D7	Smallwood Reservoir	✓ **34**	U6	Sømna	◼ **56**	F4	South Sandwich Trench	◼ **48**	H9
Siracusa	**72**	K11	Smargon'	**56**	P9	Sondags	✓ **112**	D6	South Saskatchewan	✓ **36**	D1
Sir Baní 'Yās	◼ **101**	E4	Smederevo	**74**	H5	Sønderborg Ærø	**60**	E2	South Shetland Islands	▣ **120**	
Sir Edward Pellew			Smila	**78**	F5	Sondershausen	**60**	F5			(2)MM4
Group	▣ **116**	G3	Smirnykh	**84**	Q7	Sóndrio	**70**	E4	South Shields	**64**	L7
Siret	**74**	P2	Smiths Falls	**40**	E2	Songavatn	✓ **56**	D7	South Taranaki Bight	◄ **118**	D4
Siret	✓ **74**	Q4	Smokey Hills	◄ **42**	B2	Songea	**110**	F6	South Uist	◄ **64**	E4
Sïrgän	**96**	H4	Smoky	✓ **34**	H6	Song Hông	✓ **90**	C2	South West Cape,		
Şiria	**58**	L11	Smøla	▣ **56**	D5	Songhua	✓ **86**	H1	*Auckland Island*	▣ **118**	(2)A1
Siri Kit Dam	✓ **90**	B3	Smolensk	**78**	F4	Songhua Hu	✓ **88**	D2	South West Cape,		
Sirk	**101**	G3	Smolyan	**76**	G3	Songhua Jiang	✓ **88**	D1	*Australia*	▣ **116**	H8
Sirohi	**94**	B4	Smooth Rock Falls	**40**	D1	Songkan	**86**	D5	Southwest Cape	▣ **118**	A8
Sirsa	**94**	C3	Smyrna	**42**	E3	Songkhla	**90**	C5	South West Pacific		
Sirsi	**94**	B6	Snæfell	◄ **56**	(1)F2	Songnam	**88**	D5	Basin	◄ **114**	L9
Sisak	**74**	D4	Snake	✓ **38**	C1	Songnim	**88**	C4	Southwold	**62**	D2
Sisian	**98**	L4	Snake River Plain	◄ **38**	D2	Songo	**112**	E3	Sovata	**74**	N3
Sisimiut	**34**	W3	Snåsavatnet	✓ **56**	F4	Songololo	**108**	G6	Sovetsk, *Russia*	**56**	L9
Sisŏphŏn	**90**	C4	Sneek	**62**	H1	Songpan	**86**	C4	Sovetsk, *Russia*	**78**	J3
Sisseton	**38**	G1	Snezhnogorsk	**82**	R4	Sonid Yuoqi	**86**	E2	Soweto	**112**	D5
Sistema Central	◄ **68**	E4	Snežnik	◄ **70**	K5	Sonid Zuoqi	**86**	E2	Sōya-misaki	◼ **88**	L1
Sistema Ibérico	◄ **68**	H3	Snina	**58**	M9	Son La	**90**	C2	Sozopol	**74**	Q7
Sisteron	**70**	A6	Snøhetta	◄ **56**	E5	Sonneberg	**60**	G6	Spa	**62**	H4
Sitapur	**94**	D3	Snøtinden	◄ **56**	G3	Sono	✓ **50**	H6	Spain	Ⓐ **68**	F5
Sitasjaure	✓ **56**	J3	Snowdon	◄ **64**	H8	Sonora	**44**	B1	Spalding	**62**	B2
Siteia	**76**	J9	Snowdrift	**34**	J4	Sonora	✓ **44**	D3	Sparks	**44**	C1
Sitges	**68**	M3	Snowville	**38**	D2	Sonoyta	**44**	D2	Spartanburg	**42**	E3
Sithonia	▣ **76**	F4	Snyder	**44**	F2	Sonsorol Islands	▣ **92**	(2)D1	Sparti	**76**	E7
Sitka	**34**	D5	Soalala	**112**	H3	Sonthofen	**70**	F3	Sparwood	**38**	D1
Sittard	**62**	H4	Soanierana-Ivongo	**112**	H3	Sopot	**56**	K9	Spassk-Dal'niy	**88**	G1
Sittwe	**94**	F4	Soa-Siu	**92**	(2)C2	Sopron	**70**	M3	Spearfish	**38**	F2
Sivand	**101**	E1	Sobral	**50**	J4	Sora	**72**	H7	Spencer	**40**	A2
Sivas	**98**	G4	Sochaczew	**58**	K5	Soracaba	**52**	M3	Spencer Gulf	◄ **116**	G7
Siverek	**98**	H5	Sochaux	**70**	B3	Sorel	**40**	F1	Spetses	▣ **76**	F7
Sivrihisar	**76**	P5	Sochi	**98**	H2	Sorgun	**98**	F4	Spey	✓ **64**	J4
Siwa	**104**	E1	Socorro	**44**	E2	Soria	**68**	H3	Speyer	**62**	L5
Siyäzän	**98**	N3	Socotra = Suquţrä	▣ **96**	F7	Sørø	**60**	G1	Spiekeroog	▣ **60**	C3
Sjælland	▣ **56**	F2	Socuéllamos	**68**	H5	Soroca	**74**	R1	Spiez	**70**	C4
Sjenica	**74**	H6	Sodankylä	**56**	P3	Sorochinsk	**78**	K4	Spišska Nová Ves	**58**	K9
Sjenica Jezero	✓ **74**	G6	Söderhamn	**56**	J6	Sorong	**92**	(2)D3	Spitsbergen	▣ **120**	(1)P2
Sjöbo	**58**	C2	Södertälje	**56**	J7	Soroti	**110**	E3	Spittal	**70**	J4
Skädldervíken	◄ **58**	B1	Sodo	**110**	F2	Sørøya	▣ **56**	L1	Split	**74**	D6
Skaerbaek	**60**	D1	Soe	**92**	(2)B4	Sorrentó	**72**	J8	Spokane	**38**	C1
Skagen	**56**	F8	Soest	**62**	L3	Sorsele	**56**	J4	Spoleto	**72**	G6
Skagerrak	◄ **56**	E6	Sofia = Sofiya	◼ **74**	L7	Sorso	**72**	C8	Spooner	**40**	B1
Skantzoura	▣ **76**	G5	Sofiya	◼ **74**	L7	Sort	**68**	M2	Sprague	**38**	C1
Skardu	**96**	L2	Sofiysk, *Russia*	**84**	N6	Sortavala	**56**	R6	Spratly Islands	▣ **90**	E4
Skaulo	**56**	L3	Sofiysk, *Russia*	**84**	P6	Sørvagen	**56**	G3	Spray	**38**	C2
Skawina	**58**	J8	Soforog	**56**	R4	Sosnogorsk	**82**	J5	Spree	✓ **60**	K4
Skegness	**62**	C1	Söfu-gan	**86**	L5	Sosnovo	**56**	R6	Spremberg	**60**	K5
Skellefteä	**56**	L4	Sogamoso	**50**	C2	Sosnowiec	**58**	J7	Spring	**42**	B3
Ski	**56**	F7	Sognefjorden	◄ **56**	C6	Sos'va	**78**	M3	Springbok	**112**	B5
Skiathos	▣ **76**	F5	Sogod	**90**	G4	Sos'vinskaya	**78**	M2	Springe	**60**	E4
Skidal'	**58**	P4	Sog Xian	**94**	F2	Soto la Marina	**44**	G4	Springer	**44**	F1

Springerville **44** E2
Springfield, Colo.,
  United States **44** F1
Springfield, Ill.,
  United States . . . . . ☐ **40** C3
Springfield, Mass.,
  United States **40** F2
Springfield, Mo.,
  United States **40** B3
Springfield, Oh.,
  United States **40** D3
Springfield, Oreg.,
  United States **38** B2
Springfield, Vt.,
  United States **40** F2
Spring Hill **42** E4
Springs **112** D5
Springs Junction **118** D6
Springsure **116** J4
Springville, Al.,
  United States **42** D3
Springville, N.Y.,
  United States **40** E2
Squamish **38** B1
Squinzano **72** N8
Srbija . . . . ▣ **74** H6
Srbobran **74** G4
Sredenekolymsk **84** S3
Sredinnyy Khrebet . . . . ▲ **84** T6
Srednesibirskoye
  Ploskogor'ye . . . . . ▣ **84** F3
Srednogorie **76** G2
Šrem **58** G5
Sretensk **84** K6
Srikakulam **94** D5
Sri Lanka . . . . ▣ **94** D7
Srinagar **94** B2
Stack Skerry . . . . ▣ **64** H2
Stade **56** E10
Stadlandet . . . . ▣ **56** C5
Stadskanaal **62** J2
Stadtallendorf **60** E6
Stadthagen **60** E4
Staffa . . . . ▣ **64** F6
Staffelstein **60** F6
Stafford **64** K9
Staines **62** B3
Stainz **70** L4
Stakhanov **78** G5
Stalowa Wola **58** M7
Stambolijski **76** G2
Stamford,
  United Kingdom . . . **62** B2
Stamford, United States . . . **40** F2
Standish **40** D2
Stanford **40** D3
Stanke Dimitrov **76** F2
Stanley, Australia **116** J8
Stanley, Falkland Islands . . **52** K9
Stanley, United States . . **38** F1
Stanovaya **84** T3
Stanovoye Nagor'ye . . . ▣ **84** J5
Stanovoy Khrebet . . . . ▲ **84** L5
Staphorst **62** J2
Stapleton **38** F2
Starachowice **58** L6
Stara L'ubovňa **58** K8
Stara Pazova **74** H5
Stara Planina . . . . ▲ **76** F1
Staraya Russa **78** F3
Stara Zagora **74** N7
Starbuck Island . . . . . ▣ **114** L6
Stargard Szczeciński . . . **56** H10
Starkville **42** D3
Starnberg **70** G2
Starnberger See . . . . . ◪ **70** G3
Start Point . . . . ▷ **66** B3
Staryy Oskol **78** G4
Staszów **58** L7
Statesboro **42** E3
Statesville **42** E2
Staunton **42** F2
Stavanger **56** C7
Stavoron **62** H2
Stavropol' **98** J1
Stavropol'skaya
  Vovyshennost' . . . ▣ **78** H5
Steamboat Springs **38** E2
Steens Mountains . . . ▲ **38** C2
Stefansson Island . . . ▣ **34** L2
Stege **60** H1
Štei **74** K3
Stein **60** G7
Steinach **70** G3
Steinfurt **62** K2
Steinjker **56** F4
Stenay **62** H5
Stendal **60** G4
Steno Antikythiro . . . . ▷ **76** F9
Stephenville **42** B3
Sterling **38** F2
Sterling City **44** F2

Sterling Heights **40** D2
Sterlitamak **78** L4
Sternberk **58** G8
Stettiner Haff . . . . ▷ **56** G10
Stevenage **62** B3
Stevens Point **40** C2
Stevens Village . . . . . . **44** (1)H2
Stewart **34** F5
Stewart . . . . ▨ **44** (1)K3
Stewart Island . . . . . . ▣ **118** A8
Steyr **70** K2
Stillwater **42** B2
Stinnett **44** F1
Štip **76** E3
Stirling **64** J5
Stjørdal **56** F5
Stockach **70** E3
Stockerau **70** M2
Stockholm . . . . ▣ **56** K7
Stockport **64** K8
Stockton, Calif.,
  United States **44** B1
Stockton, Kans.,
  United States **44** G1
Stockton-on-Tees **64** L7
Stŏng Trêng **90** D4
Stoke-on-Trent **64** K8
Stokksnes . . . . ▣ **56** (1)F2
Stolac **74** F6
Stolberg **62** J4
Stolin **78** E4
Stollberg **60** H6
Stonehaven **64** K5
Stony Rapids **34** K5
Stör . . . . ▨ **60** E2
Stora Lulevatten . . . . . ◪ **56** K3
Stord . . . . ▣ **56** C7
Store Bælt . . . . ▷ **60** F1
Størlien **56** F5
Store Sotra . . . . ▣ **56** B6
Størlien **56** G5
Storm Bay . . . . ▷ **116** J8
Storm Lake **40** A2
Stornoway **64** F3
Storozhevsk **78** K2
Storozhynets' **74** N1
Storsjøen . . . . ◪ **56** F6
Storsjön, Sweden . . . . ◪ **56** G5
Storsjön, Sweden . . . . ◪ **56** J6
Storuman **56** J4
Storuman . . . . ◪ **56** J4
Stour . . . . ▨ **62** C2
Stowmarket **62** D2
Strabane **64** E7
Stradella **70** E5
Strait of Belle Isle . . . . ▷ **34** V6
Strait of Bonifacio . . . . ▷ **72** D7
Strait of Dover . . . . . . ▷ **62** D4
Strait of Georgia . . . . . ▷ **38** B1
Strait of Gibraltar . . . . ▷ **68** E9
Strait of Hormuz . . . . . ▷ **101** G3
Strait of Juan de Fuca . . ▷ **38** B1
Strait of Malacca . . . . ▷ **92** (1)C2
Straits of Florida . . . . . ▷ **42** E5
Strakonice **60** J7
Stralsund **56** G9
Strand **112** B6
Stranda **56** D5
Strandavatn . . . . ◪ **56** D6
Stranraer **64** H7
Strasbourg **70** C2
Strasburg **44** F1
Strășeni **74** R2
Stratford, Canada **40** D2
Stratford, United States . . **38** F3
Stratford-upon-Avon . . . **62** A2
Strathroy **40** D2
Stratoni **76** F4
Stratton **40** F1
Straubing **70** H2
Straumnes . . . . ▷ **56** (1)B1
Strausberg **60** J4
Streaky Bay **116** F6
Streator **40** C2
Strehaia **74** L5
Strelka, Russia **84** E5
Strelka, Russia **84** S4
Strezhevoy **78** Q2
Strimonas . . . . ▨ **76** F4
Strofades . . . . ▣ **76** C7
Stròmboli . . . . ▣ **72** K10
Strömsund **56** H5
Stronsay . . . . ▣ **64** K2
Stroud **64** K10
Struga **76** C3
Strugi-Krasnyye **56** Q2
Strumica **76** E3
Stryjama . . . . ▨ **74** M7
Stryy **58** N8
Stryy . . . . ▨ **58** N8
Strzegom **58** F7
Strzelce Opolskie **58** H7

Strzelin **58** G7
Sturgeon Bay **40** C2
Sturgeon Falls **40** E1
Sturgis, Ky.,
  United States **40** C3
Sturgis, S.D.,
  United States **38** F2
Sturkö . . . . ▣ **58** E1
Šturova **58** H10
Sturt Stony Desert . . . ▣ **116** G5
Stuttgart, Germany **70** E2
Stuttgart, United States . . **42** C3
Stykkishólmur . . . . **56** (1)B2
Suai . . . . **92** (2)C4
Suakin **104** G4
Subcule . . . . ▲ **104** H5
Subi Besar . . . . ▣ **92** (1)D2
Sublette **44** F1
Subotica **74** G3
Suceava **74** P2
Suck . . . . ▨ **64** D8
Sucre . . . . ▣ **50** D7
Sudak **98** F1
Sudan . . . . ▲ **104** E5
Sudan . . . . ▣ **108** D2
Suday **78** H3
Sudbury, Canada **40** D1
Sudbury,
  United Kingdom . . . **62** C2
Sudd . . . . ▣ **110** E2
Sudová Vyshnya **58** N8
Suez = El Suweis **104** F2
Suez Canal . . . . ▨ **104** F1
Suffolk **42** F2
Sugun **96** L2
Suḩār **101** G4
Suhl **60** F6
Suide **86** E3
Suifenhe **88** F1
Suihua **84** M7
Suippes **62** G5
Suir . . . . ▨ **64** E9
Suixi **86** E6
Suizhong **86** G2
Suizhou **86** E4
Sukabumi . . . . **92** (1)D4
Sukadana . . . . **92** (1)D3
Sukhinichi **78** G4
Sukhona . . . . ▨ **78** H3
Sukkertoppen =
  Maniitsoq **34** W3
Sukkur **96** J4
Sula **78** K1
Sula . . . . ▨ **78** K1
Sula Sgeir . . . . ▣ **64** F2
Sulawesi . . . . ▣ **92** (2)A3
Sulejówek **58** L5
Sule Skerry . . . . ▣ **64** H2
Sulgachi **84** N4
Sulina **74** S4
Sulingen **62** L2
Sullana **50** A4
Sullivan **42** C2
Sulmona **72** H6
Sulphur Springs **42** B3
Sultanhani **76** R6
Sultanpur **94** D3
Sulu Archipelago . . . . ▣ **90** G5
Sulu Sea . . . . ▷ **90** F5
Sulzbach **62** K5
Sulzbach-Rosenberg . . . **60** G7
Sulzberger Bay . . . . . ▷ **120** (2)CC2
Sumatera = Sumatera . . ▣ **92** (1)C2
Sumatra = Sumatera . . . ▣ **92** (1)C2
Sumba . . . . ▣ **92** (2)A5
Sumbawa . . . . ▣ **92** (2)A4
Sumbawabesar . . . . . . **92** (2)A4
Sumbawanga **110** E5
Sumbe **112** A2
Šumen **98** B2
Sumenep . . . . **92** (1)E4
Sumisu-jima . . . . ▣ **88** L8
Sumkino **78** N3
Summer Lake . . . . . . ◪ **38** B2
Summerville **42** E3
Summit **34** B4
Šumperk **58** G8
Sumqayit **98** N3
Sumter **42** E3
Sumy **78** F4
Sunbury **40** E2
Sunch'ŏn **88** D6
Sun City **112** D5
Sundance **38** F2
Sundarbans . . . . ▣ **94** E4
Sunday Strait . . . . ▷ **116** D3
Sunderland **64** L7
Sundridge **40** E1
Sundsvall **56** J5
Sundsvallsbukten . . . . ▷ **56** J5
Sungaipenuh . . . . **92** (1)C3
Sungei Petani **90** C5

Sunnyvale **38** B3
Sun Prairie **40** C2
Suntar **84** K4
Suntsar **96** H4
Sunwu **84** M7
Sunyani **108** D3
Suomussalmi **78** E2
Suŏ-nada . . . . ▷ **88** F7
Suonenjoki **56** P5
Suordakh **84** P3
Suoyarvi **78** F2
Superior **36** H2
Supetar **74** D6
Süphan Daği . . . . ▲ **98** K4
Süqash Shuyūkh **101** B1
Suqian **86** F4
Suqutrā . . . . ▣ **96** F7
Sür **96** G5
Sura . . . . ▨ **78** J4
Surab **96** J4
Surabaya . . . . **92** (1)E4
Sürak **101** H4
Surakarta . . . . **92** (1)E4
Šurany **74** F1
Surat **94** B4
Surat Thani **90** B5
Surdulica **74** K7
Sûre . . . . ▨ **62** H5
Surfers Paradise **116** K5
Surgut **82** N5
Surgutikha **82** R5
Surigao **90** H5
Surin **90** C4
Surinam . . . . ▲ **50** F3
Surkhet **94** D3
Sürmaq **101** E1
Surovikino **78** H5
Surskoye **78** J4
Surt **106** J2
Surtsey . . . . ▣ **56** (1)C3
Susa **70** C5
Şuşa **98** M4
Sušac . . . . ▣ **74** D7
Susak . . . . ▣ **70** K6
Susanville **38** B2
Suşehri **98** H3
Sušice **60** J7
Susitma . . . . ▨ **44** (1)G3
Susuman **84** R4
Susurluk **76** L5
Sutherland **112** C6
Sutlej . . . . ▨ **94** B3
Suusamyr **82** N9
Suva . . . . ▣ **114** J6
Suvorov Island . . . . . . ▣ **114** K7
Suwałki **58** M3
Suwannaphum **90** C3
Suweilih **100** C4
Suweima **100** C5
Suwŏn **88** D5
Suzak **78** N6
Suzhou, China **86** F4
Suzhou, China **86** G4
Suzuka **88** J6
Suzu-misaki . . . . ▷ **88** J5
Svalbard . . . . ▣ **120** (1)Q2
Svalyava **74** L1
Svartenhuk Halvø . . . . ▣ **34** V2
Svatove **78** G5
Sveg **56** H5
Svendborg **56** F9
Šventoji . . . . ▨ **56** M6
Sverdrup Islands . . . . ▣ **120** (1)DD2
Svetac . . . . ▣ **74** C6
Sveti Nikole **76** D3
Svetlaya **84** P7
Svetlogorsk **58** K3
Svetlograd **98** K1
Svetlyy, Russia **58** J3
Svetlyy, Russia **82** L7
Svidnik **58** L8
Svilengrad **76** J3
Svishtov **74** N6
Svitava . . . . ▨ **58** F8
Svitavy **58** F8
Svobodnyy **84** M6
Svratka . . . . ▨ **58** F8
Svyetlahorsk **78** E4
Swain Reefs . . . . ▣ **116** K4
Swains Island . . . . . . ▣ **114** J7
Swakopmund **112** A4
Swale . . . . ▨ **64** K7
Swan . . . . ▣ **48** G3
Swan Hill **116** H7
Swan Islands . . . . ▣ **46** H5
Swan River **34** L6
Swansea, Australia **116** J4
Swansea, United Kingdom . . **64** J10
Swaziland . . . . ▲ **112** E5
Sweden . . . . ▣ **56** H6
Sweetwater **44** F2
Swider . . . . ▨ **58** L5

Name		Ref
Świdnica	58	F7
Świdnik	58	M6
Świdwin	58	E4
Świebodzin	58	E5
Swift Current	36	E1
Swindon	62	A3
Świnoujście	56	H10
Switzerland ▲	70	C4
Syalakh	84	L3
Syamzha	78	H2
Sydney, *Australia* ◉	116	K6
Sydney, *Canada*	34	U7
Syke	62	L2
Syktyvkar ◉	78	K2
Sylacauga	42	D3
Sylhet	94	F4
Sylt 〰	56	E9
Sylvania	40	D2
Sym	82	R5
Sym ⊿	82	R5
Symi 〰	76	K8
Synya	78	L1
Syracuse, *Kans., United States*	44	F1
Syracuse, *N.Y., United States*	40	E2
Syrdar'ya	96	J1
Syrdar'ya ⊿	82	L8
Syria ▲	96	C3
Syrian Desert = Bādiyat ash Shām 〰	100	D4
Syrna 〰	76	J8
Syros 〰	76	G7
Sytomino	78	P2
Syzran'	78	J4
Szamos ⊿	74	K1
Szamotuły	58	F5
Szarvas	58	K11
Szczecin	58	D4
Szczecinek	58	E4
Szczytno	58	K4
Szeged	74	H3
Szeghalom	74	J2
Székesfehérvár	74	F2
Szekszárd	74	F3
Szentendre	74	G2
Szentes	74	H3
Szerencs	58	L9
Szigetvár	74	E3
Szolnok	74	H2
Szombathely	74	D2
Szprotawa	58	E6

T

Name		Ref
Tab	74	F3
Tabarka	72	C12
Tabas	96	G3
Taber	38	D1
Table Cape 〰	118	G4
Tabong	94	G3
Tábor	58	D8
Tabor	84	B2
Tabora	110	E5
Tabou	108	C4
Tabrīz	98	M4
Tabuaeran 〰	114	K5
Tabūk	96	C4
Tacheng	82	Q8
Tachov	60	H7
Tacloban	90	H4
Tacna	50	C7
Tacoma	36	B2
Tacuarembó	52	K5
Tacurong	92	(2)B1
Tadjoura	104	H5
Tadmur	98	H6
Tadoussac	40	G1
Taech'ŏn	88	D5
Taegu	88	E4
Taejon	86	H3
Tafahi 〰	114	J7
Tafalla	68	J2
Tafila	100	C6
Tafi Viejo	52	H4
Tahoka	44	F2
Tahoua	108	F2
Tahrūd	101	G2
Tai'an	86	F3
T'ai-chung	86	G6
Taihape	118	E4
Taihe	86	E5
Taikeng	86	E4

Name		Ref
Tailem Bend	116	G7
Tain	64	H4
T'ai-nan	86	G6
T'ai-Pei ■	86	G6
Taiping	92	(1)C1
Taipingchuan	88	B1
T'ai-tung	90	G2
Taivalkoski	56	Q4
Taiwan ▲	90	G2
Taiwan Strait ⊵	90	F2
Taiyuan	86	E3
Taizhou	86	F4
Ta'izz	96	D7
Tajikistan ▲	96	J2
Tajima	88	K5
Tajo ⊿	54	D3
Tak	90	B3
Takaka	118	D5
Takamatsu	88	H6
Takaoka	88	J5
Takapuna	118	E3
Takasaki	88	K5
Takayama	88	J5
Takefu	88	J6
Takengon	92	(1)B2
Takestán	96	E2
Takht	84	P6
Takhta-Bazar	96	H2
Takhtabrod	82	M7
Takhtakupyr	82	L9
Takijuq Lake ⊿	34	J3
Takikawa	88	L2
Takoradi	108	D4
Taksimo	84	J5
Takua Pa	90	B5
Takum	108	G3
Talak 〰	106	F5
Talara	50	A4
Talas	82	N9
Tal'at Mūsá ▲	98	G6
Talavera de la Reina	68	F5
Talaya	84	S4
Talbotton	42	E3
Talca	52	G6
Talcahuano	52	G6
Taldykorgan	82	P9
Tālesh	96	E2
Taliabu 〰	92	(2)B3
Talibon	90	G4
Talitsa	78	M3
Tall 'Afar	98	K5
Tallahassee ◉	42	E3
Tallaimannar	94	C7
Tall al Laḥm	101	B1
Tallinn ■	56	N7
Tall Kalakh	100	D2
Tallulah	36	H5
Tall 'Uwaynāt	98	K5
Tālmaciu	74	M4
Tal'menka	82	Q7
Talon	84	R5
Tāloqān	82	N10
Taloyoak	34	N3
Talsi	56	M8
Taltal	52	G4
Tama	40	B2
Tamale	108	D3
Tamanrasset	106	G4
Tamanthi	94	G3
Tamási	74	F3
Tamazunchale	36	G7
Tambacounda	108	B2
Tambey	82	N3
Tambo	116	J4
Tambov	78	H4
Tambu	92	(2)A3
Tambura	110	D2
Tampa	42	E4
Tampere	56	M6
Tampico	46	E4
Tamsagbulag	86	F1
Tamsweg	70	J3
Tamworth, *Australia*	116	K6
Tamworth, *United Kingdom*	62	A2
Tana, *Kenya* ⊿	110	G4
Tana, *Norway* ⊿	56	P2
Tanabe	88	H7
Tanacross	44	(1)J3
Tanafjorden ⊵	56	Q1
Tanaga Island 〰	44	(3)C1
T'ana Häyk' ⊿	104	G5
Tanahgrogot	92	(1)F3
Tanahjampea 〰	92	(2)A4
Tanahmerah	92	(2)F4
Tanami	116	E4
Tanami Desert 〰	116	F3
Tánaro ⊿	70	C6
Tandag	90	H5
Tándärei	74	Q5
Tandil	52	K6
Tanega-shima 〰	88	F8

Name		Ref
Tanew ⊿	58	M7
Tanezrouft 〰	106	E4
Tanga, *Russia*	84	J6
Tanga, *Tanzania*	110	F5
Tanger	106	D1
Tangermünde	60	G4
Tanggu	86	F3
Tangmai	94	G2
Tangra Yumco ⊿	94	E2
Tangshan	86	F3
Tanimbar 〰	114	D6
Tanjona Ankaboa ⊵	112	G4
Tanjona Bobaomby ⊵	112	H2
Tanjona Masoala ⊵	112	J3
Tanjona Vilanandro ⊵	112	G3
Tanjona Vohimena ⊵	112	H5
Tanjung	92	(1)F3
Tanjungbalai	92	(1)B2
Tanjung Cangkuang ⊵	92	(1)C4
Tanjung Datu ⊵	92	(1)D2
Tanjung d'Urville ⊵	92	(2)E3
Tanjungkarang Telukbetung	92	(1)D4
Tanjung Libobo ⊵	92	(2)C3
Tanjung Mengkalihat ⊵	92	(1)F2
Tanjungpandan	92	(1)D3
Tanjung Puting ⊵	92	(1)E3
Tanjungredeb	92	(1)F2
Tanjung Selatan ⊵	92	(1)E3
Tanjungselor	92	(1)F2
Tanjung Vals ⊵	92	(2)E4
Tankovo	82	R5
Tankse	94	C2
Tanlovo	78	P1
Tanney	62	G5
Tanout	108	F2
Tanta	104	F1
Tan-Tan	106	C3
Tanzania ▲	110	E5
Tao'an	86	G1
Taomasina	112	H3
Taongi 〰	114	J4
Taormina	72	K11
Taos	44	E1
Taoudenni	106	E5
Taourirt	106	E2
T'ao-yuan	90	G2
Tapa	56	N7
Tapachula	46	F6
Tapajós ⊿	50	F4
Tapauá	50	E5
Tapolca	74	E3
Tappahannock	42	F2
Tapsuy ⊿	78	M2
Tapuaenuku ▲	118	D6
Taquarí ⊿	50	F7
Tara ⊿	78	Q3
Tara	82	N6
Tarābulus ◉	106	H2
Taracua	50	D3
Tarāghin	106	H3
Tarakan	90	F6
Taran	82	N3
Taranaki = Mount Egmont ▲	118	E4
Tarancón	68	H5
Taranto	72	M8
Tarapoto	50	B5
Tarare	66	K8
Tarascon	66	K10
Tarauacá	50	C5
Tarauacá ⊿	50	C5
Tarawa 〰	114	H5
Tarawera Lake ⊿	118	F4
Tarazona	68	J3
Tarbes	66	F10
Tarcoola	116	F6
Taree	116	K6
Tarfaya	106	C3
Târgovişte	74	N5
Târgu Frumos	74	Q2
Târgu Jiu	74	L4
Târgu Lăpuş	74	L2
Târgu Mureş	74	M3
Târgu-Neamţ	74	P2
Târgu Ocna	74	P3
Târgu Secuiesc	74	P3
Tarhunah	106	H2
Tarif	101	E4
Tarifa	68	E8
Tarija	52	J3
Tarime	96	E6
Tarim ⊿	82	Q9
Tarim Pendi	82	Q10
Tarīn Kowt	96	J3
Tariskay Shan	82	Q9
Taritatu ⊿	92	(2)E3
Tarko Sale	82	P5
Tarlac	90	G3
Tarn ⊿	66	H10
Tarna ⊿	58	K10

Name		Ref
Tärnaby	56	H4
Tärnäveni	74	M3
Tarnogskiy Gorodok	78	H2
Tárnovo	76	K2
Tarnów	58	K7
Tarnowskie Góry	58	H7
Taro ⊿	70	E6
Taroom	116	J5
Taroudannt	106	D2
Tarquínia	72	F6
Tarragona	68	M3
Tarras	118	B7
Tárrega	68	M3
Tarso Emissi ▲	104	C3
Tarsus	98	F5
Tartagal	52	J3
Tartu	56	P7
Ţarţūs	100	C2
Tarutyne	74	S3
Tarvisio	70	J4
Tasbuget	78	N6
Tashigang	94	F3
Tashir	98	L3
Tashkent ■	82	M9
Tash-Kömür	82	N9
Tashtagol	82	R7
Tasiilaq	34	Z3
Tasikmalaya	92	(1)D4
Taskesken	82	Q8
Tasman Bay ⊵	118	D5
Tasmania 〰	114	E10
Tasmania	116	H8
Tasman Mountains ▲	118	D5
Tasman Sea ⊵	118	B3
Tăşnad	74	K2
Taşova	98	G3
Tassili du Hoggar 〰	106	F4
Tassili-n'-Ajjer 〰	106	G3
Tasty	82	M9
Tata, *Hungary*	74	F2
Tata, *Morocco*	106	D3
Tatabánya	74	F2
Tatarbunary	74	S4
Tatariya 〰	78	J3
Tatarsk	82	P6
Tatarskiy Proliv ⊵	84	P7
Tateyama	88	K6
Tathlina Lake ⊿	34	H4
Tatta	94	J5
Tatvan	98	K4
Tauá	50	J5
Tauberbischofsheim	60	E7
Tauern ▲	70	J4
Taumarunui	118	E4
Taungdwingyi	90	B2
Taung-gyi	94	G4
Taungup	94	F5
Taunsa	94	B2
Taunton, *United Kingdom*	64	J10
Taunton, *United States*	40	F2
Taunus ◉	62	L4
Taunusstein	62	L4
Taupo	118	F4
Tauragè	58	M2
Tauranga	118	F3
Tauroa Point ⊵	118	D2
Tavda	78	N3
Tavda ⊿	78	N3
Tavira	68	C7
Tavoy	90	B4
Tavşanli	98	C4
Taw ⊿	64	J11
Tawas City	40	D2
Tawau	92	(1)F2
Tawitawi 〰	92	(1)F1
Taxkorgan	82	P10
Tay ⊿	64	J5
Tayga	82	R6
Taylorville	42	D2
Taym	96	C4
Taymä'	104	G2
Taymura ⊿	84	F4
Taymylyr	84	L2
Tay Ninh	90	D4
Tayshet	84	F5
Tayuan	74	L6
Tayyebād	96	H3
Taza	98	E2
Tazeh Kand	98	M4
Tazenakht	106	D2
Tāzirbū	104	D2
Tazovskiy	82	P4
Tazovskiy Poluostrov ◉	82	N4
Tazungdam	90	B1
T'bilisi ■	98	L3
Tchamba	108	G3
Tchibanga	108	G5
Tchin Tabaradene	106	G5
Tczew	58	H3
Te Anau	118	A7
Te Araroa	118	G3
Te Aroha	118	E3

Name	Page	Grid
Te Awamutu	118	E4
Teberda	98	J2
Tébessa	106	G1
Tebingtinggi	92	(1)B2
Téboursouk	72	D12
Techa	78	M3
Techiman	108	D3
Tecuala	44	D4
Tecuci	74	Q4
Tedzhen	96	H2
Tees	64	L7
Tegal	92	(1)D4
Tegernsee	70	G3
Tegina	108	F2
Tegucigalpa	46	G6
Tegul'det	82	R6
Te Hapua	118	D2
Te Haroto	118	F4
Tehek Lake	34	M3
Teheran = Tehrān	96	F2
Tehrān	96	F2
Teignmouth	64	J11
Tejo = Tagus	68	B5
Te Kaha	118	F3
Tekirda	76	K4
Tekirdağ	98	B3
Teknaf	94	F4
Teku	92	(2)B3
Te Kuiti	118	E4
T'elavi	98	L3
Tel Aviv-Yafo	100	B4
Telegraph Creek	44	(1)L4
Telén	52	H6
Teles Pires	50	F5
Telford	64	K9
Telfs	70	G3
Teller	44	(1)D2
Telsen	52	H7
Telšiai	58	M2
Teltow	60	J4
Teluk Berau	92	(2)D3
Teluk Bone	92	(2)B3
Teluk Cenderawasih	92	(2)E3
Telukdalem	92	(1)B2
Teluk Kumai	92	(1)E3
Teluk Sampit	92	(1)E3
Teluk Sukadana	92	(1)D3
Teluk Tomini	92	(2)B2
Tema	108	D3
Tembenchi	82	T4
Temerin	74	G4
Temerloh	90	C6
Teminabuan	92	(2)D3
Temochic	44	E3
Tempe	44	D2
Témpio Pausária	72	D8
Temple	44	G2
Temryuk	98	G1
Temuco	52	G6
Tenali	94	D5
Tendaho	104	H5
Ten Degree Channel	94	F7
Tendrara	106	E2
Ténéré	106	G5
Ténéré du Tafassasset	106	G4
Tenerife	106	B3
Tènès	106	F1
Tenggarong	92	(1)F3
Tenke	112	D2
Tenkodogo	108	D2
Tennant Creek	116	F3
Tennessee	32	K6
Tennessee	36	J4
Tenojoki	56	P2
Tenteno	92	(2)B3
Tenterfield	116	K5
Teo	68	B2
Teófilo Otoni	50	J7
Tepehuanes	36	E6
Tepic	36	F7
Teplice	58	C7
Ter	68	N2
Terceira	106	(1)B2
Terek	98	L2
Teresina	50	J5
Tergnier	62	F5
Termez	96	J2
Términi Imerese	72	H11
Termirtau	82	N7
Térmoli	74	C8
Ternate	92	(2)C2
Terneuzen	62	F3
Terni	72	G6
Ternitz	70	M3
Ternopil'	78	E5
Ternuka	118	C7
Terracina	72	H7
Terrassa	68	N3
Terre Haute	42	D2
Terry	38	E1
Tersa	78	H4
Terschelling	62	H1
Teruel	68	J4
Tervel	98	B2
Tervola	56	N3
Teseney	104	G4
Teshekpuk Lake	44	(1)F1
Teshio	88	L1
Teslin	44	(1)L3
Teslin	44	(1)L3
Tessalit	106	F4
Tét	66	H11
Tete	112	E3
Teterow	60	H3
Teteven	76	G2
Tétouan	106	D1
Tetovo	74	H8
Teuco	52	J3
Teulada	72	C10
Tevere	72	G6
Teverya	100	C4
Tevriz	78	P3
Te Waewae Bay	118	A8
Texarkana	42	C3
Texas	36	F5
Texel	62	G1
Teya	82	S5
Teykovo	78	H3
Thaba Putsoa	112	D5
Thabazimbi	112	D4
Thailand	90	C4
Thai Nguyên	90	D2
Thal	94	B2
Thale Luang	90	C5
Thamarīt	96	F6
Thames	64	L10
Thamūd	96	E6
Thane	94	B5
Thanh Hoa	90	D3
Thanjavur	94	C6
Thann	70	C3
Tharad	94	B4
Thar Desert	94	B3
Thargomindah	116	H5
Tharwāniyyah	101	E5
Thasos	76	G4
Thasos	76	G4
Thaton	90	B3
Thaya	58	E9
The Bahamas	42	F4
The Bluff	42	F4
The Dalles	38	B1
Thedford	38	F2
The Fens	62	B2
The Gambia	108	A2
The Granites	116	E4
Thelon	34	L4
The Minch	64	F3
The Naze	62	B3
Thenia	68	P8
Theniet el Had	68	N9
Theodore Roosevelt	50	E5
Theodore Roosevelt Lake	44	D2
The Pas	34	L6
Thermaikos Kolpos	76	E4
Thermopolis	38	E2
The Sisters	118	(1)B1
The Solent	62	A4
Thessalon	40	D1
Thessaloniki	76	E4
Thetford	64	N9
Thetford Mines	40	F1
The Twins	118	D5
The Wash	64	N9
The Weald	62	B3
The Whitsundays	116	J4
Thief River Falls	40	A1
Thiers	66	J8
Thiès	108	A2
Thika	110	F4
Thimphu	94	E3
Thionville	62	J5
Thira	76	H8
Thira	76	H8
Thirasia	76	H8
Thiruvananthapuram	94	C7
Thisted	56	C3
Pistilfjöður	56	(1)F1
Thívai	76	F6
Thiviers	66	F8
Þjórsá	56	(1)D3
Tholen	62	G3
Thomasville	42	E3
Thompson	34	H6
Thompson	34	M5
Thompson Falls	38	C1
Thomson	42	E3
Thonon-les-Bains	70	B4
Þórisvatn	56	(1)D2
Þorlákshöfn	56	(1)C3
Þorshöfn	56	(1)F1
Thouars	66	E7
Thrakiko Pelagos	76	H4
Three Forks	38	D1
Three Kings Island	118	C2
Three Rivers	40	C2
Throckmorton	42	B3
Thuin	62	G4
Thun	70	C4
Thunder Bay	40	C1
Thuner See	70	C4
Thung Song	90	B5
Thüringer Wald	60	F6
Thurso	64	J3
Tïäb	101	G3
Tianjin	86	F3
Tianmen	86	E4
Tianqiaoling	88	E2
Tianshifu	88	C3
Tianshui	86	D4
Tianshuihai	96	L2
Tiaret	106	F1
Tibati	108	G3
Tibboburra	116	H5
Tibesti	104	C3
Tibet = Xizang	94	E2
Tibet = Xizang	46	B3
Tiburón	46	D5
Tichît	106	C4
Tichla	106	C4
Ticino	70	D4
Ticul	46	G4
Tidjikdja	106	C5
Tieling	88	B2
Tielongtan	94	C1
Tielt	62	F3
Tienen	62	G4
Tien Shan	82	Q9
Tien Yen	90	D2
Tierra Amarilla	38	E3
Tiétar	68	E4
Tiflis = T'bilisi	102	H1
Tifton	42	E3
Tifu	92	(2)C3
Tighina	74	S3
Tignère	108	G3
Tigre	50	B4
Tigris	98	K6
Tijuana	36	C5
Tikamgarh	94	C4
Tikhoretsk	78	H5
Tikhvin	78	F3
Tikrīt	98	K6
Tiksi	84	M2
Tilburg	62	H3
Tilichiki	84	V4
Tillabéri	108	E2
Tillamook	38	B1
Tilos	76	K8
Timanskiy Kryazh	78	K2
Timaru	118	C7
Timashevsk	78	G5
Timber Creek	116	F3
Timerloh	92	(1)C2
Timimoun	106	F3
Timiş	74	J4
Timmins	40	D1
Timon	50	J5
Timon	92	(2)C4
Timor Sea	116	E2
Tinaca Point	114	C5
Tindivanam	94	C6
Tindouf	106	D3
Tineo	68	D1
Tinglev	60	E2
Tingo Maria	50	B5
Tingri	94	E3
Tingsryd	58	E1
Tiniroto	118	F4
Tinnsjø	56	C2
Tinogasta	52	H4
Tinos	76	H7
Tinos	76	H7
Tinsukia	94	G3
Ti'o	104	H5
Tipperary	64	D9
Tirana = Tiranë	76	B3
Tiranë	76	B3
Tirari Desert	116	G5
Tiraspol	74	S3
Tire	76	K6
Tiree	64	F5
Tirschenreuth	60	H7
Tirso	72	C9
Tiruchchiráppalli	94	C6
Tirunelveli	94	C7
Tirupati	94	C6
Tiruppur	94	C6
Tiruvannamalai	94	C6
Tisa	74	H4
Tišnov	58	F8
Tisza	58	M9
Tiszaföldvár	74	H3
Tiszafüred	74	H2
Tiszaújváros	58	L10
Tit-Ary	82	Z3
Titel	74	H4
Titova Korenica	70	L6
Titovo Velenje	72	K2
Titu	74	N5
Titusville	42	E4
Tivaouane	106	B6
Tiverton	64	J11
Tívoli	72	G7
Tiyäs	100	E2
Tizi Ouzou	106	F1
Tiznit	106	D3
Tjeldøya	56	H2
Tjørkolm	56	D7
Tlemcen	106	E2
Tmassah	104	C2
Toad River	34	F5
Tobago	46	M6
Tobelo	92	(2)C2
Tobermorey	116	G4
Tobermory, United Kingdom	64	F5
Tobermory, United States	40	D1
Tobi	92	(2)D4
Toblach	70	H4
Toboali	92	(1)D3
Tobol	78	M4
Tobol	78	M4
Tobol'sk	78	N3
Tobseda	78	K1
Tocantins	50	H5
Tocantins	50	H5
Tocee	70	D4
Tocopilla	52	G3
Todi	72	G6
Tofino	38	A1
Togo	108	E3
Toimin	72	H2
Toi-misaki	88	F8
Tójö	88	G6
Tok	44	(1)J3
Tokar	104	G4
Tokat, Sudan	96	C6
Tokat, Turkey	96	C1
Tokelau	114	J6
Tokmak	82	P9
Tokoroa	118	E4
Toksun	82	R9
Tok-tō	86	J3
Toktogul	82	N9
Tokushima	88	H6
Tokuyama	88	F6
Tōkyō	88	K6
Tolaga Bay	118	H4
Tôlañaro	112	H4
Tolbo	82	S8
Toledo, Brazil	52	L3
Toledo, Spain	68	F5
Toledo, United States	40	D2
Toliara	112	G4
Tolitoli	92	(2)B2
Tol'ka	82	Q5
Tol'ka	82	Q5
Tollense	60	J3
Tolmezzo	70	J4
Tolmin	70	J4
Tolna	74	F3
Tolosa	68	H1
Tolti	78	J4
Toluca	82	L7
Tom'	82	R8
Tomah	40	B2
Tomakomai	88	L2
Tomar	68	B5
Tomari	84	Q7
Tomaszów Lubelski	58	N7
Tomaszów Mazowiecki	58	K6
Tombouctou	106	E5
Tombua	112	A3
Tomé	52	G6
Tomelloso	68	H5
Tomini	92	(2)B2
Tommot	84	M5
Tomo	50	D3
Tompo	84	P4
Tom Price	116	C4
Tomra	74	E2
Tomsk	82	Q6
Tomtor	84	Q4
Tomu	92	(2)D3
Tonalá	92	(2)B2
Tondano	92	B2
Tønder	60	D2
Tonga	110	C2
Tonga	114	J7
Tonga Islands	114	K6
Tongareva	114	K6
Tonga Trench	114	K8
Tongbai	86	E4
Tongchuan	86	D3
Tongduch'ŏn	88	D5
Tongeren	62	H4
Tonghae	88	E5

Name	Page	Ref
Tonghua	88	C3
Tongliao	86	G2
Tongling	86	F4
Tongshi	90	D3
Tongue	◪38	E1
Tongyu	86	G2
Tónichi	36	E6
Tonj	110	D2
Tonk	94	C3
Tonkåbon	96	F2
Tônlé Sab	◪90	C4
Tonnay-Charente	66	E8
Tönning	60	D2
Tonopah	38	C3
Tooele	38	D2
Toora-Khem	82	T7
Toowoomba	116	K5
Topeka	▣36	G4
Topki	82	R6
Topliţa	74	N3
Topock	44	D2
Topol'čany	58	H9
Topolobampo	36	E6
Torbali	76	K6
Torbat-e Heydarïyeh	96	G2
Torbat-e Jäm	96	H3
Tordesillas	68	F3
Torells	68	N2
Torgau	60	H5
Torgelow	58	C4
Torhout	62	F3
Torino	70	C5
Tori-shima	▣88	L8
Torneälven	◪56	L3
Torneträsk	▣56	K2
Tornio	56	N4
Toro	68	E3
Toronto	▣40	E3
Tororo	110	E3
Toros Dağları	▲98	E5
Torquay	64	J11
Torrance	44	C2
Torreblanca	68	L4
Torre de Moncorvo	68	C3
Torrejón de Ardoz	68	G4
Torrelavega	68	F1
Torremolinos	68	F8
Torrent	68	K5
Torreón	44	F3
Torres Strait	▣116	H2
Torres Vedras	68	A5
Torrevieja	68	K6
Torrington	38	F2
Tortol	72	D9
Tortona	70	D6
Tortosa	68	L4
Tortum	98	J3
Torüd	96	G2
Tory Island	58	H4
Torzhok	78	G3
Tosa-wan	◄88	G7
Tostedt	60	E3
Tosya	76	S3
Totaranui	118	D5
Tôtes	62	D5
Tot'ma	78	H3
Totora	50	D7
Tottori	88	H6
Touba, *Ivory Coast*	108	C3
Touba, *Senegal*	108	A2
Tougan	108	D2
Touggourt	106	G2
Toul	66	L5
Toulépleu	108	C3
Toulon	66	L10
Toulouse	66	G10
Toummo	106	H4
Toungoo	90	B3
Tourcoing	62	F4
Tournai	62	F4
Tours	66	F6
Touws River	112	C6
Tovuz	98	L3
Towanda	40	E2
Towari	92	(2)B3
Towcester	62	B2
Towner	38	F1
Townsend	38	D1
Townshend Island	▣116	K4
Townsville	116	J3
Toxkan	◪82	P9
Toyama	88	J5
Toyohashi	88	J6
Toyooka	88	H6
Toyota	88	J6
Tozeur	106	G2
Tráblous	100	C2
Trabzon	98	H3
Tracy	40	A2
Trail	38	C1
Traiskirchen	70	M2
Trakai	56	N9
Tralee	64	C9
Tralee Bay	◄64	B9
Tramán Tepuí	▲50	E2
Tranås	56	H7
Trancoso	68	C4
Trang	90	B5
Trangan	▣92	(2)D4
Transantarctic Mountains	▣120	(2)B1
Trapani	72	G11
Trappes	62	E6
Traun	70	K2
Traunreut	70	H3
Traunsee	◪70	J3
Traversay Islands	▣48	H9
Traverse City	40	C2
Travnik	74	E5
Trbovlje	70	L4
Trébbia	◪70	E6
Třebíč	58	E8
Trebinje	74	F7
Trebišov	74	J1
Trebnje	70	L5
Trebon	70	K1
Tregosse Islets	▣116	K3
Trelew	52	H7
Trelleborg	56	G9
Tremonton	38	D2
Tremp	68	L2
Trenčín	58	H9
Trent	◪64	M8
Trento	70	G4
Trenton, *Canada*	40	E2
Trenton, *United States*	▣40	F2
Trepassey	34	W7
Tres Arroyos	52	J6
Três Corações	50	H8
Tres Esquinas	50	B3
Tres Lagos	52	G8
Trespaderne	68	G2
Treuchtlingen	70	F2
Treviglio	70	E5
Treviso	70	H5
Tricase	72	N9
Trichur	94	C6
Trier	62	J5
Trieste	70	J5
Triglav	▲70	J4
Trikala	76	D5
Trikomon	100	A1
Trilj	70	M7
Trincomalee	94	D7
Trinidad	▣50	E6
Trinidad, *Bolivia*	50	E6
Trinidad, *United States*	44	F1
Trinidad, *Uruguay*	52	K5
Trinidad and Tobago	▲50	E1
Trinity Islands	▣44	(1)G4
Trino	70	D5
Tripoli	42	D3
Tripoli = Tråblous	76	E7
Tripoli = Tarábulus	100	C2
Trischen	▣60	D2
Tristan da Cunha	▣102	B9
Trivandrum = Thiruvananthapuram	94	C7
Trjavna	98	A2
Trnava	74	E1
Trogir	74	D6
Troina	72	J11
Troisdorf	60	C6
Trois Rivières	40	F1
Troitsk	78	M4
Troitsko-Pechorsk	78	L2
Trojan	76	G2
Trollhättan	56	G7
Trombetas	◪50	F4
Tromsø	56	K2
Trona	38	C3
Trondheim	56	F5
Trondheimsfjörden	◄56	F5
Troodos	100	A1
Trotuş	◪74	P3
Trout Lake, *N.W.T., Canada*	◪34	G4
Trout Lake, *Ont., Canada*	◪34	N6
Troy, *Al., United States*	42	D3
Troy, *N.Y., United States*	40	F2
Troyan	74	M7
Troyes	66	K5
Trstenik	74	J6
Trudovoye	88	G2
Trujillo, *Peru*	50	B5
Trujillo, *Spain*	68	E5
Truro, *Canada*	34	U7
Truro, *United Kingdom*	64	G11
Trusovo	82	J4
Truth or Consequences	44	E2
Trutnov	58	E7
Tryavana	76	H2
Trzcianka	58	F4
Trzebnica	58	G6
Tsetserleg	84	G7
Tshabong	112	C5
Tshane	112	C4
Tshikapa	110	C5
Tshuapa	◪110	C4
Tsiafajavona	▲112	H3
Tsimlyanskoy Vodokhranilishche	◪78	H5
Tsiroanomandidy	112	H3
Ts'khinvali	98	K2
Tsuchiura	88	L5
Tsugaru-kaikyõ	◄88	L3
Tsumeb	112	B3
Tsumkwe	112	C3
Tsuruga	88	J6
Tsuruoka	88	K4
Tsushima	◪88	E6
Tsuyama	88	H6
Tua	◪68	C3
Tual	92	(2)D4
Tuân Giao	90	C2
Tuapse	98	H1
Tubarão	52	M4
Tübingen	70	E2
Tubize	62	G4
Tubruq	◪104	D1
Tubuai	▣114	M8
Tubuai Islands	▣114	L8
Tucano	50	K6
Tuchola	58	G4
Tucson	44	D2
Tucumcari	44	F1
Tucupita	50	E2
Tucuruí	50	H4
Tudela	68	J2
Tuguegarao	90	G3
Tugur	84	P6
Tui	68	B2
Tuktoyaktuk	44	(1)L2
Tula, *Mexico*	44	G4
Tula, *Russia*	78	G4
Tulare	38	C3
Tulcea	74	R4
Tulcán	50	B3
Tulia	44	F1
Tulkarm	100	B4
Tulle	66	G8
Tuloma	◪56	S2
Tulsa	36	G4
Tulsequah	44	(1)L4
Tulun	84	G6
Tulung La	▲94	F3
Tulu Weiel	▲110	E2
Tumaco	50	B3
Tumán	96	H2
Tumen	88	E2
Tumereng	50	E2
Tumut	116	J7
Tumkur	94	C6
Tunca	◪76	J3
Tunceli	98	H4
Tunduru	112	F2
Tundzha	◪74	P8
Tunga	◪84	L5
Tungku	92	(1)F1
Tungsten	44	(1)M3
Tunguska	◪82	S5
Tunis	▣106	H1
Tunisia	▲106	E2
Tunja	50	C2
Tupelo	42	D3
Tupik	84	L6
Tupiza	52	H3
Tupper Lake	40	F2
Tuquan	86	G1
Tura, *India*	94	F3
Tura, *Russia*	84	G4
Turan	82	S7
Turangi	118	E4
Turayf	104	G1
Turbat	96	H4
Turbo	50	B2
Turda	74	L3
Turek	58	H5
Turgay	82	L8
Turgayskaya Stolovaya Strana	◪82	L7
Türgovishte	74	P6
Turgutlu	76	K6
Turhal	98	G3
Turin = Torino	70	C5
Turinsk	78	M3
Turiy Rog	88	F1
Turka	84	H6
Türkeli Adası	▣76	K4
Turkestan	82	M9
Turkmenbashi	96	F1
Turkmenistan	▲96	G2
Turks and Caicos Islands	▣46	K4
Turks Islands	▣46	K4
Turku	56	M6
Turma	84	N6
Turnhout	62	G3
Turnov	58	E7
Turnu Mägurele	74	M6
Turpan	82	R9
Turpan Pendi	▣82	S9
Turquino	◪48	D2
Turtas	◪78	N3
Turtkul'	96	H1
Turtle Island	▣116	K3
Turu	◪82	U5
Turugart Pass	◪82	P9
Turukhan	◪84	C3
Turukhansk	82	R4
Turukta	84	K4
Tuscaloosa	42	D3
Tuscola	42	D2
Tuticorin	94	C7
Tutonchany	84	E4
Tutrakan	74	P5
Tuttle Creek Reservoir	◪42	B2
Tuttlingen	70	D3
Tutuila	▣114	K7
Tuvalu	▲114	H6
Tuxpan, *Mexico*	36	E7
Tuxpan, *Mexico*	36	G7
Tuxtla Gutiérrez	46	F5
Tuyên Quang	90	D2
Tuy Hoa	90	D4
Tuymazy	78	K4
Tuz Gölü	◪98	E4
Tuz Khurmätü	98	L6
Tuzla	74	F5
Tver'	78	G3
Tweed	◪64	K6
Twentynine Palms	44	C2
Twilight Cove	◄116	E6
Twin Buttes Reservoir	◪44	F2
Twin Falls	38	D2
Twizel	118	C7
Two Harbors	40	B1
Tyachiv	74	L1
Tygda	84	M6
Tyler	36	G5
Tylkhoy	84	U4
Tym	◪82	Q6
Tynda	84	L5
Tyne	◪64	K6
Tynemouth	64	L6
Tynset	56	F5
Tyra	▣82	S7
Tyrifjorden	◪56	F6
Tyrnavos	76	E5
Tyrrhenian Sea	◪72	F8
Tyry	◪84	P4
Tysa	◪58	N9
Tyukyan	◪84	K4
Tyumen'	82	M6
Tyung	◪84	K3
Tyva	◪84	F6

U

Name	Page	Ref
Uaupés	50	D3
Ubá	50	J8
Ubaitaba	50	K6
Ubangi	◪110	B3
Ube	88	F7
Úbeda	68	G6
Uberaba	50	H7
Uberlândia	50	H7
Überlingen	70	E3
Ubon Ratchathani	90	C3
Ubrique	68	E8
Ucayali	◪50	B5
Uchami	82	T5
Ucharal	82	Q8
Uchiura-wan	◄88	L2
Uchkuduk	82	L9
Uckermark	◪60	J3
Ucluelet	38	A1
Uda, *Russia*	84	F5
Uda, *Russia*	84	N6
Udachnyy	84	J3
Udagamandalam	94	C6
Udaipur	94	B4
Uddevalla	56	F7
Uddjaure	◪78	C1
Uddjaure Storavan	◪56	K4
Udine	70	J4
Udmurtiya	◪78	K3
Udon Thani	90	C3
Udupi	94	B6
Uecker	◪60	J3
Ueckermünde	60	J3
Ueda	88	K5
Uele	◪110	C3
Uelen	84	AA3

INDEX

Uel'kal … 84 Y3
Uelzen … 60 F4
Ufa … ☑78 L3
Ufa … ▣78 L4
Uganda … ▲110 E3
Ugep … 108 F3
Ugine … 70 B5
Uglegorsk … 84 Q7
Uglich … 78 G3
Ugljan … ▨70 L6
Ugol'nyye Kopi … 84 X4
Ugulan … 84 S4
Uh … ☑74 K1
Uherské Hradiště … 58 G8
Uherský Brod … 58 G8
Uiju … 88 C3
Uil … 78 K5
Uil … ☑78 K5
Uinta Mountains … ◣38 D2
Uitenhage … 112 D6
Újfehértó … 74 J2
Ujiji … 110 D4
Ujjain … 94 C4
Ujung Pandang … 92 (2)A4
Ukerewe Island … ▨110 E4
Ukhta … 82 J5
Ukiah … 38 B3
Ukkusissat … 34 W2
Ukmergé … 58 P2
Ukraine … ▲54 G3
Ulaanbaatar … ■84 H7
Ulaangom … 82 S8
Ulan … 86 B3
Ulan Bator = Ulaanbaatar … ■86 D1
Ulan-Ude … ▣84 H6
Ulchin … 88 E5
Uldz … 84 J7
Ulety … 84 J6
Ulhasnagar … 94 B5
Uliastay … 82 T8
Ulindi … ☑110 D4
Ullapool … 64 G4
Ullŭng do … ▨88 F5
Ulm … 70 F2
Ulog … 74 F6
Ulongue … 112 E2
Ulsan … 88 E6
Ulu … 84 M4
Ulubat Gölü … ☑76 L4
Uluggat … 96 K2
Ulukişla … 98 F5
Ulungur Hu … ☑82 R8
Ulunkhan … 84 J5
Uluru … ▲116 F5
Ulu-Yul … ☑84 D5
Ulva … ▨64 F5
Ulverston … 64 J7
Ulya … 84 Q5
Ul'yanovsk … 78 J4
Ulytau … 82 M8
Uman' … 78 F5
Umarkot … 96 J4
Umba … 78 F1
Umeå … 56 L5
Umeälven … ☑56 J4
Umfolozi … ☑112 E5
Ummal Arānib … 106 H3
Umm al Jamājim … 101 A3
Umm Durman … 104 F4
Umm Keddada … 104 E5
Umm Lajj … 104 G3
Umm Qaşr … 101 B1
Umm Ruwaba … 104 F5
Umnak Island … ▨44 (1)E5
Umtata … 112 D6
Umuarama … 52 L3
Unalakleet … 44 (1)E3
Unalaska Island … ▨44 (1)E5
'Unayzah … 100 C6
Underberg … 112 D5
Ungava Bay … ◣34 T5
Ungheni … 74 Q2
Ungwana Bay … ▲110 G4
União da Vitória … 52 L4
Unije … ▨70 K6
Unimak Island … ▨44 (1)D5
Unim Bāb … 101 D4
Unini … ☑50 E4
Union … 40 B3
Union City … 46 G1
Union Springs … 42 D3
United Arab Emirates … ▲96 F5
United Kingdom … ▲64 G6
United States … ▲32 M5
Unna … 62 K3
Unraven … 44 E1
Unst … ▨64 M1
Unstrut … ☑60 G5
Unzha … ☑78 H3
Upernavik … 34 W2
Upernavik Kujalleq … 34 V2
Upington … 112 C5

Upolu … ▨114 J7
Upper Hutt … 118 E5
Upper Klamath Lake … ☑38 B2
Upper Lake … ☑38 C2
Upper Lough Erne … ☑64 E7
Upper Sandusky … 40 D2
Uppsala … 56 J7
Upsala … 40 B1
'Uqlat al 'Udhaybah … 101 X2
Urad Houqi … 86 D2
Urakawa … 88 M2
Ural … ☑78 K5
Ural Mountains =
  Ural'skiy Khrebet … ◣54 L1
Ural'sk … 78 K4
Ural'skiy Khrebet … ◣54 L1
Urambo … 110 E5
Uranium City … 34 K5
Uraricoera … ☑50 E3
Uray … 78 M2
Urbana, Ill., United States … 40 C2
Urbana, Oh.,
  United States … 40 D2
Urbania … 70 H7
Urbino … 70 H7
Urdzhar … 82 Q8
Uren' … 78 J3
Urengoy … 82 P4
Urgench … 96 H1
Urho … 82 R8
Uritskiy … 78 N4
Urla … 76 J6
Urlaţi … 74 P5
Uroševac … 74 J7
Uro-teppa … 96 J2
Urt … 86 C2
Uruaçu … 50 H6
Uruapan … 46 D5
Urucurituba … 50 F4
Uruguaiana … 52 K4
Uruguay … ▲52 K5
Uruguay … ☑52 K5
Ürümqi … 82 R9
Urus Martan … 98 J4
Uryupino … 84 L6
Uryupinsk … 78 H4
Urzhum … 78 K3
Urziceni … 74 P5
Usa … ☑82 L4
Uşak … 98 C4
Uşak … ◣60 J3
Useless Loop … 116 B5
Usfān … 96 C5
Ushtobe … 82 P8
Usingen … 60 D6
Usk … ☑64 J10
Usman' … 78 G4
Usol'ye Sibirskoye … 84 G6
Ussel … 66 H8
Ussuri … ▨88 G1
Ussuriysk … 86 J2
Usta … ☑78 J3
Ust'-Alekseyevo … 78 J2
Ust'-Barguzin … 84 H6
Ust' Chaun … 84 W3
Ústí … 58 F8
Ústica … ▨72 H10
Ust'-Ilimsk … 84 G5
Ústí nad Labem … 58 D7
Ust'-Ishim … 82 N6
Ustka … 58 F3
Ust'-Kamchatsk … 84 U5
Ust'-Kamenogorsk … 82 Q8
Ust'-Kamo … 82 T5
Ust'-Karenga … 84 K6
Ust'-Khayryuzovo … 84 T5
Ust'-Kulom … 78 K2
Ust'-Kut … 84 G5
Ust'-Kuyga … 84 P3
Ust'-Labinsk … 98 H1
Ust'-Maya … 84 N4
Ust'-Mukduyka … 82 R4
Ust'-Muya … 84 K5
Ust' Nem … 78 K2
Ust'-Nera … 84 Q4
Ust'-Nyukzha … 84 L5
Ust'-Olenek … 84 K2
Ust'-Omchug … 84 R4
Ust' Ozernoye … 84 D5
Ust' Penzhino … 84 V4
Ust'-Pit … 84 E5
Ustrem … 78 N2
Ust'-Sopochnoye … 84 T5
Ust' Tapsuy … 78 M2
Ust'-Tarka … 82 P6
Ust'-Tatta … 84 N4
Ust'-Tsil'ma … 82 J4
Ust' Un'ya … 78 L2
Ust'-Urkima … 84 L5
Ust' Usa … 78 L1
Ust'-Uyskoye … 82 L7
Usu … 82 Q9

Usuki … 88 F7
Utah … ■36 D4
Utah Lake … ☑38 D2
Utata … 84 G6
Utena … 56 N9
Uthal … 96 J4
Utica … 40 E2
Utiel … 68 J5
Utrecht … 62 H2
Utrera … 68 E7
Utsjoki … 56 P2
Utsunomiya … 88 K5
Uttaradit … 90 C3
Utva … ☑78 K4
Uummannaq Fjord … ◢34 V2
Uummannarsuaq … ◢34 Y5
Uusikaupunki … 56 L6
Uvalde … 46 E3
Uvargin … 84 X3
Uvat … 78 N3
Uvinza … 110 E5
Uvira … 110 D4
Uvs Nuur … ☑82 S7
Uwajima … 88 G7
Uy … ☑78 M6
Uyar … 82 S6
Uyega … 82 N9
Uyo … 108 H7
Uyuni … 52 H3
Uzbekistan … ▲82 L9
Uzhhorod … 74 K1
Užice … 74 G6
Uzunköprü … 74 P8

V

Vaal … ☑112 D5
Vaasa … 56 L5
Vác … 74 G2
Vacaria … 52 M4
Vachi … 96 F1
Vadodara … 94 B4
Vado Ligure … 70 D6
Vadsø … 56 Q1
Vaduz … ■70 E3
Værøy … ▨56 G3
Vaganski Vhr … ▲70 L6
Vagay … ☑78 N3
Váh … ☑58 H8
Vakh … ☑78 Q2
Valbonnais … 70 A6
Valcheta … 52 H7
Valdagno … 70 G5
Valday … 78 F3
Val-de-Meuse … 70 A2
Valdemoro … 68 G4
Valdepeñas … 68 G6
Valdez … 34 B4
Valdivia … 52 G6
Val-d'Or … 40 E1
Valdosta … 36 K5
Valdres … ▨56 E6
Valea lui Mihai … 74 K2
Valence … 66 K9
Valencia, Spain … 68 K5
Valencia, Venezuela … 50 D1
Valencia de Alcántara … 68 C5
Valenciennes … 62 F4
Vălenii de Munte … 74 P4
Valentia Island … ◢64 B10
Valentine … 38 F2
Valenza … 70 D5
Valera … 50 C2
Valga … 78 E3
Val Horn … 36 F5
Valjevo … 74 G5
Valka … 56 N8
Val'karay … 84 X3
Valkeakoski … 56 N6
Valkenswaard … 62 H3
Valladolid, Mexico … 46 G4
Valladolid, Spain … 68 F3
Valledupar … 50 C1
Vallée de Azaouagh … ▣106 F5
Vallée du Tilemsi … ▣106 F5
Vallée-Jonction … 40 F1
Vallejo … 38 B3
Vallentuna … 56 K7
Valletta … ■72 J13
Valley City … 38 G1
Valley Falls … 38 B2
Valley of the Kings … ▲104 F2
Valli di Comacchio … ☑70 H6
Vallorbe … 70 B4
Valls … 68 M3
Valmiera … 56 N8
Valognes … 62 A5
Val-Paradis … 40 E1
Valparai … 94 C6
Valparaiso, Chile … 52 G5
Valparaiso, Mexico … 44 F4
Valsad … 94 B4

Val'tevo … 78 H2
Valuyki … 78 G4
Valverde del Camino … 68 D7
Vammala … 56 M6
Van … 98 K4
Vanadzor … 98 L3
Vanavara … 84 G4
Van Buren … 40 G1
Vancouver, Canada … 38 B1
Vancouver, United States … 38 B1
Vancouver Island … ▨34 F7
Vandalia … 42 D2
Vanderbijlpark … 112 D5
Vanderhoof … 34 G6
Van Diemen Gulf … ◣116 F2
Vänern … ☑56 G7
Vangaindrano … 112 H4
Van Gölü … ☑98 K4
Van Horn … 44 F2
Vanimo … 92 (2)F3
Vanino … 84 Q7
Vankarem … 84 Y3
Vanna … ▨56 K1
Vännäs … 56 K5
Vannes … 66 C6
Vanrhynsdorp … 112 B6
Vantaa … 56 N6
Vanua Levu … ▨114 H7
Vanuatu … ▲114 G7
Van Wert … 40 D2
Vanzevat … 78 N2
Vanzhil'kynak … 84 C4
Varāmīn … 96 F2
Varanasi … 94 D3
Varangerfjorden … ◣56 R2
Varaždin … 74 D3
Varazze … 70 D6
Varberg … 56 G8
Vardar … ☑76 E3
Varde … 56 E9
Vardenis … 98 L3
Vardø … 56 R1
Varel … 60 D3
Varèna … 58 P3
Varese … 70 D5
Vârful Moldoveanu … ▲74 M4
Vârfurile … 74 K3
Varginha … 52 M3
Varkaus … 56 P5
Varna … 58 B2
Värnamo … 56 H8
Varnsdorf … 60 K6
Várpalota … 74 F2
Varto … 98 J4
Varzi … 70 E6
Varzy … 66 J6
Vásárosmény … 74 K1
Vasilikos … 100 A2
Vaslui … 74 Q3
Västerås … 56 J7
Västervik … 56 J8
Vasto … 72 J6
Vasvár … 70 M3
Vatan … 66 G6
Vathia … 76 E8
Vatican City … ▲72 F7
Vatnajökull … ▨56 (1)E2
Vatomandry … 112 H3
Vatra Dornei … 74 N2
Vättern … ▨56 H7
Vaughn … 44 E2
Vawkavysk … 58 P4
Växjö … 56 H8
Vayuniya … 90 D7
Vazhgort … 78 J2
Vecht … ☑62 J2
Vechta … 62 L2
Vecsés … 74 G2
Vedaranniyam … 94 C6
Vedea … ☑74 N6
Veendam … 62 J1
Veenendaal … 62 H2
Vega … ▨56 F4
Vega … 44 F1
Vegreville … 34 J6
Vejen … 60 E1
Vejer de la Frontera … 68 E8
Vejle … 56 E9
Vel' … ☑82 D7
Vela Luka … 70 L7
Velenje … 70 L4
Veles … 76 D3
Vélez-Málaga … 68 F8
Velika Gorica … 70 M5
Velika Plana … 74 H5
Velikaya … ☑84 W4
Velikiye Luki … 78 F3
Velikiy Ustyug … 78 J2
Veliko Tŭrnovo … 74 N6
Vélingara … 108 B2
Velingrad … 74 L7
Velita Kladuša … 70 L5

Name	Page	Ref.
Velké Meziříčí	58	F8
Velký Krtíš	58	J9
Velletri	72	G7
Vellinge	58	C2
Vellore	94	C6
Velopoula	76	F8
Vel'sk	78	H2
Velten	60	J4
Velva	38	F1
Venaria	70	C5
Vence	70	C7
Venda Nova	68	C3
Vendôme	66	G6
Venev	78	G4
Venézia	70	H5
Venezuela	50	D2
Vengurla	94	B5
Veniaminof Volcano	44	(1)F4
Venice = Venézia	70	H5
Venice	42	D4
Venlo	62	J3
Venray	62	H3
Venta	78	D3
Ventimiglia	70	C7
Ventotene	72	H8
Ventspils	56	L8
Vera, Argentina	52	J4
Vera, Spain	68	J7
Veracruz	46	E5
Veraval	94	B4
Verbania	70	D5
Vercelli	70	D5
Verdalsøra	56	F5
Verde	50	G8
Verden	60	E4
Verdun	62	H5
Vereeniging	112	D5
Vereshchagino	84	D4
Verín	68	C3
Verkhneimbatsk	84	D4
Verkhnetulomskoe Vodokhranilishche	56	R2
Verkhneural'sk	78	L4
Verkhniy Baskunchak	78	J5
Verkhnyaya Amga	84	M5
Verkhnyaya Toyma	78	J2
Verkhnyaya Tura	78	L3
Verkhovyna	74	M1
Verkhoyansk	84	N3
Verkhoyanskiy Khrebet	84	M4
Vermillion	38	G2
Vermont	36	M3
Vernal	38	E2
Verneuil	62	C6
Vernon, France	62	D5
Vernon, United States	42	B3
Vero Beach	42	E4
Veroia	76	E4
Verona	70	F5
Versailles	62	E6
Verviers	62	H4
Veselí	70	N2
Vesijärvi	56	N6
Vesoul	60	B9
Vesterålen	56	G2
Vestfjorden	56	G3
Vestmannaeyjar	56	(1)C3
Vestvagøy	56	G2
Vesuvio	72	J8
Veszprém	74	E2
Vet	112	D5
Vetlanda	78	J3
Vetluga	78	J3
Veurne	62	E3
Vevey	70	B4
Vezirköprü	98	F3
Viana do Castelo	68	B3
Vianden	62	J5
Viangchan	90	D4
Viarégio	70	F7
Viaréggio	72	E5
Viborg	56	E8
Vibraye	66	F5
Vic	68	N3
Vicenza	70	G5
Vichuga	78	H3
Vichy	66	J7
Vicksburg	42	C3
Victor Harbor	116	G7
Victoria	80	D1
Victoria	116	H7
Victoria, Argentina	52	J5
Victoria, Canada	38	B1
Victoria, Malta	72	J12
Victoria, Romania	74	M4
Victoria, Seychelles	112	(2)C1
Victoria, United States	42	B4
Victoria de las Tunas	46	J4
Victoria Falls	112	D3
Victoria Island	34	J2
Victoria Land	120	(2)W2
Victoria Strait	34	M3
Victoriaville	40	F1
Victoria West	112	C6
Vidalia	36	K5
Vidamlja	58	N5
Videle	74	N5
Vidin	74	K6
Viedma	52	J7
Vienna = Wien	70	M2
Vienna	40	C3
Vienne	66	F7
Vienne	66	K8
Vientiane = Viangchan	90	C3
Vierzon	66	H6
Vieste	72	L7
Vietnam	90	D3
Viêt Tri	90	D2
Vigan	90	G3
Vigévano	70	D5
Vigia	50	H4
Vigo	68	B2
Viho Valentia	72	L10
Vijaywada	94	D5
Vik	56	(1)D3
Vikna	56	E4
Vila de Conde	68	B3
Vilafranca del Penedès	68	M3
Vila Franca de Xira	68	A6
Vila Nova de Gaia	68	B3
Vilanova y la Geltru	68	M3
Vila Real	68	C3
Vila-real	68	K5
Vilhelmina	56	J4
Vilhena	50	E6
Vilija	56	N9
Viljandi	56	N7
Vilkaviškis	58	N3
Villa Ahumada	46	C2
Villablino	68	D2
Villacarrillo	68	G6
Villach	70	J4
Villacidro	72	C9
Villa Constitución	36	D7
Villa de Cos	46	D4
Villafranca	70	F5
Villafranca de los Barros	68	D6
Villagarcia	68	B2
Villagrán	44	G4
Villahermosa	46	F5
Villa Huidobro	52	J3
Villalba	68	C1
Villaldama	44	F3
Villalpando	68	E3
Villamartín	68	E8
Villa Montes	52	J3
Villanueva	44	F4
Villanueva de Cordoba	68	F6
Villa Ocampo	44	E3
Villaputzu	72	D9
Villarrobledo	68	H5
Villa San Giovanni	72	K10
Villavelayo	68	H2
Villavicencio	50	C3
Villaviciosa	68	E1
Villedieu-les-Poêles	62	A6
Villefranche-de-Rouergue	66	H9
Villefranche-sur-Saône	66	K8
Villena	68	K6
Villeneuve-sur-Lot	66	F9
Villers-Bocage	62	B5
Villers-Cotterêts	62	F5
Villerupt	62	H5
Villeurbanne	66	K8
Villingen	70	D2
Vilnius	56	N9
Vilsbiburg	70	H2
Vilshofen	70	J2
Vilvoorde	62	G4
Viluyu	84	L4
Vilyuysk	84	L4
Vilyuyskoye Vodokhranilishche	84	J4
Vimoutiers	62	C6
Vimperk	70	J1
Viña del Mar	52	G5
Vinarós	68	L4
Vincennes	42	D2
Vineland	40	F3
Vinh	90	D3
Vinkovci	74	F4
Vinnytsya	78	E5
Vinson Massif	120	(2)JJ2
Vinstri	56	E6
Vinzili	78	N3
Viooldsdrift	112	B5
Vipava	70	J5
Vipiteno	70	G4
Vir	70	L6
Virac	90	G4
Viranşehir	98	H5
Virawah	94	B4
Virden	38	F1
Vire	62	B6
Virginia	36	L4
Virginia	40	B1
Virginia Beach	40	E3
Virgin Islands, United Kingdom	48	E2
Virgin Islands, United States	48	E2
Virihaure	56	J3
Viróchey	90	D4
Virovitica	74	E4
Virton	62	H5
Virtsu	56	M7
Virudunagar	94	C7
Vis	74	D6
Visalia	38	C3
Visby	56	K8
Viscount Melville Sound	34	J2
Viseu, Brazil	50	H4
Viseu, Portugal	68	C4
Vişeu de Sus	74	M2
Vishakhapatnam	94	D5
Vishera	82	K5
Vishnevka	82	N7
Visoko	74	F6
Visp	70	C4
Visselhövede	60	E4
Vistula = Wisła	54	F2
Viterbo	72	G6
Viti Levu	114	H4
Vitim	84	J5
Vitolište	76	D3
Vitória	52	N3
Vitória da Conquista	50	J6
Vitoria-Gasteiz	68	H2
Vitré	66	D5
Vitry-le-François	62	G6
Vitsyebsk	78	F3
Vitteaux	66	K6
Vittel	70	A2
Vittória	72	J12
Vittório Véneto	70	H5
Viveiro	68	C1
Vivi	82	T4
Vize	76	K3
Vizhas	78	J1
Vizianagaram	94	D5
Vizinga	82	H5
Vizzini	72	J11
Vjosë	76	C4
Vladikavkaz	98	L2
Vladimir	78	H3
Vladivostok	88	F2
Vlasotince	74	K7
Vlasovo	84	N2
Vlieland	62	G1
Vlissingen	62	F3
Vlorë	76	B4
Vltava	58	D8
Vöcklabruck	70	J2
Vodice	70	L7
Vodnjan	70	J6
Vogelsberg	60	E6
Voghera	70	D6
Vohipeno	112	H4
Vöhringen	70	F4
Voi	110	F4
Voinjama	108	C3
Voiron	66	L8
Voitsberg	70	L3
Vojens	60	E1
Vojmsjön	56	J4
Vojvodina	74	G4
Volary	60	J8
Volcán Antofalla	52	H4
Volcán Barú	46	H7
Volcán Cayambe	50	B3
Volcán Citlaltépetl	32	L7
Volcán Corcovado	52	G7
Volcán Cotopaxi	50	B4
Volcán Domuyo	52	G6
Volcán Lanin	52	G6
Volcán Llullaillaco	52	H3
Volcán San Pedro	52	H3
Volcán Tajumulco	46	F5
Volga	78	J5
Volgodonsk	78	H5
Volgograd	78	H5
Völkermarkt	70	K4
Volkhov	78	F3
Volkovysk	62	J5
Volksrust	112	D5
Volochanka	82	S3
Volodarskoye	78	N4
Vologda	78	H3
Volonga	78	J1
Volos	76	E5
Volosovo	56	Q7
Volsk	78	J8
Volta Redonda	54	M2
Volterra	70	F7
Volti	70	D6
Volzhskiy	78	H5
Voorne	62	F3
Voranava	56	N9
Vorderrhein	70	E4
Vordingborg	60	G1
Voreios Evvoikos Kolpos	76	E6
Voreria Pindos	76	C4
Vorkuta	78	M1
Vormsi	56	M7
Vorona	78	H4
Voronezh	78	G4
Vorstershoop	112	C5
Võru	56	P8
Vosges	70	C2
Voss	56	D6
Vostochno-Sibirskoye More	84	U2
Vostochnyy Sayan	82	T7
Vostok Island	114	L6
Votkinsk	82	J6
Vozhgora	78	J2
Vranje	74	J7
Vranov	58	L9
Vranov nad Toplau	74	J1
Vratsa	74	L6
Vrbas	74	E5
Vrbas	74	G4
Vrbovsko	70	L5
Vrendenburg	112	B6
Vršac	74	J4
Vryburg	112	C5
Vryheid	112	E5
Vsetin	58	G8
Vucítrh	74	J7
Vukovar	74	G4
Vuktyl'	78	L2
Vulcanesti	74	R4
Vulcano	72	J10
Vung Tau	90	D4
Vuollerim	56	L3
Vuotso	56	P2
Vyatka	78	K3
Vyazemskiy	84	N7
Vyaz'ma	78	F3
Vyborg	56	Q6
Vychegda	78	K2
Vyksa	78	H3
Vylkove	74	S4
Vynohradiv	58	N9
Vyshniy Volochek	78	F3
Vyškov	58	G8
Vytegra	78	G2

W

Name	Page	Ref.
Wa	108	D3
Waal	62	H3
Waalwijk	62	H3
Wabè Shebelê Wenz	110	G2
Waco	42	B3
Wad Banda	104	E5
Waddān	104	C2
Waddeneilanden	62	G1
Waddenzee	62	H1
Wadena	40	A1
Wâdî al Fârigh	104	C1
Wâdî al Hamîm	104	D1
Wadi Halfa	104	F3
Wâdî Mûsâ	100	C6
Wad Medani	104	F5
Wadsworth	44	C1
Wafangdian	86	G3
Wafangdian	88	A4
Wagga Wagga	116	J7
Wahai	92	(2)C3
Wahiawa	44	(2)C2
Wahpeton	38	G1
Waiau	118	D6
Waiblingen	70	E2
Waidhofen	70	K3
Waidhofen an der Ybbs	74	B2
Waigeo	92	(2)D3
Waiheke Island	118	E3
Waihi	118	E3
Waikabubak	92	(2)A4
Waikaia	118	B7
Waikaremoana	118	F4
Waikato	118	E4
Waikawa	118	B8
Wailuku	44	(2)E3
Waimate	118	C7
Waingapu	116	B1
Wainwright	44	(1)F1
Waiouru	118	E4
Waipara	118	D6
Waipawa	118	F4
Waipiro	118	G4
Waipukurau	118	F5
Wairoa	118	F4
Waitakaruru	118	E3
Waitaki	118	C7
Waitangi	118	(1)B1
Waitara	118	E4

173

Name	Page	Ref
Waiuku	118	E3
Wajima	88	J5
Wajir	110	G3
Wakasa-wan	88	H6
Wakayama	88	H6
Wakeeney	44	G1
Wakefield	64	L8
Wake Island	114	G4
Wakkanai	88	L1
Waku-Kungo	112	B2
Wałbrzych	58	F7
Walcheren	62	F3
Wałcz	58	F4
Waldmünchen	60	H7
Waldshut-Tiengen	70	D3
Walen See	70	E3
Wales	64	J9
Wales Island	34	P3
Walgett	116	J6
Walker Lake	44	C1
Walkerville	116	J7
Wall	38	F2
Wallaceburg	40	D2
Walla Walla	38	C1
Wallis et Futuna	114	J7
Walpole	116	C6
Walsall	64	L9
Walsenburg	38	F3
Walsrode	60	E4
Waltershausen	60	F6
Walvis Bay	112	A4
Wamba	110	D3
Wana	96	J3
Wanaaring	116	H5
Wanaka	118	B7
Wandel Sea	32	A1
Wandingzhen	90	B2
Wanganui	118	E4
Wanganui	118	E4
Wangen	70	E3
Wangerooge	60	D3
Wangiwangi	92	(2)B4
Wan Hsa-la	90	B2
Wanxian	86	D4
Wanyuan	86	D4
Warangal	94	C5
Warburg	60	D5
Ward	118	E5
Wardha	94	C4
Waregem	62	F4
Waremme	62	H4
Waren	60	H3
Warendorf	62	K3
Warka	58	L6
Warła	58	H6
Warmandi	92	(2)D3
Warminster	64	K10
Warm Springs	38	C3
Warren, Mich., United States	40	D2
Warren, Oh., United States	40	D2
Warren, Pa., United States	40	E2
Warrensburg	40	B3
Warrenton	112	C5
Warri	108	F3
Warrington, United Kingdom	64	K8
Warrington, United States	42	D3
Warrnambool	116	H7
Warroad	40	A1
Warsaw = Warszawa	58	K5
Warstein	60	D5
Warszawa	58	K5
Warta	58	F5
Warwick	64	L9
Wasatch Range	44	D1
Wasco	44	C1
Washap	96	H4
Washburn Lake	34	K2
Washington	38	B1
Washington, N.C., United States	40	E3
Washington, Pa., United States	40	D2
Washington, Ut., United States	38	D3
Washington D.C.	32	J6
Wassenaar	62	G2
Wasserburg	70	H2
Watampone	92	(2)B3
Waterbury	40	F2
Waterford	64	E9
Waterloo	40	B2
Watersmeet	40	C1
Watertown, N.Y., United States	40	E2
Watertown, S.D., United States	38	G1
Watertown, Wis., United States	40	C2
Waterville	40	G2
Watford	62	B3
Watford City	38	F1
Watmuri	92	(2)D4
Watrous	34	K6
Watsa	110	D3
Watseka	42	D1
Watson Lake	44	(1)M3
Wau	110	D2
Waubay Lake	38	G1
Waukegan	40	C2
Waukesha	40	C2
Waurika	42	B3
Wausau	36	J3
Waverly	40	C3
Wavre	62	G4
Wawa	40	D1
Wāw al Kabīr	104	C2
Waxxari	82	R10
Waycross	42	E3
Waynesboro, Ga., United States	42	E3
Waynesboro, Miss., United States	42	D3
Waynesville	40	D3
Weaverville	38	B2
Weber	118	F5
Webi Shaabeelle	110	G3
Webster	38	G1
Weddell Island	52	J9
Weddell Sea	120	(2)A2
Wedel	60	E3
Weed	38	B2
Weert	62	H3
Wei	86	D4
Weichang	86	F2
Weida	60	H6
Weiden	60	H7
Weifang	86	F3
Weihai	86	G3
Weilburg	60	D6
Weilheim	70	G3
Weimar	60	G6
Weinan	86	D4
Weinheim	60	D7
Weining	86	C5
Weipa	116	H2
Weiser	38	C2
Weißenburg	60	F7
Weißenfels	60	G5
Weißwasser	60	K5
Weixi	90	B1
Wejherowo	58	H3
Welkom	112	D5
Welland	62	B2
Wellesley Islands	116	G3
Wellingborough	66	E1
Wellington, New Zealand	118	E5
Wellington, Colo., United States	38	F2
Wellington, Kans., United States	42	B2
Wells	38	C2
Wellsboro	40	E2
Wellsford	118	E3
Wellton	44	D2
Wels	70	K2
Welwyn Garden City	62	B3
Wenatchee	38	B1
Wenchang	90	E3
Wenga	110	M3
Wenman	50	(1)A1
Wentworth	116	H6
Wen Xian	86	C4
Wenzhou	86	G5
Werder	60	H4
Werdēr	110	H2
Werl	62	K3
Werneck	60	F7
Wernigerode	60	F5
Werra	60	F6
Wertheim	60	E7
Wesel	62	J3
Wesel Dorsten	60	B5
Weser	60	E4
Wessel Islands	116	G2
West Antarctica	120	(2)GG2
West Bank	100	C4
West Branch	40	D2
West Cape	114	G10
West End	42	F4
Western Australia	116	D5
Western Cape	112	B6
Western Ghats	94	B5
Western Reef	118	(1)B1
Western Sahara	106	C4
Wester Ross	64	G4
Westerschelde	62	F3
Westerstede	62	K1
Westerwald	62	K4
West Falkland	52	J9
West Frankfort	42	D2
West Glacier	38	D1
West Lunga	112	C2
West Memphis	42	C2
Weston	40	D3
Weston-super-Mare	64	K10
West Palm Beach	42	E4
West Plains	40	B3
Westport, New Zealand	118	C5
Westport, Republic of Ireland	64	C8
Westray	64	J2
West Siberian Plain = Zapadno-Sibirskaya Ravnina	80	L3
West Virginia	40	D3
West Wendover	38	D2
West Yellowstone	38	D2
Wetar	92	(2)C4
Wetaskiwin	34	J6
Wete	110	F5
Wetumpka	42	D3
Wetzlar	60	D6
Wewak	92	(2)F3
Wexford	64	F9
Wexford Harbour	64	F9
Weyburn	36	F2
Weymouth	64	K11
Whakatane	118	F3
Whale Cove	34	N4
Whalsay	64	M1
Whangarei	118	E2
Wharfe	64	L7
Wheeler Peak	44	E1
Wheeler Ridge	44	C2
Wheeling	42	E1
Whitby	64	M7
White, Nev., United States	38	C3
White, S.D., United States	34	L8
White Bay	34	V6
White Cliffs	116	H6
Whitecourt	34	H6
Whitefish Point	40	C1
Whitehaven	64	J7
Whitehorse	44	(1)L3
Whitemark	116	J8
White Island	118	F3
White Mountain Peak	38	C3
White Mountains	34	S8
Whitemouth	38	G1
White Nile = Bahr el Abiad	104	F5
White River, Canada	40	C1
White River, United States	38	F2
White Sea = Beloye More	78	Q1
White Sulphur Springs	38	D1
Whiteville	42	F3
White Volta	108	D3
Whitney	40	E1
Whyalla	116	G6
Wichita	42	B2
Wichita Falls	42	B3
Wick	64	J3
Wickenburg	44	D2
Wicklow Mountains	64	F8
Widawka	58	J6
Wieluń	58	H6
Wien	70	M2
Wiener Neustadt	70	M3
Wieringermeer Polder	62	G2
Wiesbaden	60	D6
Wiesloch	60	D7
Wiesmoor	60	C3
Wigan	64	K8
Wiggins	38	F2
Wil	70	E3
Wilcannia	116	H6
Wildeshausen	60	D4
Wilhelmshaven	60	D3
Wilkes-Barre	40	E2
Wilkes Land	120	(2)U2
Willadja Bay	38	B1
Williams, Australia	116	C6
Williams, Ariz., United States	38	D3
Williams, Calif., United States	38	B3
Williams Lake	34	G6
Williamson	42	E2
Williamsport	40	E2
Willis Group	116	K3
Williston, Fla., United States	42	E4
Williston, N.D., United States	38	F1
Williston Lake	34	G5
Willmar	40	A1
Willow	44	(1)H3
Willowmore	112	C6
Willow River	40	B1
Willow Springs	40	B3
Wilmington, Del., United States	40	E3
Wilmington, N.C., United States	42	F3
Wilson	40	E3
Wilson Reservoir	42	B2
Wilson's Promontory	116	J7
Wiluna	116	D5
Winamac	40	C2
Winchester, United Kingdom	64	L10
Winchester, Ky., United States	40	D3
Winchester, Va., United States	40	E3
Windhoek	112	B4
Windischgarsten	70	K3
Windom	40	A2
Windorah	116	H5
Windsor, Canada	40	D2
Windsor, United Kingdom	62	B3
Windsor, United States	42	F2
Windward Islands	46	N6
Windward Passage	48	D2
Winfield, Al., United States	42	D3
Winfield, Kans., United States	44	G1
Wingate Mountains	116	E2
Winisk	34	P5
Winisk	34	P6
Winisk Lake	34	P6
Winnemucca	38	C2
Winner	38	G2
Winnfield	36	H5
Winnipeg	34	M7
Winona, Minn., United States	40	B2
Winona, Miss., United States	42	D3
Winschoten	62	K1
Winsen	60	F3
Winslow	44	D1
Winston-Salem	40	D3
Winterberg	60	D5
Winter Harbour	34	J2
Winterswijk	62	J3
Winterthur	70	D3
Winton, Australia	116	H4
Winton, New Zealand	118	B8
Wisbech	62	C2
Wisconsin	36	H2
Wisconsin	40	B2
Wisconsin Dells	40	C2
Wisconsin Rapids	40	C2
Wisła	58	H4
Wisła	58	H8
Wisłoka	58	L8
Wismar	60	G3
Wissembourg	60	C7
Witney	62	A3
Witten	62	K3
Wittenberge	60	G3
Wittenoom	116	C4
Wittingen	60	F4
Wittlich	62	J5
Wittmund	60	C3
Wittstock	60	H3
Witzenhausen	60	E5
W. J. van Blommesteinmeer	50	G2
Wkra	58	K5
Władysławowo	58	H3
Włocławek	58	J5
Włodawa	58	N6
Wodzisław Śląski	58	H7
Wohlen	70	D3
Wokam	92	(2)D4
Woking	64	M10
Wolf Creek	38	D1
Wolfen	60	H5
Wolfenbüttel	60	F4
Wolf Point	38	E1
Wolfratshausen	70	G3
Wolfsberg	70	K4
Wolfsburg	60	F4
Wolgast	60	J2
Wollaston Lake	34	K5
Wollaston Peninsula	34	H3
Wollongong	116	K6
Wołomin	58	L5
Wolsztyn	58	F5
Wolverhampton	64	K9
Wŏnju	88	D5
Wŏnsan	88	D4
Woodbridge	62	D2

Woodburn	38	B1
Woodland	38	B3
Woodstock, *Canada*	40	G1
Woodstock, *United Kingdom*	62	A3
Woodstock, *United States*	40	C2
Woodville, *New Zealand*	118	E5
Woodville, *Miss., United States*	42	C3
Woodville, *Tex., United States*	42	C3
Woodward	38	G3
Woody Head	▣118	E3
Woonsocket, *R.I., United States*	40	F2
Woonsocket, *S.D., United States*	38	G2
Worcester, *South Africa*	112	B6
Worcester, *United Kingdom*	64	K9
Worcester, *United States*	36	M3
Wörgl	70	H3
Workington	64	J7
Worksop	62	A1
Worland	38	E2
Worms	60	D7
Wörth	60	D7
Worthing	64	M11
Worthington	36	G3
Wosu	92	(2)B3
Wotu	92	(2)B3
Wowoni	▣92	(2)B3
Wrangell	34	E5
Wrangell Mountains	▲34	C4
Wray	36	F3
Wrexham	64	K8
Wrigley	34	G4
Wrocław	58	G6
Września	58	G5
Wu	☑86	D5
Wubin	116	C6
Wubu	86	E3
Wuchang	86	H2
Wuchuan	86	E2
Wuday'ah	96	E6
Wudu	86	C4
Wuhai	86	D3
Wuhan	86	F4
Wuhu	86	F4
Wüjang	94	C2
Wukari	108	F3
Wuli	94	F2
Wunsiedel	60	G6
Wunstorf	60	E4
Wuppertal	60	C5
Würzburg	60	E7
Wurzen	60	H5
Wushi	82	P9
Wusuli	☑86	J1
Wutach	☑70	D3
Wuwei	86	C3
Wuxi	86	G4
Wuxu	90	D2
Wuyuan	86	D2
Wuzhong	86	D3
Wuzhou	90	E2
Wye	☑64	J9
Wyndham	116	E3
Wynniatt Bay	▣34	J2
Wyoming	◼36	E3
Wyszków	58	L5
Wytheville	42	E2

X

Xaafuun	110	J1
Xàbia	68	L6
Xaçmaz	98	N3
Xaidulla	82	P10
Xainza	94	E2
Xai-Xai	112	E4
Xam Nua	90	C2
Xankändi	98	M4
Xanten	62	J3
Xanthi	76	G3
Xapuri	50	D6
Xar Moron	☑84	K8
Xàtiva	68	K6
Xiahe	86	C3
Xiamen	90	F2
Xi'an	86	D4
Xiangcheng	86	E4
Xiangfan	86	E4
Xianghoang	90	C3
Xianghuang Qi	86	E2
Xiangtan	86	E5
Xianning	86	E5
Xianyang	86	D4
Xiaogan	86	E4
Xiao Hinggan Ling	▲84	M7

Xiaonanchuan	94	F1
Xichang	90	C1
Xigazê	94	E3
Xi Jiang	☑86	E3
Xilinhot	86	F2
Xincai	86	E4
Xingcheng	86	G2
Xinghua	86	F4
Xingtai	86	F3
Xingu	☑50	G5
Xingyi	90	C1
Xinhe	82	Q9
Xining	86	C3
Xinjin	86	G3
Xinmin	88	B2
Xintai	86	E3
Xinxiang	86	E3
Xinyang	86	E4
Xinyu	86	F5
Xinyuan	82	Q9
Xinzhou	86	E3
Xinzo de Limia	68	C2
Xique Xique	50	J6
Xi Ujimqin Qi	86	F2
Xiushu	86	E5
Xiwu	94	G2
Xixia	86	E4
Xi Xiang	86	D4
Xizang	▣94	E2
Xizang Gaoyuan	◼94	D2
Xuanhua	86	E2
Xuchang	86	E4
Xuddur	110	G3
Xuwen	90	E2
Xuzhou	86	F4

Y

Ya'an	86	D3
Yabassi	108	F4
Yabëlo	110	F3
Yablonovyy Khrebet	▲84	J6
Yabrüd	100	D3
Yabuli	88	E1
Yacuma	☑50	D6
Yadgir	94	D5
Yagodnyy	78	N3
Yahk	34	H7
Yakima	38	B1
Yako	108	D2
Yakoma	110	C3
Yaksha	78	L2
Yakumo	88	L2
Yaku-shima	▣88	F8
Yakutat	44	(1)K4
Yakutsk	◼84	M4
Yala	90	C5
Yalova	76	M4
Yalta	98	F1
Yalu	☑88	D3
Yalutorovsk	78	N3
Yamagata	88	L4
Yamaguchi	88	F6
Yamarovka	84	J6
Yambio	110	D3
Yambol	74	P7
Yamburg	82	P4
Yamdena	▣92	(2)D4
Yamoussoukro	◼108	C3
Yampa	☑38	E2
Yampil'	74	R1
Yamsk	84	S5
Yan'an	86	D3
Yanbu'al Baḥr	96	C5
Yancheng	86	G4
Yandun	86	A2
Yangambi	110	C3
Yangbajain	94	F2
Yangdok	88	D4
Yangi Kand	98	N5
Yangjiang	90	E2
Yangon	◼90	B3
Yangquan	86	E3
Yangshuo	90	E2
Yangtze = Chang Jiang	☑86	D4
Yangzhou	86	F4
Yanhuqu	94	D2
Yani-Kurgan	82	M9
Yanji	88	E2
Yankton	38	G2
Yano-Indigirskaya Nizmennost'	◼84	N2
Yanqi	82	R9
Yanqing	86	F2
Yanshan	90	C2
Yanskiy Zaliv	▶84	N2
Yantai	86	G3
Yaoundé	◼108	G4
Yap	◼114	D5
Yapen	▣92	(2)E3
Yaqui	☑36	E6

Yaransk	78	J3
Yardımcı Burnu	▶76	E8
Yare	☑62	D2
Yaren	◼114	G6
Yarensk	78	J2
Yari	☑50	C3
Yarkant	☑96	L2
Yarkovo	78	N3
Yarlung Zangbo	☑94	F3
Yarmouth	34	T8
Yaroslavl'	78	G3
Yar Sale	78	P1
Yartsevo	78	F3
Yashkul'	78	J5
Yasnyy	78	L4
Yäsüj	101	D1
Yatağan	76	L7
Yathkyed Lake	☑34	M4
Yatsushiro	88	F7
Yavari	☑50	C5
Yawatongguzlangar	82	Q10
Yaya	82	R6
Yayladaği	98	F6
Yazd	96	F3
Yazdän	96	H3
Yazd-e Khväst	101	E1
Yazoo City	42	C3
Ydra	▣76	F7
Ye	90	B3
Yea	116	J7
Yecheng	96	L2
Yecla	68	J6
Yefremov	78	G4
Yegendybulak	82	P8
Yei	110	E3
Yekaterinburg	78	M3
Yelets	78	G4
Yell	▣64	L1
Yellowknife	◼34	J4
Yellow River = Huang He	☑86	C3
Yellow Sea	◼86	G3
Yellowstone	☑38	E1
Yellowstone Lake	☑38	D2
Yeloten	96	H2
Yelva	☑82	J5
Yelwa	108	E2
Yemen	▲96	D7
Yemetsk	78	H2
Yenakiyeve	78	G5
Yengisar	96	L2
Yenihisar	76	K7
Yenisey	☑82	S6
Yeniseysk	82	S6
Yeniseyskiy Kryazh	▲82	S5
Yeo Lake	▣116	D5
Yeovil	64	K11
Yeppoon	116	K4
Yeraliyev	82	J9
Yerbogachen	84	H4
Yerevan	◼98	L3
Yerington	38	C3
Yerkov	78	S5
Yerkoy	98	F4
Yermak	82	P7
Yermitsa	78	K1
Yernva	82	J5
Yershov	78	J4
Yerupaja	▲50	B6
Yerushalayim	◼100	C5
Yesil'	78	N4
Yeşilhisar	98	F4
Yeşilköy	76	L4
Yessey	82	U4
Yevlax	98	M3
Yevpatoriya	78	F5
Yeyik	82	Q10
Yeysk	78	G5
Yibin	86	C5
Yichang	86	E4
Yichun, *China*	86	E5
Yichun, *China*	86	H1
Yilan	86	H1
Yıldız Dağları	▲76	K2
Yidizeli	98	G4
Yinchuan	86	D3
Yingcheng	86	E4
Yingkou	86	G2
Yining	82	Q9
Yirga Alem	110	F2
Yitomio	78	M3
Yitulihe	84	L6
Yiyang	86	E5
Yli-Kitka	☑56	Q3
Ylivieska	56	N4
Ylöjärvi	56	M6
Yoakum	42	B4
Yoboki	104	H5
Yogyakarta	92	(1)E4
Yokadouma	108	G4
Yoko	108	G3
Yokohama, *Japan*	88	K6
Yokohama, *Japan*	88	L3

Yokosuka	88	K6
Yokote	88	L4
Yola	108	G3
Yonago	88	G6
Yonezawa	88	L5
Yong'an	90	F1
Yongdeng	86	C3
Yŏnghŭng	88	D4
Yongren	90	C1
Yongxiu	86	F5
Yonkers	40	F2
York, *United Kingdom*	64	L8
York, *Nebr., United States*	38	G2
York, *Pa., United States*	40	E3
Yorkton	34	L6
Yoshkar Ola	☑78	J3
Yōsu	88	D6
Yotvata	100	C7
You	☑90	D2
Youghal	64	E10
Youghal Bay	▶64	E10
Youngstown	40	D2
Yozgat	98	F4
Yreka	38	B2
Ystad	58	C2
Ysyk-Köl	☑82	P9
Ytre Sula	▣56	B6
Ytyk-Kyuyel'	84	N4
Yu	☑90	D2
Yuan	☑90	C2
Yuanjiang	90	C2
Yuanmou	90	C1
Yuanping	86	E3
Yucatán	◼46	F5
Yucatan Channel	▶46	G4
Yuci	86	E3
Yudoma	☑84	Q4
Yuendumu	116	F4
Yueyang	86	E5
Yugorenok	84	P5
Yugoslavia	▲74	H6
Yugo-Tala	84	S3
Yukagirskoye Ploskogor'ye	◼84	S3
Yukon	☑44	(1)E3
Yukon Territory	☑44	(1)K2
Yukorskiy Poluostrov	◼82	L4
Yüksekova	98	L5
Yukta	84	H4
Yuli	82	R9
Yulin, *China*	90	E2
Yulin, *China*	86	D3
Yuma	44	C2
Yumen	86	B3
Yumin	82	Q8
Yuncheng	86	E3
Yun Xian	90	C2
Yuogi Feng	▲82	R8
Yurga	82	Q6
Yurimaguas	50	B5
Yurla	78	K3
Yuroma	78	J1
Yur'yevets	78	H3
Yu Shan	▲90	G2
Yushkozero	56	S4
Yushu, *China*	86	B4
Yushu, *China*	86	H2
Yusufeli	98	J3
Yutian	82	Q10
Yuyao	86	G4
Yuzhno Kuril'sk	88	N1
Yuzhno-Sakhalinsk	84	Q7
Yuzhno-Sukhokumsk	98	L1
Yuzhnoural'sk	78	M4
Yverdon-les-Bains	70	B4
Yvetot	62	C5

Z

Zaanstad	62	G2
Ząbkowice Śląskie	58	F7
Zabok	70	L4
Zäbol	96	H3
Zabrze	58	H7
Zacatecas	44	F4
Zadar	70	L6
Zadonsk	78	G4
Zafora	▣76	J8
Zafra	68	D6
Zägheh-ye-Bälä	98	M6
Zagora	106	D2
Zagreb	◼70	L5
Zagyva	☑58	K10
Zähedän	96	H4
Zahirabad	94	C5
Zahlé	100	C3
Zähran	96	D6
Zaječar	74	K6
Zakamensk	84	G6

INDEX

Name	Page	Grid
Zäkhö	98	K5
Zakopane	58	J8
Zakynthos	76	C7
Zakynthos	76	C7
Zala	70	M4
Zalaegerszeg	70	M4
Zalari	84	G6
Zalaszentgrót	70	N4
Zălău	74	L2
Žalim	96	D5
Zaliv Aniva	84	Q7
Zaliv Kara-Bogaz Gol	96	F1
Zaliv Kresta	84	Y3
Zaliv Paskevicha	78	L5
Zaliv Shelikhova	84	T5
Zaliv Terpeniya	84	Q7
Zamakh	96	E6
Zambezi	112	C2
Zambezi	112	E3
Zambia	112	D2
Zamboanga	90	G5
Zambrów	58	M5
Zamora	68	E3
Zamość	58	N7
Zanda	94	C2
Zandvoort	62	G2
Zanesville	42	E2
Zangguy	96	L2
Zanjän	98	N5
Zannone	72	H8
Zanzibar	110	F5
Zanzibar Island	110	F5
Zaozernyy	82	S6
Zapadnaya Dvina	78	E3
Zapadno-Sibirskaya Ravnina	82	L5
Zapadnyy Sayan	82	S7
Zapata	44	G3
Zaporizhzhya	78	G5
Zaprešić	70	L5
Zaqatala	98	M3
Zara	98	G4
Zarafshan	82	L9
Zaragoza	68	K3
Zarand	101	G1
Zaranj	96	H3
Zarasai	56	P9
Zaraza	50	D2
Zarechensk	56	R3
Zaria	108	F2
Zărnești	74	N4
Zarqä'	100	D4
Zarqän	101	E2
Žary	58	E6
Zarzadilla de Totana	68	J7
Žatec	58	C7
Zavetnoye	78	H5
Zavidovići	74	F5
Zavitinsk	84	M6
Zayarsk	82	U6
Zaysan	82	Q8
Zayü	90	B1
Zbraslav	58	D8
Zbäk	96	K2
Zēbār	98	L5
Zeebrugge	62	F3
Zefat	100	C4
Zeilona Góra	58	E6
Zeist	62	H2
Zeitz	60	H5
Zelenoborskiy	56	S3
Zelenograd	78	G3
Zelenogradsk	58	K3
Zelenokumsk	98	K1
Zell am See	70	H3
Zella-Mehlis	60	F6
Zémio	110	D2
Zemlya Alexsandry	82	G1
Zemlya Frantsa-Iosifa	82	J2
Zemlya Vil'cheka	82	L1
Zempoalteptl	46	E5
Zenica	74	E5
Zerbst	60	H5
Zermatt	70	C4
Zeta Lake	34	K2
Zeulenroda	60	G6
Zeven	60	E3
Zevenaar	62	J3
Zeya	84	M6
Zeya	84	M6
Zeydäbäd	101	F2
Zeyskoye Vodokhranilishche	84	M5
Zgharta	100	C2
Zgierz	58	J6
Zgorzelec	58	E6
Zhailma	78	M4
Zhaksy	78	N4
Zhaksykon	78	N5
Zhaltyr	78	N4
Zhambyl	82	N9
Zhanatas	82	M9
Zhangbei	86	E2
Zhangguangcai Ling	86	H2
Zhangjiakou	86	E2
Zhangling	84	L6
Zhangwu	86	G2
Zhangye	86	B3
Zhangzhou	90	F2
Zhanjiang	90	E2
Zhaodong	84	M7
Zhaoqing	90	E2
Zhaosu	82	Q9
Zhaoyuan	86	H1
Zharkamys	82	K8
Zharkent	82	P9
Zharma	82	Q8
Zharyk	82	N8
Zhaxigang	94	C2
Zheleznogorsk	78	G4
Zhengzhou	86	E4
Zhenjiang	86	F4
Zherdevka	78	H4
Zhetybay	82	J9
Zhezkazgan	82	M8
Zhigalovo	84	H5
Zhigansk	84	L3
Zhilinda	84	J2
Zhob	96	J3
Zholymbet	82	N7
Zhongba	94	D3
Zhongdian	86	B5
Zhongning	86	D3
Zhongshan	90	E2
Zhongze	86	G5
Zhoukou	86	E4
Zhuanghe	86	G3
Zhucheng	86	F3
Zhumadian	86	E4
Zhuo Xian	86	F3
Zhytomyr	78	E4
Žiar	58	H9
Zibo	86	F3
Zichang	86	D3
Zierikzee	62	F3
Ziesar	60	H4
Zigong	86	C5
Ziguinchor	106	B6
Zikhron Ya'aqov	100	B4
Žilina	58	H8
Zillah	104	C2
Zima	84	G6
Zimbabwe	112	D3
Zimmi	108	B3
Zimnicea	74	N6
Zinder	108	F2
Zinjibär	104	J5
Zirc	58	G10
Žirje	72	K5
Zistersdorf	70	M2
Zitava	58	H9
Zittau	60	K6
Ziway Häyk'	110	F2
Zixing	90	E1
Zlaté Moravce	58	H9
Zlatoust	78	L3
Zlín	58	G8
Zlīţan	106	H2
Złotów	58	G4
Zmeinogorsk	82	Q7
Znamenskoye	82	N6
Žnin	58	G5
Znojmo	70	M2
Zoigê	86	C4
Zomba	112	F3
Zongo	110	B3
Zonguldak	76	P3
Zouar	104	C3
Zouérat	106	C4
Žovka	58	N7
Zrenjanin	74	H4
Zschopau	60	J6
Zug	70	D3
Zugdidi	98	J2
Zuger See	70	D3
Zugspitze	60	F9
Zuid-Beveland	62	F3
Zuni	44	E1
Zunyi	86	D5
Županja	74	F4
Zürich	70	D3
Zuru	108	F2
Žut	72	K5
Zutphen	62	J2
Zuwärah	104	B1
Zuyevka	82	J6
Zvishavane	112	E4
Zvolen	58	J9
Zvornik	74	G5
Zwedru	108	C3
Zweibrücken	62	K5
Zwettl	70	L2
Zwickau	60	H6
Zwiesel	60	J7
Zwolle	62	J2
Zyryanka	84	S3
Zyryanovsk	82	Q8
Żywiec	58	J8